West African Women Entrepreneurs in a Glocal World

More African women than men become entrepreneurs, with women often balancing time caring for their households with small enterprises such as setting up shops in front of their homes, renting market stalls, or setting up hairstyling businesses.

This book considers these micro-level instances of entrepreneurship, as well as cases of more established high-status entrepreneurs, to build a picture of women entrepreneurs in West African societies, and their wider role in socio-economic development. Small and medium enterprises are seen as agents of change in the global south, vital for job creation and poverty reduction, but women often face barriers which hinder their entrepreneurial success, such as lack of funding, useful networks, or inhibitive gender stereotypes. This book highlights cases of gender and economic success, to demonstrate the significant potential of the female economy to generate progress and change.

This book will be an important read for students and researchers of entrepreneurship, business, gender, development, and economic sociology in Africa.

Ulrike Schuerkens studied at the Universities of Cologne (Germany) and Rennes (France). She has doctorates in both sociology, and social anthropology and ethnology, from the *École des Hautes Études en Sciences Sociales* in Paris. She received the diploma *Habilitation à diriger des recherches* from the University Paris V – René Descartes. Currently, she is a professor of sociology at the University Rennes 2, France. She taught in the master's and PhD programmes of the *École des Hautes Études en Sciences Sociales*, Paris, France. She also taught as a lecturer at the University Lille 3 (France) and Humboldt University, Berlin (Germany). She was a visiting professor at the Universities Paris 1 and Paris V, the University of Cologne (Germany), Rouen Business School, Université Cheikh Anta Diop in Dakar (Senegal), and others. Ulrike Schuerkens has served for many years in different functions as a member of the board of the Research Committee on Social Transformations and Sociology of Development, RC 09 of the International Sociological Association. She is on the editorial board of several international journals. She has published extensively on globalisation, glocalisation, socio-economic development, social change, transnational migrations, multiculturalism, and colonialism. Her latest monographs are *Entreprises, entrepreneurs et travail au Sénégal*, *Pour une sociologie du management en Afrique et dans le monde arabe,*

Social Changes in a Global World, Soziale Transformationen und Entwicklung(en) in einer globalisierten Welt, Global Management, Local Resistances (ed., Routledge, 2014), *The Socio-economic Outcomes of the Global Financial Crisis* (ed., Routledge, 2012), *Globalization and Transformations of Social Inequality* (ed., Routledge, 2010), *Globalization and Transformations of Local Socio-Economic Practices* (ed., Routledge, 2008), *Transnational Migrations and Social Transformations, Global Forces and Local Life-Worlds: Social Transformations, Changement social sous régime colonial: Du Togo allemand aux Togo et Ghana indépendants, Transformationsprozesse in der Elfenbeinkueste und in Ghana.*

Routledge Research in Business and Economics in Africa

Routledge Research in Business and Economics in Africa features innovative and original research on business and economics from scholars both within and outside of Africa. The series particularly promotes comparative and interdisciplinary research targeted at a global readership. The series welcomes submissions from both established and junior authors, and considers high-quality edited collections as well as authored monographs.

Multinational Corporations in West Africa
Building Decentralized Partnerships
Souleymane Doumbia

West African Women Entrepreneurs in a Glocal World
Edited by Ulrike Schuerkens

For more information about this series, please visit: https://www.routledge.com/Routledge-Research-on-African-Economics/book-series/RROAE

West African Women Entrepreneurs in a Glocal World

Edited by Ulrike Schuerkens

Routledge
Taylor & Francis Group
LONDON AND NEW YORK

First published 2025
by Routledge
4 Park Square, Milton Park, Abingdon, Oxon OX14 4RN

and by Routledge
605 Third Avenue, New York, NY 10158

Routledge is an imprint of the Taylor & Francis Group, an informa business

British Library Cataloguing-in-Publication Data
A catalogue record for this book is available from the British Library

ISBN: 978-1-032-79597-3 (hbk)
ISBN: 978-1-032-79598-0 (pbk)
ISBN: 978-1-003-49293-1 (ebk)

DOI: 10.4324/ 9781003492931

Typeset in Times New Roman
by Deanta Global Publishing Services, Chennai, India

Contents

Tables

Figures

Contributors

Asante, Philomena is an Executive member of the Association of Ghana Industries, Accra (AGI). She is a serial entrepreneur with a keen interest in youth employment. She is the CEO of Minana Services Ltd., a Human Resource consulting business, co-founder of ANP Consulting and Crop Afrik. Philomena Asante holds an MBA in Business Development and social entrepreneurship from *Universita Cattolica Del Sacro Cuore-Altis*, Milan, Italy. From Catholic Institute of Business and Technology (CIBT), she holds a bachelor's degree in economics, University of Ghana. In her ten years of work experience, she has trained over 500 youth with employable skills under Nation Builders Corps. She was a participant in *Women in Technology Conference* 2019 and in Ghana Tech Summits.

Badini, Haoua Koné holds a doctorate in management science and is a lecturer and researcher, director of the professional master's programme in labour economics and human resources at the economics and management training and research unit of the University Félix Houphouët-Boigny in Abidjan, Côte d'Ivoire. Her areas of expertise include partnership governance, corporate social responsibility (CSR), socially responsible human resource management, and female entrepreneurship.

Dembelé, Abdul-Aziz is a PhD candidate in sociology at the University Rennes 2, in the *Laboratoire interdisciplinaire de Recherche en Innovations Sociétales* (LiRIS EA 7481). Under the supervision of Ulrike Schuerkens, he is working on a thesis on digital transformations in relation to development issues in Côte d'Ivoire. As a member of the ManaGlobal project, he was granted a scholarship to conduct research on the emergence of women digital entrepreneurship in Senegal.

Diallo, Aboubacar is a PhD student in socio-anthropology at Cheikh Anta DIOP University in Dakar (ED-ETHOS, LASAP, Senegal), specialising in rural sociology. He works on land conflicts in the Republic of Guinea, in particular the conflict between the Dar-Es-Salam district and the Sekhou Sorya district in the Madina-Oula sub-prefecture over the Fossikhouré and Tadara lowlands.

Diédhiou, Paul Mamba is a joint doctoral student in socio-anthropology, specialising in Economy and Society (UR2, LiRIS EA 7481 and UCAD). His PhD thesis is entitled "La multinationale 'Auchan' au Sénégal: entre controverses et logiques d'appropriation". His thesis analyses the problem of the implantation of a French multinational (Auchan) in one of its former colonies, Senegal, seeking to understand its management, administration, and distribution methods. This is an analysis of the globalisation of commercial and cultural practices, questioning the management and social marketing of Auchan in Senegal in an interconnected world. Paul Mamba Diédhiou works on issues related to the establishment of multinational companies, in particular large-scale food retailers in Senegal, and the controversies and social reactions to which they give rise. He is an adjunct lecturer in quantitative research methodology at UCAD. A book chapter from his thesis has just been published in *Entreprises, entrepreneurs et travail au Sénégal*, 2023, Paris: L'Harmattan, Ulrike Schuerkens (ed.).

Ekodo Bekono, Brigitte Audrey is a doctoral student jointly supervised by the University of Douala in political science and the University of Rennes 2 (LiRIS EA 7481) in sociology. She is working on the implementation of gender policies in the management of entrepreneurship by Cameroonian public policies. Specifically, she analyses the effectiveness of local public initiatives to promote women's entrepreneurship.

Fletcher, Kathy-Ann is an academic with over one decade of experience split between professional contexts of marketing and advertising agency in the Caribbean and the United Kingdom and growing academic experience in the UK. She currently lectures in marketing in the Division of Accounting, Business, and Management teaching largely within the digital marketing area but also some strategic marketing modules. She is also the programme leader for MSc in Digital Marketing and E-Business. Her research experience is within the digital marketing and consumer area with publications on the role of live stream social media on consumer behaviour and the influence of digital marketing on consumer behaviour in developing countries among others. Her PhD focused on the development of consumer identity in social media brand communities. Her current research focuses on the dynamics of digital marketing in SMEs and internationalisation strategies within emerging economies.

Forbes, Sharon L. is currently a Lecturer in marketing at Abertay University, Scotland, UK. Her previous academic role was at Lincoln University, New Zealand, from 2009 to 2019. Sharon Forbes's academic qualifications are also from Lincoln University; in 2004, she completed a Bachelor of Viticulture & Oenology undergraduate degree; in 2005, a Commerce Honours degree; and in 2009 a PhD in Marketing. Sharon Forbes's research interests centre on business and consumer studies in the wine and food sectors. In particular, she has led or participated in national and global studies that have examined sustainability, consumer behaviour, supply chain management, disaster resilience, social media marketing, and philanthropy.

Gning, Sadio Ba is a Lecturer in the sociology department at Gaston Berger University in Saint Louis, Senegal. Since completing her PhD in sociology in

2010 at the University of Picardie Jules Vernes in Amiens (France), her research has focused on women's entrepreneurship in the context of religious pluralism (Islam, Catholicism, Protestantism, animism) and gender-sensitive public policies.

Kouadio, Jean Claude holds a PhD in Sociology from the University of Rennes 2 and is a research associate at LIRIS (EA 7481, University of Rennes 2) and PhiLab (University of Quebec in Montréal). His areas of interest include philanthropy, globalisation, labour and employment, and development issues. Since October 2022, he has been a contract research assistant on a research project entitled "Impact strategies of African foundations", supported by the Telfer School of Management at the University of Ottawa (Canada). He has published several articles such as Jean Claude Kouadio and Saouré Kouamé (2022) "Transparency in African foundations: between opportunity, tension, and constraint", *The Philanthropic Year*, 4: 43–46.

Ndione, Mamadou is a research professor at ISTEC in Paris and a lecturer in management science at the University of Orleans. He holds a doctorate in management science from the University of Burgundy. He is a member of CREGO (*Centre de Recherche en Gestion des Organisations*) and the *Val de Loire Recherche en Management* laboratory (VALLOREM). His research focuses on entrepreneurship, particularly in Africa, microfinance, and sustainable development.

Oladejo, Mutiat Titilope is a Senior Lecturer in the Department of History, University of Ibadan, Nigeria. She is the coordinator of Oral History, Information Retrieval, and Documentation Unit of the Department of History, University of Ibadan. Her research focuses on women's studies and cross-cutting issues in African History. She has published four books relating to women, child health, textiles, and fashion. She is a fellow of the Council for Development of Social Research in Africa (CODESRIA) and the American Council of Learned Societies (ACLS).

Salla Bezanga, Estelle Vérine is a Lecturer at the University of Yaoundé II in political science. She holds a PhD in political science. She published with Gérard Amougou and Victorine Oyane Ossah (2021) "De l'assujettissement à la subjectivation. Parcours de jeunes gardiens domestiques originaires de la région de l'Extrême-Nord à Yaoundé", *Revue internationale des études du développement*, 246 (2): 181–206. Another book chapter from her is Estelle Vérine Salla Bezanga (2018) "L'universitaire dans l'administration d'Etat: La légitimation des politiques publiques par la mobilisation de l'expertise académique au Cameroun", in B. Biard (ed.), *L'État face à ses transformations,* pp. 169–179. Louvain-La-Neuve, Académia-L'Harmattan.

Sbai, Hicham is Director of the Interdisciplinary Laboratory for Research on Organizations (LIRO) at the National School of Commerce and Management of El Jadida (ENCGJ) where he is a Professor in the management department. He is also an associate member of CREOP (Center for Research on Companies, Organizations and Heritage, EA 4332) at the University of Limoges. He holds a doctorate in management sciences from the University of Limoges. His research focuses on mergers and acquisitions, bank governance, CSR, dividend policy, and gender diversity.

St-Jean, Étienne holds the Canada Research Chair in Entrepreneurial Careers at the *Université de Québec à Trois-Rivières* (UQTR). He is a Full Professor at the same university and director of the *Institut de Recherche sur les PME* (InRPME). He is responsible for the Global Entrepreneurship Monitor in Quebec. His work focuses on entrepreneurship and entrepreneurial intention, the training, coaching, and development of entrepreneurs through mentoring, and entrepreneurship as a specific career.

Schuerkens, Ulrike is a University Professor of Sociology and Social and Cultural Anthropology at the University Rennes 2, where she coordinated the EU-funded ManaGlobal (https://managlobal.hypotheses.org/) project within LiRIS EA 7481 from 2019 to 2023. Her research focuses on businesses and entrepreneurs in Africa. She has published some 15 books on social transformations and globalisation. Her books include: Schuerkens, Ulrike (ed.) (2023) *Entreprises, entrepreneurs et travail au Sénégal*. Paris: L'Harmattan; Schuerkens, Ulrike et al. (eds) (2019) *Pour une sociologie du management en Afrique et dans le monde arabe*. Paris: L'Harmattan; Schuerkens, Ulrike (2017) *Social Changes in a Global World*. London: Sage.

Scotto, Marie José is a Professor at IPAG Business School in Paris and Nice, and Head of the Human Resources and CSR Department. She is also responsible for various master's programmes in Nice and Paris. She teaches Human Resources, Corporate Organization, and Management Theories. She holds an MBA from the HEC business school and a PhD in Management Sciences (University of Auvergne, Clermont 1), and worked for several years as a project manager in a French IT services company. Her research focuses on Human Resources Management and Gender Diversity. She regularly publishes academic articles in peer-reviewed journals, symposia, and as book chapters. Marie José Scotto is also a member of ANDRH, National Association of Human Resources Directors and AGRH, Association of Researchers in Human Resources Management.

Toche, Lolita holds a doctorate in economics and society from Rennes 2 University and is a qualified lecturer in management science (France). She is a postdoctoral researcher in entrepreneurship at the *Institut de recherche sur les PME* (InRPME) at the *Université de Québec à Trois-Rivières*. She also works as a financial analyst at the *Réseau d'Investissement Social du Québec* (RISQ). Her research focuses on women's entrepreneurship, collective entrepreneurship, youth entrepreneurship, and the social economy. Her doctorate analysed the entrepreneurial dynamics of women setting up collective enterprises. She also published an article on offshoring and its impact on work-based support establishments and services, a book chapter on the informal sector and female entrepreneurship in Africa, and another on youth entrepreneurship in Quebec.

Preface

I want to thank the Senior Editor, Global Development & African Studies at Routledge, Ms Helena Hurd who suggested to write this edited book on women entrepreneurs and who has supported the preparation of the manuscript with many valuable comments. My special thanks go to the European Association of Development Research and Training Institutes and its conference in Lisbon (Portugal, June 2023), the World Congress of the International Sociological Association in Melbourne (Australia, July 2023), and the Association for the Anthropology of Social Change and Development and its conference in Liège (Belgium, May 2024). At these conferences, I could give talks on these topics in individual sessions and several of the chapters of this book were presented. I would like to especially thank the publishers of two reviews that kindly authorised me to publish in English largely modified versions of two articles recently published in French. I would also like to thank L'Harmattan that kindly authorised me to publish in English an article that I published in French in a book in 2023. I would also like to thank the Research Committee 09 Sociology of Development and Social Transformations of the International Sociological Association that I have been honoured to chair for several years. The Research Committee's sessions organised at the World Conference in Melbourne (Australia, July 2023) made possible several edited chapters of this book that were presented as individual papers on this occasion. Thanks to the many conference participants, the young students, and experienced colleagues who have contributed with their case studies to this volume. My thanks also go to my colleagues at the Université Cheikh Anta Diop in Dakar (Senegal) and to my current and former PhD students at the University Rennes 2 who have contributed to this research on global-local aspects of the life of women entrepreneurs. Furthermore, I would like to thank my students at the University Rennes 2 who have commented on the various chapters and the individual topics of this book with their enthusiasm, which has contributed to improving my understanding of these research fields. For many years, I have greatly enjoyed teaching and research with these groups interested in similar topics.

Finally, I want to thank the anonymous reviewers for their valuable comments on my book proposal and the first chapters of this book at Routledge. They have ensured that some of my ideas could develop in a most productive way. Finally,

I am responsible for any remaining shortcomings that were hard to avoid in the width of the tackled topics.

I dedicate this book to my late mother who always supported my projects and ideas as the wife of an entrepreneur. I have to thank her for her continuous understanding of my objectives.

Paris, August 2024

Acknowledgements

Chapter 3: This chapter was published in French and is here published with the kind authorisation of the review: Haoua Badini Koné (2021) "Entrepreneuriat féminin à domicile à Abidjan en Côte d'Ivoire: Gouvernance partenariale et perpétuation de la relève", *Revue Organisations & Territoires*, 30 (2): 39–52. https://doi.org/10.1522/revueot.v30n2.1348

Chapter 7: This chapter was published in French and is here published with the kind authorisation of the publisher: Ulrike Schuerkens (2023) "Les femmes entrepreneures au Sénégal et le contexte géographique plus large de l'Afrique et de l'Europe", in Ulrike Schuerkens (ed.) *Entreprises, entrepreneurs et travail au Sénégal*, pp. 237–254. © L'Harmattan, Paris, 2023.

Chapter 9: This chapter was published in French and is here published with the kind authorisation of the review: Sadio Ba Gning (2021) "Biographies relationnelles d'entrepreneures sociales au Sénégal", *RECMA, Revue internationale de l'économie sociale,* 362 (4): 66–80.

Part 1

Introduction

West African Women Entrepreneurs in a Glocal World

1 West African Women Entrepreneurs in a *Glocal* World

Ulrike Schuerkens

The initiative to write this book was based on three sessions that I organised at the 20th World Congress of the International Sociological Association in Melbourne, Australia, in June 2023 and a second one at the General Conference of the European Association of Development Institutes in Lisbon in July 2023. A third session was organised at the University of Liège, Belgium, at the Conference of the Association for the Anthropology of Social Change and Development in May 2024. These three sessions reunited several papers that were supplemented by other papers from colleagues that I have contacted asking them if their research could be integrated in this edited book. This volume constitutes a part of the ManaGlobal RISE project financed by the European Commission[1] that includes three countries South of the Sahara, such as Senegal, Cameroon, and Ghana. Several other countries could be included in the book such as the Ivory Coast and Nigeria.

Entrepreneurship is here conceived as the process of managing and creating an income-generating activity as a combination of personal factors that permit women to act more rapidly and more effectively than others do (Cf. de Bruin et al., 2007; Amine and Staub, 2009; Brush et al., 2009; Brush and Cooper, 2012), and of economic conditions of the environment in which opportunities are widespread (Berry, 2019: 457; Ojong et al., 2021: 236). As Ojong et al. write: "Micro-level factors (individual resources and different forms of capital) interact with macro-level factors (the economy and wider institutional framework) affecting female entrepreneurs to help shape entrepreneurial strategies".

African women are rarely caring full-time of their household, husband, and children. Many of them have created small shops in front of their homes, or they rent stalls in the market or establish shops where they take care of a hairstyling business or where they sell food (Spring, 2009). A study by the World Bank in 2018 (World Bank Economic Report) already revealed that in Africa more women than men become entrepreneurs (cf. also World Economic Forum 2012 and 2015; World Bank, 2022 and 2023). The purpose of this book is thus to explore women entrepreneurship in sub-Saharan West Africa. This topic has rarely been discussed in entrepreneurship and there only exists some recent articles in French published in journals, mainly based on PhD theses on the French side (Etim and Gervase Iwu, 2019) and articles on some countries in English-speaking Africa (cf. Ojong et al., 2021). A recent book on African women entrepreneurs was focused on a historical perspective and above all life stories of women (Anyansi-Archibong, 2021).

DOI: 10.4324/9781003492931-2

This new book focuses on current and actual topics on West African women entrepreneurship that can be discussed in business schools and universities of the continent that too rarely consecrate courses on the female part of entrepreneurs. These limited research and teaching correspond to the perceived roles of women in the development of African regions and the existing gender differences. I want to change this discourse and this knowledge with this book. The different chapters of the book tackle micro-entrepreneurs but also more established entrepreneurs. They display that the topic is highly significant for students and their life stories to be defined, for researchers to include the focus of women entrepreneurs in their teaching, and for political actors that can find here the presentation of an overview of recent research topics that need political actions.

Focusing on women entrepreneurs and their employment situation will help us to improve the national, regional, and continental socio-economic development that needs perspectives that can be looked for by women entrepreneurs who may engage in entrepreneurship because of economic necessity and/or new opportunities. Knowing possible solutions will permit a young generation of female students to engage in paths that they are encouraged to undertake by teachers, political actors, and husbands thus contributing to slowly changed gender roles in the region linked to a fast-changing *glocal* economy. This book will raise awareness on employment situations in the wider region of sub-Saharan West Africa and the multifaceted aspects of women entrepreneurship. The authors of the different chapters discuss topics that need further efforts to understand West African socio-economic systems. Questions such as informal work, social entrepreneurship, philanthropy of women entrepreneurs, sustainable economic projects, and different forms of entrepreneurship such as poverty-induced economic situations, but also employments in the IT sector, will permit to clarify the activities of these female entrepreneurs. Advances in technology, globalisation, and other forms of innovation ask for new ways of creating businesses.

This book innovates our knowledge on West African women entrepreneurs and hopefully contributes to improve the knowledge on female entrepreneurship in West Africa. We aim to recover the voices, works, and experiences of women through field studies whose descriptions will permit business school lecturers to choose topics for their classes with students who wish to know more on female entrepreneurship.

The disciplines of the different authors are multiple: anthropology, sociology, economy, gender studies, and management studies. We will show how women of different backgrounds engage with new socio-economic situations in their everyday life. We will not focus on men but on the topic of how women make places and cultural choices. This book is thus influenced by a history of below and displays women entrepreneurs that are fundamental for larger societies on the continent. A Eurocentric perspective isn't chosen but instead life situations that are mainly influenced by local cultural traditions and the impact of globalisation on West African societies. The different chapters are meant to address recent important challenges that may become the focus of teaching for the next generation of women entrepreneurs. This teaching must be open to new research results and the necessity to create jobs for millions of young people that arrive on the African job market every year.

In fields otherwise dominated by a white, male, and Euro-centric perspective, a focus on women entrepreneurs will renew teaching and trigger new courses that include the diversity demands of today's students. We hope that this book will be a starting point for a wider change in entrepreneurship taught in business schools and universities of the African continent but also in African studies sections in Europe or the United States.

Being linked to the ManaGlobal project, we are interested to learn more about the possible factors that contribute to the socio-economic success of female entrepreneurs in sub-Saharan West Africa. We believe that socio-cultural dynamics that are close to gender stereotypes influence the success of women entrepreneurs. The underrepresentation of African women in entrepreneurship and in SMEs contributes to the difficult move from a subsistence-based form to a modern economy, based on industrialisation and services.

Entrepreneurs are those men and women who create new businesses based on new needs and new services that may be successful if adopted by customers who need these goods and services. Skills, raw materials, and low-end technology may impact the socio-economies of West African countries (Matsoso and Gervase Iwu, 2016; Lo, 2016). Yet, women don't receive the same level of funding as their male counterparts with the consequence that they are less productive regarding socio-economic development. The World Economic Forum (2012) considered that Western governments and NGOs should emphasise female entrepreneurs whose activities are considered to lead to improved social situations of their families and communities (cf. Etim and Gervase Iwu, 2019: 2). Growth and development should be attained through activities destined to women. So far, fewer women than men have success in leading businesses (Vossenberg, 2013). These women are more often exposed to failure and exit the businesses that they may have created (Etim and Gervase Iwu, 2019: 2). To enlarge the participation of women in the economy, it is important to create jobs and improve socio-economic development. However, there are gaps in our knowledge because women entrepreneurs are underrepresented in successful businesses in sub-Saharan West Africa. This book will contribute to having a closer look on this situation and will suggest ways to improve the living of millions of African women entrepreneurs.

Some of the constraints of female entrepreneurs are the lack of funding, few useful networks, and poor management knowledge to be applied. However, SMEs are regarded as agents of change that create jobs and reduce poverty to contribute finally to an improvement of living standards in African countries (cf. Lo, 2016). Other problematic factors are linked to stereotypes, patriarchal and family situations that are demanding and hinder entrepreneurial success. These disadvantages are seen as barriers to women's professional uptake. As such they contribute to gender differences that are hard to change. As the article of Etim and Gervase Iwu (2019: 12) suggests, women have difficulties to obtain loans as they are "unlikely to offer a collateral". Moreover, "there is very little confidence in her ability to run a business" (13).

The studies in this book are thus intended to focus on gender and economic success. Traditional roles of women but also knowledge defiance are contributing to difficult female socio-economic situations that are moreover influenced by a class structure that attributes better chances to women of privileged origins. By the variety of the topics of this book, the opportunity is given to approach women entrepreneurship in West Africa in a significant way that should permit progress and change.

A final chapter insists on the future of women entrepreneurship in West Africa and its contribution to continental development and economic growth. A decisive factor will be entrepreneurship education for women that encourages them to engage in an entrepreneurial career based on knowledge that permits them to obtain loans, create social networks locally and internationally, and get positions in enterprises besides their roles as mothers and wives. Teaching has thus to develop entrepreneurial thinking and skills through internships that contribute to the creation of effective human capital, linking traditional knowledge with new experiences of entrepreneurial development. The results of the ManaGlobal project can be introduced in these learning processes that need to understand *glocal* economic situations influenced by traditional African cultural processes and the new knowledge obtained by management studies taught in business schools, whose courses are often based on Western knowledge. Curricula must be developed that insist on the link of these traditional and Western knowledge pieces that must be critically understood as possible *glocal* forms of management so that business successes will only be secured by an understanding of these *glocal* economic situations. Moreover, ways must be found to change traditional gender roles as new economic opportunities for women are created and cultural norms are being transformed in the *glocal* world that influences African economies and societies (cf. Schuerkens, 2017 and Schuerkens (ed.), 2023). The female economy is in fact a large emergent market with the possibility to add $12 trillion to the global GDP (Anyansi-Archibong, 2021: 169) on the African continent where more women than men create enterprises even if most of them are small, with fewer gains as those of male entrepreneurs as they are often in the informal sector.

In West Africa, necessity-driven entrepreneurs often linked to the past will be supplemented by opportunity-driven entrepreneurs who base their success on knowledge acquisition in business schools and universities. Today, female physicians and pharmacists are looking for their own clinics and stores instead of seeking employment in hospitals and enterprises. A more global reach and links to the African diaspora will be assets for parts of women entrepreneurs that look for innovative solutions (cf. Schuerkens (ed.), 2023 and the chapter on women entrepreneurs in Senegal). Political support for women entrepreneurship will assist these women to look successfully for funding, such as that given by the *Délégation Générale à l'Entreprenariat Rapide des Femmes et des Jeunes* (DER/FJ) in Senegal (Schuerkens (ed.), 2023) that gives loans and business support to women entrepreneurs since 2018.

Globalisation and the Problem of Global Cultural Diversity

The processes here described must be considered as a new cultural diversity that has been intensively influenced by *glocal* (global-local) socio-economic processes

(Hannerz, 1992). To clarify, I refer to earlier publications on this topic (Schuerkens, 2017 and Schuerkens (ed.), 2019) that permit inserting the lifeworld of West African female entrepreneurs in the context of glocalisation.

Currently, the processes of local absorptions of global cultural flows and the mix between global and local cultural elements are frequently examined (Peterson, 2009). It has been shown that the global cannot exist without the local. The local is the space, "in which a variety of influences come together, acted out perhaps in a unique combination, under those special conditions" (Hannerz, 1996: 27).

The essential elements of the local can be found in the local daily lifeworld. Hannerz called it the "form-of-life context". This framework includes daily activities at home, at work, and in the neighbourhood, daily emotional face-to-face relationships with other people in the region, and daily uses of symbolic forms, in short, all those elements that last long and are part of the local life (Hannerz, 1996: 28). These events and experiences of local everyday life are considered as direct and genuine. Often, these elements have a great impact on people's lives. The local daily life is regarded as the central area of the organisation, production, and dissemination of culture. Here we find a constant circulation of meanings, including any person participating in local life, each consumer, and each worker. Hannerz (1996: 73) wrote: "It is by way of people's attentions to one another in situations within the form-of-life frame (…) that meanings are most continuously and precisely constructed".

This means that the central role of the life framework regarding external cultural inflows must be negotiated with local daily actions and interactions. A cultural inflow is filtered by local human experiences that allow the adoption, rejection, interpretation, and transformation of actions and forms. Long (1996: 50) wrote: "In fact, globalization itself can only be meaningful to actors if the new experiences it simultaneously engenders are made meaningful by reference to existing experiences and cultural understandings".

What is now the central role of globalisation in the construction of meanings and in the reception of external cultural elements? Because of this cultural power of the local, everyday possibilities of cultural influences from the global culture are strongly limited. But this local living environment will change; it is limited in time so an unchanged cultural continuity cannot be guaranteed. New cultural elements are introduced by TV series, Western consumer goods, and values of migrants; they may become elements of the local everyday life, often in changed forms and adapted to the local conditions. Families are the most important places of cultural reproduction and transmission of traditions of immense external influences through processes of globalisation: A trans-generational continuity of attitudes, beliefs, and desires is thus more and more undermined.

The local culture and the local daily life can no longer be considered as a space where practices and dispositions are transmitted (Appadurai, 1990: 18). The life and the cultural identity of a people are becoming less constructed according to a traditional setting. Due to mass media and other aspects of globalisation, numerous possible lifestyles and identification models are currently used by different actors in local dimensions. They represent ideas, fantasies, and inspire perspectives that are not the same as traditional local representations and lifestyles. Imagination and tentative adaptation play an increasingly important role in the creation of an individual life. Individual lifestyles, values, and behaviours of people are thus more and more different from local cultural traditions.

The mutual influence of the local and the global means a continuous interaction of local cultural elements and global cultural influences in the local cultural construction of local meanings and cultural forms.

Globalisation and the Emphasis on Local Cultures

Parallel to global integration and the increasing importance of transnational levels, we find an intensification of local cultural traditions that must be considered as a countertrend in the current global world. We can thus find an increasing importance of local characteristics and differentiation (cf. Freeman, 2001).

These processes can be found in numerous societal fields: economics, politics, environmental movements, cultural values, etc. They can be an expression of enrichment, revitalising and reinventing local cultural identities and traditions, considering common ethnic, social, or religious elements. Several factors explain the appearance of these trends: local groups, global connections, and their influence on local elements interpreted as an attack on vague fears in the face of their own culture. The speed and extent of global change and the complexity of global systems may also help to strengthen the desire for stability and continuity. This new sort of localism permits to establish a refuge from the difficult larger world. References to local communities and local values, the revitalisation of traditional cultures, and an emphasis on local cultural identities may permit a feeling of stability and confidence in the face of globalisation processes.

From this perspective, the focus is not directed at one's own culture against another real culture – even if groups who are concerned often emphasise this factor – but against the feared effects of processes of globalisation. At the same time, the emphasis on local cultures may mean in Western and Southern countries the opposition to globalisation processes and their origin.

Another trend needs to be considered here: The worldwide development of a new cultural self-consciousness. This cultural self-awareness is growing due to the global spread of ideas and values and the worldwide recognition of culture and cultural elements as a universal value. A global recognition of the right to an own culture and cultural self-determination accompanies these processes. As the idea of landscapes studied by Appadurai shows, a global spread of ideas and values is part of the current globalisation processes. The fact that more and more groups consider their culture and lifestyle as a political right lets them put an emphasis on their own culture. Today, due to mass media and global migration flows, global cultural differences are thus easier to determine and find out.

In conclusion on this theoretical part, we can state that many of the inflowing cultural elements are transformed during the processes of integration and embedding in new local environments. They are interpreted by local populations in terms of local cultures and experiences. They are accepted with the help of local requirements and are filled with appropriate content and functions. Hannerz (1992: 238) showed that this process takes its time in reshaping the global culture. But these processes of local appropriation and transformation of cultural elements allow the emergence – due to the mixture of local and imported cultural elements – of something new and unique. The local clash of different cultural elements is a creation of new cultural forms, new lifestyles, and new representations. According to a global perspective, this means a global cultural diversity: but a diversity resulting from the current global cultural relations, from the cultural appropriation of external elements by local populations, and from the creative mixture of "global" elements with local cultural meanings and forms.

The global culture is certainly not a one-way street but may rightly be interpreted as "a global intercultural interplay", as Nederveen Pieterse (1993: 9) described it. The countries of the South export, for example, their music, their literature, their spirituality, or healing methods in the countries of the northern hemisphere. These trends are not new, but due to processes of globalisation, their importance increases: migrants and the media, tourists and scientists are constantly looking for innovations in other cultures and are interested in "exotic" and "authentic" cultures.

Overview of the Different Chapters of the Volume

The first part of this book includes a short introduction written by Ulrike Schuerkens and her first chapter on "West African Women Entrepreneurs in a *Glocal* World" where a theoretical discussion is outlined and an overview over the different chapters is given. The second chapter includes an historical chapter on wealth making in marriage by the example of Simbiat Abiola of Southwestern Nigeria, 1938–1992. This historical chapter permits to describe the historical phenomena of wealth making in the region during the last decades of colonisation, over the first years of independence until the beginning of a global era in West Africa.

The chapter "Wealth Making in Marriage: Simbiat Abiola of Southwestern Nigeria, 1938–1992" was written by Mutiat Titilope Oladejo. In many accounts of family businesses in Africa, it is rare to find women visibly involved. In precolonial Yorubaland, women work to promote family vocations in lineages because life is communal. Within homes, women work, fulfil domestic roles, and converge at market centres to trade simultaneously; thus, it was difficult to separate work and domesticity. Basically, colonialism changed the dynamics of gender and kinship relations in families. Men in the colonial era had the opportunity to work out of towns and family farms, thus leaving women behind. Yet, women were rarely entitled to inherit properties. The milieus affected women's livelihood in colonial Yorubaland. It is in this context of colonialism that Simbiat Abiola was born in Abeokuta in 1938. Wealth creation for women was stifled during this era, but Simbiat Abiola's life history was atypical.

The Family Embeddedness Perspective is used to explain the transitions, social norms, and resources derived from the family as stimulators of entrepreneurial growth. Thus, the chapter analyses Simbiat Abiola's transition from girlhood to wife and the implication on the wealth-making life she shared with her husband till her death in 1992. With emphasis on the change and dynamics in the entrepreneurial patterns across time, this study explains the factors that aided the growth of wealth in her marriage and gender relations in the family business. The explanations feature the rarity of having women build and manage businesses in the formal sector in Nigerian business history. The study uses prosopography to present the realities in the wealth-making life of Simbiat Abiola, with a view to establish her roles in building family businesses into an organised private sector in Nigerian business history.

The second part of the book includes four chapters that describe the processes of the creation of women enterprises mainly on linking informal and formal practices that one can find in current urban and partly rural places of the region.

The first chapter on "Women's Home-Based Entrepreneurship in Abidjan, Côte d'Ivoire: Partnership Governance and Succession Planning" from Haoua Badini Koné on female entrepreneurship in Africa shows that women use specific management characteristics. The chapter highlights entrepreneurship practised at home by women with the support of the family network. This type of entrepreneurship still lacks a strong theoretical foundation. The aim of this chapter is to show how this home-based female entrepreneurship, analysed through the prism of partnership governance, contributes to learning responsible behaviour conducive to succession. The study is rooted in the theories of social capital, corporate social responsibility (CSR), and partnership governance. Interviews conducted with 16 women entrepreneurs from different backgrounds in Abidjan, Côte d'Ivoire, show that in addition to seizing business opportunities, these women share a desire to pass on entrepreneurial know-how to the next generation.

The chapter of Estelle Salla Bezanga "Digital Businesses and the Construction of Social Legitimacy for Women in Cameroon" wants to understand the capacity of women entrepreneurs in the informal economy sector to overcome the changes brought about by COVID-19. To do this, the analytical approach is structuralist, based on a network of symbolic relationships that make possible a political analysis of the position of women in Cameroon, the crisis, and their empowerment.

One of the major social transformations brought about by COVID-19 in Cameroon with the internet is the development of e-shop commercial activities. At the heart of this movement are women whose socio-economic profiles are in a situation of financial vulnerability. These women's commercial activities range from the clothing industry to the food industry, including cosmetics, catering, and natural health products. While their motivations are part of a personal development dynamic that is linked to their backgrounds, most of these women are using digital platforms to make money and get out of their precarious situation. Relying on a network of wholesale suppliers based in China, Turkey, and the major shopping centres of Yaoundé and Douala, these saleswomen are helping to dematerialise the sales areas and digitise them. This is due to the many advantages offered by the phenomenon: The payment of rent replaces the payment of an internet package for the various transactions. This form of utilitarian accumulation of digital capital provides information not only on the socio-economic transformation of Cameroon by social cadets but also on the meaning of the relationships between these online vendors, their customers and suppliers, and the patriarchal structure of the social system.

The chapter "Analysis of the Motivations and Constraints of Pre-existing Women's Groups in the Process of Creating a Collective Enterprise: The Case of the Creation of a Cooperative by a Women's Group in the West Region of Cameroon" from Lolita Toche and Etienne St-Jean tackles a cooperative that Lolita Toche accompanied for her PhD thesis at the University Rennes 2.

What happens when a women's group seizes a collective entrepreneurship opportunity in Africa? This is the question that guides this chapter, based on an analysis of the constraints and motivations of women entrepreneurs to understand their presence in the informal sector and the interest of the collective. The authors present a project to set up a women's cooperative to process avocados into oil, in the western region of Cameroon. To do this, Lolita Toche carried out intervention research with a pre-existing women's group that was behind the project in question. The main findings were that the idea for setting up a business does not always come from the group concerned, but that the prior existence of the group encourages a predisposition to collective entrepreneurship. In addition, the group encourages the mobilisation of local collective savings to finance the project, reflecting the importance of solidarity-based finance in development projects led by women and subsequently by men. In addition, the endogenous nature of the initiative and confidence in their "collective strength" could increase the chances of success of this women's collective project.

The chapter "The Auchan Brand in Senegal: A Source of Supply for Women Stallholders in Mbour – A Link to Working-Class Consumers" was written by Paul Mamba Diédhiou, PhD student at Université Cheikh Anta Diop, Senegal, and University Rennes 2, France. In Senegal, local markets (fixed and weekly), wholesalers, and neighbourhood stores have always been the places where consumer products are purchased. However, the liberal and/or anarchic pricing of products is increasingly forcing local traders, particularly stallholders, to explore other sources of supply.

In the department of Mbour, located in the Thiès region of Senegal, the multinational Auchan has become a source of supply for women stallholders. In fact, to diversify their sources of supply, and to innovate their managerial and marketing strategies, and diversify their offers, these women buy from Auchan some of the products (local and imported) that they display and sell afterwards. The study of this phenomenon allows us to better understand the logic of supply and the rationalities that structure them, as well as the managerial and marketing practices of these women at Auchan.

The third part of the book describes women entrepreneurs and their enterprises. It is based on qualitative research with owners of formal enterprises that have been growing this last decade with an increase in female education at secondary and university levels. These groups of women have rarely become the topic of research in the social sciences so that the chapters present empirical cases that are relatively hidden in the social sciences literature.

The chapter "Women Entrepreneurs in Senegal and the Wider Geographical Context of Africa and Europe" by Ulrike Schuerkens was prepared as part of the ManaGlobal project. The existing research on women in entrepreneurship has improved our understanding of structural inequalities in markets. However, this research focuses on women entrepreneurs in the North, including the United States and Europe (Edoho 2015; Sheriff and Muffatto, 2015). There is a lack of information on the challenges and obstacles of women in Africa (both North Africa and sub-Saharan Africa) to manage and start a new business (cf. Diop Thiam, 2015; Mbodji Diop, 2019). The research question was: How do female entrepreneurs perceive and describe the experience of running a successful formal business in West Africa and beyond? This chapter intends to understand how women entrepreneurs make meaning from their lived experiences. Empirical case studies from Senegal and the African diaspora are presented.

The chapter gives an overview on successful women entrepreneurs in Senegal who link the African continent and France in their professional activities. The life stories of these women have been collected in Dakar during the fieldwork of the ManaGlobal project that was funded by the European Union. These stories show how successful women can enter economic fields that are neglected by large business owners, such as the beauty sector and the food sector. Theoretical reflections could also be deducted from this case study. The chapter was published in a book that Ulrike Schuerkens edited in 2023 in French: *Entreprises, entrepreneurs et travail au Sénégal* (Paris and Dakar: L'Harmattan).

The chapter written by Abdul-Aziz Dembélé "New Figures in Women's Entrepreneurship in Sub-Saharan Africa: Dakar Women Entrepreneurs between the Global and the Local in Digitalisation" argues that the literature on women's entrepreneurship in sub-Saharan Africa is characterised by two main figures: that of "success", embodied by the businesswoman involved in transnational trade networks, and that of "survival", illustrated by the trader in the informal economy. Based on a field study conducted in Dakar, Senegal, in July and August 2023, financed by the European RISE project ManaGlobal, this chapter paints a portrait of 15 women entrepreneurs. Most of these women have a high level of education, and their businesses operate in the formal sector. Using a comprehensive sociological framework, the aim of this chapter is to give an account of the subjective meaning that these women give to their entrepreneurial commitment and the ways in which it unfolds. The analysis is divided into two parts. The first looks at the rationale behind their entrepreneurial activities. This part shows that business creation, a complex and multidimensional phenomenon, is expressed by these women through personal dispositions, individual or family aspirations, the discovery of business opportunities, and economic constraints. Far from being solely confined to subjective dimensions, the analysis of these women's entrepreneurial commitment is set in a broader socio-economic context characterised by migratory phenomena, the increased responsibility of women in the household economy, the tightening of conditions of access to employment for young people, and the recent pandemic of COVID-19. The second part looks at the economic, cognitive, social, and institutional resources on which these women rely to develop their businesses. By showing that a large proportion of these resources is acquired or has been acquired through social trials and institutional selection mechanisms, it is argued that these women's entrepreneurial commitment is experienced and expressed as a form of "self-affirmation" in contrast to the public role. The implications of the results of this study are discussed both at the level of the academic field, where there is little existing work on these new figures of women's entrepreneurship in Africa, and at the level of policymaking, where the need to redefine current policies to promote entrepreneurship in Africa is emphasised.

Based on a qualitative analysis of the trajectories, the chapter "Relational Biographies of Women Social Entrepreneurs in Senegal" by Sadio Ba Gning reveals the process of social construction of female entrepreneurs through the prism of the analysis of relational networks – on the one hand, the embedding of the trajectories in family and associative links (including religious and political) at different professional and institutional levels – and on the other hand, the diversity of female social entrepreneur figures whose trajectories depend on a long process of (re)construction and (de)construction of multiple links.

The aim of this research[2] was to study the dynamics of networks in the trajectories of female social entrepreneurs and to show the extent to which they are embedded in multiplex links to access the resources available in their networks. In the first part, the author presents the data from the survey, showing the general and specific characteristics of these women entrepreneurs. The second part of her presentation displays the space of these networks by describing a series of sometimes overlapping links that cross the trajectories. In the third part, the overlap of these old, recent, and new social relationships enables the author to show, in a dynamic way, how family and associative ties are embedded in pathways and networks, through the regularities, continuities, changes, ruptures, and (re)configurations during entrepreneurial trajectories.

The diversification of networks at the heart of these trajectories reveals a long and complex process of embedding and decoupling. The multiplex nature of these networks reflects the ability of women entrepreneurs to embed their professional trajectories in relationships that *ultimately* prove instrumental, enabling them to achieve their goals through the synchronisation of different time horizons. The dual strategy of anchoring (family and religion) and conquering (political and institutional), both serve to legitimise and moralise women's entrepreneurship, which in turn fosters recognition and enhancement of the career paths of social entrepreneurs. Through the plurality of anchors and logics of totalising conquests, the construction of women entrepreneurs' paths reveals both the complexity of the embedding process and the decoupling, which through these interdependent, interwoven, and multiplex relational links allows us to grasp the multidimensional character of the woman entrepreneur and her plural figures.

Creating jobs, maintaining high labour force participation rates, and improving the quality of the workforce are among the major challenges that Africans face in the labour market. This must undoubtedly also involve entrepreneurship, since this is the key to success for young people in Africa (Lam, 2019). However, in addition to the informal situation, insalubrity, and the problem of acquiring places or workshops faced by women dressmakers in Senegal, the lack of financial resources is the main cause of their difficulties. One effective strategy for these women dressmakers to access finance is to form associations. In this context, since 2015, the *Association des Femmes Couturières de Colobane* (AFC) has been created, with a state-recognised receipt, moving from the informal to the formal and able to ensure their claims at the level of the authorities. However, despite the financial opportunities it offers, many women of the AFC are disaffiliating, described by Paul Mamba Diédhiou and Aboubacar Diallo.

The qualitative methodology used, based on a categorical thematic content analysis (N'Da, 2015), suggests that the disaffiliation of women dressmakers from AFC stems not only from the dysfunction but also from the illegitimacy and lack of leadership of the women responsible for ensuring its viability. Added to this were the rumours that led to a crisis of confidence between leaders and other members. Despite this, the presence of people with political experience is an undeniable asset in the search for funding. Disaffiliated members of the AFC have found alternatives, such as participating in tontines and selling their products online to boost their activities, and become more independent.

The fourth part of the book is dedicated to women entrepreneurs and new upcoming challenges, such as participatory financing, public policies to promote female entrepreneurship, women as philanthropes, and business sustainability adoption by Ghanaian women entrepreneurs.

The chapter "Participatory Financing in Senegal and Its Role in Financing Female Entrepreneurship: An Empirical Case Study" by M. Ndione, H. Sbai, and M.-J. Scotto intends to make an inventory of participatory finance in Senegal and to see its role in the financing of female entrepreneurship. This research tackles a topic that has rather been neglected so far and that displays interesting aspects that need to be better known. The authors collected information by web scraping on the crowdfunding sites that exist for Senegal through the Google search engine. In addition, they administered a questionnaire to 44 entrepreneurs to examine the place occupied by crowdfunding in their entrepreneurial activities. This exploratory empirical study, the first stage of a more in-depth research, makes it possible to identify the actors of participatory financing in Senegal and to display, moreover, the widespread ignorance of this mode of financing among women entrepreneurs in Senegal.

The chapter "Factors in the Success and Failure of Public Policies to Promote Female Entrepreneurship in Cameroon" written by Brigitte Audrey Ekodo Bekono looks at the success and failure factors of public policies to promote female entrepreneurship in Cameroon. The study, conducted among 20 women entrepreneurs in the city of Yaoundé, is structured around three categories of public policy impact: regulation and administration, support and capacity-building structures, and financing structures.

The regulation and administration of public policies for women's entrepreneurship are supposed to guarantee equal opportunities but do not consider the specific challenges faced by women. As far as support and capacity-building structures are concerned, institutional structures such as the Ministry for the Promotion of Women and the Family have been created to combat gender disparities, particularly in entrepreneurship. However, these efforts remain theoretical and are struggling to bring about concrete change. Financing structures are another challenge. Although initiatives have been put in place to facilitate access to finance for women entrepreneurs, studies show that complex procedures, lack of information, and the low penetration rate of financial services in rural areas hamper their effectiveness.

The chapter concludes that public policies to promote women's entrepreneurship in Cameroon have significant shortcomings, and that research shows that without in-depth knowledge of the specific needs of women entrepreneurs and appropriate implementation, public policies often fail to achieve their objectives.

The chapter "Women Entrepreneurs in Côte d'Ivoire's Philanthropic Landscape" by Jean Claude Kouadio analyses female philanthropy measures. In Côte d'Ivoire, apart from the philanthropy of businessmen, politicians, and first ladies (or the philanthropy of the wives of politicians), there is a new phenomenon in the philanthropic landscape with the activities of women entrepreneurs. A few women who have succeeded in the business world are increasingly involved in philanthropic activities. These actions mainly take the form of one-off donations to help vulnerable populations. For those who are more committed, they set up foundations to support causes such as education, health, or the empowerment of women. This chapter looks at the profiles of these women and the motivations at the heart of their commitment.

The chapter "Business Sustainability Adoption by Ghanaian Women Entrepreneurs" written by Philomena Asante, Kathy-Ann Fletcher, and Sharon L. Forbes tackles a topic that is one of those that will know tremendous developments in the coming years not only in the northern hemisphere but also in the South. The sustainability challenge is a worldwide important task that needs to be analysed in the North and the South to obtain sustainable practices that can influence positively the climate challenge.

Sustainability adoption among businesses is a priority for a range of stakeholders. The UN's Sustainable Development Goals drive adoption among a range of sectors and motivate academic interest. While much investigation of sustainability adoption has focused on corporations and developed countries, more attention needs to be paid to emerging markets, a gap that is being addressed by this study that makes three main contributions. Firstly, it provides insights to businesses and entrepreneurs about designing sustainability into their operations. Secondly, the authors are giving policymakers an understanding of the barriers that exist and the importance of creating a facilitating environment for sustainable adoption in businesses. Thirdly, the study shows academics a practical application of the use of Sustainable Design Theory from the context of women entrepreneurs in Ghana. Using a quantitative method of questionnaires, the study finds a positive correlation between thinking of the environmental and social impact of a business with planning and implementing sustainable actions within a company.

The fifth and last part of the book includes some concluding remarks and perspectives for future research on women entrepreneurs in Africa.

Conclusion

The different chapters of this book reveal important new research results on women entrepreneurs in West Africa that display a social reality that is different from what has been described at the beginning of this century. The chapters show multiple aspects that describe a social reality that is on the move. The life histories presented let appear the *glocal* situation of these women who are influenced by globalisation and management knowledge that parts of them learnt in universities of the northern hemisphere. These women are also influenced by local traditions and the knowledge they have on local African cultures that contribute to their success. They are no longer the poor women of West African societies that are exposed to global processes but actors that redefine their roles in African societies. As such, these studies reveal new processes that should be taught in business schools and universities to inform students on these social realities that are on the move. While several chapters are dedicated to women who have privileged origins and lead successful lives as entrepreneurs, others focus on women stall holders, or women that are active in businesses organised before their homes. All these women entrepreneurs lead lives that connect them to African and global sources. Their activities are different from profiles that were described at the end of the 20th century and the beginning of the 21st century. Scholars on African societies most often described the lives of poor women, some years ago. Publications continue to have a focus on poor women, such as Lam (2019) and Kane and Chroqui (2021). The latter describes entrepreneurs that choose their activities to survive. They are not challenged by opportunities that they are looking for themselves and their environment. Our focus in this book is mainly female entrepreneurs who had success with their enterprises and live lives that are different from most of the necessity-driven creation of enterprises often described in the literature. Another focus was put on the practices of female entrepreneurs that display a search for formalisation shown in the third part of the book. All chapters show new socio-economic realities of the West African continent that let appear the mix between global and local practices, *glocal* practices of West African women entrepreneurs (cf. also World Bank, 2022).

Notes

1 See http://managlobal.hypotheses.org/. The project was financed by the European Commission under the Grant agreement N° 823744 and coordinated by Ulrike Schuerkens at the University Rennes 2 from 2019 to 2023 (Grant time: 1/2019-6/2024).
2 Cf. the conclusion of her article in this book: p 205.

References

Amine, P. S. and K. M. Staub (2009) "Women entrepreneurs in sub-Saharan Africa: An institutional theory analysis from a social marketing point of view", *Entrepreneurship and Regional Development,* 21 (2): 183–211.

Anyansi-Archibong, C. (2021) *The Foundation and Growth of African Women Entrepreneurs. Historical Perspectives and Modern Trends*. Cham: Palgrave Macmillan, Palgrave Studies of Entrepreneurship in Africa.

Appadurai, A. (1990) "Disjuncture and difference in the global cultural economy", *Public Culture,* 2 (2): 1–24.

Banque africaine du développement (2019) https://African_Gender_Equality_Index_2015-FR.pdf, accessed 7 August 2023.

Berry, S. S. (2019) "Entrepreneurial labour", in S. Bellucci and A. Eckert (eds) *General Labour History of Africa, Workers, Employers and Governments, 20th–21st Centuries,* pp. 456–474. James Currey: Suffolk, GB and Boydell & Brewer Ltd: Rochester, US in association with ILO Regional Office for Africa: Abidjan, Côte d'Ivoire.

Brush, C., A. de Bruin, and F. Welter (2009) "A gender-aware framework for women's entrepreneurship", *International Journal of Gender and Entrepreneurship,* 1 (1): 8–24.

Brush, C. G. and S. Y. Cooper (2012) "Female entrepreneurship and economic development: An international perspective", *Entrepreneurship and Regional Development,* 24 (1–2): 1–6.

De Bruin, A., C. G. Brush and F. Welter (2007) "Advancing a framework for coherent research on women's entrepreneurship", *Entrepreneurship Theory and Practice*, 31 (3): 323–339.

Edoho, F. M. (2015) "*Entrepreneurship and socioeconomic development*", *African Journal of Economic and Management Studies*, 6 (2): 127–147.

Etim, E. and C. Gervase Iwu (2019) "A descriptive literature review of the continued marginalisation of female entrepreneurs in sub-Saharan Africa", *International Journal of Gender Studies in Developing Societies,* 3 (1): 1–20.

Freeman, C. (2001) "Is local: global as feminine: masculine? Rethinking the gender of globalization", *Signs: Journal of Women in Culture and Society*, 26 (4): 1007–1037.

Hannerz, U. (1992) *Cultural Complexity: Studies in the Social Organization of Meaning.* New York: Columbia University Press.

Hannerz, U. (1996) *Transnational Connections: Cultures, People, Places.* London and New York: Routledge.

Kane, N. and R. Chroqui (eds) (2021) *L'entrepreneuriat féminin en Afrique, entre bricolage et survie.* Paris: L'Harmattan.

Lam, I. T. (2019) *L'entrepreneuriat féminin en Afrique, "Une mine d'or inexploitée"!* Paris: L'Harmattan.

Lo, M. S. (2016) "*En route* to New York: Diasporic networks and the reconfiguration of female entrepreneurship in Senegal", *Gender, Place & Culture*, 23 (4): 503–520.

Long, N. (1996) "Globalization and localization: New challenges to rural research", in H. L. Moore (ed.) *The Future of Anthropological Knowledge*, pp. 37–59. London and New York: Routledge.

Matsoso, M. L. and C. Gervase Iwu (2016) "Women and small-scale entrepreneurship. Perspective from the SADC Region", in J. Etim (ed.), *Introduction to Gender Studies in Eastern and Southern Africa. A Reader*, pp. 197–213. Rotterdam: Sense Publishers.

N'Da, P. (2015) *Recherche et méthodologie en sciences sociales et humaines: Réussir sa thèse, son mémoire de master ou professionnel et son article*. Paris: L'Harmattan.

N'Da, P. (2015) *Recherche et méthodologie en sciences sociales et humaines: Réussir sa thèse, son mémoire de master ou professionnel et son article*. Paris: L'Harmattan.

Nederveen Pieterse, J. (1993) *Globalization as Hybridization.* Working Paper 152. The Hague: Institute of Social Studies.

Ojong, N., A. Simba, and L.-P. Dana (2021) "Female entrepreneurship in Africa: A review, trends, and future research directions", *Journal of Business Research,* 132: 233–246.

Peterson, V. S. (2009) "Interactive and intersectional analysis of globalization", *Frontiers: A Journal of Women Studies*, 30 (1): 31–40.

Schuerkens, U. (2017) *Social Changes in a Global World.* London: Sage.

Schuerkens, U. et al. (eds) (2019) *Pour une sociologie du management en Afrique et dans les pays arabes*. Paris: L'Harmattan.

Schuerkens, U. (ed.) (2023) *Entrepreneurs, entreprises et travail au Sénégal*. Paris: L'Harmattan.

Sheriff, M. and M. Muffatto (2015) "The present state of entrepreneurship ecosystems in selected countries in Africa", *African Journal of Economic and Management Studies*, 4 (1): 17–54.

Spring, A. (2009) "African women in the entrepreneurial landscape: Reconsidering the formal and the informal sectors", *Journal of African Business*, 10 (1): 11–30.

Vossenberg, S. (2013) *Women Entrepreneurship Promotion in Developing Countries; What Explains the Gender Gap in Entrepreneurship and How to Close it?*, Working Paper No. 2013/08, Maastricht School of Business.

World Bank Economic Report (2018) *The World Bank Annual Report*, accessed 6 August 2023.

World Bank (2022) *Breaking Barriers: Female Entrepreneurs Who Cross Over to Male-Dominated Sectors*. https://openknowledge.worldbank.org/entities/publication/36106601-3d89-54b2-9475-853c7e569302, accessed 6 August 2023.

World Bank (2023) https://live.worldbank.org/events/spring-meetings-2023-empowering-women-entrepreneurs-leaders, accessed 6 August 2023.

World Economic Forum (2012) *Global Gender Gap Report 2012*. http://www.weforum.org/reports/globalgender-gap-report-2012, accessed 6 August 2023.

World Economic Forum (2015) *Entrepreneurial Ecosystems around the Globe and Company Growth Dynamics*. https://www.weforum.org/reports/entrepreneurial-ecosystems-around-globe-and-company-growth-dynamics/, accessed 6 August 2023.

2 Wealth Making in Marriage

Simbiat Abiola of Southwestern Nigeria, 1938–1992

Mutiat Titilope Oladejo

Introduction

In many accounts of family businesses in Africa, it is rare to find women visibly involved. In precolonial Yorubaland, women work to promote family vocations in lineages, because life is communal. Within homes, women work, fulfil domestic roles, and converge at market centres to trade simultaneously, so that it was difficult to separate work and domesticity. Basically, colonialism changed the dynamics of gender and kinship relations in families. Men in the colonial era had the opportunity to work out of towns and family farms, thus leaving women behind. Yet, women were rarely entitled to inherit properties in African societies. The milieus affected women's livelihood in colonial Yorubaland. It is in this context of colonialism that Simbiat Abiola was born in Abeokuta in 1938. Wealth creation for women was stifled during this era, but Simbiat Abiola's life history was atypical.

The Family Embeddedness Perspective is used to explain the transitions, social norms, and resources derived from the family as stimulators of entrepreneurial growth. Thus, the chapter analyses Simbiat Abiola's transition from girlhood to wife and the implication of the wealth-making life she shared with her husband till her death in 1992. As a spouse, she lived most of her adult life to build family wealth with Moshood Kasimawo Olawale (MKO) Abiola. With an emphasis on the change and dynamics in the entrepreneurial patterns across time, this chapter explains the factors that aided the growth of wealth in her marriage and gender relations in the family business. The explanations feature the rarity of having women build and manage businesses in the formal sector in Nigerian business history. This research uses prosopography to present the realities in the wealth-making life of Simbiat Abiola, with a view to establishing her roles in building family businesses into an organised private sector in Nigerian business history.

Family Business in Africa

Family business has been profound to Africa since ancient times. It largely features in Africa considering the all-encompassing nature of inclusion of everyone. The family in Africa from ancient times is interwoven and cuts across communities and lineages. Family businesses as it were in precolonial Africa feature labour and expertise that circulate within the lineage across generations. According to Colli

DOI: 10.4324/9781003492931-3

(2003: 9), family businesses are submerged in the real sense of the existence of large corporations and big businesses, because over time, middle-level managers take over its organisation. Hence, family business only remains at the take-off stage and is characterised by informal credit sources, self-financing, and internal succession. Casson (1982: 205) described the pattern as that of traditional economics. Colli and Casson considered family business models as non-existent in modern corporations, except for in a few places like Italy, among others. But, in Nigeria, family embeddedness features in the pattern of business. Since the 20th century, family and family business have existed as a mix of traditional and modern economics. The African culture of communalism and vocational expertise profound in the precolonial era, made the nature of family business spectacular when compared to business set up in the world. Family businesses are usually layered and interfaced in several forms. This is linked to the character of the family and the business. There are tensions in the growth of family businesses that come with funding and succession. Rose and Colli (2009) identify the role of women in the making of family capitalism. The dynamics of familial relations require a sociological understanding of family politics in the growth of businesses. Iliffe explained the diversity in the pre-capitalist mode of production in the 20th century (Iliffe, 1983: 2). This was a period when colonial modernity took shape. Yet, entrepreneurial growth was still based on traditional systems that factored in the African realities of friendship and communalism in industrial settings.

Colli's studies of family businesses overtime resorted to building evidence. The method is taken further to explain the peculiarity of MKO Abiola as an example of growth in an African setting of the 20th century. The evidence on gender involvement in family businesses from the Arab Middle East shows the prevalence of patriarchy as women are ceremonially appointed to leadership positions in rare cases (Samara, 2020). Similar patterns occurred in the growth of indigenous business set-ups in Nigeria in the 20th century. Several industrial business capitalists' businesses were owned by men who really lacked a succession plan after their exit.

In 19th century Yorubaland, few women recorded success in businesses, although they were entangled in the challenges of the commercial activities triggered by the Trans-Atlantic trade. The most prominent of these women was Madame Tinubu (Yemitan, 1987). While few women excelled in businesses, Madame Tinubu's experience was unique, although she was not lucky with marriage (Yemitan, 1987: 2). Invariably, wealth was not defined by her marital history as she had the course to move from one marriage to the other. This status deviated from the Victorian ideals fostered by British colonialism in the 20th century. Therefore, Simbiat's life in the 20th century was largely influenced by Victorian ideals, and being from a Muslim home, a woman was not encouraged to live outside the marital setting. This accounted for Simbiat's spousal status in business and entrepreneurship.

Simbiat was born in colonial Nigeria at a time when women in Lagos struggled a lot to advocate for women's education, by seeking the colonial government's attention to establish schools for girls (Oladejo, 2019). These activities according to Faseke defined the role of Yoruba women in nationalist struggles (Faseke, 2001: 26). The foundation laid from this struggle led to the establishment of schools for wider inclusion. As such, Simbiat's schooling at Nawairudeen schools in Abeokuta was a product of the sensitisation for girls' education and efforts made by Muslims to pull resources for the education of Muslim children in southwest Nigeria. Simbiat's position as a business leader in the family enterprise as well as similar businesses is rarely captured in the scholarly works on the business history of Nigeria. Ogbeidi (2007), in the book *Fundamentals of Nigerian Business History,* focused on structural business set-ups handed over from colonial trading conglomerates. However, it rarely bothered to seek out the few indigenous businesses that attempted to organise formally.

Girlhood in the Soaga Family

The Soaga family was a typical Yoruba Muslim family used to making wealth from trade as it was the tradition in the precolonial economic system. While colonialism, western education, and Christianity intersected from the 19th century, Yoruba Muslims slowly embraced Western education, for the fear of conversion to Christianity (Nolte, 2017), and they also held on to making wealth from trade. These dynamics tilted the direction of elitism in southwestern Nigeria as it enhanced the rise of the educated Christian elite, thus leaving the Muslims to occupy trading activities in the informal sector. Danmole (2019) explicitly describes the Muslimness that evolved among the Yoruba as all-encompassing as it created a community of everyday life interwoven with bonds of livelihood. It is within this milieu that Rafiu Isola and Rabata Soaga built their wealth from Soaga Ilawo lineage of Gbagura, Abeokuta. The Soaga lineage was a notable Muslim family that provided patronage for the growth of the Nawairudeen Society in Abeokuta. The Nawairudeen was a grouping of Yoruba Muslims across western Nigeria, whose vision was to create a modern Muslimness considering the 20th-century changes. While growing up as a girl in the Soaga paternal ancestry, she was one of the few women that participated in football matches at Abeokuta Grammar School in 1954. Her interest in sporting activities was a rarity in Abeokuta. Only a few girls from rich families could find support for such interests. The typical Yoruba society of the 20th century was still in the stage of separating girls from certain roles, as girls were restricted to tasks in domestic and agricultural works. However, Simbiat's experience differed considering the elite status of the Soaga family: Simbiat's exposure was enlightening. She belonged to the Muslim elite family of the mid-20th century. Then, the Nawairudeen Society was prominent in Egbaland, her sub-ethnic Yoruba ancestry. The sophistication of Nawairudeen at this period was enabled by the coastal trade relations that enhanced import-export trade in Lagos and the integration of Brazilian Muslim migrants into Yoruba culture as profound in Lagos, Abeokuta, and Ijebu.

Marriage into Abiola Family and Spousal Entrepreneurship

Simbiat married MKO Abiola in 1961. By marriage, she relocated from Nigeria to Glasgow, Scotland. Her life in Glasgow manifests her versatile nature because she enrolled to study nursing at Robroyston Hospital, and studied for a diploma in fashion design at the Rodimus College of Art (The Cable, 2022). Her choice of courses was influenced by the Victorian ideals of womanhood fostered among the elites and obtainable in England. Most of the curriculum for girls' education was based on domestic science training, which had started in Nigeria in the 1920s (Denzer, 1992). Simbiat's role in building the family business is an extension of the Victorian ideals of womanhood. Having lived in England, and considering the Nigerian colonial encounters with Britain, what was expected of women at that time was to be supportive spouses. This was obvious across all the spaces occupied by the British colonisation in Africa. It became women's way of expressing nationalism, by submerging under a masculine system. Mougoue (2019) and Oladejo (2023) explained that Cameroonians in Anglophone spaces used the philosophy of spousal support to express nationalism so that it defined what society expected for a woman's life. This view depicts Simbiat's life in the 1970s and 1980s as her career revolved around building the family business.

While in England, the idea of domestic sciences influenced the layers of learning Simbiat engaged in. Furthermore, she obtained a certificate course in interior decoration at the School of Domestic Science in Glasgow. These qualifications enhanced her appointment to teach in the Arts Department of Yaba College of Technology, Lagos. Studies in fashion and interior education motivated the entrepreneurial spirit in her. She returned to Nigeria in 1966, and resigned as a lecturer in 1969. Wealth within the family manifests as a vision. First, she established Tinu Fashion House coined from her name. The fashion house became a space to practise dressmaking, interior decoration, and the production of tie and dye clothes.

Her entrepreneurial work in tie and dye clothes can be explained by Egba society where she grew up. Women from several Egba families engaged in the work of tie and dye, hence, it was a circular economy within lineages in the first half of the 20th century. In fact, the protest against the high costs of dyes was part of the issues Egba women had with the king (Alake) and the colonial state (Oladejo, 2019). The tie and dye production system was part of Simbiat's girlhood experience in Egba society, which made it easier for her to develop a pedagogical activity and entrepreneurial practice. Beyond the growth of core businesses, she engaged in socially stimulated entrepreneurship of sports during her secondary school days.

Simbiat was fully involved in her husband's businesses and played a large role in the growth of Abiola's business empire. She was the Vice-President of Concord Group of newspapers, where she overviewed the setting up and the maintenance of the publications and later on, of other ventures like the Wonder Bakery. Unique in Nigeria, the Wonder Baking Company opened in 1980 in Lagos, and by 1981, it had already employed over 140 people. Marketing under the brand name Mother's Pride, the enterprise made use of the same Wonder Bread recipe used in the United States and the United Kingdom (The Unknown Nigeria, 2014). The factory gulped a sum of N2.5 million (Forrest, 1994).

The family embeddedness perspective was displayed in the entrepreneurial styles of Simbiat. While MKO was publicly known as the founder of the businesses, Simbiat deputised and controlled the operations. She also used global business prototypes to make meaning of the family-owned ventures. Indigenising the family entrepreneurial ventures was enabled by the Nigerian Enterprise Promotion Decree (NEPD) of 1972, which mandated Nigerian ownership of a business. Simbiat's impact in business building was novel at this period in Nigerian history because the Nigerian economy was in a transition from the colonial to the postcolonial phase. The postcolonial phase in Nigeria's economy favoured the growth of private capital as the state ceded privileges for the growth of businesses. In this phase, Austen (1987: 228) analysed the process of decolonisation displayed by the entrepreneurial elite in the growth of private businesses. Simbiat's business initiatives fit into the decolonisation of this business phase as it was also the period when foreign experts in multinational companies handed off their subsidiaries in Nigeria. As part of the national integration policies in Nigeria, the NEPD favoured the growth of the family business so that it contributed to the rise of indigenous entrepreneurship in Nigeria. The period features newness because Nigeria was evolving its nationhood after independence. Business and politics were considered synonymous with Simbiat. Having enhanced the growth of the National Party of Nigeria in Abeokuta, grassroots mobilisation became a business opportunity to tap into. This influenced the couple's decision to establish Concord Press in 1980. The fundamental aim of the press was to produce newspapers and engage in the business of information dissemination. Simbiat was able to attract a think tank of media professionals such as Dele Giwa, Laila Dogonyaro, and Doyin Abiola (one of Simbiat's co-wives).

In the traditional Yoruba political system that existed before colonialism, the institution of Iyalode was designated for women. The Iyalode played prominent roles in Yorubaland and their leadership manifested in the market spaces across cities in modern Yoruba societies (Oladejo, 2015). The Iyalode institution is structured to have several women in the chieftaincy line. In Egbaland, Simbiat was installed as the Otun Iyalode Lisabi: this position attempted to her role as an elite woman and a businesswoman in the society. In Yoruba philosophy, holding this title indicates that she belongs to the category of the rich and influential classes. While building the family wealth, she was able to create fame and attract attention while using the family embeddedness perspective. This development was reflected in the fuji music lyrics of Sikiru Ayinde Barrister, as he attests to her level of fame and power in driving the family (Sikiru Ayinde Barrister album on Dimensional Fuji, 1993).

Political Influence and Business Networking

Simbiat and MKO were prominent members of the National Party of Nigeria (NPN). NPN became an avenue for them to connect with their space of origin in Abeokuta. Their place in NPN affirms how politicians used local capital to finance political activities of the party (Forrest, 1994: 77). Politics in Nigeria of the 1970s was interwoven with economic growth, especially at the grassroots level. To aid the growth of the family businesses at the grassroots level, political participation was used by Simbiat to leverage the prestige and to create awareness. With her husband, she organised their political relevance through the National

Party of Nigeria (NPN): NPN was used as a platform to return to the grassroots in Abeokuta.

NPN fostered MKO's economic connections with companies and government agencies. Through Concord Newspaper, business news and its entanglement with politics were analysed for the advancement of free market policies (Forrest, 1994: 236). From the mid-1980s, MKO parted with the Social Democratic Party (SDP) after the 1985 coup that destabilised Nigeria's second republic. Basically, Simbiat worked to grow the business, while MKO, her husband, used political connections to advance the businesses. During General Ibrahim Babangida's administration, MKO's companies got government contracts worth $845 million (Meredith, 2005: 395).

Simbiat and MKO's membership of NPN and later SDP was based on the long-term ambition to hold political posts but also aimed at making profits from their business interest over the long term. Profit as envisaged in the long term is considered to be interconnected with political strength in the Nigerian governance system that promotes brand awareness within the wider community. This is typified by Handley (2020) who described how business interests intercept with social realities and politics in Africa.

Beyond politics, the social reality in Africa entails the modern camaraderie of sporting activities. Having been a footballer in her teen years at Nawairudeen school, she extended philanthropy to sports in adult life. In building a national and global spectrum for the family business brand, she promoted women's football by the establishment and finance of Kakanfo Queens, a female football team. She also funded the Simbiat Abiola Cup in Kano in February 1986, which drew over 10,000 spectators as well as the 1987/88 National Under-16 Girls Soccer Championship Trophy.

While Simbiat had been in the background working for the growth of MKO Abiola businesses as the spouse, she had co-wives that were married to her husband. Polygyny is typical in many African societies and corresponds to the ideal image of masculinity. In traditional Yoruba societies, marrying women and child-bearing was a source of wealth regeneration as women and children worked on the farms and in the cottage industries. In the 20th-century modern life, men still practised polygyny, typically MKO's wives were numerous so he had written a will in the late 1980s, to clarify his estate and claims for the heirs (The Unknown Nigeria, 2014). Despite Simbiat's legacies in the growth of the businesses, the challenges of polygyny culminated in cases of rift over the control of family businesses after the death of Simbiat and MKO (The News, 7 January 2020). The rift appeared in a court case cantering around the management of Radio Communications Limited. The projection of the case to the judicial system was atypical of the traditional Yoruba system of conflict resolution in large families, especially in cases involving children from different women. This development implied a fallout of Simbiat's family embeddedness and the struggle for inclusion caused by the complexities that come with family embeddedness in business.

Conclusion

In popular perceptions about MKO family history, there is a pointer to the fact that Simbiat influenced his presidential ambition to lead Nigeria, which later failed. However, her first child proclaimed that:

> *She told my father to drop his ambition until Ibrahim Babangida, a retired Nigerian Army General who was President from August 27, 1985 to August 26, 1993 finished his tenure before contesting for Presidency.*
>
> (Daily Post, 23 June 2018)

The warning stemmed from the fact that the military head of state Ibrahim Babangida was making the political space difficult for a return to civilian rule in the late 1980s. Yet, MKO was optimistic to become the civilian president of Nigeria. While on the sick bed at a London hospital shortly before her death on 10 November 1992, she watched the earthquake occurrence and its devastating effect on a school in Egypt. This moved her to pledge $100,000 for rebuilding the school. Her entrepreneurial styles were all-encompassing as they interfaced with business expansion, brand awareness, politics, and philanthropy.

References

Austen, R. (1987) *African Economic History*. Melton: James Currey.

Casson, M. C. (1982) *The Entrepreneur: An Economic Theory.* University of Illinois at Urbana-Champaign's Academy for Entrepreneurial Leadership Historical Research Reference in Entrepreneurship, Available at SSRN: https://ssrn.com/abstract=1496173

Colli, A. (2003) *The History of Family Business, 1850–2000.* Cambridge: Cambridge University Press.

Colli, A. and M. Rose (2009) "Family Business" in Geoffrey Jones and Jonathan Zeitlon (eds) *The Oxford Handbook of Business History,* pp. 194–218. Oxford: Oxford University Press.

Daily Post (23 June 2018) "Kola Abiola reveals what mother, Simbiat told MKO about ambition, Babangida" - Daily Post Nigeria, accessed 23 July 2024.

Danmole, H. O. (2019) *Perspectives on History of Islam in Southwestern Nigeria.* Ibadan: Connell Publications.

Denzer, L. (1992) "Domestic Science Training In Colonial Yorubaland, Nigeria" in K. T. Hansen (ed.) *African Encounters with Domesticity,* pp. 116–139. New Jersey: Rutgers University Press.

Faseke, M. (2001) *The Nigerian Woman: Her Economic and Socio-Political Status in Time Perspective.* Ibadan: Agape Publication.

Forrest, T. G. (1994) *The Advance of African Capital: The Growth of Nigerian Private Enterprise.* Edinburgh: Edinburgh University Press.

Forrest, T. G. (1995) *Politics and Economic Development in Nigeria.* Oxford: Western Press.

Handley, A. (2020) *Business and Social Crisis in Africa.* Cambridge: Cambridge University Press.

Iliffe, J. (1983) *The Emergence of African Capitalism.* London: Macmillan Press.

Meredith, M. (2005) *The State of Africa: A History of Fifty Years of Independence.* London: Simon & Schuster Press.

Mougoue, J. T. (2019) *Gender, Separatist Politics and Embodied Nationalism in Cameroon.* Ann Arbor: University of Michigan Press.
Nolte, I., O. Ogen, and R. Jones (eds) (2017) *Beyond Religious Tolerance: Muslim, Christian & Traditionalist Encounters in an African Town.* Melton: James Currey
Ogbeidi, M. (2007) *Fundamentals of Nigerian Business History.* Ilisan: Babcock University Press.
Oladejo, M. T. (2015) *Ibadan Market Women and Politics, 1900–1995.* Lanham: Lexington Books.
Oladejo, M. T. (2019) *The Women went Radical: Petition Writing and Colonial State in Southwestern Nigeria, 1900–1953.* Ibadan: BookBuilders Africa Edition.
Oladejo, M. T. (2023) "Jacqueline-Bethel Tchouta Mougoué. Gender, separatist politics and embodied nationalism in Cameroon, Ann Arbor: University of Michigan Press, 2019", *African Studies Review* 66 (4): 1066–1068.
Samara, G. (2020) "Family business in the Arab Middle East: What do we know and where should we go?" *Journal of Family Business Strategy,* 12 (5): 1–16.
Sikiru Ayinde Barrister (1993) *Album on Dimensional Fuji.* Nigeria. help_outline
The Cable (11 November 2022) "'Loved, missed' — Wura Abiola remembers mum, Simbiat, on 30th death anniversary".
The News (7 January 2020) "Serious! MKO Abiola's children fight over his company" – The News (thenewsnigeria.com.ng) https://thenewsnigeria.com.ng/2020/01/07/serious-mko-abiolas-children-fight-over-his-company/, accessed 24 August 2024.
The Unknown Nigeria (4 June 2014) "The Story of Love And Courage". https://theunknownnigeriablog.blogspot.com/2014/06/simbiat-abiola-story-of-love-and-courage.html, accessed 24 August 2024.
Yemitan, O. (1987) *Madame Tinubu: Merchant and King-Maker.* Ibadan: University Press.

Part 2

Processes Linked to the Creation of Women Enterprises

3 Women's Home-Based Entrepreneurship in Abidjan, Côte d'Ivoire

Partnership Governance and Succession Planning[1]

Haoua Badini Koné

Introduction

Women's home-based entrepreneurship is on the increase in African societies. This self-employment activity, which is dominant in sub-Saharan Africa, is a response to the need to reconcile family life with professional life, with a view to integrating into the socio-economic fabric. In a socio-cultural context where women are confined to a secondary role (family tasks, women's place in society), entrepreneurial micro-enterprise initiatives within the home strengthen their social relationships and their autonomy. This home-based activity is one aspect of informal entrepreneurship. According to the Organisation for Economic Co-operation and Development (OECD, 2014), female entrepreneurship in Africa is illustrated by the marked presence of women in informal self-employment. In its study, the United Nations Development Fund for Women (UNIFEM, 2009) shows that almost 70% of women in sub-Saharan Africa work mainly in the informal sector.

Most conceptual and empirical studies conducted in Africa focus on women's entrepreneurship (Onana, 2009; Nordman and Vaillant, 2014; Tchouassi et al., 2018; Nkakleu, 2018; Glidja, 2019; Bony et al., 2021). However, although interesting, the data from these studies place little emphasis on home-based entrepreneurship. Yet women's entrepreneurial practices, especially those based at home, have always existed.

For Leclair and Redien-Collot (2013), entrepreneurial activity in the home is part of a socio-cultural environment and coexists with the family's domestic management methods. This explains the transmission of know-how from generation to generation. For Metaiche and Bendiabdellah (2016), the desire to perpetuate a received entrepreneurial tradition drives women to undertake their informal home-based activity simultaneously with their domestic tasks. According to these authors, entrepreneurial activity is carried out with the support and involvement of family members. The relational network in the entrepreneurial project calls for a partnership mode of governance (Peyroux et al., 2019).

Studies of partnership governance emphasise cooperation between stakeholders (Aoki, 2000; Charreaux and Wirtz, 2007; Dupuis and Le Bas, 2007). In their study, Paradas and her colleagues (2013) show that cooperation is a relational process favourable to female entrepreneurship, in that the domestic sphere in which women evolve gives a more integrated view of social relations. For St-Pierre and Cadieux

DOI: 10.4324/9781003492931-5

(2011), the management of women's entrepreneurial activities is driven by a more participatory and socially responsible practice.

My interest in corporate social responsibility (CSR) directs my theoretical anchoring towards the lineage of work on female entrepreneurship (Fayolle, 2010; Paradas et al., 2013; Metaiche and Bendiabdellah, 2016; Peyroux et al., 2019) which accommodates the theories of partnership governance (Charreaux and Wirtz, 2007; Dupuis and Le Bas, 2007). The latter approach the subject from the angle of the transmission of know-how in the context of home-based female entrepreneurship. In this sense, the question that motivates this study is the following: *Which values and norms do African women home-based entrepreneurs pass on to their family circle to perpetuate the entrepreneurial activity?* In other words, the aim is to analyse home-based female entrepreneurship as a form of partnership governance that is conducive to the transmission of socially responsible behaviour. The aim is to understand the entrepreneurial logic at home, which is a source of transmission of know-how and perpetuation of the succession at family level in Côte d'Ivoire.

The empirical research methodology is based on interviews with a sample of 16 Abidjan women entrepreneurs working in retail or services. The aim was to examine their entrepreneurial lives at home, but also to highlight their CSR practices, which are a source of knowledge and know-how transmission within the family unit.

To address the issue of female entrepreneurship in the home, this chapter is divided into four parts. The first part summarises the literature review on female entrepreneurship in the home and sheds some light on its links with partnership governance and CSR. The second part is devoted to the empirical and methodological study. The third part, which presents the results, focuses on the socially responsible determinants of female entrepreneurial activity as a source of knowledge and know-how transmission. The fourth part is a discussion of the results.

Literature Review

As mentioned above, most studies of women's entrepreneurship pay little attention to their relationship with the home. However, the few literature reviews that approach entrepreneurship from the perspective of the home include it in their partnership perspectives and in connection with corporate social responsibility (Redien-Collot and Léger-Jarniou, 2018).

Women's Entrepreneurial Dynamism in the Home and Partnership Governance Methods

Women's entrepreneurial activity in Africa is driven by a desire to break down barriers and prejudices (Mebtoul et al., 2010). According to these authors, women who are culturally assigned to domestic tasks find time to engage in entrepreneurial activities to better reconcile their household responsibilities with their professional lives. It is the need to assert themselves socially and to escape from precariousness that drives them to entrepreneurship. However, their resistance to regulatory standards means that their home-based activities fall within the informal sector.

In Côte d'Ivoire, nearly 98% of women work in the informal sector, according to the *National Survey on the Situation of Employment and the Informal Sector* (ENSESI) carried out by the National Institute of Statistics (2019). In addition, the *General Census of Population and Housing* (RGPH), carried out in 2014, shows that 67% of self-employed women have no formal education and 21% have pre-school education. This shows a low level of education among Ivorian women in the entrepreneurial ecosystem.

Women use the home, which is essentially a community space, to obtain support and to assert their entrepreneurial capacity (Onana, 2009). The home emphasises interaction between family members. The community is a privileged space for flexibility, creativity, and social innovation.

The field of analysis of partnership governance lends itself well to the study of home-based women's entrepreneurship. Partnership governance means considering the interactions between stakeholders who can influence decisions or be influenced by decisions (Meier and Schier, 2008). Partnership governance sees the organisation as a collective, rather than a knot of contracts (Charreaux and Wirtz, 2007). The home is presented as an organisation in which the members of the family are represented as a production team in which the creation of value comes from synergies between them. The woman entrepreneur, running the small retail business or craft industry, works in concert with family members, who assist her in her day-to-day activities. This partnership approach to governance is presented as a system of social norms encouraging cooperation between all stakeholders (Charreaux and Pitol-Belin, 1991).

This finding is also supported by Vier-Machado and Rouleau (2002), who show that women are more sensitive to interpersonal relationships. These social relationships within the family are important in women's entrepreneurial activity at home. Dutta and Banerjee (2011) note that 58% of female managers make decisions in consultation with key family members. This finding is in line with some studies that have looked at the role played by family in women entrepreneurs' decisions regarding the location of their premises, for which they tend to favour proximity to their place of residence (Borges et al., 2005). Female entrepreneurship seems to be linked to complex factors, which is why Brush and her colleagues (2009: 11) suggest "digging deeper into the family context and its internal relationships".

For Chabaud and Lebègue (2013: 43), "women build harmonious relationships with their colleagues, inviting them to take their place in the decision-making process". Such a collaborative strategy enables them to secure the full support of the family so that they can take over the business.

In their entrepreneurial role, women are forced to make more compromises in their careers (Le Loarne-Lemaire, 2013). Thus, Santoni and Barth (2014) find that women's perception of the notion of business opportunities remains influenced by their reality as women, spouses, and mothers. Women bring a more social and human dimension to their businesses. According to Santoni and Barth (2014: 81), "women integrate their business into their personal and social life, seeing it more as a cooperative network of relationships". They are much more attached to the notion of mental well-being and personal relationships than men.

To finance their entrepreneurial activities, Ba (2019) believes that women entrepreneurs rely on a spiritual network to develop their entrepreneurial activities in the short and long term. For example, Islam, with its values of solidarity, favours an interest-free loan (the *Zakat*). In this way, women can benefit from interest-free financing to develop their activities. As a result, religion is becoming an inescapable factor in the process of setting up a business for African women, as well as a structuring factor. It has an ethical basis that puts people at the heart of the action.

According to Guérin and Servet (2005), Africa also has the social practice of tontine,[2] which helps to finance businesses: people pool money and share it out among tontine members in turn. These informal financial circuits are also a means of financing entrepreneurial activities.

The mode of governance of women's activities in the home is participative and interactive (Carrier et al., 2006; St-Pierre and Cadieux, 2011). Their management approach is "more personal, more maternal and closer to employees' concerns. While they lack certain qualities related to self-esteem or recognition of a female entrepreneurial role, they rely more on listening and encouragement and delegate more easily" (Paradas et al., 2013: 187). To carry out their small business or craft activities, women give priority to the people they know best, i.e. family ties and close friends. They are not reticent about sharing power and information (Mione, 2002; Carrier et al., 2006). Their leadership style is therefore more "democratic and relational". Women entrepreneurs also seem to pay particular attention to "equity and the well-being of the community" (St-Pierre and Cadieux, 2011: 33). They are looking for effectiveness and affectivity, rather than efficiency and effectiveness (Mione, 2004). They want to be useful and make a difference in the lives of their loved ones.

Taking account of close relations, or even stakeholders, in the entrepreneurial process also means including partnership governance in the principles of CSR (Persais, 2013).

Women Entrepreneurs and the Specificities of CSR

Women's entrepreneurship is more focused on social causes; they seek above all to add value to social needs (Lambrecht et al., 2003; Zouiten and Levy-Tadjine, 2005; Paradas et al., 2013). In other words, these women entrepreneurs are more interested in contributing to social needs than in seeking personal gain, status, or money. For women entrepreneurs, success is not just about sales; satisfying others is an undeniable factor in success (Vier-Machado and Rouleau, 2002). This is why studying women in an entrepreneurial ecosystem raises the question of corporate social responsibility (CSR). Women seem to be more sensitive to CSR, although research in this area is scarce (Paradas et al., 2013). According to St-Pierre and Cadieux (2011), women show a keen interest in socio-environmental factors with a view to satisfying those around them and their personal needs through CSR practices.

CSR refers to participative management in which priority is given to the search for social well-being through harmonious relations, the creation of an optimal working environment, and the involvement of employees in decision-making (Gond and Igalens, 2012). Léger-Jarniou et al. (2015) highlight ethical practices in women's entrepreneurship that give CSR a moral meaning. For Postel and Rousseau (2008), the moral current of CSR is based on rules of conduct to act legitimately. The involvement of close family members leads to a moral commitment (Gianfaldoni et al., 2005).

For Chabaud and Lebègue (2013), women's involvement in less productive sectors leads them to develop ethical values. For Boussoura and Benslimane (2015), ethical values call for good morality and refer to the way of acting that is considered good and appropriate. It is a moral obligation marked by respect for human rights, the right to work, and the environment. It is therefore a question of acting justly through managerial values based on ethics, kindness, altruism, and benevolence.

CSR therefore refers to a form of organisational learning motivated by the desire for a mutual arrangement of ethical value systems and the challenges of entrepreneurial activity (Gond, 2006). This learning refers to the knowledge accumulated by the family unit. This is what enables entrepreneurial activity to continue and, therefore, to be sustainable. This learning is also seen as a portfolio of productive skills that gives greater visibility of the entrepreneurial environment so that resources can efficiently be allocated. Home-based projects allow actors to work together; taking collective skills into account in an activity that generates synergies. Interaction within the home is thus conducive to the transmission of entrepreneurial knowledge and know-how.

Methodology

My study seeks to analyse the discourse and interactions between different actors. I have opted for a qualitative approach because its main aim is to explore and understand a phenomenon (Miles and Huberman, 2003), which is in line with the aim of my research. In fact, my aim is to understand the link between the socially responsible management orientations of women working in retail or services in the different municipalities of Abidjan. The qualitative approach adopted consisted of exploratory interviews with 16 Abidjan women working in retail or home services. This qualitative approach had three objectives:

1. To explore the meaning and importance that women entrepreneurs attach to the notions of partnership governance, responsible behaviour, and business succession;
2. To examine the relationship between entrepreneurial status and the perpetuation of the business within the family circle;
3. To gain an insight into the cultural and organisational context in which the respondents operate, as well as their interpersonal relationships, and learning processes.

These objectives stem from my research, which focuses on the socially responsible norms and values conveyed by women home-based entrepreneurs in their family network, which is a stakeholder in their activities.

During December 2020, most of the participants were interviewed in their homes. Those who had little time to spare asked to be interviewed by telephone. The semi-structured interviews, lasting an average of 30 minutes, were based on structured but open-ended questions (Roussel and Wacheux, 2006). The 16 women interviewed came from a variety of social backgrounds and were involved in retail, craft, or catering activities across the ten municipalities of Abidjan. They run their businesses from home with the help of their spouse and other family members. Some participants have managed, through their informal home-based activities, to set up formal micro-businesses in which they are the managers. The women interviewed were aged between 20 and 50. Table 3.1 shows some of the participants' characteristics.

The choice of the sample, which included a variety of profiles, was made to gather different points of view so that an objective analysis could be carried out. I interviewed only women entrepreneurs working in their home.

Content analysis was adopted to examine the rich transcripts (verbatim) on the participants' experiences. This analysis follows the thematic logic of Bardin (2013). The themes adopted are those I initially selected from the literature review. They put forward the status of women entrepreneurs in the home as a determining criterion for family loyalty and mutual aid. These values reflect the CSR practices inherent in the perpetuation of entrepreneurial activities.

Results

My results show that the home supports women's entrepreneurial careers. They also explain home-based entrepreneurial activity as a means of reconciling family and work.

Home-Based Women's Entrepreneurship: A Legacy to Be Passed on from Generation to Generation

The initiative to run a home-based business for women is not an innate process, let alone a natural one. It is the product of a long process of maturation, which often has its origins in the social group to which the family belongs. For example, one respondent said: "I refused to go to school myself. My aunt, who brought me up, is a big shopkeeper. From the beginning until today, there have been changes for me. My business is linked to my family history. My aunt sold jewellery and pearls, that's what she sold" (R4-1) (Assétou Y., 7 December 2020).

Another respondent explained: "Yes, my older sister used to sell. When I came to live with her in Abidjan, I used to help her and that's how I took over the space after she passed away in 2016. I inherited it from my older sister. But I'd like to expand my space and make it nicer to attract customers" (R4- 2) (Emmanuella A., 4 December 2020).

In fact, the analysis of family control over the entrepreneurial ability of women within the family has its own specific features, some of which I describe here.

Table 3.1 Characteristics of the sample

Type of activity	*Breakdown*	*Workforce*	*Duration (min)*	*Level of study*	*Municipality*
Sewing (service or manufacture)	R1	1	28	Primary (CM2)	Cocody
		2	30	Secondary (3)	Yopougon
	Total R1	**2**			
Catering (service)	R2	1	27	No formal level	Koumassi
		2	31	Higher education (BTS)	Adjamé
		3	26	Primary (CM1)	Adjamé
		4	32	Higher education (4 years)	Yopougon
		5	25		Treichville
		6	29	Secondary (4)	Marcory
		7	30	No formal level	Port-Bouet
		8	29	Higher education (4 years)	Marcory
	Total R2	**8**			
Telephone booth (service)	R3	1	25	Secondary (3)	Yopougon
	Total R3	**1**			
Clothing and fashion goods (retail or manufacturing)	R4	1	33	No formal level	Cocody
		2	28	Higher education (BTS)	Abobo
		3	27	No formal level	Abobo
		4	26	Primary (CM1)	Bingerville
	Total R4	**4**			
Food products (retail)	R5	1	30	No formal level	Bingerville
	Total R5	**1**			
Total respondents		**16**			

The Omnipresence of Standards and Values in a CSR Policy

Corporate social responsibility, as a process of corporate governance, focuses on societal aspects that go well beyond the profit-seeking aspect of traditional business. Refuting the idea that the pursuit of profit should be the essence of business, women's CSR at the home has specific features that allow it to be adapted to policy measures. Its characteristics, both structural and symbolic, respond to a set of objectives relating to ethical standards and values that encourage the interaction of family members in entrepreneurial activities. In this regard, a respondent who runs a home-based restaurant said: "My business is all about cleanliness. Hygiene is important for me. My surroundings must be clean to attract more customers. With the advent of COVID-19, I installed a hand-washing facility right at the entrance and hand gel on every table. The family is obliged to comply with these measures" (R2-1) (Astou T., 6 December 2020).

The entrepreneurial experiences of women at home range from the most informal activities to attempts to set up a micro-business at home. It is through these activities that they transfer their know-how, which ensures that the entrepreneurial activity is perpetuated by family members. One respondent explained: "This business is not mine alone. Tomorrow, it's the children who will inherit the spin-offs. They can continue the business if they want to" (R2-3) (Myriame K., 30 December 2020).

Home-based entrepreneurial activity is governed by standards and codes that set out a series of provisions to be implemented in the search for a balance with life as a housewife. On this point, one respondent said: "Before making any decisions, I first talk to my husband and my eldest son and then to the younger ones. Together, we see what's right. Obviously, today, it's thanks to the advice and decisions of my eldest son that the business is more profitable than it was before. So, for me, their opinions count" (R4-3) (Abiba F., 8 December 2020).

On the other hand, standards and codes deal with a certain ability to behave and manage a market environment: "It was my aunt and my older sister who taught me how to behave with a customer, how to do this or that, in short, they taught me everything" (R2-3) (Myriame K., 30 December 2020). All these norms passed on by elderly women and internalised by younger women and men are the bearers of a cultural identity that plays a decisive role in the act of entrepreneurship and constitutes a specificity, a symbolic element of social distinction and recognition.

As a socialisation process, the transmission of norms, codes, and values in the entrepreneurial act from elderly women to younger women is often carried out by coercion. During the interviews, the respondents said that it was their duty to perpetuate this entrepreneurial know-how to allow themselves to obtain autonomy in their lives as housewives. As the assimilation and internalisation of these codes governing the business are not necessarily self-evident, it is up to the elderly women to regulate them. This learning process is restrictive, as it involves adopting standards of conduct for young people. This is a response to the issues of inaction, dropping out of school, unemployment, and economic vulnerability that young girls and boys sometimes face.

It should be noted that the idea of entrepreneurship for these women appears to be a need to reconcile their family and the professional life. The aim is to forge the learner's identity and perpetuate an "ancestral" tradition that has deep cultural roots. It is therefore part of a socialisation process undertaken long before by family members. As one respondent put it: "In our family, we've always been big shopkeepers. It didn't start with us, did it? It was the old lady [the grandmother] who trained us all, in fact. She used to tell us: it's all about tomorrow" (R4-1) (Assétou Y., 7 December 2020).

As the vehicle for primary socialisation, the family group represents for these women the environment par excellence for training, learning, and internalising the norms and codes that frame entrepreneurial activity. These values are in fact passed on to them by the family, which intends to use them to determine the image of itself that it wants to be seen by the rest of society. In this way, these women become "ambassadors" of an entrepreneurial cultural heritage that they must not only perpetuate but also pass on to future generations.

In addition to the transmission of entrepreneurial values from elderly to younger women, a transmission that sometimes takes on a coercive air, we should also note the desire of some respondents to reproduce the behaviour of their parents, thereby assuming the identity of which they are the product: "Yes, my aunt and older sister are great dressmakers. I wanted to be like them" (R1-1) (Joelle A., 3 December 2020).

Whether forced or desired, women's entrepreneurial capacity is therefore linked to the environment and to the entrepreneurial abilities of the members of the family unit. The entrepreneurial skills of current generations clearly perpetuate the entrepreneurial family tradition.

A Sense of Social Responsibility Built around the Social and Physiological Needs of the Family

Home-based entrepreneurship among Abidjan's women is a response to the problem of social imbalance, marked as much by school dropouts, as by the lack of jobs, and other forms of economic vulnerability. It's true that perpetuating the entrepreneurial spirit among the study participants is a social imperative, given the identity characteristics it encompasses.

The social implications of these women taking responsibility for their home-based activities are manifold, and can be seen in a few ways, some of which are outlined below.

The Ability to Work Independently

By *relational autonomy*, I mean the social process by which these women, who carry out these income-generating activities, construct their identity as traders. Their personal identity is constructed as a function of the social relationships they maintain: "To this day, the first customers I had in this business are still with me, and they're still bringing me other customers. [...] My husband is there; he supports me as much as he can. He often irons customers' clothes. So does my daughter. She often does the buttons and things like that" (R1-1) (Joelle A., 3 December 2020).

In other words, social interdependence plays a role not only in the construction of a businesswoman's identity but also in the possibility of action and autonomy. This autonomy, which is not simply a matter of having financial resources at one's disposal, often contributes to the family's social equilibrium and endogenous decision-making processes: "It's not doing anything that's good. Even though I don't earn enough money, people respect me. I also get a lot of respect from my family. Even my husband, when he wants to decide, he asks for my opinion" (R5-1) (Viviane N., 5 December 2020).

This shows that the benefits of responsible entrepreneurial activity are not just pecuniary. They sometimes take on abstract forms and much greater proportions that Bourdieu (1980) might describe as social capital (e.g., honour, distinction, and prestige).

In the case of the participants in this study, it is a category of players who have previously had a lower social profile given the nature of their activities, consisting of small retail or service businesses. Through their home-based economic activities, these women are trying to reposition themselves at the forefront by combining work and family life. This initiative, which has socio-cultural and economic implications, aims to reduce inequalities in a world that has long been dominated by men.

The Partnership Governance Channel

I summarise partnership governance as a social process for coordinating the skills of each player or group of players in the home-based business production system. This participatory approach has its roots in stakeholder theory.

In my study, this social process originates in the identification by family members of the woman entrepreneur as a role model who promotes family well-being by enabling them to benefit from the spin-offs of the activity through remuneration or the assumption of certain domestic burdens. In addition, the responsible behaviour shown by the woman entrepreneur towards those close to her only strengthens her moral commitment.

The value of such an approach in the context of home-based women's entrepreneurship lies in the willingness of household members to demonstrate that multiple interests, very often going beyond the purely economic dimension, are given priority. The economic interests of the woman setting up the business should not be given priority over those of other family members (spouse, children, brother/sister, etc.) who also contribute to the economic production. As a result, the woman entrepreneur strives to contribute to the social balance of the family by satisfying the expectations and demands of the other members. It would be inconceivable to reduce the expectations and concerns of the other members to the "head entrepreneur" because the search for social balance in the family implies that each member contributes to satisfying the opportunity objectives of the entrepreneurial activity.

Any behaviour by members in the opposite direction could prove counterproductive and affect the desired balance.

It should also be noted that the home is a place where a woman learns a skill that is supposed to bear the hallmarks of her entrepreneurial identity and that it is important to promote it within the family to encourage involvement. This know-how contributes to family equilibrium through the synergistic involvement of the other members of the household, so that the profits and income obtained are reinvested to meet basic needs:

> I can't spoil their name[3]. In the house, here, everyone helps me. When my husband's here and he sees I'm busy, he goes and serves the customers himself... It helps me cover the small expenses around the house, so I don't have to wait for my husband to do that" (R2-1) (Astou T., 6 December 2020).

In the light of the above, addressing the issue of partnership governance in the context of women's home-based entrepreneurship means first recognising the involvement of household members in the production system of the entrepreneurial activity. They appear as shareholders or employees of the business, depending on their level of involvement. Secondly, it means ensuring that the tasks tacitly or explicitly assigned to the members converge towards the same goal, as defined by the entrepreneurs.

The Importance of the Home

In this study, the home plays an important role in structuring entrepreneurial activity. More than a symbol, it is the place where family life and entrepreneurial life come together. This situation is significant for CSR, insofar as it confers on women entrepreneurs the responsibility of honouring their social requirements *vis-à-vis* their entrepreneurial environment, of which the home is the receptacle. This responsibility gives these women entrepreneurs a sedentary lifestyle that encourages them to respond quickly to the concerns that fall to their various statuses (wife, mother, etc.); "Running my business from home means I can keep an eye on everything at the same time. If my husband or children need me, I'm already there" (R2-2) (Mawa F., 15 December 2020).

In other words, the importance of the home in customer relations enhances the quality-of-service provision. Customers are close to the home and constantly comment on the quality of the service provided. What's more, the home frees these entrepreneurs from the precariousness of setting up in business, which in turn has a positive impact on the popular representation of the quality of the service offered in the market relationship: "When you work from home, the customer has more confidence in you" (R2-3) (Myriame K., 30 December 2020).

As a vehicle for a relationship of trust between the business owner and her customers, the prominence of the home puts a high value on the skills and credibility of the entrepreneur and, by extension, implicitly on those of the other members of the home who contribute to her success.

The home also helps to provide an opportunity to escape economic insecurity. The inequalities experienced by women in accessing finance to achieve a fulfilling working life are at the heart of their entrepreneurial prospects. In so doing, the respondents are seeking to correct a social "wrong" that gives them less visibility in society. This reduced visibility, legitimised by cultures that put men first, constitutes an inequality between men and women that is in turn reproduced by modern society.

In addition to their plans to reduce inequalities, the act of entrepreneurship for these women goes hand in hand with their goals of autonomy and self-fulfilment. Not only do they become contributors to household costs, but they also restore an image that had been socially diminished, as one respondent put it: "It's my business that allows me to do this. It's true that my husband is here, but I don't have to wait for him to do anything. That's all I want" (R5-1) (Viviane N., 5 December 2020).

The Family Home as a Factor in Perpetuating the Entrepreneurial Activity of Abidjan Women

The process of entrepreneurial socialisation, which takes account of the internalisation of procedures, standards, and codes of conduct, is designed to perpetuate the entrepreneurial tradition nurtured within the family, ensuring that it is passed on to future generations, as one participant emphasised: "I want my daughter to be a civil servant, but we also need to show her how to look for money. These days, there's only one thing you can count on: doing other things to earn extra income... That will really help her" (R4-1) (Assétou Y., 7 December 2020).

Home-based female entrepreneurship contributes to a climate of cooperation, sharing, and transmission of values. It provides jobs and stimulates resilience to precariousness among these women entrepreneurs. By creating and developing their informal entrepreneurial activities, these women break down barriers and stereotypes, and position themselves as an essential link in the national production system.

Admittedly, the capital they invest in their activities is modest, but the objectives associated with such investments are not necessarily to make a large-scale economic profit: "It allows us to react to difficulties. If, for example, your child comes to tell you he hasn't got a notebook or there's a little problem here at home, you're not going to wait until your husband gets home in the evening" (R2-3) (Myriame K., 30 December 2020).

By adopting responsible practices, these objectives aim firstly to promote social balance within the family, secondly to meet basic economic needs and, thirdly, to pass on know-how to future generations through socialisation. What's more, it reduces inactivity and all the vices associated with it: "I've always told my friends to be enterprising. It means you're always busy, and you get by. You don't have time to go and sit at your friend's house and criticise people" (R4-4) (Noura F., 16 December 2020).

The interviews reveal that women's home-based entrepreneurship aims, on the one hand, to reduce the economic vulnerability faced by housewives. On the other hand, it is betting on the development of a type of entrepreneurial activity inherent in a woman's life course.

Discussion

From the study I conducted, it appears that the cooperative and responsible behaviours developed by women home-based entrepreneurs are conducive to business perpetuation in general and in Abidjan, Côte d'Ivoire, in particular. In the light of my main findings, I support the idea that behaviour and attitudes are partly determined by socially responsible governance practices.

My results show that the status of women at the head of the home confers a certain notoriety and engenders cooperative behaviour. The importance given to women entrepreneurs contributes to the creation of a feeling of recognition that stimulates cooperation and the transfer of entrepreneurial learning. This result confirms the idea that entrepreneurial status is now an asset for reducing divisions and stereotypes against women (Carrier et al., 2006).

For Laurice (2016), women are no longer confined to a traditional role in society (mother, housewife, etc.). They are developing entrepreneurial skills that make it easier for them to reconcile family and professional life. They are called upon to play a role in setting up businesses to become involved in the search for income to meet the family's needs, in addition to the men's contribution (Simen and Diouf, 2013). Beyond this aspect, the status of women entrepreneurs also enables them to showcase their talent for innovation and risk-taking. Through their upbringing, which is underpinned by the spirit of perseverance and solidarity in the family environment, women are more inclined to take risks in their entrepreneurial activities (Badia et al., 2013).

On the other hand, my results suggest that the autonomy and access to income provided by entrepreneurial activity improve the ability of family members to work together. Behaviours associated with organisational learning and the interaction of actors' skills appear to be determined by women's degree of autonomy in the family sphere. Women entrepreneurs compensate for the absence of a commercial space by appropriating the home as a place to conduct their business. This result sheds light on the stereotypes that confine women to a domestic role. In the literature, these difficulties have been explained by the absence of a policy of involvement or support from political and government bodies. For example, in Côte d'Ivoire, this form of entrepreneurship has not been formalised by a legal framework, as there are currently no legal provisions relating to home-based income-generating activities. Even *Law No. 2014-140 on the orientation of the national policy for the promotion of small and medium-sized enterprises* sidesteps the issue. This lack of recognition means that women invest in much less productive sectors. On the other hand, they do have the distinction of bringing a more social and human dimension to their businesses (Santoni, 2016).

Above all, women entrepreneurs are looking to be their own boss, to gain external recognition, to seize an opportunity, and to exert influence on their family and friends (Carrier et al., 2006). The fact that there is no explicit communication about home-based entrepreneurial activity means that it is often confused with domestic chores. Yet this activity is an important lever for learning by doing.

Ultimately, the results of my research suggest the need to pay particular attention to social capital and the organisational context in which the entrepreneurial activity takes place. Thus, the perpetuation of home-based entrepreneurial activities would be determined by the ability of entrepreneurs to maintain an organisational learning process. These results are important in the field of entrepreneurial management, insofar as these home-based experiences reveal norms of practice.

Conclusion

My study is based on the need to move away from the traditional approach to entrepreneurship, which has long been defined by the search for profits and a profit-making purpose. Responsible female entrepreneurship in the context of the home in Abidjan shows that the prism of the traditional approach is not relevant in all cases. Through a content analysis of the discourses, the emphasis is first placed on the cultural nature of the act of entrepreneurship by these women. This cultural aspect presents the family as the environment par excellence for entrepreneurial socialisation, which is then perpetuated intergenerationally. By considering a CSR policy, which is consubstantial with partnership governance in the act of home-based entrepreneurship, attention is paid to the members of the household who contribute to the productivity of the home-based business.

Distanced from the aid and support policies of public bodies and international organisations, this type of entrepreneurship advocates policies conducive to job creation and guaranteeing all women the resources they need for real empowerment. Highlighting the factors that determine the structuring of entrepreneurial activities in the home contributes to a better understanding of the self-employment ecosystem. The home appears to be a powerful marker because it conveys women's entrepreneurial identities. Home-based entrepreneurship is part of a local management style based on the values of respect for the family, careful management of business funds, and the involvement of all members of the household, including the spouse.

In this context, entrepreneurship can be a lever for learning, i.e. a process of exchange and cooperation. Women entrepreneurs at home train the younger generations in entrepreneurial practices. This approach is part of mentoring practices and family support networks that facilitate the transfer of experience and the perpetuation of entrepreneurial activities. The glass ceiling faced by women in the workplace could steer them towards home-based entrepreneurship.

Limits

My study has three limitations. Firstly, the sample (n = 16) covers only Abidjan, the economic capital of Côte d'Ivoire, which is not representative of the country's other cities. Secondly, my study only focuses on women working in the informal sector, whereas the home can be used as a setting for formalising entrepreneurial activity. Finally, it would be interesting, in an empirical study, to seek the views of both parties; on the one hand, the family network and, on the other, the woman entrepreneur at home.

Research Avenues

For a more in-depth analysis, studies could look at how well women are represented in rural areas, where their home-based activities are more prevalent. The methodological framework could be geared towards statistical studies to build a more representative model. In addition, a study on the transmission of know-how to the younger generation could highlight the link between female entrepreneurship and organisational learning.

Notes

1 This chapter was published in French and is here published with the kind authorisation of the review: "Entrepreneuriat féminin à domicile à Abidjan en Côte d'Ivoire: gouvernance partenariale et perpétuation de la relève", *Revue Organisations & Territoires*, 2021, 30 (2): 39–52.
2 Tontine associations operate in a context where banks are not involved. They are made up of groups of friends, family, colleagues, or neighbours.
3 Spreading lies about someone.

References

Aoki, M. (2000) "Information and governance in the Silicon Valley model", in X. Vives (ed.) *Corporate Governance: Theoretical and Empirical Perspectives*, pp. 169–200. Cambridge: Cambridge University Press. https://doi.org/10.1017/CBO9781139175333.006

Ba, S. (2019) "Religion as a resource for female entrepreneurship in Senegal", *Sociologies pratiques*, 2 (39): 133–144. https://www.cairn.info/revue-sociologies-pratiques-2019-2.htm

Badia, B., F. Brunet, and P. Kertudo (2013) "Les freins et obstacles à l'entrepreneuriat féminin: étude qualitative auprès de créatrices d'entreprise dans l'agglomération de Nancy", *Recherche sociale*, 4 (208): 7–57. https://www.cairn.info/revue-recherche-sociale-2013-4.html

Badini Koné, H. (2021) "Entrepreneuriat féminin à domicile à Abidjan en Côte d'Ivoire: gouvernance partenariale et perpétuation de la relève", *Revue Organisations & Territoires*, 30 (2): 39–52.

Bardin, L. (2013) *L'analyse de contenu* (2nd ed.). Paris: Presses Universitaires de France.

Bony, N. K., H. G. R. Tiéffi, and L. Diarra (2021) "Utilité perçue de la formalisation de l'entreprise selon le niveau d'études et l'auto-efficacité entrepreneuriale des femmes entrepreneures à Abidjan (Côte d'Ivoire)", *Revue africaine de management*, 6 (1): 53–67. https://revues.imist.ma/index.php/RAM/article/view/24911

Borges, C., G. Simard, and J. Filion (2005) *Création d'entreprises – femmes entrepreneures* [research report], HEC Montréal. http://web.hec.ca/creationdentreprise/CERB_Backup-12-mai-2008/pdf/2005-17-CEFEDonneesA.pdf

Bourdieu, P. (1980) "Le capital social", *Actes de la recherche en sciences sociales*, 3: 2–3. www.persee.fr/doc/arss_0335-5322_1980_num_31_1_2069

Boussoura, E. and O. Z. Benslimane (2015, June) *Corporate social responsibility and organisational performance: what convergence?* Paper presented at the XXIVth AIMS International Conference on Strategic Management, Paris.

Brush, C. G., A. De Bruin, and F. Welter (2009) "A gender-aware framework for women's entrepreneurship", *International Journal of Gender and Entrepreneurship*, 1 (1): 8–24. https://doi.org/10.1108/17566260910942318

Carrier, C., P.-A. Julien, and W. Menvielle (2006) "Un regard critique sur l'entrepreneuriat féminin : une synthèse des études des 25 dernières années", *Gestion*, 31 (2): 36–50. https://doi.org/10.3917/riges.312.0036

Chabaud, D. and T. Lebègue (2013) "Femmes dirigeantes en PME: Bilan et perspectives", *Revue interdisciplinaire Management, Homme & Entreprise*, 3 (7): 43–60. https://www.cairn.info/revue-rimhe-2013-3.htm

Charreaux, G. and J.-P. Pitol-Belin (1991) "Conseil d'administration et pouvoirs dans l'entreprise", *Revue d'économie financière*, 6 (31): 49–79. https://doi.org/10.3406/ecofi.1994.2103

Charreaux, G. and P. Wirtz (2007) *Gouvernance des entreprises: nouvelles perspectives*. Paris: Economica.

Dutta, S. and S. Banerjee (2011) "Ethical practices towards employees in small enterprises: A quantitative index", *International Journal of Business Management & Economic Research*, 2 (3): 205–221. http://ijbmer.com/docs/volumes/vol2issue3/ijbmer2011020302.pdf

Dupuis, J.-C. and C. Le Bas (2007) "SMEs and corporate social responsibility", *Revue internationale P.M.E*, 20 (3–4): 7–15. https://doi.org/10.7202/1008521ar

Fayolle, A. (2010) "Organisation entrepreneuriale et orientation vers les opportunités: Un cadre intégrateur", *Revue française de gestion*, 7 (206): 149–169. https://www.cairn.info/revue-francaise-de-gestion-2010-7-page-149

Gianfaldoni, P., G. Colletis, and N. Richez-Battesti (2005) "Social and solidarity economy, territories and proximity", *International Review of the Social Economy*, 296: 8–25. https://doi.org/10.7202/1021859ar

Glidja, B. J. M. (2019) "Les déterminants du succès de l'entrepreneuriat féminin au Benin, le rôle modérateur de l'appui institutional support: le cas de la WBPC", *Gestion 2000*, 36 (2): 39–59. https://bec.uac.bj/uploads/publication/4c80897e128430ebf7ef3be78f2b23e6.pdf

Gond, J.-P. (2006) "Construire la relation (positive) entre performance sociétale et financière sur le marché de l'ISR: de la performation à l'autoréalisation?", *Revue d'économie financière*, 85: 63–79. https://doi.org/10.3406/ecofi.2006.4143

Gond, J.-P. and J. Igalens (2012) *La responsabilité sociale de l'entreprise*. Paris: Presses Universitaires de France.

Guérin, I. and J.-M. Servet (2005) "L'économie solidaire entre le local et le global: l'exemple de la microfinance", *Revue internationale de l'économie sociale*, 296: 83–99. https://doi.org/10.7202/102

Institut national de la statistique (INS) (2019) *Enquête nationale sur la situation de l'emploi et le secteur informel*. République de Côte d'Ivoire.

Lambrecht, J., F. Pirnay, P. Amedodji, and Z. Aouni (2003) *Entrepreneuriat féminin en Wallonie*. Centre de recherche PME et d'entrepreneuriat de l'Université de Liège and Centre d'études pour l'entrepreneuriat.

Laurice, A. (2016) "Typology of entrepreneurs, a gender approach", *Entrepreneurship Review*, 15 (3): 109–127. https://doi.org/10.3917/entre.153.0109

Leclair, A. and R. Redien-Collot (2013) "L'intention entrepreneuriale des femmes: Le cas de l'Égypte", *Revue internationale P.M.E*, 26 (1): 93–113. http://dx.doi.org/10.7202/1024272ar

United Nations Development Fund for Women (UNIFEM) (2009) Annual Report 2008-2009. UNIFEM. http://www.albacharia.ma/xmlui/bitstream/handle/123456789/30825/0590UNIFEM%20Rapport%20Annuel%20%202008_2009.pdf?sequence=1

Léger-Jarniou, C., T. Nelson, and S. Chasserio (2015) "Research on women entrepreneurs: Putting the French-speaking perspective into context", *Revue de l'entrepreneuriat*, 14 (3): 7–17. https://doi.org/10.3917/entre.142.0007

Le Loarne-Lemaire, S. (2013), The couple, pillar of female entrepreneurship", *Expansion Management Review*, 1 (148): 109–116. https://doi.org/10.3917/emr.148.0109

Mebtoul, M., J.-L. Olive, and C. Campergue (2010) *Le soin Sociomorphose*. Perpignan: Presses universitaires de Perpignan.

Meier, O. and G. Schier (2008) "Quelles théories et principes d'actions en matière de gouvernance des associations?", *Management & Avenir*, 6 (20): 179–198. *https://doi.*org/10.3917/mav.020.0179

Metaiche, F. T. and A. Bendiabdellah (2016) "Les femmes entrepreneures en Algérie: savoir, vouloir et pouvoir", *Marché et organisations"*, 2 (26): 219–240. https://doi.org/10.3917/maorg.026.0219

Miles, M. B. and A. M. Huberman (2003) *Analyse des données qualitatives* (2nd ed.). Paris: De Boeck Supérieur.

Mione, A. (2002, October) *Comparaison des femmes entrepreneurs France-Canada*. Proceedings of the 6th *Congrès international francophone sur la PME*, Montréal. http://www.airepme.org/images/File/2002

Mione, A. (2004, March) *CIGALINE, entre affectivité, effectivité et efficacité : bilan des cinq premières années de vie de l'unique Club d'investissement pour la gestion alternative de l'épargne solidaire, au féminin*. Paper presented at the 7th CIFEPME, Montpellier.

Nkakleu, R. (ed.) (2018) *Accompagnement des petites entreprises au Cameroun et au Sénégal*. Paris: Éditions EMS.

Nordman, C. J. and J. Vaillant (2014) "Informal entrepreneurship and gender in Madagascar: The role of solidarity norms and domestic responsibilities in performance gaps", *Developing Worlds*, 2 (166): 59–72. https://doi.org/10.3917/med.166.0059

Onana, F. X. (2009, May) *Les motivations des femmes à entrer en affaires au Cameroun*. Paper presented at the 11th *Journées scientifiques du Réseau entrepreneuriat de l'AUF*, Trois-Rivières (Canada).

Organisation for Economic Co-operation and Development (OECD) (2014) *Women and Enterprise 2014: Accelerating Entrepreneurship Development in the North Africa and Middle East Region*. Paris: OECD. https://www.oecd.org/fr/publications/les-femmes-et-l-entreprise-2014-9789264227521-fr.htm

Paradas, A., C. Debray, C. Revelli, and J.-M. Courrent (2013) "Les femmes dirigeantes de PME ont-elles des pratiques de RSE spécifiques? *Recherches en sciences de gestion*, 4 (97): 187–207. https://doi.org/10.3917/resg.097.0187

Persais, É. (2013) "RSE et gouvernance partenariale", *Gestion 2000*, 30 (1): 69–86. https://www.cairn.info/revue-gestion-2000-2013-1-page-69.htm

Peyroux, C., I. Bories-Azeau, F. Fort, and F. Noguera (2019) "Partnership governance of support structures and territorial entrepreneurial dynamics", *Revue internationale P.M.E*, 32 (3–4): 175–205. https://doi.org/10.7202/1067737ar

Postel, N. and S. Rousseau (2008) "RSE et éthique d'entreprise: la nécessité des institutions", *M@n@gement*, 11 (2): 137–160. http://dx.doi.org/10.3917/mana.112.0137

Redien-Collot, R. and C. Léger-Jarniou (2018) "Delayed CSR in French SMEs? The caution and hybrid ethical discourse of female leaders of high-growth SMEs", *Revue de l'entrepreneuriat*, 17 (2): 7–33. https://www.cairn.info/revue-de-l-entrepreneuriat-2018-2.htm

Roussel, P. and F. Wacheux (2006) *Management des ressources humaines*. Paris: De Boeck Supérieur.

Santoni, J. (2016) "Specificities, obstacles and potential leverage of women's entrepreneurship: State of the francophone and anglophone literatures", *International Journal of Psychosociology and Management of Organisational Behaviour*, 22 (54): 207–228. https://doi.org/10.3917/rips1.054.0207

Santoni, J. and I. Barth (2014) "The role of the network in the development of female entrepreneurship: The case of an entrepreneurial centre within a business school", *@GRH*, 2 (11): 81–113. https://doi.org/10.3917/grh.142.0081

Simen, S. and I. D. Diouf (2013, May) *Women's entrepreneurship in Senegal: towards an entrepreneurial model of 'necessity' in developing countries.* Paper presented at the CAM Congress, Dakar. https://halshs.archives-ouvertes.fr/halshs-01782047

St-Pierre, J. and L. Cadieux (2011) "La conception de la performance: quels liens avec le profil entrepreneurial des dirigeants de PME?" *Revue de l'entrepreneuriat,* 1 (10): 33–52. https://doi.org/10.3917/entre.101.0033

Tchouassi, G., N. Ngwen, H. T. Oumbe, and S. Temfack (2018) "Youth and women's entrepreneurial knowledge and economic development", *International Review of Organizational Science*, 1 (5): 57–79. https://doi.org/10.3917/riso.005.0057

Vier-Machado, H. and L. Rouleau (2002, October) *Identité sociale et entrepreneuriat féminin : étude comparative entre le Brésil et le Canada.* Paper presented at the 6th *Congrès international francophone sur la PME*, Montréal. http://www.airepme.org/images/File/2002

Zouiten, J. and T. Levy-Tadjine (2005, November) *Do women and immigrants need specific entrepreneurial support?* Paper presented at the 4th *Congrès de l'Académie de l'entrepreneuriat et de l'innovation*, Paris. http://entrepreneuriat.com/congres-aei/

4 Women's "Invisible" Paths to Empowerment in Cameroon

The Case of Digital Companies

Estelle Vérine Salla Bezanga

Introduction

The 2020s began with the health crisis, notably COVID-19, the corollary of which was the adoption of restrictive measures by the State (Benveniste, 2020). While the aim of these measures was to limit the spread of the pandemic, for the younger members of society (Bayart, 1985) and women in particular, the adoption of this emergency policy intensified the gaps that already existed with advantaged groups. Although women's equality and empowerment (Guérin and Palier, 2006; Calvès, 2009) is the theme of the 17 Sustainable Development Goals and of a national policy focusing on gender, adopted in 2014, as part of the priority areas of the National Development Strategy, the sovereign power of the Cameroonian state as employer, protector, and developer has been weakened (Ngo Nyemb-Wisman, 2011). The discourse to be found in certain social media expresses how political actors conceive the world and the means they use to transform it (Zittoun, 2013). The instruments used initially reflected a political will to promote women's empowerment and were aimed at combating gender inequality (Bacqué and Biewener, 2013; Jacquot and Mazur, 2019). However, the current socio-economic reality shows that change is minimal. The minimal effectiveness of the programmes developed is firstly opposed to the period of containment that is putting the issue of women's financial empowerment back on the agenda. That said, women develop certain skills in the use of social networks, particularly online sales, as a way of circumventing financial insecurity. At the same time, these measures reveal in their own way the inability of the public authorities to provide a credible response to the aspirations of this new category of women entrepreneurs (Amougou, Salla, and Oyane, 2021). While investing in digital entrepreneurship makes it possible to manage the imbalance arising from job losses in several sectors of activity, it also highlights women's ability to act on themselves and on the transformation of society. This commitment to online sales seemed to be the best solution to the crisis, but at the same time it reveals that women's digital entrepreneurship is a response to the State's inability to take charge of this innovative sector.

This chapter aims to analyse the place of women in public action, the purpose of which is to tackle the problem of their financial independence. I look at the contribution of women entrepreneurs to the transformation of public action (cf. Crozier and Friedberg, 1977; Nguelieutou, 2008). This line of research draws

DOI: 10.4324/9781003492931-6

on a body of literature that includes complementary work on gender and public policy.

A gender analysis of public issues reveals concerns about women's inequality and invisibility, women's empowerment, women's knowledge, and women's needs in development processes (Sreberny, 2005). This approach seems to exclude the positioning of women at the heart of economic policies that defend women's empowerment (Garcia, 2010) in society (Taborga, 2007). However, thinking based on gender studies (Talahite, 2014) shows that African women have had entrepreneurial skills for decades (Sylvanus 2006), following the example of the "Nana Benz" during the colonial and post-colonial period in West Africa, who made their fortune selling loincloth through trade with the Hollandais and the Anglais. At the same time, the role of women in informal economic activity is being highlighted in Morocco (de Henau and Puech, 2003), an informality encouraged to arouse less interest in political issues. This context, considered to be "patriarchal", is extended in Cameroon, where the "Bayam Sellam" play a decisive role in women's entrepreneurial dynamics (Kaoutoing et al., 2017). While Bayam Sellam are a category of women entrepreneurs who sell food in urban markets (Nyemb-Wisman, 2011), occupying physical sales spaces, online sellers use digital platforms as a sales space. Although both categories are ways out of precarious situations, they reveal the inadequacies of state intervention in women's empowerment processes and reveal the practical implications of women's self-engagement (Bergamashi, 2014). In examining the relationships between women digital entrepreneurship actors and women's empowerment tools in Cameroon, I include in the analysis the possibility that platformisation transforms radically women's business activity and participates in their economic inclusion. This inclusion is materialised using digital tools as a resource in the fight against precariousness and the financial exclusion of women.

The aim of my research is to examine how digitisation is reconfiguring women's commercial activity and strengthening their capacity for empowerment. Even though digital technologies are transforming women's entrepreneurial careers, the lack of regulation of their activities enables them to develop dynamics of subjectivation. Adopting an inductive approach, my research is based on field surveys and semi-structured interviews conducted with ten operators of digital micro-enterprises in May 2024.

Women's Life Experience and Entrepreneurial Path through Online Sales

Looking at women's entrepreneurship through the prism of digital platforms involves analysing their relationship with the transformation of sales practices and leads us to reflect on the meaning of the regularities of these digital practices producing new agents of social change.

A Link between Precarious Social Status and the Limits of the Wage System

For want of anything better, online sales are a gateway to social stability and are straddling the line between formality and informality: Get by on social networks to survive is the slogan. The variety of profiles and backgrounds of the women described means that there are some common threads in the motivations behind their choice of business. These women are starting up online retailing to "*round off*" the ends of the month,[1] in other words to supplement their wages by doing odd jobs, with the aim of supporting their family and saving money. For those who are employed, the move towards online sales can be explained by various forms of suffering at work, by low-paid jobs for young people, and by unfair dismissals (Beaud and Cartier, 2008), all of which are indicators of the precariousness of employment in Cameroonian society. Online sales therefore seem to be a necessary step (Amougou et al., 2021) for those who don't want to and can't do nothing.

The secondary school teacher among our interviewees has been selling online since 2014, when she graduated from the *Ecole Normale Supérieure* in Yaoundé. She started out selling fashion accessories – shoes, hair pieces, clothes, jewellery – while waiting to be integrated into the civil service.[2] She joined the civil service in November 2016 as a teacher at the age of 29 and received her first salary in 2017 that was set at 179,366 F-CFA, even though she was married with a young child. The time available between leaving school and joining the civil service was not in vain; it enabled her to invest in online trading to meet her personal needs and contribute to her family's expenses. Selling online thus helps to diversify the sources of income with the aim of improving the quality of life.

The common narrative shared by these women and their reasons for entering online retailing in the expectation of "*something better*", is constitutive of the mental and practical dispositions that make it possible to act in each social sphere (Herman, 2007). This social environment is marked by the stagnation of the Cameroonian economy and the deterioration of the urban labour market (Calvès and Kobiané, 2014), following the failure of structural adjustment programmes (Dujardin et al., 2003), the implications of which are leading to profound changes in individual behaviour. Indeed, the "individual-producer" (Heba, 1993) is affected by wage and employment policies, with the gradual disengagement of the state leading to the extension of the labour market into the informal sector (Dongmo, 2022). In this respect, online sales compensate for the wage gap and ensure a degree of autonomy and respect within family and community frameworks (Amougou et al., 2021).

Gaëlle B. is 36 years old[3] and is a civil servant with a Master's degree and qualification as an e-tailer; she is married and the mother of four children. Like the secondary school teacher, online sales were "an opportunity in 2015, when I was unemployed and everything was still in its infancy", she confides. And she continues: "I had to do something while waiting for a stable job". She is forced to take limited action (Kefi, 2010), which influences her intention to act and to engage in online sales helping her to develop her financial independence. In this respect, the words that "something had to be done" are the result of a subjective motivation influenced by the personal experience that gave rise to her desire for independence.

A Change in Perception: From Resourcefulness to Passion

My survey shows the extent to which the rise of digital platforms in Cameroon has changed social relations by placing some women not at the heart of vice-related scandals, but at the heart of household survival mechanisms (Gning, 2013), and the desire to rise socially to "look around" (Touraine, 2000). With the flexibility offered by online sales, which can be made anywhere, women are investing their Internet capital to fund targeted online advertising campaigns to reach potential customers.

Isabelle D.[4] is 40 years old, the eldest of a family of six children, a single mother of three, and a holder of a probationary diploma in the literary series and a training certificate in secretarial office automation obtained in 2005. Online sales became her main source of income when, after her training, she wanted to fulfil her potential and look after her family. She says:

> I must admit that I was just starting out in online sales and that I was doing it as a test, a hobby, because I was hoping that a manager from where I had submitted my recruitment files, would call me. What's more, the benefits were insignificant. There was nothing to encourage me to persevere other than my personal needs and those of my children.

It is thus a non-preferred life course, insofar as it reflects a second option in the absence of what she hopes for. By being part of a long wait, Isabelle D. has finally made the online sale her rational choice, thanks to a combination of actions and beliefs (Boudon, 2004). Limited access to formal employment makes online entrepreneurship an opportunity for social and financial inclusion. From being a simple relay agent between the shops and a virtual clientele, this secretary has turned her phone into her main work site through sales groups on Facebook and WhatsApp. Today, she can testify to the opportunities offered by online sales: "It's pretty free now, relax, you don't need to put in too much effort to make money. Just your internet connection and that's it".

Like Isabelle D., Laurence F.[5] has a degree in veterinary sciences. She confides:

> I started selling online at the end of 2018 after my training at the Mfouban veterinary school. I already had a friend who practised this activity. What's more, I was waiting for the competition to join the civil service to be launched[6]. I had already taken the exam four times without success.

Laurence F.'s failures in this competition encouraged her to persevere with her decision to sell online.

These dynamics are taking place in a precarious environment where the lack of support in the search for employment is giving rise to a new sector such as online sales. At the same time, these motivations provide information about the relationship between professional integration and the advantaged and disadvantaged sections of the population. This social integration is often the result of the social reproduction of advantaged positions. The employment crisis is leading women who do not have social capital to take charge in the informal sector, where the

Internet provides a window of opportunity to earn money. Over and above their limited access to formal employment, these women transform the Internet credit they have into business capital.

Rationalisation in the Feminine: When Women Commit to Producing Profits Online

Starting an online business with little financial capital and making a profit are possible. Rationalisation involves optimising online sales processes and strategies to improve efficiency, productivity, and results. To do this, committed players use digital data to understand the behaviour of customers around them and on social networks to optimise sales strategies (1) and reinvest profits in new life projects (2).

Studying Customer Behaviour and Optimising Sales Methods

Laurence F.'s starting point was the observation that "many young women no longer had enough time to do their own shopping because of their multiple commitments. So, I said to myself, they could order online, and we'd simply deliver to their home or to their place of work at their convenience". This situation of "busy" women encourages Laurence F. to play the role of *personal shopper* and earn commission fees. She began the link between her customers and suppliers in the markets of Douala, then extended her sales network abroad with Chinese and Turkish suppliers. The needs of her customers play an important role in the choice of sales method and suppliers.

Laure F.,[7] in turn, explains how she optimises her earnings:

> When I offer a product, when I go to deliver it, another product is requested. For example, a lady picked up some children's clothes from me, and once the delivery was made, she asked me for lingerie for herself. What I do at this point is carry out a study of the market, which allows me not only to process her order but also to extend the demand for lingerie by canvassing to find out how many people this purchase might interest. If I find more people interested, I order a bundle and that's how I win.

The opportunistic situations are therefore conducive to innovation. In fact, they show the conditions for reinventing sales by developing a certain agility that contributes to the implementation of new life projects.

The Production of Induced Female Subjects

The introduction of new sales technologies is changing the economic production and individual behaviour. The transformation into digital work is enabling a new configuration of social relations at work. Digital platforms are seen as levers for empowering women (McCarrick and Kleine, 2020), although this approach seems reductive because it feminises the digital conditioning of goods production, without which women cannot undertake. The perception of change is linked to an overall reduction in the structural inequalities that slow down women's emancipation in Cameroon. However, the women in my sample are involved in individual dynamics of change that correspond to a rather marginalised sector. This leads me to question the practices of subjectivation at work in online sales. Thinking about women subject to the yardstick of entrepreneurial commitment means considering the processes by which they manage to occupy positions other than those that have been assigned to them socially and institutionally (Roche, 2007).

For these women, projecting themselves through online sales means considering future opportunities and the possibility of changing their status as "women consumers". Laure F. defines herself as "a woman concerned with supporting her household", and such an exit only makes sense in a specific social and historical context (Tarragoni, 2016). Women are therefore freeing themselves from a social order that keeps them in the category of "social cadets". By their investment in online sales, the aim is to capitalise on the discursive logics assigning women to the subordination of men and institutions. However, the women's optimistic accounts overlook the social roots that structure their relationship with the dominant patriarchal order in Cameroon, which has a subtle impact on their professional socialisation pathways that are linked to motherhood and caring for children. The intersection between the desire for emancipation and the partial persistence of their invisibility in decision-making spheres means that they have appropriate mechanisms, techniques, and know-how. Their spontaneity reflects a dormant subjective position that was waiting to be mobilised (Rossi, 2004) and enables them to make the choice to blossom by online sales.

From Formalising Sales to Building Entrepreneurial Leadership

If digital platforms are renewing forms of financial inclusion, thanks to the analysis of the various paths taken by my sample, they are also bringing about a social change in the status of women. The profits generated by sales are undoubtedly helping to restructure gender relations, however insignificant they may seem. Over and above this, an economic habitus emerges (Jourdain and Naulin, 2019) incorporated into the various transactions they carry out within their network created.

Approximate Construction of an Entrepreneurial Identity

How do women construct their identity as entrepreneurs? What factors influence this construction? Platform-based sales have a significant impact on women's empowerment. By using online platforms to sell their products, women are accessing a wider audience and expanding their customer base (2) beyond geographical constraints. This quest for customers can be achieved by developing digital and marketing skills (1).

Digital Skills Culture

The desire to increase the customer base and maximise profits requires know-how linked to the mastery of digital tools (Mell, 2018), which places them in a difficult position, that of the saleswomen's academic, professional, and digital backgrounds. It must be said that these women have a relative digital culture (Cardon, 2019), and are socialised to handle digital platforms for long periods of time, such as Facebook, WhatsApp, Instagram, and more recently Snapchat: A disposition they leverage and convert into marketing capital. Yvonne S.,[8] who holds a master's degree in management science and a diploma in telecommunications administration, tells us some of the tricks she uses to attract a wider customer base:

> I go into a shop selling fashion accessories, which could be hair pieces, handbags, or kitchen utensils. I offer to act as a point of sale for the promoter or supplier. If he agrees, I give him my WhatsApp number, which he uses to include me in his sales group that is supplied with images of the products or items offered for sale. Then, I save these images which I post on my WhatsApp status and my story on Facebook. I also make sure to send them to my contacts with whom I have more affinity. I offer various products on my social networks depending on the season. When a contact is interested in my posts or sales statuses, they write to me with a screenshot of the product or item they are interested in and the discussion continues in private messaging". She continues: "This method is effective in that I don't invest any capital up front, but I make sure I increase the price initially set by the main seller. This is how I manage to make a profit ranging from 1,000 F-CFA to 10,000 F-CFA per item.

This strategy guarantees a profit when an agreement is reached between the online saleswoman and the potential customer. My fieldwork supports the idea that many of these young, enterprising online women are building a personal brand to stand out from the crowd. This can be seen in the advertising slogans (Dowling and Kabanoff, 1996), which they disseminate via WhatsApp posts and statuses, or even Snapchat stories: "Come to my air-conditioned inbox", "Free delivery", "I sell, I lose", "Top quality", "Who takes?" etc. These posts illustrate customer attraction strategies regarding the subscribers, the contacts, and the various relationships. Slogans have a significant effect on the quality of products or items, as well as on sales offers. The sum of the slogans can reflect support for the brand or the seller, as well as undermining it (Boush, 1993).

Unlike Yvonne S. and others who use colloquial language or Cameroonian slang to help their business prosper, Laure N.[9] behaves differently because she is influenced by her main job, teleworking. Aged 37, she has been a teleconsultant for 12 years. This position shapes her sales practices in terms of marketing and advertising and shows a rather technical method, unlike her colleagues. She uses a less trivial vocabulary, revealing her professional background. She is more familiar with both persuasion and dissuasion in her field. As a result, she can pride herself on having made the "right decision" (Ferry, 2023) by choosing online sales as a secondary activity. She implicitly affirms this during our discussions:

> Online sales are my secondary activity, which goes hand in hand with my main activity. When I experience low periods in the business, I keep the same thoughts about teleoperations, which make up most of my bread and butter. These are not products that I sell as a teleoperator, but services that require a great deal of delicacy in language. I want to pass on this same sensitivity to my customers, even though they are a different audience.

In her words, it's a use of her talent as a saleswoman, one who knows how to convince and survive.

It must be said that all these provisions have an integrative function that gives social value to femininity commonly considered "depraved" on social networks because of the negative image of influencers and the role stereotypes of women as mothers and wives. This discourse on femininity operates beyond sales exchanges on digital platforms where it acquires symbolic and social notability. From the discussions that take place for minutes or even hours between the saleswoman and her customers, and then in the quality of the products or items, and the service, a network, and a community are built that simultaneously contribute to the self-fulfilment of women and the enhancement of the profession of online saleswoman.

Social Capital Built Up through the Sales Network

Interpersonal relationships are being forged. The eclecticism of online sales practices is not without consequences for relations between social classes. The quality of the products sold (mainly fashion accessories and cosmetics) responds to the needs of a specific category of woman. During an interview with a promoter of a virtual online sales page, she told us about her loyal customers, most of whom are socially well-placed women from Yaoundé and Douala. Her account shows that she plays the role of "personal shopper" for businesswomen, the wives of senior civil servants, and children from well-off families.

This social capital of the female customer base, initially formed "by word of mouth", translates into considerable economic opportunities. "Imagine what it means to dress the grandsons of Cameroon's First Lady", says a promoter of an online children's clothing boutique. Social networks can be used to reach the target audience, with offers tailored to the type of customer. Although they operate on the fringes of formal recognition of their business, they interact with their virtual and material community, building relationships, and reinforcing their identity as entrepreneurs (Amougou, 2016).

An interprofessional network is being built up from the local to the global level. In the structuring of this informal work, we can read the influence of the globalisation process by describing the recompositing of organised social spaces that are dependent on the most diverse forms of solidarity (Constantin, 1996). Over and above declared affinities, selling online means building, at both local and global levels, a community of digital exchanges over a long period of time between different players involved in the chain of transactions from ordering the product to consuming it. This relationship appears linear when we are in the customer-consumer position. However, there is a complex upstream process that takes place virtually. This dynamic of transnational informality, standardised on websites, accounts for the territoriality of trading zones that promote the circulation of goods between China, India, Turkey, and Cameroon, and thus reveals the fluidity of digital borders (Delannoy and Olivier, 2019). These three countries constitute the main suppliers of items to be marketed online to Cameroon. These transactional networks are veritable places of power where suppliers, forwarding agents, and the owners of trading sites are deployed, as well as withdrawal points or delivery agencies, defining the standards of online sales.

Laure F. tells us all about *dropshipping*:

> It's a way of selling online without having to manage stocks. With a supplier who may be in China, Thailand, Turkey, or anywhere in the world with whom you have an agreement, who is not going to tell you, for example, that in order to sell such and such a product, you need to order 100, order 1000, etc. That's your arrangement with the supplier. You have your products on the catalogue but no stock. But when the customer places an order on my shop online, visits my catalogue, and orders x, y, z, and puts it in his shopping basket, I'm responsible for passing the order on to the supplier. Now, if I can put a product online for €100, my supplier can supply it for €80. The supplier prepares the order and delivers the products. I deduct my profit and the supplier's share from the customer's payment.

Accessing an international market becomes possible via social networks, which can be beneficial for remote customers or customers who find it difficult to access local markets. However, this flexibility also benefits disadvantaged groups such as women working in this sector. It is therefore an opportunity for financial inclusion, but it is also important to consider the associated challenges and risks.

Digital Risks: A Random Activity

While online sales sites offer sellers the opportunity to promote and market their products without the traditional barriers to market entry, such as the need for large amounts of capital or an established distribution network, they also present factors of imbalance that do not seem to be widely perceived. Considering the forms of resistance encountered by sellers requires to study the situations of risk-taking, and the irregularity and lack of formal regulation of content on social networks.

Risk Situations: Securing Data and the Uncertainty of Transactions with Partners

Risk is perceived as a determining variable in the decision to buy and sell online (Gallen and Cases, 2007). In the same way that these practices are building new sociability (Mercklé, 2004), they contribute to an imbalance in digital activity. My fieldwork tells me that there is no such thing as zero risk in a company. In the current context, there is no specific law governing the protection of personal data. Due to this infrastructural weakness, women engaged in online sales run the risk of facing cyber-attacks (Douzet et al., 2009). These are criminal actions by a category of deviant individuals who have the cybernetic capabilities to control the information posted online. This permanent risk contributes to social polarisation by reinforcing existing inequalities in terms of the use of the Internet. Similarly, dependence on technology makes personal data vulnerable to cyber-attacks, with inevitable questions of identification.

Engaging in online sales also means signing up to a logic of dependence on foreign suppliers which leads to the risk of data security and accentuates the uncertainty that resides in bank card transactions (Guseva, 2010). What's more, there are still moments of uncertainty about the quality of the products and the timing of the order and delivery. Laure N. readjusts her enthusiasm to the cost of selling:

> I've had low periods and even interruptions. Interruptions, because as you know, there is no such thing as zero risk in any business. They are due to delivery failures, because sometimes we order from outside the country and it's so uncertain because the supplier doesn't always meet the delivery deadlines. On the other hand, someone will call to say that the boats have caught fire, and you lose everything. And when you don't have a lot of capital to rebuild your business, you stop.

In this extract, the online saleswoman presents us with unforeseen situations that alter her abilities through a set of constraints (Ferrière, 2011), such as technical breakdowns and increased customs duties. These uncertainties – linked to the digital transformation of commercial exchanges, reducing the intervention of a legal third party in transactions between suppliers and entrepreneurs – reinforce the idea of the need for support in the digital entrepreneurship sector.

The Lack of Formal Regulations of the Online Sales Profession

The platformisation of selling plays a crucial role in empowering women by providing them with a platform to express their creativity, reach a global audience, and exercise greater control over their business activity. However, these women face a lack of material and intellectual symbolic resources (Menye and Guetsop Sateu, 2017). The investment in online sales is being feminised despite the patriarchal environment in which these women evolve. Taking charge using digital devices requires a renewal of resources. My sample includes young women who are absent from the discourse on digital advances in the retail sector. Yet training courses are an integral part of the women's empowerment policies defined by the Ministry for the Promotion of Women and the Family. If these policies do not have a major impact on the actions taken by women on social networks, these women have no interest in government initiatives for technical support. According to a report by the *Institut National de la Statistique* (National Statistics Institute), they are in a marginal position in the entrepreneurial category (2020) indicating that 37,5% of businesses are run by women. Biwolé Ondoua's work reveals that 89.5% of Cameroonian women were involved in teleworking during the COVID-19 period (Biwolé, 2021). The strong presence of women in teleworking leads us to think about the subjective *a priori* attitudes towards them in relation to success in digital entrepreneurship.

Conclusion

The objective of this study is to analyse the possibilities for empowering women through online sales. The aim was to assess the motivations behind women's choice of this economic activity, and to take account of the environment in which they operate. The fieldwork reveals the precarious nature of the employment sector, which leads women to take up online sales as their main or secondary activity. This result can be explained, in part, by the fact that women are choosing to be autonomous and taking advantage of the opportunities offered by social networks in terms of flexibility and gain. However, as digital frontiers open, they come up against the risks of cybercrime and the uncertainties of the global economic market. Similarly, the variable informality that characterises this sector does not engage the public authorities, and the impact of this is that they are slow to make a qualitative leap forward.

Notes

1 The interview with an IT teacher at a secondary school in Douala, Cameroon's economic capital, took place in May 2024.
2 The process of joining the civil service in Cameroon after graduating from ENS ends on average two years after the end of the training.
3 The interview took place in May 2024.
4 The interview took place in May 2024.
5 The interview took place in May 2024.
6 It should be noted that joining the civil service in Cameroon is not direct after this type of training. Generally speaking, you have to submit applications or a curriculum vitae to the National Employment Fund or generate the necessary funds to set up your own business.
7 The interview took place in May 2024.
8 The interview took place in May 2024.
9 The interview took place in May 2024.

References

Amougou, G. (2016) "Jeunesse entreprenante et processus d'auto-prise en charge au Cameroun", *Revue Jeunes et Société*, 1 (2): 79–97.

Amougou, G., E. V. Salla Bezanga, and V. Oyane Ossah (2021) "De l'assujetissement à la subjectivation. Parcours de jeunes gardiens domestiques originaires de la région de l'Extrême-Nord à Yaoundé", *Revue internationale des études du développement*, 246 (2): 181–206.

Bacqué, M.-H. and C. Biewener (2013) "L'empowerment, un nouveau vocabulaire pour parler de participation", *Idées économiques et sociales*, 173 (3): 25–32.

Bayart, J.-F. (1985) *L'État au Cameroun*. Paris: Presses de Sciences Po.

Beaud, S. and M. Cartier (2008) "De la précarisation de l'emploi à la précarisation du travail. La nouvelle condition salariale", in S. Beaud (ed.) *La France invisible*, pp. 560–573. Paris: La Découverte.

Benveniste, A. (2020) "En mésure de confinement", *Chimères*, 97 (2): 81–85.

Bergamashi, I. (2014) "Building state capacities?: The case of the poverty reduction unit in Mali", in J. P. Olivier de Sardan and T. Bierschenk (eds) *States at Work: Dynamics of African Bureaucracies*, pp. 271–300. Brill: Leiden.

Biwolé, V. O. (2021) "Impact de la COVID-19 sur l'emploi au Cameroun. Résultats d'une étude empirique", *Mondes en développement*, 196 (4): 27–47.

Boudon, R. (2004) "Théorie du choix rationnel ou individualisme méthodologique", *Revue du MAUSS*, 24 (2): 281–309.

Boush, D. M. (1993) "Comment les slogans publicitaires peuvent orienter les évaluations des extensions de marque", *Psychologie et marketing*, 10 (1): 67–78.

Calvès, A.-E. (2009). "'Empowerment': Généalogie d'un concept clé du discours contemporain sur le développement", *Revue Tiers Monde*, 200 (4): 735–745.

Calvès, A.-E. and J.-F. Kobian (2014) "Genre et nouvelles dynamiques d'insertion professionnelle chez les jeunes à Ouagadougou", *Autrepart*, 71 (3): 33–56.

Cardon, D. (2019) *Culture Numérique*. Paris: Presses de Sciences Po.

Constantin, F. (1996) "L'informel internationalisé ou la subversion de la territorialité", *Cultures et Conflits*, 1–2 (21–22): 1–25.

Crozier, M. and E. Friedberg (1977) *L'acteur et le système. Les contraintes de l'action collective*. Paris: Seuil.

de Henau, J. and I. Puech (2003) "Rabat: Mettre du genre à l'ouvrage au Maghreb", *Travail, genre et sociétés*, 10 (2): 219–223.

Delannoy, A. and L. Olivier (2019) "L'e-réputation de la marque dans le commerce en ligne: Risques juridiques au coeur de la gestion de l'identité numérique", *Question de management*, 1 (23): 53–66.

Dongmo, W. J. (2022) *Activités de production et syndicalisme en Afrique et au Cameroun: XIXème et XXème siècles*. Paris: L'Harmattan.

Douzet, F., J.-L. Samaan, and A. Desforges (2009) "Les pirates du cyberspace", *Hérodote*, 134 (3): 176–193.

Dowling, G. R. and B. Kabanoff (1996) "Analyse de contenu assistée par ordinateur: Quel est le point commun entre 240 slogans publicitaires", *Lettres de marketing*, 7: 63–75.

Dujardin, B., M. Dujardin, and I. Hermans (2003) "Ajustement structurel, ajustement culturel", *Santé publique*, 15 (4): 503–513.

Ferrière, M. (2011) "Les principales critiques de la théorie du choix rationnel", *Idées économiques et sociales*, 165 (3): 37–45.

Ferry, M. (2023) "Elles triment, ils flambent", *Terrain. Anthropologie et sciences humaines*, 78: 70–89.

Gallen, C. and A.-S. Cases (2007) "Le rôle du risque perçu et de l'expérience dans l'achat de vin en ligne", *Décisions Marketing*, 1 (45): 59–74.

Garcia, M. (2010) "La femme est-elle un homme économique comme les autres?", *Multitudes*, 42: 94–99.

Gning, S. B. (2013) "Les femmes dans le secteur informel", in M. Maruani (ed.) *Travail et genre dans le monde: L'état des savoirs*, pp. 336–344. Paris: La Découverte.

Guérin, I. and J. Palier (2006) "Microfinance et empowerment des femmes: La révolution silencieuse aura-t-elle lieu?", *Finance et Bien Commun*, 2 (25): 76–82.

Guseva, A. (2010) "Incertitude et complémentarité: le marché des cartes de crédit en Russie", *Genèses*, 79 (2): 74–96.

Heba, N. A. (1993) "Quelques conséquences sociales des programmmes d'ajustement structurel", *Égypte/Monde arabe*, 12–13: 145–177.

Herman, E. (2007) "La notion d'autonomie et ses impensés dans la socialisation enfantine", *Mouvements*, 49 (1): 46–52.

Institut National de la Statistique du Cameroun (2020) *Entrepreneuriat et genre au Cameroun*. Yaoundé: Institut National de la Statistique.

Jacquot, S. and A. Mazur (2019) "Genre et politiques publiques", in S. Jacquot et al. (eds) *Dictionnaire des politiques publiques*, pp. 289–297. Paris: Presses de Sciences Po.
Jourdain, A. and S. Naulin (2019) *La sociologie de Pierre Bourdieu.* Paris: Armand Colin.
Kaoutoing, S., T. Maï Django Wambé, and Hourenatou (2017) "La croissance de micro et très petites entreprises féminines au Cameroun: Une analyse par les modes de financement", *Management et Avenir*, 91: 65–85.
Kefi, H. (2010) "Mesures perceptuelles de l'usage des systèmes d'information: Application de la théorie du comportement planifié", *Humanisme et Entreprise*, 297 (2): 45–65.
McCarrick, H. and D. Kleine (2020) "Inclusion numérique, entrepreneuriat féminin et sujets néolibéraux", in C. Leterme (ed.) *Impasses numériques. Points de vue du Sud,* pp.133–146. Paris: Éditions Syllepse, "Alternatives Sud".
Mell, L. (2018) "À travers les hypostases du numérique dans l'enseignement supérieur: Réflexion critique sur le développement de la culture et des compétences numériques", *Lien social et politiques*, 81: 173–191.
Menye, O. A. and F. Guetsop Sateu (2017) "L'entrepreneuriat féminin au Cameroun: Enjeux et perspectives", *Revue Congolaise de Gestion*, 24 (2): 11–42.
Mercklé, P. (2004) *La sociologie des réseaux sociaux.* Paris: La Découverte.
Nguelieutou, A. (2008) "Évolution de l'action publique au Cameroun: L'émergence de l'État régulateur", *Polis. Revue camerounaise de science politique*, 15 (1–2): 1–25.
Nyemb-Wisman, M. N. (2011) "Crise de l'État et stratégies de survie des Bayam-Sellam au Cameroun", *Les Politiques Sociales*, 1–2 (1): 68–84.
Roche, P. (2007) "La subjectivation", in V. de Gaulejac (ed.) La *sociologie clinique*, pp. 161–185. Toulouse: Érès, "*Sociologie clinique*".
Rossi, P. (2004) "Les voies de la subjectivation", *Dialogue*, 163 (1): 37–49.
Sreberny, A. (2005) "Genre, autonomisation et communication: Rétrospective et prospectives", *Revue internationale des sciences sociales*, 184 (2): 309–327.
Sylvanus, N. (2006) "L'habileté entrepreneuriale des Nana Benz du Togo", *Africultures*, 69: 179–184.
Taborga, C. (2007) "L'émancipation économique des femmes. Réalités et défis pour l'avenir", *Revue internationale des sciences sociales*, 1: 33–41.
Talahite, F. (2014) "Genre et théorie économique", *Regards croisés sur l'économie,* 15 (2), 13–28.
Tarragoni, F. (2016) "Du rapport de la subjectivation politique au monde social. Les raisons d'une mésentente entre sociologie et philosophie politique", *Raisons politiques*, 62 (2): 115–130.
Touraine, A. (2000) *Sociologie de l'action.* Paris: Gallimard, Le Livre de Poche.
Zittoun, P. (2013) *La fabrique politique des politiques publiques. Une approche pragmatique de l'action publique.* Paris: Presses de Sciences Po.

5 Analysis of the Motivations and Constraints of Pre-Existing Women's Groups in the Process of Creating a Collective Enterprise

The Case of the Creation of a Cooperative by a Women's Group in the West Region of Cameroon

Lolita Toche and Étienne St-Jean

Introduction

Over the last 20 years or so, entrepreneurship has become a tool used by governments to help people, such as women, who are far from the labour market, into work (Boutillier and Uzunidis, 2015). Many women have a spirit of creativity, initiative, and resourcefulness, but how many of them are not only willing but also able to set up a business (Guérin et al., 2009)? The trend in developing countries is to focus on strengthening women's entrepreneurial capacities, and they are being encouraged by governments and NGOs to organise themselves collectively, in cooperatives, professional groups, and in other ways that take advantage of the collective.

Although the theme of collective entrepreneurship seems to be gaining ground naturally today, it must be admitted that thinking is clearly lagging behind practice (Levesque, 2002). In several countries, such as Cameroon, solidarity initiatives have existed for longer than the literature on the subject. Women come together in associations, and formal and informal organisations to improve their living conditions and meet basic economic and social needs (Charlier, 2011). Women's involvement in collective organisations is presented as a factor of emancipation, and women's groups have even become a condition for governments and NGOs to grant financial or technical support. A few groups do form to receive financial and technical support, but most already exist as self-help groups or tontines (Saussey, 2011). In the informal sector, women organise themselves into solidarity networks based on tontines or collective purchases of goods (Ba Gning, 2013). They mobilise and form collective organisations (groups, cooperatives, associations) "considered to be conducive to the development of 'capabilities' while contributing to the emergence of 'empowerment' among poor women" (Saussey, 2011). It is these existing women's groups that interest us in this chapter.

These groups are a source of collective dynamics and collective entrepreneurial projects. One question that arises here is that of the capacity for autonomy of these

DOI: 10.4324/9781003492931-7

women, who are certainly dynamic, but often ill-prepared for the task of creating and managing a collective enterprise, even if they may already be carrying out small income-generating activities. Collective enterprises have two dimensions: a collective dimension to their objectives and a collective dimension to their internal operation (Spaey and Defourny, 2004). The prior existence of a women's group probably has an influence on the group's collective entrepreneurial process. In fact, when entrepreneurial teams are formed based on social reasons, the project is adapted to the pre-existing group; it adheres to the capacities of the group that conceives it, whereas when teams are formed based on strategy, it is the project that decides on the necessary skills and resources. The team must therefore be shaped to meet the requirements of the project (Moreau, 2006). However, although the literature on entrepreneurship is now focusing on its collective dimension, moving beyond the idea of individual entrepreneurship and towards the mobilisation of collective approaches (Razafindrazaka and Fourcade, 2016), it has underestimated the impact of the prior existence of the group on collective entrepreneurship. What are the consequences of the prior existence of the group on the motivations and constraints of a women's group for the creation of a collective enterprise? This is the question that guides this chapter through an analysis of the motivations and constraints of a women's group with a project to set up a collective enterprise. To answer this question, we carried out intervention research with a group of women in the West Cameroon region who were planning to set up a collective unit to process avocados into oil. We begin by outlining the motivations and constraints of women entrepreneurs in general, then present our research methodology, and finish by presenting our results.

Cooperate, Associate, Emancipate: Women's Collective Organisation for Greater Empowerment

Increasingly, setting up a business is the act of a group of people rather than a single individual (Moreau, 2006). On the face of it, collective entrepreneurship means more income, more ideas, and more talent (Barringer and Ireland, 2010). It is also true that belonging to a group enables women to raise sufficient start-up capital, make group purchases, negotiate prices, and limit travel. It is also a way of distancing themselves from family obligations while helping women to take ownership of the commercial world (Guérin, 2003). For Guérin and Nobre (2015), women often have little choice. Difficult access to resources and the weight of domestic obligations contribute to women's collective organisation. By pooling their resources, they can lighten their load and improve their daily lives. These women's groups are based on "collective strength". In many solidarity initiatives in the North and South, women are in the majority (Guérin et al., 2009; Saussey, 2011). In the social economy, two-thirds of employees are women, and some sectors are even more feminised, such as local services, production cooperatives, mutual health, and social protection organisations, and savings and credit institutions (Guérin, 2014). They want to promote activities that demonstrate their concern for the common good and their capacity for initiatives and show that they cannot be excluded from the public sphere (Laville, 2017). They are therefore moving towards collective enterprises. These have two dimensions: a collective dimension to their objectives and a collective dimension to their internal operation (democratic operation, one person-one vote) (Spaey and Defourny, 2004). Collective enterprises act for the community and see member participation as an end. In the West Cameroon region, for example, groups enable people to forge bonds of belonging to a community and create solidarity networks. These groups are made up of people who have come together to carry out an economic and/or social project. Women come together to save, access credit, produce, sell, and process. It is at the heart of local communities that mutual aid and solidarity organisations have been created and developed, particularly to deal with costly social events (weddings, deaths, births, etc.). Women have other expectations of these organisations apart from their economic interests. They can receive training, increase their autonomy and self-esteem, and take part in political life (Verschuur, 2011). What's more, these collective women's initiatives seek first and foremost to meet needs that cannot be satisfactorily met by the market or the state. Women are expected to be business leaders who can be taught how to draw up business plans, "whereas women are claiming a unique way of building the economy through collective entrepreneurship and porosity between the different private and public spheres" (Hersent, 2015: 266). Women's groups now appear to be genuine tools for emancipation.

Motivations of Women Entrepreneurs

Motivations influence the behaviour of entrepreneurs during the creation phase (Giacomin et al., 2016), hence the interest in analysing women's motivations in the context of a project to create a collective enterprise.

The act of creation is the result of a decision, but this decision can be voluntary (Duchéneaut and Orhan, 2000). In fact, the decision to start a business may be born of a genuine desire to create or a need to create. In the literature, authors speak of *push* factors or negative events for factors that drive women to start up out of necessity and *pull* factors or positive events for those that attract women to entrepreneurship through a genuine desire to do so (Table 5.1). These factors generally refer to entrepreneurship by necessity (*push* factors) and entrepreneurship by opportunity (*pull* factors). However, entrepreneurs are generally motivated by a combination of *pull* and *push* factors (Kirkwood, 2009). Necessity entrepreneurs are made up of women, older people, the unemployed, immigrants, people with few qualifications, ethnic minorities, lone parents, people with no bank accounts, people with health problems, and young people without qualifications (Tessier-Dargent and Fayolle, 2016). According to Gorissen et al. (2006), women tend to create more out of necessity than men. According to GEM's 2016/2017 report on women's entrepreneurship[1] (19), women are 20% more likely than men to cite reasons of necessity, and in sub-Saharan Africa, 36% of women entrepreneurs cite reasons of necessity whereas in North America for example only 13% of women entrepreneurs cite reasons of necessity. Malach-Pines et al. (2010) consider that in developed countries, women are in a *pull* position, whereas in developing countries, they are more in a *push* position. Women entrepreneurs in Africa who set up

Table 5.1 Pull and push motivations

Entrepreneurship out of necessity	*Entrepreneurship by opportunity*
Negative motivation – push, reactive, extrinsic factors	***Positive motivation – pull, incentive, intrinsic factors***
• Frustration with an employer • Lack of interest and stimulation at work • Unemployment • Divorce • Job dissatisfaction • Need for flexibility • Insecurity in current job • Individual or family needs	• An entrepreneurial spirit • Choice • Desire for independence • Discovering an opportunity • Profit income • Personal fulfilment • The social mission • Social status • Power
Defensive reaction	Proactive response
Last resort	Pursuing a business opportunity
Generally speaking, women entrepreneurs are motivated by a combination of these two factors	
Push + pull	
Examples:	
Desire + need	
Unemployment + personal fulfilment	
In Cameroon: + Community altruism	

businesses to avoid exclusion and alleviate their poverty problems seem, on the face of it, to be closer to *forced entrepreneurs (push)*. In Cameroon, for example, a study of women's motivations for going into business, conducted by Onana (2006) among 117 Cameroonian women entrepreneurs, showed that "ensuring the future of her children" and "ensuring the security and well-being of her family" are at the forefront, although "being her own boss", "making the most of her training and talents", and the need for money also appear to be important motivations. However, community altruism is by far the strongest motivation among Cameroonian women entrepreneurs. Community altruism is associated with a culture that values the group more than the individual, and in which an individual's value is measured by what he or she contributes to the community. Traditional Cameroonian society is attached to values that revolve around sharing.

Furthermore, Giacomin et al. (2007) point out that certain motivations recognised as *push* or *pull* in the literature may be the opposite for some people. For example, they observe that an unemployed person from an entrepreneurial background does not develop an entrepreneurial activity primarily to combat his/her unemployment situation, because they have had the opportunity to develop an entrepreneurial culture. In addition, access to the position of company director can often be the result of chance, luck, an opportunity that has arisen, or an obligation to take over the family business. Fouquet (2005) uses the term "favourable chance" to describe the sometimes-improvised nature of access to the position of company manager.

Several authors have proposed typologies of women entrepreneurs based on motivations. Morris et al. (2006), for example, distinguish between two types of female entrepreneurs, depending on their motivation for business growth: *high growth entrepreneurs,* who aim for strong growth, and *modest growth entrepreneurs,* who aim for weak growth. For the former, the business comes before the family, and for the latter, the family comes before the business. Lewis (2013) adds a third type to this classification: those who do not seek growth. D'Andria and Gabarret (2016) identify three types of entrepreneurs based on a review of the literature over the last 30 years on the motivations of women entrepreneurs: women who start a business out of necessity (mainly for economic reasons), women who choose an entrepreneurial career transition (women who already have a job and decide to start a business), and women seeking to balance work, family, and motherhood (mampreneurs).

However, being an entrepreneur is not simply a question of motivation. Women entrepreneurs must be able to "assess risk, access and process information, negotiate, argue and negotiate with suppliers, customers, the administration, and law enforcement agencies" (Guérin et al., 2009: 51), but their socio-economic environment is not always favourable.

Constraints Faced by Women Entrepreneurs

Swati Panda's (2018) study of constraints faced by women entrepreneurs, covering 90 developing countries, identifies seven major constraints faced by women entrepreneurs in developing countries: gender discrimination, work-family balance, financial constraints, poor infrastructure, lack of entrepreneurship-related training, personality constraints, and an unfavourable economic and political environment. In addition to the constraints that can hamper any entrepreneur, such as political instability, high production costs, inadequate infrastructure, and an unfavourable environment, women entrepreneurs face specific constraints. Women generally must work harder than their male counterparts to ensure their legitimacy with stakeholders (Vera and Dean, 2005), as they suffer from a lack of credibility. Women also face barriers related to the technical or masculine side of certain jobs, as stakeholders do not expect to see a woman in management (Crutzen et al., 2012). They also face difficulties in accessing finance linked to the lack of solid material guarantees (e.g., land title in Africa), the sector of activity, the size and level of liquidity of the business, but not necessarily to their gender (Carrington, 2006). Women also often cite the difficulty of reconciling work and family life. Women work at least 50% longer hours than men (ADB and ADF, 2015). This phenomenon of the "double day" (De Vreyer and Roubaud, 2013), which women face, limits the time they can devote to their businesses and thus hampers their performance. However, some studies in Africa, such as that by Metaiche and Bendiabdellah (2016) in Algeria, show that women have a remarkable ability to multitask and that the work-life balance is well managed.

Difficulty in accessing networks is also a constraint for women entrepreneurs (Santoni and Barth, 2014). Fewer women belong to a professional network.

As a result, they turn less to their professional circle than to their family circle (Alexandre, 2016). As a result, women are often at a disadvantage in terms of access to networks, resources, advice, and information.

In addition to these constraints linked to the woman entrepreneur's environment, there are also constraints linked to the woman entrepreneur herself, such as a lack of self-confidence and determination. Studies show that women entrepreneurs have little belief in their ability to become and succeed as entrepreneurs (Dempsey and Jennings, 2014). It even seems that this lack of self-confidence is one of the biggest obstacles for women entrepreneurs (Koellinger et al., 2007). Women generally face what Bourdieu (1998) called "symbolic violence". This refers to a form of domination in which the victim is complicit. Even when they are in managerial positions, they may be afraid because their mental structure is unconsciously linked to a form of domination. Women are often inclined to resemble the pejorative image that men portray of them, and they end up accepting it as the truth.

As a result of these constraints, many women entrepreneurs in Africa work in low-productivity units in the informal sector. However, faced with their constraints, women are often the first to mobilise and self-organise (Guérin and Nobre, 2015).

Methodology: Intervention Research Carried Out with a Group of Women Planning to Set Up a Cooperative

Our desire to understand and interpret the entrepreneurial process of a group of women led us to carry out intervention research (IR), because as well as interpreting what we observed in the field, we wanted to contribute to making the project a reality. We knew that our neutrality as researchers in the field would be virtually impossible. Interaction between researchers and stakeholders is at the heart of IR. Our research is therefore based on methodological choices (qualitative methods) and on an analysis system (interactive approach) adapted to the research project (Plane, 2018). The data collected does not serve to validate previously constructed hypotheses, but it does contribute to the construction of these hypotheses. We have chosen to focus on a specific case: a cooperative being set up in the West Cameroon region, to capture in real time, through participant observation, the entrepreneurial process of a group of women involved in this project. This region seems to offer a particularly interesting field of research because of its socio-economic and cultural originality, the adaptability of local farmers and the growth of an associative movement that is attracting attention because of its vitality and diversity (Guillermou, 2007).

The data was collected mainly from a group of women who were planning to set up a women's cooperative to process avocados into oil, and who were accompanied by a retired zone extension officer (AVZ). The AVZs play a very strategic role in the formation and formalisation of groups in Cameroon. They play the role of facilitating advisers (Ngouambe, 2016). They encourage farmers to form groups and provide them with support in all areas: institutional (structuring, formalisation, role of the various members), technical (implementation of production activities, training), and managerial (record keeping, management, and monitoring of financial activities).

The group in question comprises 80 women, whose main activities are farming and trading (with two midwives), and whose ages range from 25 to 70 (with 60 women aged between 36 and 55). Sixty-eight of the women in the group are married, and there are seven widows and five single women (notably the youngest aged between 25 and 35). However, the project is open to all women in the village who wish to take part (there are at least 300 women in the village, according to the AVZ). In terms of level of education, the group includes 50 women with primary education, 20 with secondary education, and 10 with no formal education.

The group of women involved in the project to set up the cooperative has already formed an informal neighbourhood solidarity association, in which the women organise tontines, mutual aid, and discussions on collective social activities (traditional dance groups, for example). This association has been in existence for over 50 years. The women were unable to give us the exact date it was set up because it goes back so far. The group enables women to support each other during social events such as weddings, bereavements, and births. These women are bound together by a sense of closeness and trust that enhances the spirit of collective solidarity. They had no plans to set up a collective business. We conducted three group interviews with the group of women, semi-structured individual interviews with around 30 women in the group, participant observations during their regular tontine sessions, and we took part in several meetings to discuss the project collectively. It was also relevant to meet other structures and other people who had information useful for our research. These included

- Two AVZs (one of whom is involved in the project) with whom we conducted non-directive interviews, as we had no knowledge of this profession prior to our field study.
- The head of the register of joint initiative groups (JIG) and cooperatives in the West region (COOP/JIG register) to get an idea of the dynamics of women's cooperative creation in the region.
- The Head of Surveys and Statistics at the Regional Delegation for Agriculture and Rural Development in Bafoussam, who had been a project expert in supporting women's groups to set up cooperatives as part of a project by the Bafoussam Centre for the Promotion of Women and the Family, from 2010 to 2014.

Our field data collection took place in three stages. The first stage took place from 10 February to 6 March 2017. It consisted mainly of carrying out an overall inventory (contacting the group, documentary research, locating relevant institutions, collective interviews, getting to know the project). The second stage, which took place from 5 August to 9 September 2017, consisted of participating in reflections with the various project stakeholders, observations, and interviews. And the third stage, which ran from 18 January to 9 February 2019, allowed us to continue our observations, interviews and reflections on the project. However, we are still in contact with the players in the field by telephone, as we want to follow the project's progress until the cooperative is set up.

Results

Our results focus on the events that triggered the project in question and the potential constraints on this project, as the cooperative has not yet been in existence for several years.

The Idea behind the "Avocado" Project: The Prior Existence of the Group and Encouragement from a Support Person

The idea for the project arose from discussions between the AVZ and the village producers during reforestation activities in 2013 and the construction of a nursery for the avocado seedlings selected in 2014, and builds on the long-standing collaboration between the AVZ and the village population in setting up a responsible tourism project since 2008. During these reforestation activities, avocado seedlings were distributed to the local population, who questioned the relevance of continuing to plant avocados, given the commercial difficulties and the value of existing production. The avocado is a fragile fruit that perishes quickly. The AVZ therefore proposed to the villagers that they should recoup the losses from uneaten fruit by processing it into oil. As the women's group already existed, it suggested that they set up a women's processing cooperative. The AVZ is contributing its know-how, in a participative way, to the formulation of this project. The retired AVZ's former profession is not neutral in this project proposal. His training as an agro-economist also makes him a resource person for this project. He knows the group of women involved very well, and the women also know him and trust him: "He wants to help us"; "It's when daddy X tells us that we're only going to follow him too"; "It's when we set up the project that I'll really know what it's about".

Even if the questions that led to the formalisation of this project came from the population, the incentive to set up the project was stimulated by the AVZ. It is therefore important to note here that the women needed this resource person, this person who encouraged them to create, to think that they could carry out such a project. We can therefore describe the women involved in the project as entrepreneurs "by chance", as they were not a group formed to create a business or a group looking for entrepreneurial opportunities. This is in line with the concept of "favourable chance" used by Fouquet (2005) to describe the sometimes-improvised nature of access to the position of entrepreneur. However, pure chance does not exist. The simple fact of accepting an opportunity and making oneself available for this project may constitute a form of unconscious preparation. The women involved in the project were available and seized the project opportunity as soon as it presented itself. Availability here means not anticipating (Germain, 2010), but not anticipating does not mean that this opportunity was pure chance, because the women's environment had an influence on their acceptance of this opportunity (prior existence of the group, confidence in the AVZ, several avocado plantations in the village). The triggers for this project were the prior existence of the group and the intervention of a third party, and subsequently, it was the collective dynamics of the project that fuelled the motivation of the women in the group. Without the prior existence of the group and the collective will to carry out the project, each of the women, taken individually, would not have been motivated for this project. However, their collective motivation was born as soon as they were informed of the idea of the project: "When you're in a group, you get more done than if you were on your own"; "If you're on your own, you can't do anything"; "The group is good"; "First of all, there's love between us, ideas come out everywhere and you can succeed just as quickly"; "When you're in a group, you work together, you share ideas"; "When there are a lot of people and everyone has the will to do what we say, it will always be good"; "At the beginning it was just a meeting of women from the neighbourhood, it evolved into an association of women in solidarity and today into a cooperative". They seized this business opportunity unprepared, even though it was proposed by a third party. The prior existence of the group explains the motivation to accept this collective project and, consequently, the collective action. Informal women's groups can be a springboard for collective entrepreneurship. We were able to ascertain from what was left unsaid that some women accepted this project to maintain good relations with their group. They were afraid to get involved in such a project, but they did not want to be the ones to prevent the group from carrying it out. In addition, we noted that the women in the group are also motivated to learn how to transform avocados into oil: "We eat a lot of avocados, but we don't know how to make oil"; "We were told that they were going to teach us how to make avocado oils"; "I'm interested because the project is going to teach us a lot of things". The various typologies drawn up in the literature on motivational factors, "push" and "pull", concern the individual entrepreneur. But this is a case of collective entrepreneurship. The collective dynamic alone can be an important motivator. It is therefore difficult to determine whether their motivations are "push" or "pull", or whether it is a case of entrepreneurship by necessity. There is no desire for independence as in the case of "pull" motivations, or insufficient family income as in the case of "push" motivations, for example. However, it should be noted that these women are not in paid employment, hence their availability for this project. This lack of salaried employment is considered a "push" motivation in the literature (D'Andria and Gabarret, 2016), but it does not emerge explicitly in the women's discourse. It is likely that this is because they do field work and small-scale trading in food crops. The increase in women's income is highlighted indirectly by the AVZ, but not by the women themselves. One of them told us that she has "never run out of food" in her house, and another added that "even when it's complicated, there's always something to help us in the field". They grow a variety of food crops (maize, beans, groundnuts, yams, manioc, etc.). Financial difficulties are, however, among the main constraints identified in this project.

Financing Collective Projects: "Structural" Solidarity Finance?

As far as constraints are concerned, funding is their main fear: "It's only finance that will be difficult"; "The problem is mainly financial"; "It's funding that can set us back"; "Financial resources are the group's real problem"; "If we don't have the money, how are we going to buy the fruit"? The women involved in the project are aware that they will have to find funding and make the most of their existing resources: "First, we have to build up a fund to finance the purchase of avocados".

Through our discussions with the women, collective savings emerged as the preferred means of financing: "We'll see at the meeting if we can collect the savings to finance this"; "We'll see as a group if we can collect the money amongst ourselves", "Savings can help us"; "We'll use the tontine". In concrete terms, we suggested that they choose a few sessions of their usual tontines, during which each member would contribute a pre-defined sum, the total of which would be used to finance parts of the project. If this is in line with their tontine system, with the same amount to contribute and the same frequency of contributions, members could keep the same contribution habit. Access to bank finance is not really a limit for them, as they don't even think about it when they are thinking about financing. However, the AVZ pointed out that "financing through the tontine alone will be complicated, as the women will already have to pay for the cooperative's shares". But for them, microfinance is a last resort: "We'll see. If we can't contribute everything, we'll borrow". The fact that the group exists in the first place means that collective savings can be mobilised, and part of the funding required for the project can be raised, highlighting the importance of solidarity-based finance in a collective women's project. It is not each of the women who contributes her financing capacity; it is the group that mobilises the collective savings, thanks to the tontine system already well established in the pre-existing group.

In addition, to get the project off the ground quickly, it proved necessary to supplement the collective savings with a solidarity loan from a microfinance institution. To do this, we proposed including a microfinance institution as a partner in the project, rather than simply applying for funding. We therefore studied the terms and conditions of a partnership with a microfinance institution located close to where the project is to be set up. This institution wishes to participate in the project to contribute to a village development project and achieve its social objectives. This partnership will make it possible to adapt the credit conditions to the members of the cooperative, which will be jointly and severally liable for its members. The AVZ also offered to apply for funding from international NGOs, which they did. An NGO in France agreed to provide financial and technical support for the construction of the semi-industrial processing unit and a first payment was made to the AVZ in January 2019. However, the cooperative had not yet been set up in April 2024 and the AVZ seems to be more concerned about meeting the NGO's requirements than launching a processing unit, even an artisanal one, depending on the resources available. To obtain substantial funding from the NGO, the AVZ had to draw up a business plan for a large-scale project, and the downside is that they must justify the use of every penny paid in. This has led to a growing lack of self-confidence among the women, who had imagined setting up a collective small-scale unit to process avocados into oil, based on their available resources (collective savings, current production in the village, etc.), and who are now afraid to embark on such a large-scale project. A nursery for selected avocado seedlings has now been set up, a water tower has been built and a plot of land for the processing plant has been purchased from a village patriarch.

"Triple Days": Domestic Work, Farming, and Cooperative Management

Despite their current work in the fields and at home, these women believe that they will be able to reconcile all their activities, including the cooperative: "The avocado project cannot interfere with our work growing maize"; "We will always find time to work on our maize. We can't run out of time"; "I think we can manage our time. Which day I do my field, which day I do the avocado. If we don't do it that way, what are we going to eat? It depends on the field"; "There won't be any time problems, we'll plan our activities". Female entrepreneurship in our Cameroon fieldwork does not seem to be affected by the obstacles inherent in women's time management. This is because women have long been accustomed to working long hours. They are multitaskers and multi-skilled. They do both domestic and rural work, as well as running small businesses. They don't just have "double days" (De Vreyer and Roubaud, 2013), they even have "triple days". They are a source of innovation in terms of working time management. However, the primary and secondary nature of the activities must be considered. What we have been able to note in the women's discourse is that work in the fields or on the farm takes priority over the cooperative's activities. Subsistence farming is the main activity for women in rural areas in West Cameroon, as it enables them to feed their families. The order of priorities is first and foremost the home, followed by farming activities, and finally the business. In fact, the value of women in this rural context is measured more by their role as wife and mother than by the success of their businesses. Even if, according to these women, time management is not a constraint, they are nonetheless obliged to make a compromise in their activities, and in this case they give priority to rural activities. This can be a hindrance to the development of their entrepreneurial activity. The women in our study correspond to the '*modest growth entrepreneurs*' described by Morris et al. (2006). These are entrepreneurs who put family before business, which leads to modest growth in their businesses. These entrepreneurs are the opposite of the '*high growth entrepreneurs*' who put the business before the family. Consideration has been given to the possibility of part-time work in the cooperative. On this subject, the AVZ proposed that "in the processing unit, there can be, at most, five permanent women and others who will come on a temporary basis".

Women's Entrepreneurial Skills: Training Needed?

As far as the need for training is concerned, their main concern is the transformation of lawyers: "Transform the lawyer first and we'll see about the other training later"; "If we knew how to transform the lawyer, it would be good"; "We need to be trained first before we can start". Technical training is important because you must produce before you can sell it. The women also pointed out that although "we don't know what we need to do for management, we'll know when we start"; "We can learn directly in the business". Here we find the "learning by doing" that gives meaning to the "push" in the women's collective entrepreneurship observed. One of the women (the current secretary of the pre-existing group) added, however, that training would be needed in lawyer transformation and management: "We'll also need training in accounting, balance sheets, and the input-output book". However, thanks to the collective movement, these women don't really see their low levels of training as a constraint, because each of them doesn't feel that they have any limits or hindrances compared with the others. This enthusiasm and positive spirit that drives the group is a strength for the project. This "learning by doing" seems to be a recurring theme among women entrepreneurs in the Western region of Cameroon. The person in charge of training at the *Centre de Promotion de la Femme et de la Famille* in Bafoussam told us: "We don't even see women entrepreneurs for training. They don't even come to us. Sometimes, it's us who go to women's associations, even though there are also women who often come to us". Moreover, women are not always aware of the problems they will face (Schmidt and Parker, 2003), especially in the case of entrepreneurship out of necessity or in this specific instance where the project was proposed by someone outside the group. In fact, the more the entrepreneur is motivated by opportunities, the more he or she will seek advice and assistance at the start of the business (Fontier, 2019).

We also found that these women already have several skills that simply need to be exploited for entrepreneurship. For example, the president of the pre-existing association has skills in managing a group and dealing with conflict. The treasurer has developed skills in keeping cash books (receipts, disbursements, interest rates, calculating balances, profit and loss). The secretary has developed her skills in drawing up agendas and minutes of meetings. The censor has developed skills in team management and maintaining order within the group. In addition to the officers, all the members have multi-tasking skills that they have been able to develop throughout their lives as daughters, wives, mothers, and widows through all the activities for which they are responsible in the household. A widow who takes over her husband's plantations, for example, develops her ability to adapt and learn. What's more, women's long working days require a strict organisational system to be put in place, and this organisational capacity can be used as part of the project. We can also mention the management of their agricultural plantations, which requires knowledge of the type of soil, the appropriate type of crop, multi-crop management according to the seasons, the purchase of seeds, negotiating the selling price of their crops, and so on. But the qualities specific to the female workforce are often not considered as know-how, but rather as "innate" aptitudes (Saussey and Degrave, 2015: 167). Women must therefore accept the potential they have. The idea behind this project is to re-qualify women's devalued skills, to recognise each woman's contribution to carrying out the project, and to enhance the wealth of local people. However, even when it comes to their small businesses, or the production and sale of crops, they don't see themselves as entrepreneurs. They told us that they "get by" because they don't consider their activities to be "businesses". However, for Laville (2015: 57), the term "initiatives" is more relevant, because "it designates a capacity to act, a power to take or influence decisions, a beginning that is not a matter of simple adaptation or functional reaction to constraints". He adds that (65) the preference for "enterprise" "normalises the phenomenon and prevents recognition of individual support".

Lack of Self-confidence and Integrating Men into the Project

We also noted a lack of self-confidence, as the women were reluctant to take on responsibilities and said they "just wanted to be members". This lack of self-confidence was particularly noticeable during our second fieldwork stage when the women decided to include men in the project to set up the cooperative, which was initially supposed to be a women's cooperative. During our first field visit, these women agreed that the cooperative should be "women only". The main reason given was that they were already living in a community with men in the neighbourhood and that it would be frowned upon for them to embark on such a project just between themselves without including the men. They also think that there are things that men can do that they can't, such as picking the avocados, packing them, and transporting them to the processing plant. They also think that men can come up with good ideas and that working with them would be a plus: "Yes, it's better to have a mix of men, women and young people, because even if we collect from the field, can we carry?" The head of the region's COOP/GIC register told us that "there are no women's cooperatives in the region. If there are any, it's probably because the men don't want to join". The idea is above all to understand the rationale behind this desire in our field. In fact, the points raised during the interviews relate above all to the question of the men's "physical strength" in supplying the lawyers. This male domination has been rooted in societies for centuries, through the valorisation of virile characteristics, strength, and confidence in business (Burke, 1997). In principle, the women's cooperative only concerns the avocado oil processing plant. Thus, the supply of avocados, i.e. the picking, packaging and transport to the processing plant, can be the responsibility of the men who have avocado plantations in the village, without including them in the processing cooperative. "Women don't have confidence in themselves. They think you always must rely on a man to succeed. We first need to work on the mindset and make women aware of the need for self-confidence" (Head of surveys, and statistics, Regional Delegation for Agriculture and Rural Development). When setting up a business does not correspond to an emotional desire, it is already a constraint, making it difficult for entrepreneurs to make profound changes to their lifestyle (Couteret, 2010). The interviews also raised the issue of the fear of being perceived by the men in the village, who are mainly their husbands, if they decide to set up the cooperative, solely between women. The person in charge of surveys and statistics at the Regional Delegation for Agriculture and Rural Development gave us her opinion, along the same lines, on the use of the word "female" for the cooperative. For her, "it's not important. As we live in a society, we can't work without men. That means we're trying to segregate. Men may not see it that way. Women may be in the majority, but even men's ideas are important. There are things that men can see that women can't". In the context of this "lawyer" project, the decision to include men was made without consulting them beforehand. We also asked them about their ability to put forward their ideas in the presence of men, most of whom are their husbands. They agree that everything will go well, thanks to the dialogue and understanding that exists within the neighbourhood: "There won't be any problems negotiating with the men". However, they point out that in any collective system, there are conflicts: "There are bound to be problems when men and women get together, because even children from the same house have problems"; "There are always inconveniences such as arguments". Nonetheless, we made a relevant observation in the field: the women manage to get together, among themselves, for tontines or dance groups, for example, but as soon as an economic activity is involved, they express a desire to integrate men. However, some women (about ten) do not agree with the inclusion of men in the cooperative project:

> "Men are too much of a nuisance".
>
> "Women can get along just fine without men".
>
> "You can't reproach a man in any way, because he's a man and you can't speak out because they'll say you're insulting them, whereas when we're just women, it's better".
>
> "They have the right to ask us that, but we don't. We're just women. We're just women. Houses are for men. Everything is for men!"
>
> "Yes, it's good to create something just for women, for love and peace between us. Men create too much disorder".

If they include men in the project, they will be the ones taking all the decisions, as "it will be difficult for women to contradict their husbands or get their ideas accepted, for fear of being seen as disrespectful women who don't submit to their husbands" (AVZ). These women who expressed their dissatisfaction with the inclusion of men are, however, in the minority and are therefore obliged to follow the group, since all the other women want the men in the neighbourhood to be included in the project. In this way, the collective takes precedence over the individual, forcing them to take a collective approach.

Women are sensitive to what men think. Whether they are those who want to integrate men or those who want to keep the women's cooperative, they are all guided by the "fear" of the reaction of the men in the village, both inside and outside the cooperative. One AVZ told us that he accompanies a group of women, but that he has not noticed any differences between the groups of women and the groups of men. On the other hand, he points out that when the group is mixed, "the men always want to get the upper hand". And when there are couple relationships in the group, "the women talk even less, because they're afraid of their husbands. It's the man who's at the centre of decision-making. The land belongs to the man and women manage it. It's generally the woman who manages the family farm when the man has another activity, but when both manage the farm there's always a relationship where the man dominates". This domination is also felt by the women themselves, as Bourdieu (1998) points out. According to this sociologist, in his book entitled "La domination masculine", women incorporate the dominant values constructed by men and naturally see themselves as dominated. This is what he called "symbolic violence". However, as the AVZ told us, women in the region are generally community-minded and supportive. They would be happier if the project benefited the whole village, and everyone was involved. The real challenge would

Table 5.2 Levers offered by collective entrepreneurship to deal with the constraints identified

Constraints	*Features*	*Leverage offered by the collective*
Financing	Financial difficulties Reluctance to deal with financial institutions	Group savings, tontine, choice of self-financing, possibility of joint activity and several guarantees in the event of a loan
Entrepreneurial skills	Technical training Cooperative management training Know-how to develop	Complementary skills, learning together, no feeling of inferiority, because the whole group is involved, know-how developed in the pre-existing grouping
Reconciling work and family life	Balance between farm, domestic, and cooperative work	Part-time work, organised so that each woman can reconcile her usual activities with running the cooperative
Women's lack of self-confidence	Patriarchal system, inclusion of men in the project without consulting them beforehand, fear of occupying decision-making positions	Structuring producers to supply raw materials, mainly female processing units

be for them to manage to retain a significant role in the project. It therefore seemed important to point out to the group of women involved in the project that creating a women's cooperative does not rule out the possibility of working with men on the project (AVZ, husbands, etc.), as a project involves several stakeholders. Finally, a three-tier structure has been devised: a first tier made up of avocado growers who will indicate their production potential and available acreage, a second tier made up of cooperative sections grouping production by neighbourhood for sale to the processing unit; and a third tier responsible for processing and marketing (the women's cooperative). More concretely, in the cooperative sections, each member will produce avocados and the total production of the section will be sold to the central processing cooperative. The representatives of the sections will then distribute the sum of the sales among the members of the section according to their individual production, and the processing unit will be for the pre-existing women's group.

Summary of Constraints Identified and Levers Offered by the Collective

Collective entrepreneurship offers opportunities to overcome women's constraints, as shown in Table 5.2.

Conclusion

The aim of this chapter is to understand the potential motivations and constraints of a pre-existing group of women who undertake unpremeditated ventures. This chapter highlights the pre-existence of the group as an initial element for collective entrepreneurship. Entrepreneurship is "collective" here because the entrepreneur is a pre-existing "collective", independent of the entrepreneurial project. We need thus to look beyond the economic aspect, to consider the value of the collective dynamic, and the enhancement of the know-how and interpersonal skills of these women, who are entrepreneurs "by chance". In our fieldwork, we are not talking about a group of women entrepreneurs who have decided to join forces to cope better with their constraints, but about an existing group of women, with no entrepreneurial project, who seizes an opportunity for collective entrepreneurship. Our results make it possible to distinguish between the motivations of the individual entrepreneur and those of the 'collective' entrepreneur. Collective dynamics, the prior existence of the group, encouragement from a trusted person, and the preservation of the social image within the group appear to be collective motivations specific to collective entrepreneurship. These motivations are neither *pull* nor *push,* they are collective and linked to the pre-existing group. Individual motivations, if they exist, are absorbed by these collective motivations. In this way, the collective takes precedence over the individual. We have highlighted the know-how and interpersonal skills that these women already possess, thanks to the group's pre-existence, but which are not yet valued for collective entrepreneurship. Support structures wishing to intervene in this region should start by developing these skills to boost their self-confidence. It is also important to highlight a particular feature of our fieldwork, which is the intervention of a retired AVZ to encourage the formal creation of a collective organisation. What's more, the fact that the group had already been set up gave us the leverage we needed to deal more effectively with the constraints we identified. The women implement innovations in their entrepreneurial process to make the most of the resources of the pre-existing group (tontines, collective savings, administrators, know-how) before seeking resources from outside the group.

The motivations and constraints identified could be used by local support structures and other pre-existing women's groups wishing to set up collective enterprises. Governments and NGOs promoting women's collective entrepreneurship could make use of existing collective dynamics and help facilitate the transition from an informal social group to a collective enterprise.

In terms of methodology, very few studies have carried out an IR of women's solidarity groups in Cameroon and Africa, and have studied women's entrepreneurship from the perspective of the collective, with the group as the focus of analysis and not the individual within the group. Future research on women's collective entrepreneurship could consider the individualities within the group of women entrepreneurs in order to highlight the influence of the group on the opinions and personal interests of each member.

The cooperative in question in this study has not yet been set up, but as Levesque (2002) points out, the transition from project to business is very laborious. This collective dynamic of the women in our field is at the heart of the success of their project. They will have to show even greater solidarity as the project progresses and become aware of the advantages of the prior existence of their group for the creation of a collective enterprise.

Note

1 Women's entrepreneurship 2016/2017 report, WWW.gemconsortium.org, accessed 12 June 2024

References

AfDB (African Development Bank Group) and ADF (African Development Fund) (2015) "Empowering African Women: Action Plan. Africa Gender Equality Index". http://www.afdb.org/fileadmin/uploads/afdb/Documents/Publications/African_Gender_Equality_Index_2015-FR.pdf, accessed 12 June 2024.

Alexandre, L. (2016) "Typologie des entrepreneurs, une approche par le genre", *Revue de l'entrepreneuriat*, 15 (3): 109–127.

Ba Gning, S. (2013) "Les femmes dans le secteur informel", in Margaret Maruani (ed.) *Travail et genre dans le monde*, pp. 336–344. Paris: La Découverte "Hors collection Sciences Humaines".

Barringer, B. R. and R. D Ireland (2010) *Entrepreneurship: Successfully Launching New Ventures*, 3rd ed. New York: Pearson Limited.

Bourdieu, P. (1998) *La domination masculine*. Paris: Seuil.

Boutillier, S. and D. Uzunidis (2015) "IV. *Joseph Aloïs Schumpeter* - L'entrepreneur force vive du capitalisme", in Karim Messeghem (ed.) *Les grands auteurs en entrepreneuriat et PME*, pp. 87–104. Caen: EMS Editions.

Burke, R. J. (1997) *Valeurs féminines, le pouvoir de demain*. Paris: Village Mondial.

Carrington, C. (2006) "L'entrepreneuriat au féminin", *Journal of Small Business & Entrepreneurship*, 19 (2): 95–106.

Charlier S. (2011) "Empoderamiento des femmes par l'économie populaire solidaire: participation et visibilité des femmes en Bolivie", in I. Guérin, M. Hersent and L. Fraisse (eds) *Femmes, économie et développement. De la résistance à la justice sociale*, pp. 155–184. Toulouse: Érès.

Couteret, P. (2010) "Peut-on aider les entrepreneurs contraints? Une étude exploratoire", *Revue de l'entrepreneuriat / Review of Entrepreneurship*, 9 (2): 6–33.

Crutzen, N., F. Pirnay and Z. Aouni (2012) "La place des femmes dans les entreprises familiales belges francophones en 2012", *Research commissioned by the Institut de L'Entreprise Familiale*, Liège. https://orbi.uliege.be/handle/2268/202569, accessed 30 July 2024.

D'Andria, A. and I. Gabarret (2016) " Femmes et entrepreneurs: Trente ans de recherches en motivation entrepreneuriale féminine", *Revue de l'entrepreneuriat*, 15 (3): 87–107.

De Vreyer, P. and F. Roubaud (2013) *Urban Labour Markets in Sub-Saharan Africa*. Paris/Washington: World Bank/Agence Française de Développement (AFD).

Degavre, F. and M. Saussey (2014) "La fabrique des chercheur-e-s mise à l'épreuve des normes globales d'éthique", *Journal des anthropologues*, 136–137 (1–2): 137–158.

Dempsey, D. and J. Jennings (2014) "Gender and entrepreneurial self-efficacy: Learning perspective", *International Journal of Gender and Entrepreneurship,* 6 (1): 28–49.

Ducheneaut, B. and M. Orhan (2000) *Les femmes entrepreneurs en France*. Paris: Editions Seli Arslan.

Fontier, V. (2019), "L'insertion professionnelle par la création d'activité: Le cas des entrepreneures-salariées", *Marché et organisations*, 3 (36): 83–100.

Fouquet, A. (2005) "Les femmes chefs d'entreprise: Le cas français", *Travail, genre et société*, 1 (13): 31–50.

Germain, O. (2010) "Quand l'opportunité rencontre la stratégie", *Revue française de gestion,* 206 (7): 171–187.

Giacomin, O., F. Janssen, and J. Guyot (2016) "Entrepreneurs de nécessité et d'opportunité: quels comportements durant la phase de création?", *Revue de l'Entrepreneuriat / Review of Entrepreneurship*, 15 (3–4): 181–204.

Giacomin, O., J.-L. Guyot, F. Janssen, and O. Lohest (2007) "Novice creators: Personal identity and push pull dynamics", IAG - LSM, *Working Papers*, 7 (10), Louvain: DIAL. Research Publications.

Gorissen A., F. Bernard, T. Graas, and M. Selmouni (2006) *Starters 2006: Carte d'identité des créateurs d'entreprise en Région Bruxelles Capitale*. Brussels: ABE / ICHEC-PME.

Guérin, I. (2003) "Economie solidaire et inégalités de genre: une approche en termes de justice sociale", *Revue internationale de l'économie sociale RECMA*, 3 (289): 40–57.

Guérin, I. (2014) "The poor and their savings: protection or discipline?", *Techniques Financières et Développement*, 115 (2): 29–43.

Guérin, I. and M. Nobre (2015) "L'économie solidaire revisitée à la lumière du genre: Changement social ou subordination féminine?", in C. Verschuur, I. Guérin, and H. Guétat-Bernard (eds) *Sous le développement, le genre*, pp. 425–448, Marseille: IRD Éditions, Collection Objectifs Sud.

Guérin, I., J. Palier and B. Prévost (2009) *Femmes et microfinance: Espoirs et désillusions de l'expérience indienne*. Paris: Archives Contemporaines.

Guillermou, Y. (2007) "Organisations de producteurs et dynamiques paysannes dans l'Ouest-Cameroun", *Afrique contemporaine*, 222 (2): 251–271.

Hersent, M. (2015) "Les initiatives solidaires de femmes et les pouvoirs publics: Une dure confrontation", in C. Verschuur, I. Guérin, and I. Hillenkamp (eds) *Une économie solidaire peut-elle être féministe ? Homo oeconomicus, mulier solidaria*, pp. 257–273, Paris: L'Harmattan.

Kirkwood, J. (2009) "Motivation factors in a push-pull theory of entrepreneurship", *Gender in Management, an International Journal*, 24 (5): 346–364.

Koellinger, P., M. Minniti, and C. Schade (2007) "I think I can, I think I can: Overconfidence and entrepreneurial behaviour", *Journal of Economic Psychology*, 28 (4): 502–527.

Laville, J. L. (2015) "Féminisme et économie solidaire", in C. Verschuur, I. Guérin, and I. Hillekamp (eds) *Une économie solidaire peut-elle être féministe? Homo œconomicus, mulier solidaria*, pp. 51–69. Paris: L'Harmattan.

Laville, J.-L. (2017), "Féminisme et économie solidaire: Penser les rapports entre le politique et l'économique", in I. Guérin, I. Hillenkamp, and C. Verschuur (eds) *Genre et économie solidaire, des croisements nécessaires*, pp. 241–260. Cahiers Genre et Développement, n°10, Geneva, Paris: Graduate Institute Publications.

Lévesque, B. (2002) "Entrepreneurship collectif et économie sociale: entreprendre autrement", *Forum l'entrepreneurship en économie sociale: oser l'entrepreneuriat différemment*, organised by the *Centre local de développement des Moulins and Emploi-Québec* on February 21, 2002.

Lewis, P. (2013) "The search for an authentic entrepreneurial identity: Difference and professionalism among women business owners", *Gender, Work & Organization*, 20 (3): 252–266.

Malach-Pines, A., M. Lerner, and D. Schwartz (2010) "Gender differences in entrepreneurship: Equality, diversity, and inclusion in times of global crisis", *Equality, Diversity and Inclusion: An International Journal*, 29 (2): 186–198.

Metaiche, F. T. and A. Bendiabdellah (2016) "Les femmes entrepreneures en Algérie: savoir, vouloir et pouvoir!" *Marché et organisations*, 26 (2): 219–240.

Moreau, R. (2006) "La formation des équipes d'entrepreneurs", *Revue de l'entrepreneuriat*, 5 (2): 55–68.

Morris, M. H., N. Miyasaki, C. E. Watters, and S. M. Coombes (2006) "The dilemma of growth: Understanding venture size choices of women entrepreneurs", *Journal of Small Business Management*, 44 (2): 221–244.

Ngouambe, N. (2016) "De la vulgarisation rapprochée à l'encadrement à distance: Le pouvoir des TIC à l'ouest du Cameroun", 16 (4), Series: ICTs for Agriculture, Working paper.

Onana, F. X. (2006) *Motivations et modes de gestion des femmes entrepreneurs au Cameroun: une étude exploratoire.* PhD in Management Sciences, Bordeaux.

Plane, J.-M. (2018) "Publier une recherche-intervention de type ethnométhodologique: le cas d'une publication dans la revue *Journal of Business Ethics*", in A.F. Buono, H. Savall and L. Cappelletti (eds) *La recherche-intervention dans les entreprises et les organisations: De la conception à la publication*, pp. 221–228. Charlotte: Information Age Publishing.

Razafindrazaka, T. and C. Fourcade (2016) "L'entrepreneuriat collectif: un outil du développement territorial?", *Revue d'économie régionale et urbaine*, 5: 1017–1042.

Santoni, J. and I. Barth (2014) "Le rôle du réseau dans le développement de l'entrepreneuriat féminin: Cas d'un centre entrepreneurial au sein d'une business school", *@GRH*, 2 (11): 81–113.

Saussey, M. (2011) "Initiatives féminines et économie sociale et solidaire dans la production du beurre de karité au Burkina Faso", in I. Guérin, M. Hersent, and L. Fraisse (eds) *Femmes, économie et développement: De la résistance à la justice sociale*, pp. 107–128, Toulouse: Érès.

Saussey, M. and F. Degrave (2015) "Sécuriser l'existence des femmes et résister. Raisons d'agir des initiateurs et initiatrices d'organisations de l'économie sociale et solidaire", in C. Verschuur, I. Guérin, and I. Hillekamp (eds) *Une économie solidaire peut-elle être féministe?: Homo œconomicus, mulier solidaria*, pp. 155–175. Paris: L'Harmattan.

Schmidt, R. A. and C. Parker (2003) "Diversity in independent retailing: Barriers and benefits – the impact of gender", *International Journal of Retail & Distribution Management*, 31 (8), 428–439.

Spaey, M. and J. Defourny (2004) "Introduction et objectifs de l'étude", in M. Spaey (ed.) *Entrepreunariat collectif et création d'entreprises dans un cadre d'économie sociale*, Study for the Walloon government.

Swati, Panda (2018) "Constraints faced by women entrepreneurs in developing countries: Review and ranking", *Gender in Management: An International Journal*, 33 (4): 315–331.

Tessier-Dargent, C. and A. Fayolle (2016) "Une approche typologique de l'entrepreneuriat de nécessité", RIMHE: *Revue Interdisciplinaire Management, Homme & Entreprise*, 22 (3): 74–92.

Vera, C. F. and M. A. Dean (2005) "An examination of the challenges daughters face in family business succession", *Family Business Review*, 18 (4): 321–345.

Verschuur, C. (2011) "Mouvements et organisations populaires en milieu urbain: identité de genre et brèches pour le changement", in I. Guérin (ed.) *Femmes, économie et développement: De la réussite à la justice sociale*, pp. 185–204. Toulouse: ERES.

6 The Auchan Brand in Senegal

A Source of Supply for Women Stallholders in Mbour – A Link to Working-Class Consumers

Paul Mamba Diédhiou

Introduction

If ever there were a place or space in Senegal where consumer goods were procured, these are the local markets (fixed and weekly), wholesalers, neighbourhood shops, and so on. However, the nature of the prices of products sold in these spaces, which are set liberally and/or anarchically (Kébé, 2014: 109–126) and the transformation of Senegalese cultural identities by the globalisation of food practices, is supported by the emergence of large-scale distribution (Varman and Belk, 2012). These changes are forcing local traders, and stallholders in particular,[1] to explore other alternatives (Claval, 2012).

Established in Senegal in 2014, the Auchan chain has given rise to controversy: on the one hand, there have been strong protests by local traders (e.g., shopkeepers, stallholders, wholesalers, street vendors, etc.) and national movements (*Auchan dégage*, *UNACOIS/Jappo*, etc.) (Ndiaye, 2022; Diédhiou, 2023) castigating these commercial practices[2] and, on the other hand, clear reconfigurations of the local market: diversity of products (imported and local), modernisation of sales outlets, digitisation, innovative managerial and marketing practices, and so on. In this way, Dominique Raynaud (2018) suggests, in a debate, rejecting the use of the term "controversy" by referring to five essential criteria: (1) no goal of knowledge; (2) no defined question; (3) no different interpretations; (4) absence of scientific researchers on both sides; (5) finally, non-public debate. In this respect, the authors consider that scientific controversies refer to "the persistent and public division of several members of a scientific community, whether coalesced or not, who support contradictory arguments in the interpretation of a given phenomenon" (Raynaud and Bunge, 2018: 40). The social mobilisations sparked by Auchan in Senegal are in line with this line of thinking. In fact, these commercial practices have given rise to numerous debates in the mass media and/or social media between those in favour (adherents or opportunists) and those opposed (objectors or opponents).

In this context, in Mbour, a department in the Thiès region of Senegal, the Auchan brand has become a source of supply for women traders, particularly stallholders. Along the way, it is worth asking whether the behaviour of the Senegalese towards the Auchan offers can be understood based on the way in which practices (re)constitute themselves (purchasing and consumption behaviour). Finding the answer to this question is the subject of this chapter.

DOI: 10.4324/9781003492931-8

Extracted from our socio-anthropology thesis in preparation on "The multinational Auchan in Senegal. Between controversies and logics of appropriation", this chapter seeks to find out to what extent the Auchan brand is a source of supply for women stallholders in Senegal, and in the town of Mbour at 86 km from Dakar, by examining their relationship between the local and the global, i.e., globalisation. The latter being "a global cultural diversity, but a diversity resulting from current global cultural relations, from the cultural appropriation of 'global' elements with local cultural meanings and forms" (Schuerkens 2019: 40; my translation). In the present study, it refers to the fact that the women stallholders' supply logics are hybrid (local and imported products) via the Auchan chain.

Going behind the scenes of this phenomenon, which appears to be new in the qualitative method, coupled with an ethnographic approach to sales systems and locations, has enabled me to gain a better understanding of the way these women shop at Auchan, by identifying not only the types of products they buy there, but also by questioning their choices, preferences, and rationales. Using these methods, the managerial practices[3] and the marketing[4] of these women and customer perceptions of their services (stalls) are documented.

Content analysis is a way of organising the data collected by theme (Paillé and Mucchielli, 2016; N'Da, 2015) and was extremely useful in analysing the data. To make the analysis more robust, I have used the principle of verbatim quotations of the respondents' comments. The random assignment of nicknames – "Fatou S., Bineta L., Oulimata T., and Bintou S." – enabled the interviewees to remain anonymous.

Research Methodology

The present study targets women stallholders who buy their supplies at Auchan and at the same time at local markets. Given the impossibility of meeting all these women, it seemed appropriate to use the non-probabilistic technique of reasoned choice, as I was conducting a qualitative study. It was an iterative survey, with repeated rounds, a maximum of three rounds in 15 days. This reflective feedback enabled me to better confirm or refute and complete certain data collected. This approach (reasoned and repeated visits) sought to reproduce as correctly as possible the different profiles of women stallholders who buy products at Auchan, considering their common characteristics. As it was difficult to find these women, the "snowball or network sampling" technique (N'Da, 2015: 106) made it possible to identify, through a close acquaintance, an influential woman in the town of Mbour. On this basis, the other women who were in a relationship with this influential woman: friends, relatives or neighbours, sisters, etc., were found for interview purposes.

The women interviewed who buy their supplies at Auchan are generally aged between 20 and 50, married, single, and/or widowed. Most of the married women live in polygamous households. Those who are polygamous, practice this activity for their autonomy, enabling them to support their husbands, who sometimes have a very low level of income. Single women are for the most part "breadwinners".

Widows who are heads of household engage in this activity to support their households. Previously, these women were involved in income-generating activities, with commercial experiences such as participation in economic interest groups (EIG) or tontines, associations, etc. The consumers (men and women) who frequent these sales outlets are generally people with low purchasing power, friends, and teachers living in the neighbourhoods. The evidence suggests that women who sell food and non-food products from the stalls help their husbands provide for their families. They come from modest families with a low level of education, almost all of them having only completed primary school.

As this study aims to document the logics/rationalities and perceptions that drive women stallholders to buy from Auchan, the use of semi-structured interviews seemed more appropriate. Furthermore, this study focuses on an ethnographic approach (Geertz, 1998; Roucous and Dauphragne, 2015) of sales outlets, products, and customer purchasing behaviour. Interviews with women stallholders document the types of products supplied at Auchan, questioning their choices and rationales. Similarly, interviews with the stallholders' customers were crucial for understanding their assessments and perceptions of customer service, product quality, and accessibility in relation to their expectations and needs. The information saturation method (Beaud, Gravier, and de Tolédo, 2006; Paugam, 2012) determined the number of interviewees. In fact, I conducted a total of 17 interviews. Ten interviews were conducted with women stallholders, and seven interviews were conducted with the stallholders' various customers, trying as far as possible to diversify their profiles (age, level of education, marital and socio-economic status, types of products sold and/or purchased, etc.). Moreover, during the survey period, I paid close attention to the interactions between customers and employees, and at the same time, I sporadically observed shopping moments. This enabled me to get a better ethnographic picture of the most popular products (local and/or imported) and the rationales behind these choices (Table 6.1).

Table 6.1 Respondents' profiles

Types of players	*People the author met*	*Material*
Women window dressers	Supporting women Women with business experience (tontines, MSEs) Polygamous, single women	10 interviews Ethnography of product types Description of stall service organisation Assess product diversification logics
Customers	People with low purchasing power Surroundings (friends, family, etc.) Neighbourhood teachers	7 interviews Appreciation of the types of products (local and imported) Appreciation of prices and product quality Appreciation of sales areas

Presentation and Discussion of Results

This chapter is divided into two main parts. In the first part, I present the supply logics of women stallholders in Mbour. In fact, the focus is on the ethnography of the types of products supplied, by questioning the choices and rationalities that shape them and the relationships between the logics of the use of Auchan, and the food and socio-economic cultural system of the Senegalese population. In the second part, I analyse customer perceptions of the products supplied by Auchan. Specifically, I study the perceptions of the services offered by these women, showing how they intersect with the local and the global. Similarly, a comparative analysis of the types of products supplied at Auchan and at local markets has been very useful.

Sourcing Patterns of Women Stallholders in Mbour

The supply logic of women retailers at stall level is at the crossroads of local and global (glocalisation) food practices. They correspond to the current food and cultural systems of Senegalese consumers in a globalised context.

Ethnography of the Types of Products Supplied at Auchan: Choices and Rationalities

Meat, vegetables, fish, dairy, oil, cereal, and vinegar products are usually the types of products that women stallholder's source, display, and retail in Senegal as a whole and in Mbour in particular. Until recently, these products were sourced from the local sales outlets mentioned above.[5] Why are they now also buying from Auchan? Does Auchan have anything special to offer compared to other local sources of supply? This diversity of products has led to innovations in the management and marketing systems of women stallholders. This is why the only alternative available to them was to go to Auchan to buy a certain number of products that they display and sell. These purchases include both local and imported products. The types of products they buy at Auchan include fish products, vegetables, clothing, and cosmetics (Table 6.2).

Table 6.2 provides a detailed categorisation of the various products supplied by Auchan. The reasons why women stallholders buy from Auchan include its

Table 6.2 Types of products supplied at Auchan

	Types of products	*Product details*
Auchan	Market garden products	Fresh vegetables (tomatoes, carrots, peppers, cucumbers)
	Fish products	Fish (sea bream, thiof, badaise)
	Cosmetic products	Toiletries (body lotion, perfumes, soaps, etc.)
		Clothing (t-shirt, Lacoste, towel)
	Clothing products	Shoes (bare feet, flip-flops)
		Bags (satchels, wallets)
		Accessories (watches, bracelets)
	Other products	Toys, sweets, biscuits, fresh mints, etc.

difference from other local markets: modernisation of sales areas (digitisation, self-service, etc.), quality (cold chain, imported brand, etc.), and accessibility (perceived prices) of products. In this respect, the women interviewed feel that they are buying from Auchan because it offers "sometimes lower prices" than other local food outlets (markets, shops, wholesalers, etc.) where prices are set liberally and/ or anarchically for the same products. Similarly, the Auchan brand offers, according to the interviewees, a certain level of comfort in terms of shopping and security (clean, air-conditioned space). It also offers a warm welcome to its customers. Senegalese society is characterised by a strong presence of collectivism rooted in particular African or religious traditions, and a communitarianism that values time spent with the group (Diallo, Sall, and Seck, 2014).

Senegalese society, it seems worth pointing it out, is marked by a strong sense of affectivity that often prevails over rationality. For example, the endless greetings, the "palaver", the taste for gifts, the sense of hospitality, and the permanent smile are all signs of the human warmth that is typical of this society (Ollivier and de Maricourt, 1990; Diallo, Sall, and Seck, 2014). The work of Amadou Lamine Dia (1991) highlights the collateral relational orientation of the Senegalese population, who tends to favour their community, family, and clan (Dia, 1991). In the same vein, Fatou Diop (2013) in her writings on the clothing behaviour of Senegalese shows that values such as warm relationships based on sociability, bodily well-being, a sense of belonging characterised by social visibility (the importance of appearance) and community identity strongly influence the behaviour of Senegalese consumers (Diop, 2013).

The Auchan chain offers a self-service distribution system with wide opening hours (from 8 a.m. to midnight): This is an innovation in terms of convenience and shopping. The diversity of products (local and imported – especially branded) that respond positively to the needs and expectations of women stallholders is a key indicator of the innovation of their services. Not only does this show that "the hybridisation of local practices and ideas from elsewhere is a source of innovation" (Schuerkens, Branine and Mamman (eds), 2019: 10, my translation) But still better, understanding purchasing and consumption behaviour is a means of building customer loyalty (Diédhiou, 2023). It is in this context that the comments of this woman stallholder become quite illustrative:

> In Senegal, local markets used to be places to buy food and non-food products. But now, with the arrival of food distribution companies like Auchan, I prefer to go and get my supplies there to satisfy my customers by ensuring quality and safety, by which I mean hygiene, and above all, by offering them imported products. Extract from an individual interview, Oulimata T., 25 years old, stall vendor, married, polygamous, without formal education, December 2022.[6]

These comments point to an innovation in the sales service provided by women stallholders. This innovation takes account of hybrid food needs to satisfy customers, by opting for a diversified offer: a range of imported products and food safety, hygiene, etc. (Démettre, 2022), which, in turn, force these women to go and buy products at Auchan. Food needs reintegrating what could be described as a mixture of the local and the global (Schuerkens, Branine, and Mamman (eds), 2019; Ka and Leport, 2023). This is further evidence of how, in an interconnected world, the cohabitation of Auchan and local Senegalese commerce seems unavoidable (Diédhiou, 2023). Seen from this angle, this innovation can be compared to the work of Den Hertog and Brouwer (2000), who highlight a model of commercial innovation with four dimensions: a new concept (e.g., format), a new customer interface (e.g., level of personalisation), a new distribution system (e.g., self-service), and a new technological option (e.g., electronic payment system). In addition to these dimensions, I have added a fifth one, which is applicable to Auchan: the loyalty card, which makes it possible to manage change after payment.

Better still, the Auchan brand is able to meet the current cultural and dietary needs of women stallholders more than other existing offers – local markets (Diédhiou, 2023). Still better, its offer is innovative and therefore becomes a source of supply (Bahoken et al., 2016). As Mbour is a touristic area with an increased presence of middle-class people (who tend to show the importance of their social position by going to buy at Auchan), it is therefore favourable for these women to diversify their offers. This adaptability of their offers (purchases of local and imported products) reinforces the comments made by Varman and Belk (2012) who felt that Senegalese and Indian food identities are transformed by the emergence of shopping centres (Varman and Belk, 2012). Having set out the types of products stocked at Auchan, let's now look at the ways in which Auchan is used.

Cultural and Economic Facts[7]: Two Ways of Using Auchan

The way in which Auchan is used is closely linked to economic and cultural factors. The current food culture of the Senegalese population is part of what might be termed food studies or the socio-anthropology of food (Poulain, 2017; Berg, Nestle, and Bentley, 2021). This could be defined as all the methods used to determine the historical, cultural, behavioural, biological, and socio-economic consequences of food production and consumption (Berg, Nestle, and Bentley, 2021). The existing literature (Hofstede, 1980; Triandis, McCusker, and Hui, 1990. ; Michon and Chébat, 2004) shows that culture has considerable effects on purchasing and consumption behaviour via shopping centres and food distribution shops. Culture is said to be a system of collective values held by individuals which influence their beliefs and behaviour. It is therefore a set of values shared by individuals, or groups in society (Hofstede, 1980; Munene et al., 2000). This definition shows the differences that exist in the way food is consumed in different cultures.

This being the case, social consumption practices are strongly embedded in the economic logic of the market (Le Velly, 2012; Ka and Leport, 2023). The success of the Auchan chain seems to depend on its ability to meet the current food needs of the Senegalese population better than existing offers (Ulaga and Reinartz, 2011; Bahoken et al., 2016; Diédhiou, 2023). This is why Varman and Belk (2012) consider that Senegalese consumers, like Indian consumers, are in the process of transforming their food identities via shopping centres (Varman and Belk, 2012).

As a result, consumers are both caught up in the systems and equipped by them to make sovereign decisions (Dubuisson-Quellier, 2009). The alternative forms of consumption developed in this way convey a critique of the dominant modes of consumption (Dubuisson-Quellier, 2009), which are extroverted and disconnected from those of the lower middle and working classes.

Having understood that the cultural identities of Senegalese people are being transformed by the globalisation of food practices, and accentuated by the emergence of mass retailing (Varman and Belk, 2012; Ka and Leport, 2023; Diédhiou, 2023), in their supply strategies, women stallholders adopt a diversity of products (local and imported). This hybrid strategy is supported by the rise of the middle class, which seems to favour the establishment of supermarkets and agri-food companies that are taking over local Senegalese markets (Diallo, Sall, and Seck, 2014). This means, in the sense of the sociology of uses, that the "meaning", "advantage", "usefulness", "ease of use", "simplicity of the idea", and "perceived added value" (Mallein and Toussain, 1994) of the Auchan brand encourage the sourcing of consumer products (food or non-food). At present, multinational companies operating in the food retail sector are considerably changing the purchasing and consumption behaviour of the Senegalese population. This is all the more true as these patterns of use correspond to a current food culture system: a hybrid system, connected to globalisation (Poulain, 2017).

It seems appropriate to emphasise the close relationship between food studies and the globalisation of Senegalese eating habits. Indeed, as a phenomenon of accelerating trade between countries, the globalisation of market economies brings most of the world's countries into interrelation, if not interdependence, impacting lifestyles, consumption, and cultures (Diemer, 2001; Schuerkens et al., (eds), 2019). In Senegal, this food culture is reflected in the spread of distribution methods, marked by the emergence of chains such as Auchan (Diédhiou 2023), food representations: ingredients, diversity of both local and imported dishes with the use of bouillons, etc. (Ka and Leport, 2023), and the emergence of new restaurant concepts (Myerson, 2012; Poulain, 2017; Berg, Nestle, and Bentley, 2021). In this sense, globalisation favours the circulation of products and dishes of foreign origin which, in Senegal, regularly fill the shelves of hypermarkets, supermarkets, and local markets, not to mention restaurant menus: egg rolls, burgers, pizzas, KFC, etc. In this context, cooking becomes an essential part of the meal. Cooking becomes a process of cultural transformation, moving from the "raw" to the "cooked" (Lévi-Strauss, 1968), or even a transformation of food, by moving from the natural state to the cultural state .

In this respect, the diversity of cooking methods and cooking stocks appears to be a fundamental element of differentiation between cultures. This being the case, the cooking methods of the Senegalese are influenced by the emergence of food retailers (Varman and Belk, 2012). These current Senegalese cultural food logics therefore appear to be forms of cultural hybrids: They mix the original French model with certain elements of Senegalese food culture (Ka and Leport, 2023; Diédhiou, 2023). This hybridisation of modes of consumption and distribution thus becomes a factual indicator of the practices of women stallholders at Auchan to meet customer expectations. Thus, it appears that while globalisation has certainly changed Senegalese food practices through the emergence of large-scale food retailers (e.g., Auchan), its influences have been subject to a form of integration and acculturation. In other words, they have not taken the place of pre-existing practices, but rather have become part of a French food model that is still quite pronounced, with a particular emphasis on quality, hygiene, food safety rules, etc. In addition to cultural considerations, economic considerations[8] represent the aim of diversifying suppliers or sources of supply. Although there are[9] structures for state regulation and control of prices, the prices charged on local markets are still not harmonised and are therefore set in a liberal manner. At Auchan, on the other hand, there is a certain predictability of expenditure, as prices are not negotiated and are known in advance.[10] It is worth looking at how shoppers perceive the different products from the Auchan chains.

Customer Perceptions of Products Supplied by Auchan

The diversity of products, particularly imported products, that women retailers stock at Auchan boosts their managerial and marketing strategies and, at the same time, innovates their sales service. This has led customers to appropriate (frequent) these services.

Consumer Perceptions of Products on Display: Between Local and Global

The Auchan brand has enabled women retailers, who once had no choice but to sell local products, to sell imported products, and innovate their service. When I talk about innovation, I am referring to the work of Joseph Alois Schumpeter (1883–1950), who defined it as a "process of creative destruction" (Akrich, Latour, and Callon, 1988; Gallouj, 2007; Alter, 2010; Funel et al., 2012; Goldman and Little, 2015). In this study, I look at innovation not from the technical point of view, but from the commercial point of view (Reynolds et al., 2006; Gallouj, 2007). This being the case, women retailers have realised that the current purchasing and consumption patterns of Senegalese people are undergoing radical change with the emergence of the Auchan brand (Villette, 2001; Schuerkens, 2014; Diédhiou, 2023), and have embarked on a strategy of diversifying their service offerings. Embedded in the local and the global, the current food needs of the Senegalese population are reflected in "integration into the global food market and the presence on the local market of many imported products" (Ka and Leport, 2023: 1).

Perceptive women retailers at the stall level are going to focus more on the display, promotion, and sale of products, not only those imported but also local goods. An informed observer will ask to what extent these hybrid supply logics correspond to the needs of buyers in a globalised context. In trying to shed some light on this, I must point out that the service is perceived in a mixed way. Indeed, the interviewees have a good perception of the quality of Auchan products displayed on the stalls because they are well preserved (cold chain) and are original, given that they are imported and defy all competition: "They keep the same quality as those from the country of origin (France)". (Extract from individual interview, Bintou S., aged

25, customer, cleaning lady, secondary education, December 2022.) Even though these products are well appreciated, their prices are perceived as expensive; they often do not consider the socio-economic situation of the buyers. The retail strategy has made it possible to take account of this adaptability to the socio-economic realities of households. Regarding product preference, one customer replied:

> I know that there are both imported and local products. But I prefer to go to these stalls and buy imported products because they are so rare in this neighbourhood. I mean, to get them, you must go to Auchan, and that's a long way away. Since this lady sells the same products from Auchan, if I bought them here, it would be more advantageous for me. Extract from an individual interview, Bintou S., 25 years old, customer, cleaning lady, secondary education, December. 2022.

Imported products are more popular because they come from Auchan, which is a long way from consumers. These customers feel that going to Auchan, including the cost of transport to and from the store and the price of the products to be bought, is the same thing as buying from stalls closer to them, and help to empower these women. This shows that these women are "relays" for Auchan among working-class consumers. In addition, the diversity of products (imported and local) meets customers' expectations and, from this point of view, is an important indicator of stall traffic. This situation contributes greatly to the commercial innovation of their sales services.

Despite this, the sales areas still leave much to be desired due to their lack of modernisation and organisation: Product shelves, open-air products, lack of hygiene, non-fixed and negotiable prices. Consumers' perceptions of the service (stalls) are on the roads between the local and the global (Berg, Nestle, and Bentley, 2021; Ka and Leport, 2023). These facts take us into the comparative universe of the types of products supplied at Auchan and at local markets.

Comparative Analysis of the Types of Products Supplied: Auchan and Local Markets

A comparative analysis of the supply rationales of women stallholders makes it possible to see to what extent they choose products at Auchan rather than at the local markets, and vice versa. Table 6.3 summarises, from a comparative perspective, the types of products supplied at Auchan and at local markets, showing the preferences and rationales structuring them.

Vegetables (tomatoes, carrots, peppers, and cucumbers) are bought at local markets because they can be supplied in sufficient quantities (in bulk), with negotiable prices to cover after-sales profit margins. On the other hand, when these vegetables are bought at Auchan, the women consider their quality (frozen, location of shelves, and cleanliness of sales areas). Women stallholders buy fish not only at local markets but also from Auchan. When they buy them at the local markets, these women consider the nature of the prices, which are affordable and debatable.

Table 6.3 Comparative analysis between Auchan and local markets

Where to buy	*Types of products*	*Rationalities/logics*
Local markets	Vegetables	Enough (wholesale), negotiable prices to cover profit margins
	Fish	Fresh produce, affordable and questionable prices
Auchan	Vegetables	Product quality (frozen foods), cleanliness (hygiene) of sales areas
	Fish	Proximity to Auchan, fixed and displayed prices Product quality (frozen)
	Skill and accessories	Rare (but expensive) products, originality (brand), unbeatable prices (promotions)
	Cosmetic products	High quality and rare imported products
	Toys, biscuits, etc.	Design, ease of use, perceived quality, etc.

On the other hand, when these women buy their fish from Auchan, they base their decision on proximity, fixed prices, and quality (frozen).

Clothing products: clothes (t-shirts, Lacoste, and towels), especially sold during the summer; shoes: slippers, flip-flops; bags: purses, and wallets; and accessories: watches, bracelets, etc. are exclusively bought at Auchan. They are highly priced for their rarity and originality – even if they are admittedly expensive – because they are imported (retail brands) and their unbeatable prices defy all competition, with promotion opportunities (ranging from 30 to 50%) during the festive period (Christmas and Tabaski[11]), and Ramadan, or Lent. Other products such as toys, sweets, and biscuits, which are also bought at Auchan, are much sought-after by children, especially in pre-school and primary schools, because of their design, attractive packaging, and ease of use. With these products, women stallholders would be able to obtain supplies (from Auchan) in sufficient quantities (in bulk) with the possibility of negotiating and setting profit margins after the sale.

> It's true that the products I buy at Auchan are really good quality and comply with hygiene rules, but they're expensive if you compare them to the ones I buy at the market. I go to Auchan to buy them because my customers like them, even if I make a small profit. For example, I buy a packet of 'Gina' brand biscuits for 1,000 F-CFA, but after the sale, I end up with 1,250 F-CFA, i.e., a profit margin of 250 F-CFA. Extract from an individual interview, Bineta L., 23, stall vendor, widow (head of household), primary education, December 2022.

Or:

> For example, I buy a kilogram of 'Thiof' fish at Auchan for 2,900 F-CFA, which I sell for 4,000 F-CFA, 4,500 F-CFA and sometimes even 5,000 F-CFA. On the other hand, if I buy it at the market for 1,500 F-CFA, I sell it for 2,000 F-CFA or even 2,500 F-CFA profit. Extract from an individual

interview, Fatou S., 33, stall vendor, widow (head of household), primary education, December 2022.

These verbatims show that the preferences and rationales of women stallholders in terms of sourcing from Auchan take into account the quality of Auchan products that comply with food hygiene and safety rules (Ponce et al., 2007) even if the profit margins are not negligible. However, these margins evolve and change depending on the products supplied (vegetables, fish, clothing, etc.). In the case of fish products from local markets, for example, profit margins vary between 500 and 1,000 F-CFA. But if they come from the Auchan chain, profits start at 1,100 F-CFA and rise to 2,100 F-CFA. From this comparison, however, I can deduce that the types of products bought either from Auchan and/or from the local markets depend largely on whether the customers' food needs are met, and on the profits that the women stallholders receive after the sale.

Conclusion

Thanks to food exports and imports, Senegal is increasingly becoming a fertile ground for the study of dietary changes. In other words, the influence of globalisation and integration into the world food market has led to changes in Senegalese dietary practices.

In this chapter, I have attempted to identify the supply patterns of women retailers at the Auchan stalls in the town of Mbour, using a qualitative analysis combined with an ethnographic approach. The results suggest that Senegalese consumption practices and cultural food identities are undergoing major changes. This has a strong influence on the rationales underlying the supply of women stallholders at Auchan. Among other factors favouring the use of Auchan, I could note its difference from other local markets: Modernisation of sales areas, digitisation of services, self-service system, hygiene, imported product brands, and affordability of products, especially promotions during the festive and Lenten periods. These supply logics therefore have an ambivalent status, at the crossroads between the local and the global. This hybridity has helped to boost the profitability of these women and satisfy customer demands, by offering a diversified range of products (local and imported) that comply with hygiene and consumer regulations. In other words, the types of products supplied to Auchan and/or local markets largely depend on the food needs of satisfied consumers and the perceived benefits after the sale (costs and opportunities). In other words, in Senegal, women stallholders who also own local businesses are relays for Auchan among working-class consumers. They can also compete with multinational food and non-food retailers (such as Auchan) by offering a differentiated and innovative customer experience.

Nevertheless, the results of this study cannot be extrapolated to all shop assistants in Senegal. This is a major prospect for the future. There are two points to bear in mind here. Firstly, a possible comparison between men and women would make it possible to determine the extent to which there are gender-based disparities in sourcing patterns. Finally, another comparative analysis of the supply rationales of women who exclusively use Auchan and those who buy their supplies only from local markets, enables me to understand how the former innovate their services, and managerial and marketing strategies and, in turn, boost their appropriation in this globalised world.

Notes

1 Stall sellers are local traders who display items for sale in the open air, on the street, or in front of their homes. This is a small business generally run by women seeking to empower themselves with the possible gains.
2 The Auchan chain is criticised for having developed these managerial and marketing practices into unfair competition for local traders, small local retail shops, and small businesses often run by women.
3 Management is an innovative approach based on standards (working hours and standards, etc.) to boost the profitability of stall vendors.
4 Marketing is a sales strategy (communication, lower prices, advertising, promotions, networks, weak or strong links, etc.) that stallholders use to attract and retain customers.
5 We're talking about neighbourhood shops, wholesalers, weekly and fixed markets, street vendors, etc.
6 The quotations (extracts from individual interviews) used to support my analysis are the words of the surveyed women and customers. These extracts are taken from the transcripts of the interviews from Wolof to French (translated by P.D.).
7 These two facts (cultural and economic) are certainly the main drivers of usage, but other indicators are also corollaries. These indicators, which revolve around these two facts, are developed throughout the argument: innovation, product quality, food hygiene, self-service, and digitisation, product diversity, costs, and opportunities.
8 The economic aspect is not the subject of a specific section; it is interwoven into the analysis.
9 These include the Directorate of Economic Control (DEC) that monitors prices and stocks, and the Directorate of Domestic Trade and Prices (DDTP), which has regional and/or departmental offices responsible for implementing the government's pricing and distribution policies.
10 However, the prices shown do not include VAT. VAT only appears on the invoice. So, the real price is the one including VAT. This marketing strategy is also one of the indicators of the Auchan brand's logic.
11 Known as the "feast of the sheep" or "Aïd el-kebir", Tabaski is celebrated annually by Muslims, as a reminder of Ibrahim's submission to God, when the latter asked him to sacrifice his son, Ismael or Ismayil.

References

Akrich, M., B. Latour, and M. Callon (1988) "A quoi tient le succès des innovations?" 1: "L'art de l'intéressement"; 2:"Le choix des porte-parole", *Gérer et Comprendre, Annales des Mines*, June: 4–17 and 14–29.

Alter, N. (2010) *L'innovation ordinaire* (3rd ed.). Paris: Presses Universitaires de France.

Bahoken, F., C. Blanquart, E. Gaubert, and T. Zeroual (2016) "Une typologie spatiale des commerces intra-urbains fondée sur l'analyse de leurs relations d'approvisionnement", *Revue d'Économie Régionale et Urbaine,* 3: 619–647.

Beaud, M., M. Gravier, and A. de Tolédo (2005) *L'art de la thèse: comment préparer et rédiger un mémoire de master, une thèse de doctorat ou tout autre travail universitaire à l'ère du Net.* Paris: Découverte.

Berg, J., M. Nestle, and A. Bentley (2021) "Food studies", in S. H. Katz et W. W. Weaver (eds) *The Scribner Encyclopaedia of Food and Culture*, vol. 2, pp. 16–18. New York: Charles Scribner and Sons.

Claval, P. (2012) "De la nature à la culture: La médiation alimentaire", in P. Claval (ed.) *Géographie culturelle: une nouvelle approche des sociétés et des milieux*, pp. 172–193. Paris: Armand Colin.

Démettre, L. D. (2022) "Une lecture géographique du voyage de la rose kenyane: De l'éclatement de la chaîne d'approvisionnement aux innovations logistiques", *Revue belge de géographie (Belgeo)*, 2: 234–238.

Dia, A. L. (1991) "Le management africain: Mythe ou réalité", *Revue internationale P.M.E*, 4 (1): 29–48.

Diallo, M. F., F. D. Sall, and A. M Seck (eds) (2014) G*estion des activités publiques et privées en milieu africain: L'exemple du Sénégal*. Paris: L'Harmattan.

Diédhiou, P. M. (2023) "Ethnographie d'une boutique locale: Cas d'*Auchan Keur Massar à Dakar*", in Ulrike Schuerkens (ed.) *Entreprises, entrepreneurs et travail au Sénégal*, pp. 255–280. Paris: L'Harmattan.

Diemer, A. (2001) "Mondialisation et spécificités socioculturelles", Formation continue, SES, IUFM d'Auvergne.

Diop, F. (2013) "Tradition et comportement de consommation au Sénégal: Une étude exploratoire sur la tenue vestimentaire", *La Revue des sciences de gestion, Direction et Gestion,* 3 (261–262): 121–130.

Dubuisson-Quellier, S. (2009) *La consommation engagée.* Paris: Presses de Sciences Po, Collection Contester.

Funel, C., M. Vigoureux, and A. Vittori (2012) "L'innovation commerciale: quelles innovations commerciales au regard des attentes des consommateurs", *Cahier de recherche* C291: 1-105. Paris: CREDOC.

Gallouj, G. (2007) *Innover dans la grande distribution.* Paris: De Boeck Supérieur. Perspectives et marketing.

Geertz, C. (1998) "La description dense: Vers une théorie interpretative de la culture", *Enquête,* 6 (October): 73–105.

Goldman, M. J. and J. S. Little (2015) "Innovative grassroots NGOs and the complex processes of women's empowerment: An empirical investigation from Northern Tanzania", *World Development*, 66 (February): 762–777.

Hofstede, G. (1980) "Culture and organisations", *International Studies of Management & Organisation*, 10 (4): 15–41.

Ka, A. and J. Leport (2023) "Le ceebu jën: Un plat révélateur de la dualité de l'alimentation sénégalaise entre approbation sociale et dévalorisation sanitaire", *Anthropology of Food*, 17 (1–2): 122–137.

Le Velly, R. (2012) *Sociologie du marché*. Paris: La Découverte.

Lévi-Strauss, C. (1968). *Mythologiques – L'origine des manières de table*. Paris: Plon.

Mallein, P. and Y. Toussain (1994) "L'intégration sociale des technologies d'information et de communication. Une sociologie des usages", *Technologies de l'information et société*, 6 (4): 315–335.

Michon, R. and J.-C. Chébat (2004) "The interaction effect of background music and ambient scent on the perception of service quality", 8th International Research Seminar in service management, La Londe Les Maures – France.

Myerson, P. (2012) *Lean Supply Chain and Logistics Management*. New York: McGraw Hill Education.

N'Da, P. (2015) *Recherche et méthodologie en sciences sociales et humaines: Réussir sa thèse, son mémoire de master ou professionnel et son articl*e. Paris: L'Harmattan.

Ndiaye, A. (2022) "La protestation AUCHAN DÉGAGE à Dakar. De l'éthique d'une résistance au plaidoyer pour le consommer Local", *Anthropology of Food*, 17: 118–168.

Olivier de Sardan, J.-P. (1995) "La politique du terrain: Sur la production des données en anthropologie", *Enquête,* 1: 71–109.

Ollivier, A. and R. de Maricourt (1990) *Pratique du marketing en Afrique*. Paris: Coll. Universités francophones, Ed. Edicef/AUPELF.

Paillé, P. and A. Mucchielli (2016) *L'analyse qualitative en sciences humaines et sociales*. Paris: Armand Colin.

Paugam, S. (ed.) (2012) *L'enquête sociologique*, 2nd ed. Paris: Presses Universitaires de France.

Ponce, S., S. Landry, and J. Roy (2007) "De l'organisation scientifique du travail à la gestion de la chaîne d'approvisionnement: Les 100 ans de la gestion des opérations, de la production, et de la logistique", *Gestion,* 32 (3): 52–65.

Poulain, J.-P. (2017) "Socio-anthropologie du fait alimentaire ou food Studies. Les deux chemins d'une thématisation scientifique", *L'Année sociologique*, 67 (1): 23–46.

Raynaud, D. and M. Bunge (2018) *Sociologie des controverses scientifiques.* New, revised and expanded ed. Paris: Éditions Matériologiques.

Reynolds, M., F. Dreccer, and R. Trethowan (2006) "Drought-adaptive traits derived from wheat wild relatives and landraces", *Journal of Experimental Botany*, 58 (2): 177–186.

Roucous, N. and A. Dauphragne (2015) "La chambre d'enfant: Une construction partagée entre parents et enfants", *La revue internationale de l'éducation familiale*, 37 (1): 87–113.

Schuerkens, U. (ed.) (2014) *Global Management, Local Resistance: Theoretical Discussion and Empirical Case Studies.* New York and London: Routledge.

Schuerkens, U., M. Branine, and A. Mamman (eds) (2019) *Pour une sociologie du management en Afrique et dans le monde arabe.* Collection Vivre l'entreprise. Série Management et ressources humaines. Paris: L'Harmattan.

Triandis, H. C., C. McCusker, and C. Hui (1990) "Sondages multi-méthodes de l'individualisme et du collectivisme", *Journal of Personality & Social Psychology*, 59 (5): 1006–1020.

Varman, R. and R. W. Belk (2012) "Consuming postcolonial shopping malls", *Journal of Marketing Management*, 28 (1–2): 62–84.

Villette, M. (2001) "Le commerce n'adoucit pas les mœurs. La grande distribution a-t-elle besoin de vendeurs", *Gérer et Comprendre, Les Annales des Mines*, 64 (1): 61–71.

Part 3

Women Entrepreneurs and Their Enterprises

7 Women Entrepreneurs in Senegal and the Wider Geographical Context of Africa and Europe[1]

Ulrike Schuerkens

Introduction

There are many research findings on women in entrepreneurship, such as literature on challenges and barriers. However, most of this literature focuses on women entrepreneurs in the North, particularly in the United States and Europe, and to a lesser extent in Africa (Rajemison, 1995; Moore and Buttner, 1997; Sarr, 1998; Denieul, 2004; Ouattara, 2007; Kamdem and Ikelle, 2011; Edoho, 2015; Sheriff and Muffatto, 2015; Sumathi and Gunasundari, 2016; Isiwu and Onwuka, 2017; Said and Enslin, 2020). Studies on Senegalese women can be found in two doctoral theses whose approach was mainly quantitative (Diop Thiam, 2015; Mbodji Diop, 2019). However, there is a lack of information on the challenges and obstacles faced by Senegalese women in managing and launching a new formal business (Sarr, 1998). Thus, the research question is: How do women entrepreneurs perceive and describe the experience of running a successful business in Dakar and elsewhere? This research aims to understand which meaning women entrepreneurs have given to their experiences. As Memili et al. (2015) point out, value creation requires innovation and resources to build new profitable businesses. You need to be able to seize opportunities and have ideas if you want to create a new business venture. Women entrepreneurs in the South face barriers to success such as lack of support and cultural perceptions (Rajemison 1995; Ouattara, 2007; Kamdem and Ikelle, 2011; Kumar, 2019). These difficulties differ according to culture, age, education, and ethnic origin. In Africa, social and cultural perceptions are decisive in the choice of business, including so-called feminine sectors such as the beauty sector or hair-dressing.

The life stories of the three women presented here deal with the education and knowledge they acquired in business schools and universities to be able to plan, organise, control, and run a business (cf. Sumathi and Gunasundari, 2016). It was in European higher education institutions that these women acquired the scientific knowledge they needed to analyse and solve problems. They were helped to analyse and define market opportunities for their new businesses. However, these women put a particular emphasis on their being Africans who know the Senegalese culture and how to have success in an economic sector that they understand better than those that are not familiar with this environment.

The aim of this chapter is to understand the specificities of three personal biographies and the belief systems to which individuals adhere to account for their

DOI: 10.4324/9781003492931-10

experiences. I will attempt to integrate the study of the macro and micro levels of African women's lives into a single methodological framework. The analysis of their experiences will expose not only the convergent and divergent meanings of values and the contradictions within those values but also the motivations and choices whose complex meanings could not have been discovered by any other means. This chapter looks at the stories of three African women pursuing personal and professional interests. I highlight the lived experiences as the subjective creation of a life course that reveals links based on factors of gender, ethnicity, and class, as well as the political, economic, and social context of these experiences. I present the subjectivities displayed as being linked to a process of creating meanings constructed in relation to social and economic interests. By demonstrating the multiple roles of these women, I can identify the beliefs, ideas, and objectives at work in integrated ideological systems.

These three women are entrepreneurs who are combining their experiences in Africa and France to rise to the top of the economic and societal players in the African sub-region. Their early exposure to a commercial environment has encouraged them to pursue their goal and break through the glass ceilings that women also face in African societies. All three have benefited from the sponsorship of companies that have facilitated their upward social and economic mobility. The decision-making processes they have adopted and the interactions in which they have taken part have enabled them to attain highly valued social positions.

The information was gathered through in-depth interviews, supplemented by information gathered from the Internet and from the web pages of their companies and other sites. The interviews had an informal character, resembling cordial conversations. The mix of micro and macro was at the heart of these data sources. From a micro perspective, these women accept the macro ideologies governing the economic and political system that guides their career paths. They apply innovative thinking to create an entrepreneurial practice that places them at the forefront of African businesswomen. I study their individual motivations and interpretations of their career development to show how these relate to macro processes.

A few comments on the methodological implications of these case studies. In mainstream sociology, preference is given to quantitative approaches based on large-scale studies involving many actors. However, to understand the complexity of processes and motivations, experiences and hybrid situations, case studies make sense. Studying the lives of these women will help to illustrate the multiplicity of places and interpretations. I'm looking for new ideas and new points of view that are neglected in quantitative studies.

In these personal biographies, the axes and structural levels come together to provide a fundamental understanding of structural and individual processes, through the analysis of certain practices.

These women told me the story of their careers and how they built their businesses. Their stories are interesting because they demonstrate their contradictions and illustrate their position as women. They occupy privileged positions compared to the mass of Senegalese women, but their experiences show that even women with a high level of education suffer structural discriminations in the economic sphere. These women do not identify with the causes of disadvantaged African women. Their experiences reveal their privileged positions and roles in relation to other women. The arguments they put forward reveal their experiences of class and gender in society.

As it is difficult to understand the significance of personal perceptions, the three-case study approach encourages us to be cautious in interpreting real-life experiences that reveal the impact of class and gender. African women occupy different positions depending on their socio-economic status. The conditions in which they play their roles can be difficult to combine and analyse in a comprehensive way. As researchers, we work our way through career narratives to uncover African women's ambivalences, emotions, arguments, and explanations of the relationships between self, social group, and society.

Presentation of the Case Studies

The empirical basis for this chapter are the stories of Seynabou Dia, a 43-year-old entrepreneur; Aminata Thior, a 38-year-old entrepreneur; and Khadja Diop, a 48-year-old entrepreneur in 2024. The full stories, as told to me, are very long, and I will only use here the chapters that cover their professional lives in relation to the company. Allow me, however, to give some background information on these biographies first.

The Genre

For these studies, the feminist views expressed by the three women can be seen as indicating a "progressive" view of gender. The lack of identification with the cause of African women may be linked to their position in the Senegalese class structure. On several occasions, they present as positive values (1) the pursuit of high aspirations, (2) respect for marriage, and (3) race consciousness. The idea of personal change as the primary condition for social change has implications for the way they experience their role in the struggle for African development. They emphasise individual responsibility and individual action: "Africans with property must make efforts for the benefit of African countries, and Africans without property must acquire greater aspirations" (S. Dia). They insist on the symbolic significance of their projects for the African community. They provide individual support to African women on the continent according to them. They believe that taking care of themselves will help them break the vicious circle of "poverty".

Assumptions

Through these case studies, we analyse three hypotheses: (1) self-efficacy as a psychological factor positively influences the entrepreneurial intentions of African women: "*Self-efficacy* is confidence in the ability to control one's motivation, behaviour, performance and social environment" (cf. https://www.apa.org/pi/aids/resources/education/self-efficacy, accessed 19 January 2024); (2) professional involvement positively influences the entrepreneurial intentions of African women; (3) the pursuit of a goal positively influences the entrepreneurial intentions of African women.

"Entrepreneurial intentions" refer to a person's desire to become an entrepreneur. A personal intention to become an entrepreneur is influenced by an individual intention. Certain psychological factors have an impact on an entrepreneur's innovation and success. These factors include entrepreneurial commitment and self-efficacy, as well as the positive impact on the growth of female entrepreneurship. Self-efficacy enables women to create and sustain businesses because it increases the level of motivation of female entrepreneurs and encourages them to act.

Professional involvement measures the degree of investment in work. The skills associated with this factor enable women to succeed in the marketplace. Women's commitment is a determining factor in their entrepreneurial activities, as well as in setting up and running their own businesses. The training programmes organised by Global Mind Consulting can then reinforce the self-sufficiency of other African women.

Seynabou Dia, Global Mind Consulting[2]

Founding President of Global Emergence Corporation and Global Mind Consulting Gabon, Seynabou Dia is a public relations specialist with in-depth knowledge of communications. She founded her first agency, Global Emergence, in Paris. As a young consultant, she coordinated the gala launch of the World Festival of Black Arts in France at UNESCO in 2010.

Since 2012, she has been running the first consultancy dedicated to public relations management for economic and political players in Africa, Global Mind Consulting, based in Libreville, which is tending to establish itself as a major player in the promotion of agents of transformation on the continent and is involved in supporting initiatives with a high societal impact, with companies and organisations but also political candidates, by preparing their public and media interventions at events taking place on the African continent. The firm focuses on supporting young entrepreneurs and initiatives that empower women in Africa.

Seynabou Dia organises business meetings and communication-building sessions, speaks at forums, organises and runs conferences, and coaches and advises entrepreneurs. Seynabou Dia has also taken on other important roles. She has been vice-president of the European Collective for the Development of African Countries (CEDA), ambassador for the *Women in Africa* network, and expert consultant on the activities of the African Union. In 2017, she was voted Woman Entrepreneur of the Year at the Hub Africa Awards in Casablanca. Seynabou Dia was one of the winners of the 7th AS de La Com Awards, held in Abidjan, and received the 2019 ASCOM Award for Excellence, which honoured Ivorian and African communication players dedicated to female leadership. She also took part in a round table organised during the event on "customer experience, a performance lever for businesses". Also in 2019, she won the Diaspora Awards and was included in the Financial Afrik ranking of the "100 who are transforming Africa" several times. In 2021, she was included in the #NaoleMedia40 ranking, an unprecedented list of the

40 most inspiring African women in the media and communications professions in French-speaking Africa and the diaspora.

Seynabou Dia was born in France to a father who owned a company in the security sector and a mother who brought up her children and had some commercial activities. She has dual French and Senegalese citizenship. After growing up in the north of France, she began studying economic and social administration at the University of Paris 8 and obtained a diploma in technology, particularly in business and organisation management. This diploma combined theory and practice, with an apprenticeship in a company that gave her the opportunity to discover new businesses and a passion that she would never lose. At the age of 19, she founded her first company, which did not prosper but enabled her to make contacts with personalities who would be decisive for the rest of her career. Ever since she was young, she has been interested in the African continent and its challenges. Her life project is to contribute to the transformation of the African world, an activity she thought she could carry out in international organisations, but after her first responsibilities at the Senegalese embassy in Paris and the organisation of an event at UNESCO in 2010, she decided to pursue her career in the private sector, working on projects in both the public and private sectors. She became a member of a network of African companies in France and another network of leading African managers. She joined these networks because she was interested in contacts with the African diaspora. She very quickly became communications manager, one of whose tasks is to organise meetings and influence the decision-makers she meets. It was in this capacity that she met influential members of the African diaspora in France who wanted to invest in the African continent. She has also accompanied groups of Africans who have come to France to perfect their knowledge. Very close to the African diaspora in the United States, she set up a business there, which she soon abandoned as she left France for Africa. It was then that international and African organisations started asking her to speak at events such as the World Economic Forum in Addis Ababa in 2011. These events enabled her to expand her network. She was asked to organise public events, which she did, despite some initial reluctance. But her mentors were convinced that she could do the job. Customers were soon so interested in her qualifications that she was able to develop the practice she set up in Libreville in 2012, specialising in consultancy, mainly in communications, leading to practical solutions and objectives. She started her business with a partner who left 18 months later. In 2019, she set up a second regional office, in Dakar, where she works with a dozen or so associates at maximum. The firm's strategy, which includes practical solutions, usually supports companies for a year or more. Finally, the enterprise carries out an evaluation to identify what works and what doesn't in its consultancy practice.

The agency prepares and organises public events and is also active in the education sector. Its website offers a PDF file presenting a wide range of educational activities as well as prices for these events and training courses. The team, which has no more than ten qualified permanent members working in the various areas of activity in Dakar and specialising according to regional focus, provides advice in management, legal affairs, communication, media, and training. The agency also has a rich list of potential consultants of African origin who can be entrusted with tasks that the small permanent team cannot carry out. For example, in the field of corporate social responsibility or anthropology, qualified consultants are available to carry out audits and respond to specific questions and issues.

The agency has been working with the African Union for over eight years, organising sessions on leadership, public speaking, young entrepreneurs, and women entrepreneurs. Such sessions have been organised in Gabon, Uganda, Rwanda, Kenya, and Zanzibar, and have included practical exercises to make them useful to participants.

COVID-19 has forced the agency to change its approaches, a task that the CEO sees as challenging but interesting. Global Mind Consulting's corporate clients include AXA, UNESCO, the African Union, the World Bank, Business France, Orabank, Gabon Oil, Royal Air Morocco, L'OREAL, Women in Science, Global Entrepreneurship Week, Women in Africa, African Media Agency, France 24, Canal+, BBC News, etc. Despite this impressive international list, S. Dia claims that her company has contracts with 20% European companies and 80% African companies. However, the list above reveals a slightly different picture, as it contains many international organisations.

According to its CEO, the agency promotes African expertise and knowledge in solving the continent's problems, even though its founder has a European university degree and is originally from France, where she spent her childhood, youth, and early career. The offices in Libreville and Dakar and S. Dia's Senegalese citizenship enable the company to address its clients from a point of view that should, in all probability, often be influenced by the knowledge of the problems of the African continent and preliminary scientific knowledge acquired in European or American universities. The staff at the Dakar office are creative, dynamic, and intergenerational, and have been recruited mainly by recommendation and unsolicited applications. According to S. Dia, the main criterion for selecting staff members is motivation.

The regions covered by the two offices are CEMAC and UEMOA, but S. Dia also wants to extend her activities to English-speaking Africa. The reason for this is that English-speaking companies want to invest in the French-speaking part of Africa and need a certain amount of support. This strategy should be implemented over the next few years, so that central management can observe, study, and adapt its consultancy activities. S. Dia maintains that the national approach of most companies and their micro-status must be extended to the regional and continental scale. "The many opportunities in the field of energy and industrialisation need to be seized if we are to address the problem of unemployment in African urban centres", she says. In her opinion, women and young people are interested in setting up businesses, in implementing new ideas, and in finding solutions to current challenges. In particular, the digitisation of African economies can be achieved by young women entrepreneurs specialising in these new techniques, which will enable African economies to develop and cooperate with European or American companies in the years to come.

The focus on women and young entrepreneurs is in line with a continental policy and a Senegalese approach supported by the *Délégation générale à l'entrepreneuriat rapide des femmes et des jeunes* (https://der.sn) linked to the Senegalese Presidency.

According to Seynabou Dia, the approaches to be adopted in African countries must focus on national or regional particularities. The criteria defining these approaches may be different in West Africa and Central Africa, as the socio-economic characteristics vary from one country or region to another. In particular, the CEO says that it is important to carry out site visits and look for specific local characteristics where factories and organisations are located.

In the seminars that the agency organises, Seynabou Dia tries to communicate her passion for African development to young people and women. The videos that can be viewed on the agency's website provide an insight into her various activities as one of Africa's most influential women leaders. The agency organises seminars with Junior Achievement, HUB Africa, and the African Entrepreneurship Award, with the aim of helping project leaders and entrepreneurs to develop and sustain their businesses. In 2021, the intention was to address the new generation of communication managers and journalists who are learning their trade on a changing African continent that needs the support of people who are making a difference and influencing the African narrative.

Aminata Thior, Setalmaa[3]

Aminata Thior left Senegal in 2005 after her secondary education to study agronomy and then telecommunications in Lyon. After her university studies, she started work in a consultancy agency. Five years later, she decided to return to her favourite field: journalism. In 2017, she left her job to create Setalmaa. She wanted to create a media outlet focusing on the economy, which she couldn't find in the Senegalese media landscape. Radio France Internationale was organising competitions for entrepreneurs working with the media. In 2015, Aminata Thior proposed a project that RFI liked, but found it too big for her so she was asked to propose something smaller. Aminata Thior then focused on fashion and beauty and created a website tasked with finding market information for major international brands and African cosmetics brands. She chose WhatsApp to send useful information to women who were looking for information, for example about the brands and products they were selling. But she soon realised that it would be better to leave WhatsApp and create a web platform that would offer interviews and videos with women who had created African beauty brands. She promoted these brands on her site, whose products were then bought by the women in her network so that some of the companies' merchandise quickly sold out. Aminata Thior has frequently travelled in French-speaking Africa to prepare these interviews and videos: Senegal, Cameroon, Côte d'Ivoire, Benin, Congo Brazzaville, and Burkina Faso. She has spent several weeks in these countries and has regularly returned. She uses her travels to interview and meet women entrepreneurs she finds on the Internet. The stories she tells have contributed to the success of the businesses they have set up in the beauty sector.

Aminata Thior also runs a blog on RFI, which gives her access to a large French-speaking network. She asked the members of this network to send her important names in the beauty sector in their region; people she then met in their own countries. The information she gathered was then put on the Setalmaa website. Today, Aminata Thior has a large network of 548 African cosmetics brands at her disposal, and she no longer simply provides information, as she did in the early years of her journalistic activity: she organises the communication of these African brands within their own networks. These companies want to be visible on the Internet. Setalmaa creates content for them for between 300 and 800 euros, based on the positive aspects of their products that they have communicated to her. The most important thing about Setalmaa is that the story of these companies is told in attractive words to customers, 80% of whom are from the African diaspora living mainly in France. This *storytelling* involves writing articles and posting photos of the company online. A team of three people supervise these posts in Dakar, Abidjan, and Douala. Aminata Thior's French and Senegalese citizenships enable her to travel easily in the region.

The company's turnover has risen from 56,000 euros in 2019 to 100,000 euros in 2020. In addition to the communication service, the company has prepared a report, published in March 2021, and sold for 150 euros, which has increased turnover in 2021. Three members of the staff in Senegal receive a salary and are declared to the tax authorities. Staff in other regions receive honoraria and are paid on a *freelance basis* by the company's Senegalese subsidiary. A Paris-based consultancy company oversees Setalmaa's accounts. The long-term plan is to market European and African brands from an office in Dakar and to handle the marketing and sales of products in Africa. This will enable international brands to be sold in Africa and African brands to be bought by the African diaspora.

On social networks such as Instagram, Facebook, and Twitter, now X, Setalmaa has 100,000 subscribers. Its YouTube channel features videos of the company. According to Aminata Thior, 241 women in her network have beauty salons, brands, or commercial activities. The rest of the several thousand women are customers who were interviewed by telephone or at meetings in their various businesses. For example, in Côte d'Ivoire, Aminata Thior and her team went to the local market in Adjamé to ask questions. The answers are used to estimate the market and are included in the annual report on beauty in French-speaking Africa. Aminata Thior's husband helps her to collect and analyse the data, as he is a professional in data collection and analysis. She has also set up an agency to provide advice to brands looking to invest in Africa, at a cost of around €3,000 per hour. She can give between three and five consultations a month.

In 2019, Aminata Thior organised a forum at Pullman Dakar, attended by politicians, French entrepreneurs, and 62 people who paid an entrance fee of 100,000 F-CFA (152 euros), which enabled her to publicise her company and its consultancy activities. Air Sénégal and Pullman quickly decided to participate in her company's activities. And other companies are expected to follow, as they see the market opportunities in the beauty sector. International brands such as L'Oreal, Inoya, and Turkish brands have called on her services. As Aminata Thior frequently travels to beauty fairs in New York, Shanghai, and Dubai, she meets company managers who call on her services as an African who knows the African markets and has a medium through which to contact potential clients. Aminata Thior tries to create a win-win situation for brands wanting to enter the African market and for her own benefit for the international brands working with her company. This activity has enabled her to compile a directory of African brands and beauty salons which is not available on the Internet, but which helps her in her consultancy work. In 2023, she published a book on the African skin based on her beauty knowledge with the title "Ma peau, saine et belle, au naturel", which she has sold on her webpage.

Setalmaa markets two products from each of the ten international and African brands with which it works. Plans to expand these activities are underway and will be implemented soon. In all these activities, competitors could be doing the same thing as Setalmaa, but this enterprise occupies a strong position in the market, presided over as it is by a Senegalese/French woman who can communicate between the two regional zones, Africa and Europe, and who is selling her knowledge at a time when international brands are conquering African markets.

Because Aminata Thior has written articles on political subjects for her blog at RFI, she has been able to connect with important political players in Senegal who continue to follow her activities and are interested in linking their image with her activities. As a result, she has risen to a high position in Senegalese society where she is well connected, so much so that she was even able to turn down a cooperation offer from a French agency for a monthly salary of 15,000 euros: She prefers to do herself the tasks that the agency's French owner wanted her to do for his firm. She has built her reputation on her own network in Senegal and beyond. Born into a privileged Senegalese family with a father who was an engineer in a state-owned company and a mother who owned a fashion business, she was exposed to the lifestyle of Senegal's privileged groups, which gave her access to the political and economic elites. She was able to create a link between the Western way of life and the African world because she was able to live in both worlds, in Paris and its suburbs, but also in Dakar, where she spent her youth until the end of her secondary education and where she has recently returned.

Khadja Diop, O'Royal[4]

K. Diop studied economic and social administration up to Master's level at the University of Reims, where she met her husband, who was studying the same subject, before continuing with a postgraduate degree in management at the Faculty of Economics and Management at UCAD. After graduating in France, Khadja Diop returned to Senegal with the idea of putting the knowledge she had acquired in management at university to good use by setting up her own business and contributing to the work of Africans committed to Africa. Her father was a self-employed technician in the private sector. Her mother was an executive secretary in an NGO and studied up to the first year of secondary school. Her paternal grandfather was an immigrant in France and his wife was a vegetable seller at the market in Dakar. Her maternal grandfather was a marabout from the Tijane brotherhood and taught the Koran. Her maternal grandmother owned several houses and looked after the family and children. On her husband's side, his paternal grandmother traded between northern Senegal and Mauritania, while his father worked in a telecommunications agency. So, both had role models in their families who should have influenced their decision to take an interest in the business world.

On her return to Senegal, K. Diop worked for 13 years in the private sector: she began her "adventure" in a telecommunications agency (Tigo), where she stayed for eight years. She then worked for a Swedish company for four years before setting up her own telecoms distribution company, thanks to her knowledge of the sector. Through these activities, she acquired knowledge on how companies operate in Senegal. She rose through the ranks at Tigo to become close to the head of sales. At the Swedish company Ericsson, she was Sales Director. In her own company, she was a director before working as a director in the company where her husband was the majority shareholder. At the request of her husband and his partners, she became director of O'Royal in 2016, where she put her experience in the service sector in Senegal to good use and developed this soft drinks company that was in economic difficulties.

O'Royal is an industrial company that specialises in packaging water in bottles ranging from 33 cl to 19 litres. The company began with soft drinks before focusing in 2019 on a water source in Pout, which it leases and operates to the tune of 10%. The company has enjoyed strong growth in recent years, with sales of around €2 million a year. The small 33cl bottle is sold for religious ceremonies and can be customised to suit the type of ceremony. Companies can also order labels with their name on them, which will be produced with short lead times, a considerable success for O'Royal since the launch of this range in June 2022. Companies frequently order between 100 and several hundred bottles, as O'Royal is the only company to offer this service. These bottles are not sold for 100 F-CFA, but for 125 or 150 F-CFA. These individualised bottles are bought by all social groups, from the middle-income earners to the wealthy. They can be ordered online the day before the event. These products are promoted on social networks such as Facebook and Instagram, rather than in the traditional media. A service provider oversees this promotion, which is tailored to the Senegalese public.

The company employs around 100 people, 65% of whom work in production in Pout, 60 km from Dakar, and 35% in the company's administration in Yoff, a district of Dakar where the 48-year-old director also lives with her family. The company is prospering and is the country's third or fourth largest water producer, a sector that is growing rapidly. O'Royal is active in the plastic sector, recovering 19-litre bottles for reuse. It takes them back from the premises of client companies. Its small 33cl bottle replaces water bags that cannot be recycled and are still sold in some of Dakar's poorer neighbourhoods.

We can conclude that this entrepreneur was able to learn through her management activities in various companies in Senegal before being appointed director of O'Royal by her husband and his partners, a company that is entirely profitable. Plans are also afoot for the company's soft drinks division in the medium term. The future of the company is assured, as two of K. Diop's children have also chosen university courses in France and Canada to prepare them for corporate roles.

Conclusion

The analysis of these three biographies has shown how the three women construct their social reality in such a way as to reinforce the positive image they have of themselves in the eyes of the African community, and to ensure the survival of their businesses. The social class to which they belong has an impact on their perception of social change. They see it in the context of the existing economic system. Acting as role models for other African women is consistent with their belief that they have a role to play to improve difficult economic situations in Africa.

Through these case studies, I have argued that theorising the structures that shape African women's experiences is relevant, but not sufficient. Awareness of belonging to Africa has had an impact on their perceptions of gender and class. The notion of being African has been experienced in terms of dimensions such as income, lifestyle, and status.

Women entrepreneurs in the South and North face common challenges such as gender discrimination, lack of information and business resources such as lack of funds, and often, the small size of their professional support networks (Kumar, 2019). The three women whose journeys were presented enjoy higher income and education levels than the population average, which could only have been achieved by having high aspirations geared towards upward mobility.

The experience of these women shows that they could transform and change their situation and become major economic players in Senegal. They dared to launch a new business, and experienced stress and anger. However, they felt powerful and motivated thanks to their private and professional support systems. They have enjoyed learning more and improving their skills to come up with new ideas and make their business prosper. They are creative and innovative, but also ambitious and determined to contribute to the African economy. They believe in their ability to overcome obstacles, be they financing, government support, or adapting to social expectations. As a result, they have been able to produce positive results in their personal and social lives. The experiences of these women have the potential to be multipliers for other women in terms of their contribution to the economy, financial independence, and women's empowerment. These examples can provide other women with models of success for their own businesses, thereby contributing to the Senegalese economy and the well-being of their families. These women have demonstrated risk-taking, courage, a thirst for learning, ambition, consistency, and self-confidence. They have succeeded in transforming their social situation by creating and running a successful business in Senegal and abroad.

As for the political implications, they lie in the need for women to work together through networks to better support each other. Political leaders need to support women entrepreneurs and provide an attractive environment to attract new people. For their part, these women must persist in their endeavours, learn from their mistakes, and not give up.

Notes

1 The information used in this chapter was gathered during fieldwork carried out as part of the ManaGlobal programme, which is supported by the European Union's Horizon, 2020 framework programme through Marie-Sklodowska Curie Grant Agreement 82374. The paper was published in a book that I edited in 2023 in French: *Entrepreneurs, entreprises et travail au Sénégal*, pp. 237–254. Paris: L'Harmattan. The chapter is published here with the kind authorisation of the editor.
2 This part of the article is based on an interview I had with S. Dia on 8 July 2021 and on information gathered from the Global Mind consulting web page: https://globalmindconsulting.com/seynabou-dia-ceo-global-mind-counsulting-monde-de-communication-relations-publiques-na-de-secret/; https://globalmindconsulting.com/interview/; https://globalmindconsulting.com/webinaire/; https://globalmindconsulting.com/replay-femmes-leaders-au-senegal-les-competences-avant-tout/.
3 This part of the article is based on a lengthy exchange with Aminata Thior on 23 December 2021 in Dakar, as well as information found on her website and the Internet.
4 A meeting was arranged the 13 October 2022 at the company's head office in Yoff.

References

Denieul, N. (2004) *Femmes et entreprises en Tunisie: Essai sur les cultures du travail féminin.* L'Harmattan: Paris.

Diop Thiam, N. (2015) *L'entreprenariat féminin au Sénégal: déterminants de la croissance des PME dirigées par des femmes.* PhD thesis in economics, Université Cheikh Anta Diop, Dakar, Senegal.

Edoho, F. M. (2015) "Entrepreneurship and socioeconomic development", *African Journal of Economic and Management Studies*, 6 (2): 127–147.

Isiwu, P. I. and I. Onwuka (2017) "Psychological factors that influences entrepreneurial intention among women in Nigeria: A study based in South-East Nigeria", *The Journal of Entrepreneurship*, 26 (2): 176–195.

Kamdem, E. and R. Ikelle (2011) "Management de la diversité et genre au Cameroun: Une approche en termes d'accompagnement de l'entrepreneuriat féminin", *Humanisme et Entreprise*, 5 (305): 49–64.

Kumar, N. P. (2019) "Paving the way for transformational future – Women entrepreneurs in Uttar Pradesh", *Productivity*, 60 (1): 42–56.

Mbodji Diop, Ndéye Sira (2019) *Le processus entrepreneurial féminin: Une approche compréhensive dans le contexte sénégalais.* PhD thesis in management, Université de Lille.

Memili, E., H. C. Fang and D. H. B. Welsh (2015) "Value creation and value appropriation in innovation process in publicly traded family firms", *Management Decision*, 53 (9): 1921–1952.

Moore, D. P. and E. H. Buttner (1997) *Women Entrepreneurs: Moving Beyond the Glass Ceiling*. Thousand Oaks: Sage Publications.

Ouattara, A. (2007) "L'entrepreneuriat féminin en Côte-d'Ivoire: Obstacles et opportunités", *Management international,* II (2): 53–64.

Rajemison, S. (1995) *Femmes entrepreneurs et dynamique entrepreneuriale: cas de Madagascar; les facteurs de performance de l'entreprise*. Paris: Edition AUPELF-UREF, John Libbey Eurotext.

Said, I. and C. Enslin (2020) "Lived experiences of females with entrepreneurship in Sudan: Networking, social expectations, and family support", *Sage Open*, October–December: 1–12.

Sarr, F. (1998) *L'entrepreneuriat féminin au Sénégal, la transformation des rapports de pouvoir*. Paris: L'Harmattan.

Schuerkens, U. (ed.) (2023) *Entreprises, entrepreneurs et travail au Sénégal.* Paris: L'Harmattan.

Schuerkens, U. (2023) "Les femmes entrepreneures au Sénégal et le contexte gégraphique plus large de l'Afrique et de l'Europe", in U. Schuerkens (ed.) *Entreprises, entrepreneurs et travail au Sénégal*, pp. 237–254. Paris: L'Harmattan.

Sheriff, M. and M. Muffatto (2015) "The present state of entrepreneurship ecosystems in selected countries in Africa", *African Journal of Economic and Management Studies*, 4 (1): 17–54.

Sumathi, V. and K. Gunasundari (2016) "Problems faced by the women entrepreneurs in India", *International Journal of Management Research and Reviews*, 6 (3): 348–354.

Websites:

https://der.sn/
https://globalmindconsulting.com/
https://setalmaa.com/
https://oroyal.sn/contact/

8 New Figures in Women's Entrepreneurship in Sub-Saharan Africa

Dakar Women Entrepreneurs between the Global and the Local in Digitalisation[1]

Abdul-Aziz Dembélé

Introduction

In sub-Saharan Africa, women's economic activity is generally measured as one of the highest levels in the world (Charmes, 2005; ILO, 2016). At the end of the economic crisis caused by the COVID-19 pandemic, the International Labour Organisation (ILO) estimated that the employment rate for women in this region was 48.7%, compared with a world average of 43.2% (ILO, 2021). However, these figures conceal major discrepancies both in the sectoral distribution of jobs and in their quality. Over 60% of women workers are employed in agriculture in rural areas (ILO, 2016). In urban areas, although women are present in some government departments and modern businesses, protected salaried employment remains essentially male (Charmes, 2005; Locoh, 2013). Women are most active in the informal economy, the main source of employment in sub-Saharan Africa (ILO, 2016). Most of their activities are carried out as family helpers in generally precarious conditions, or through the creation of commercial activities ranging from street or itinerant saleswomen to wholesale trade in marketplaces (Locoh, 2013).

In the literature on women's economic activity in sub-Saharan Africa, the emphasis is generally placed on their entrepreneurial skills (Sylvanus, 2006; Schuerkens, 2008) illustrated by two major figures. The first, a "figure of economic success and power" (Banéga and Warnier, 2001), is that of the businesswoman involved in transnational trade networks. This figure was embodied by the famous Nana Benz (Cordonnier, 1987; Boni, 2008; Coquery-Vidrovitch, [1994] 2012). These Togolese businesswomen historically dominated the loincloth trade in West Africa before seeing their activities decline in the late 1980s under the effects of competition from low-end products from China (Sylvanus, 2008, 2009; Toulabor, 2012; Vampo, 2021). The second pattern is that of "survival and coping" (Kane and Chroqui, 2021). It can be seen in work on informal economies through the image of petty trade. In the wake of neoliberal reforms, numerous studies have shown how the deterioration in living conditions and the increase in socio-economic inequalities have led more and more African women to multiply this type of income-generating activity to help their families survive (Adjamagbo and Calvès, 2012; Mbembe, 2013). This phenomenon has been described as a "silent revolution" (Locoh, 1996) which has led to a recomposition of male and female roles within households.

DOI: 10.4324/9781003492931-11

While these two major figures continue to leave their mark on the literature on women's entrepreneurship in sub-Saharan Africa, other works have highlighted the emergence of a new generation of female entrepreneurs. Locoh (2013) has already pointed out that, as school enrolment increases, more and more women with qualifications who are affected by unemployment are turning to entrepreneurship. The research of Sylvanus in Togo (2008, 2009) shows how the Nana Benz business has been turned upside down by the emergence of a new generation of transnational traders: The *Nanettes*, who have established new connections with Chinese production centres. In this bygone era of Nana Benz, Toulabor (2012) describes how their daughters and granddaughters took over their businesses. The author points out that these "heiresses" differ from their mothers in terms of their educational capital, a strategy of commercial diversification and discretion and sobriety in the conduct of business. Also in Togo, Vampo (2021) highlighted the emergence of a new generation of female entrepreneurs. In a context where women's entrepreneurship is still associated with the image of women traders in the informal economy, the author describes women entrepreneurs, most of whom are university graduates, who define themselves as "modern" entrepreneurs in reference to a model of entrepreneurship associated with the formal sector. The emergence of new women entrepreneurs in sub-Saharan Africa is also attested by Ulrike Schuerkens in her recent study on Senegal (Schuerkens, 2023b and 2023c). The author describes women entrepreneurs from the upper and middle classes who draw on the educational capital and professional experience they acquired during their migration to Europe to set up and develop businesses. Ulrike Schuerkens emphasises that this new generation of women entrepreneurs, situated at the crossroads of global and local dynamics (Schuerkens, 2023) gives symbolic meaning to their businesses as a contribution to the African community, while at the same time demonstrating ethics based on individual responsibility and action.

Following on from the work just mentioned, this chapter explores the trajectories of Senegalese women belonging to this new generation of entrepreneurs. It is based on fieldwork carried out in Dakar, Senegal.[2] The survey began with interviews with managers of public, private, and voluntary organisations dedicated to supporting entrepreneurship.[3] The initial methodological assumption was that these institutional players in the entrepreneurial ecosystem could point me in the direction of women entrepreneurs who met the initial research criteria, i.e., women entrepreneurs operating in the formal sector. These initial exploratory interviews gave me access to women entrepreneurs who had already received support or financing. The survey was then conducted using the "snowball" method (Noy, 2008) which consists of asking a respondent to nominate other potential respondents, thus creating a chain of "*close contacts*" (Blanchet and Gotman, 2017). In the Dakar context, where women's entrepreneurship is most visible among informal economy traders, this research method proved particularly effective. By mobilising the social relations of the respondents (Blanchet and Gotman, 2017), some of whom belong to associative groups, the close-in method provided access to the hidden population of women entrepreneurs in the formal sector. One of the disadvantages of this method, however, is the selection bias likely to lead to the constitution of a homogeneous sample from a socio-demographic point of view. In order to overcome this limitation and maximise the probability of the appearance of strong cases (Becker, 2013) interviews were conducted with other female entrepreneurs contacted via the LinkedIn social network or through informants met during the survey. This approach made it possible to broaden the scope of the research and to include women entrepreneurs who did not work in the formal sector but whose level of education made it possible to assimilate them into the overall study population.

Table 8.1 summarises the profile of the respondents. The sample is made up of 15 female entrepreneurs aged between 24 and 42. Most of their businesses are less than five years old, with the oldest dating back to 2013. They operate in sectors such as digital, fashion, para-pharmacy, personal services, audio-visual production, business consultancy, agro-industry, and agribusiness.

Based on an analysis of life stories, this chapter looks at the reasons, resources, and subjectivities at work in these women's entrepreneurial endeavours. The chapter is divided into three parts. Firstly, I situate my research in relation to the literature on entrepreneurship and women's entrepreneurship more generally, and in Africa in particular. By delimiting the contours of entrepreneurship, I propose to consider it as a sociological object constructed from a comprehensive approach (Grossetti and Reix, 2014). Based on the categories of female entrepreneurs identified by the analysis of the corpus (see Table 8.1), the second part describes the logic at work in the act of entrepreneurship. Placed in a broader socio-economic context, these logics will be discussed in the light of global and local phenomena such as migration, the increased responsibility of women in the household economy, the tightening of conditions of access to employment for young people and the recent pandemic of COVID-19. Entrepreneurship is first and foremost a question of resources, especially at the start-up stage. The third and final section looks at the resources on which these women rely to develop their businesses. By showing that a significant proportion of these resources are acquired through social trials and institutional selection processes, this section will support the hypothesis that entrepreneurship is experienced by these women as a form of self-affirmation in contrast to the mainstream.

The Entrepreneurial Phenomenon in the Literature: The Gradual Expansion of a Field to Include Women's Entrepreneurship

An abundance of literature has been produced on entrepreneurship, a major contemporary theme. As Fayolle argues (2004), an attempt to provide a complete and detailed representation of its coverage by academic research seems illusory. This section aims to highlight several salient points within a field covered by different disciplines.

It was the economic sciences that initially questioned the entrepreneurial phenomenon from the point of view of its supposed role in the development of capitalism. Tracing the evolution of the economic theory of the entrepreneur, Boutillier and Tiran (2016) show how it has evolved from the Schumpeterian

Table 8.1 Categorisation and summary presentation of respondents

Categories	*Forename*	*Age*	*Study level*	*Place of graduation*	*Company creation date*	*Company statute*	*Number of employees*
Returning migrant entrepreneurs	Mariama T.	34	University	France/Canada	2013	Formal	15
	N'Deye N.	36	University	France	2021	Formal	5
	Siny S.	31	University	France/Canada	2021	Formal	7
Expatriate women entrepreneurs	Aicha D.	35	University	France/Canada	2021	Formal	1
	Sabrina C.	40	University	France	2020	Formal	5
"Ordinary" women entrepreneurs	Aissatou L.	33	University	Senegal	2020	Formal	15
	Fatou D.	37	Secondary	Senegal	2015	In the process of being formalised	0
	Kalista S.	42	University	Senegal	2019	Formal	15
	Yandé T.	37	University	Senegal	2020	Formal	4
Student entrepreneurs	Betty K.	24	University	Senegal	2020	Formal	0
	Cathy D.	29	University	Senegal	2022	Formal	0
Women entrepreneurs in the pandemic	Awa D.	37	University	Canada/United States	2021	Formal	5
	Jeanne S.	33	University	France	2021	Formal	0
	Latifa D.	28	University	Senegal	2020	Formal	3
	Sina G.	32	University	Senegal	2021	Formal	0

Note: Although some of the surveyed female entrepreneurs reported not having employees, most of them have partners, usually family members with whom they work. Others reported using contractors for delivery services or to meet occasional surges in demand.

entrepreneur (Schumpeter, [1951] 2021) introducing new combinations of factors of production to the Kirznerian entrepreneur (Kirzner, 2009), vigilant for profit opportunities.

Outside economics, entrepreneurship has been studied by psychology and the behavioural sciences. This is particularly true of the famous "push/pull" theory of Shapero and Sokol (1982), which explains the entrepreneurial phenomenon on the basis of a number of motivational factors. According to this theory, individuals set up a company either for so-called "positive" reasons, such as a desire for independence or the discovery of a business opportunity, thus *pulling* them (*pull*) away from the company that employs them; or for "negative" reasons, such as unemployment, pushing them (*push*) to take their future into their own hands. This theory, while interesting, has been challenged by the fact that, although presented as mutually exclusive, these two dimensions can overlap and vary over time (Gabarret and Vedel, 2015). Another striking approach is that of personality traits (Gartner, 1989). Focusing on individuals, research conducted from this perspective aims to produce knowledge on psychological characteristics, behaviour, origins, and social trajectories, with the aim of identifying typical entrepreneurial profiles. The main limitation of this approach lies in its essentialism (Gartner, 1988; Pesqueux, 2012) suggesting that certain individuals have an "entrepreneurial instinct".

It is in management sciences that new approaches to entrepreneurship have recently emerged. These have opened up new perspectives insofar as the approach aims less to explain the entrepreneurial phenomenon than to understand how it unfolds (Fayolle, 2004; Pesqueux, 2012). The research carried out within this framework espouses two main perspectives. The "situationist" perspective integrates the environment into the analysis of entrepreneurship by looking at how business opportunities are discovered and exploited. The second perspective, "interactionist", focuses on the way in which individuals interact with their environment in carrying out an entrepreneurial project. By integrating social dimensions into the study of entrepreneurship, these new approaches are in line with the perspectives opened by the literature on entrepreneurial ecosystems and their role in business creation (Isenberg, 2010; Laperche et al., 2019; Cao and Shi, 2021; Stam and van de Ven, 2021).

Academic interest has also focused on women's entrepreneurship. This is particularly true of feminist studies, which highlight the invisibility of women in relation to the implicit male norm around which representations of entrepreneurship have historically been constructed (Chasserio et al., 2016). Research from this perspective focuses on the specific motivations of women entrepreneurs, their profiles, and their ways of being in business (Alexandre, 2016; D'Andria and Gabarret, 2016). The main focus is on gender, defined as the "socially constructed sex" (Constantinidis, 2014). Approaches in terms of gender question the asymmetrical differentiations of masculine and feminine as well as the power relationships between the sexes considered as structuring factors likely to account for the disparities between women and men in entrepreneurial activity (Chasserio et al., 2016). Numerous studies can be found, such as those by Gupta and Turban (2012),

Balanchandra et al. (2019), and Bellier and Idi Cheffou (2019), which point to the impact of stereotypes on the perception of women entrepreneurs. However, most of these studies focus on northern countries.

As far as the countries of the South are concerned, the literature on women's entrepreneurship generally focuses on the obstacles they face in launching an entrepreneurial activity. Based on a review of the literature, Goyal and Yadav (2014) identified five main barriers: (1) difficulties in accessing finance; (2) cultural factors such as male dominance and domestic roles assigned to women; (3) individual and social factors such as lack of confidence and social recognition; (4) weak legal and institutional structures, and (5) lack of entrepreneurial skills and education. Although women's entrepreneurship is now recognised as a factor in job creation and socio-economic development in southern countries, particularly in Africa (Boateng, 2018), the dominant image that emerges from the literature, with the notable exception of the works cited in the introduction (Sylvanus, 2008, 2009; Toulabor, 2012; Vampo, 2021; Schuerkens, 2023c), is still that of entrepreneurs out of survival or necessity (D'Andria and Gabarret, 2016).

This chapter aims to fill this gap by highlighting new figures in women's entrepreneurship in Senegal. The approach adopted is not so much to start from a prior definition of the object "entrepreneur" as to consider entrepreneurship as a social activity in the Weberian sense of the term, i.e., an activity whose progress relates to the behaviour of others (Weber, [1956] 2008). It is therefore understandable that this study does not focus on the economic performance of the women entrepreneurs I met. In fact, most of them expressed reservations about declaring their annual sales figures. This was not the case for the number of employees, which provides an indication of the level of development of their business. In the context of sub-Saharan Africa, where entrepreneurship has been promoted for some years now in view of its expected socio-economic impact (Chapus et al., 2021), an approach that focuses on job creation seemed appropriate. Nor does this work focus on the gendered dimensions of entrepreneurship, although gender relations will be mentioned in the discussion. Instead, this study is part of a comprehensive sociology whose aim is to give an account of the subjective meaning given by these women to entrepreneurial activity and the ways in which it is carried out.

Reasons to Do Business

The women entrepreneurs surveyed stand out in Senegal in two ways. With the exception of one, they are all higher education graduates in a country with just over 200,000 students (Sagna, 2022) out of a population of 18 million.[4] Above all, most of them run formal businesses in a context where 97% of the economic fabric is made up of informal enterprises (Dieng and Diaw, 2023). These distinctive features do not, however, make them a homogeneous class. Our analysis based on emerging categories (Paillé, 2011) will show that there are significant differences in the reasons for business creation.

Return from Migration and Entrepreneurship

The first category of entrepreneur is that described in the literature as a "returnee entrepreneur". Before presenting the cases belonging to this category, it will be interesting to carry out a brief review of the literature to get a general idea.

Defined as an individual who has studied and/or acquired professional experience abroad – in the countries of the North in particular – before setting up a business in their country of origin (Drori et al., 2009). In recent years, the returning entrepreneur has been the subject of sustained attention in academic research (Gruenhagen et al., 2020). In fact, these men and women are reputed to be individuals with skills, and some authors see them as "knowledge brokers" (Lin et al., 2016). In other words, they are agents for disseminating and adapting knowledge and technologies produced in the North to countries in the South. So, unlike the "brain drain" issue that has long characterised research on student or professional migration (Jamid et al., 2020), the literature on return entrepreneurship embraces the paradigm of transnationalism by emphasising the importance of "brain circulation" (Saxenian, 2002).

Although important, the literature on return entrepreneurship focuses mainly on emerging Asian countries, particularly China, India, and Taiwan (Kenney et al., 2013; Pruthi, 2014; Qin et al., 2017; Gruenhagen et al., 2020). In existing work on sub-Saharan Africa, the focus is more on the conditions likely to encourage return migration than on return entrepreneurship as such. This work, carried out in several countries such as Mali (Mary, 2014), Senegal, the Democratic Republic of Congo (Flahaux, 2015), the Comoros, and Togo (Bréant, 2019, 2020), indicates that migrants who choose to return are generally those from the upper classes and/or whose initial objective was to acquire diplomas and professional skills. Following on from the research already begun by Cerase (1974) and Cassarino (2004) on return migration, these studies emphasise that return plans are closely linked to the economic and social resources available to migrants, as well as to the prospects for professional reintegration in their country of origin. My survey sample allows me to envisage several cases of return migration leading to entrepreneurship.

The first category includes those who chose to return to work directly after their university education. They initially held a salaried position before setting up their own business. N'Deye N. is the daughter of retired parents who had previously worked as managers in the Senegalese public sector. She returned to France after completing a management degree at a leading business school. Although as a teenager, she regularly went on holiday to France, she explains that she "never envisaged living outside Senegal".[5] After graduating, she sought to gain initial professional experience, without success, before being offered the opportunity to join a major auditing and consulting firm in Dakar. Describing herself as a "hands-on person" who was quickly won over by the "boredom of office work", N'Deye N. became an entrepreneur alongside her salaried activity. First in 2017, with the creation of an events structure offering services dedicated to women, but the project didn't work out; then in 2021, with the creation of an agricultural services business. Through her company, which now employs five people, N'Deye N. offers "solutions to all those who want to invest in agriculture in Senegal", with advice on land and crop selection as well as business planning. Mariama T.'s career path is like that of N'Deye N. Her return, justified by her attachment to Senegal, was also facilitated by the opportunity to take up salaried employment in Dakar after obtaining a degree in journalism in Canada. But unlike N'Deye N., who describes herself as a "serial entrepreneur", Mariama T. confides that she "never thought about entrepreneurship before starting".[6] Her business plan is based on the discrepancy between the ways in which she lived out her passion for dance: on the one hand, in the streets of Dakar out of sight of her parents when she was a teenager, and on the other, in formal structures during her time as a student in Canada. After four years as a communication officer in a public agency, she has been running a company offering dance lessons since 2013, with 15 employees. Mariama T. believes she has turned her passion into a business opportunity.

Siny S.'s story offers a second example of entrepreneurship on return from migration. Unlike the previous interviewees, Siny S. did not choose to return to Toulouse after her studies. After graduating as an agri-food engineer, she had her first job in Research and Development with a multinational specialising in baby food. Although she "saw herself pursuing a career in the big multinational food companies",[7] Siny S. explains that she was "triggered" during a holiday in Senegal when she noticed that the baby food market was essentially made up of imported products: "I saw that there was a market opportunity in the baby food sector, I had the professional skills and experience in the field [...]; there were also local resources that were not being exploited and I said to myself why not transform them and offer a local product". That's how she came to the decision to return for good: "I was 25 and I told myself that if worse came to worst, if it didn't work out, I'd have my CV and I wouldn't have any trouble finding a job". Siny S. now runs a company with seven employees offering a "100% Made in Senegal" range of baby food products.

Expatriate Entrepreneurs

The stories of Sabrina C. and Aicha D. illustrate an original situation that has received very little attention in the literature on migration and entrepreneurship. Unlike the previous stories, these two interviewees do not come from families settled in Senegal. One was a French-Senegalese woman who was born and lived in France before marrying a Senegalese man, while the other, married to a Chadian like herself, lived between France and Canada for 12 years. Rather than returning, we should be talking here about a diaspora expatriation process that has led to the creation of businesses. The plan to leave their countries of residence, which these respondents say, they formulated jointly with their respective partners, is expressed in different ways.

Sabrina C. explains that she and her husband felt "limited in their professional development" and no longer "felt they were serving a purpose in their respective jobs"[8] in France. The couple also aspired to "a better life for their children". For Aicha D. and her husband, the plan to leave was more in line with a "desire to return to Africa after achieving professional fulfilment".[9] She also explains that she did not want to follow in the footsteps of previous generations of immigrants who "return for retirement or when they are too old". The decision to leave Canada was taken when her husband was offered a job in Senegal. With her diploma as a dental assistant and her professional experience, Aicha D. didn't stay unemployed for long. Alongside her work as a consultant for dental practices, she is continuing her entrepreneurial activity, initially launched in Canada, of selling eco-responsible hygiene products.

For Sabrina C. and her husband, the choice of Senegal seemed more obvious. As they had become accustomed to staying there regularly during their holidays, she says she was able to observe changes in the socio-economic context and thus describes their resettlement process:

> This famous growing middle class is a reality. We saw leisure activities developing, and that's what clicked for us. We also had a few Senegalese people around us in France who were looking to move back home, so my husband and I started talking about it. And we saw that French companies based in Senegal had adopted a new policy of hiring Senegalese from the diaspora. We jumped on the bandwagon, and within two years it was a done deal. All we had to do was to find a job so that we could pay the bills, because we've got children after all, and then we had a few things to sort out in France. Once everything was validated, well, we quit our jobs. We kept the house we had to see what it would be like when we got back.

In 2015, after her husband was offered a job, the couple resettled in Senegal. Sabrina C. initially sought salaried employment before setting up a consultancy business, which was re-founded in 2020 with a partner, who was also an expatriate. By pooling their expertise, in law for Sabrina C. and in management for her partner, their five-employee business offers advice on legal security and corporate strategy.

"Ordinary" Women Entrepreneurs

The famous theory of Shapero and Sokol (1982) mentioned above, distinguishes two ideal types of entrepreneurship: "push" entrepreneurship linked to not having a job or dissatisfaction at work, and "pull" entrepreneurship resulting from the discovery of a business opportunity or a desire for independence. It was by looking at this theory that I developed the second category of entrepreneurs: "ordinary" women entrepreneurs.

Fatou D. is an exemplary case of entrepreneurship in a "push" situation. A resident of Guédiawaye, a working-class district in the suburbs of Dakar, she comes from a sibling group whose members migrated to Europe "to try their luck".[10] Left with a widowed mother, Fatou D. dropped out of school at secondary level. For her, "in general, when you come from the suburbs and you haven't had an advanced education, you start your own business". Thanks to remittances from her migrant brothers, Fatou D. first tried her hand at livestock farming, which she saw as a hobby to earn pocket money. When she got married, she gave up her activities for a while: "In Senegal, when you get married, they say it's the husband who has to take care of everything", before taking them up again later: "With my husband, it was starting to be hard to make a living and there was no one to help us". Faced with the economic constraints in her household, Fatou D. set up a sewing workshop from which she sold dresses via Facebook. This was in 2015, when, according to her, this sales technique had not yet been developed in Senegal. The success of this activity led her to transform her Facebook page first into a platform for selling various products, and then into a system of digital tontines:

> I saw that there were a lot of people asking me for the price of goods online but who didn't have the option of paying in cash. So, I came up with the idea of bringing them together and setting up groups with weekly contributions. It was a bit difficult at first because people didn't know me and didn't trust me. The first people came to see me [...], I started with ten people and then these ten people told other people about it and that's how we set up the tontine. From 100,000 F-CFA in contributions every ten days, we went up to 9 million, because we created a lot of tontines after that.

Fatou D. has won several national competitions for her success in digitalising the informal tontine system via Facebook, and her story has been described as a *success story* by *Forbes Afrique* magazine.[11] However, her activities came to a halt at the time of the COVID-19 pandemic. Fatou D. is now working on formalising her business and setting up an application to stand out from the competition, which has copied her model.

Fatou D.'s story is an illustration of the changes taking place in contemporary Senegalese and African patriarchal societies, where the rise in the precariousness of the working and middle classes is leading more and more women to take on responsibilities for household "survival" (Locoh, 1996; Adjamagbo and Calvès, 2012; Mbembe, 2013; Pinard, 2016). Another illustration is provided by the case of Yandé T. This woman, a computer and industrial electronics engineer, became an entrepreneur after losing her job. A "mother"[12] who for a time had to move back into her parents' house when her couple could no longer afford the cost of their flat. Yandé T. has set up a poultry farm that she plans to develop through a circular economy project.

"Ordinary" entrepreneurship is not only the result of economic constraints. It can also arise from a desire for professional fulfilment and independence. This is the case of Kalista S. Trained as a journalist, she worked for 15 years in Senegal's public broadcasting system before becoming head of a television series production company. Included on the BBC's list of the "100 most inspiring women" of 2019,[13] this creator of internationally successful series sees her move into entrepreneurship as a "professional and passionate reconversion"[14] at a time when she was much more attracted to activities such as scriptwriting and directing that "spoke to her and [allowed her] to be invested, whatever the time and the moment". Aissatou L. follows a similar path. After ten years' experience in human resources consultancies in Dakar, this human resources graduate decided to set up her own business for reasons of autonomy and professional advancement: "During my last experience as an HR manager in a consultancy, I was doing almost 80% of the tasks [...], which is why I said to myself why not set up my own business and do them myself".[15]

Students and Entrepreneurs

In a recent study conducted in Senegal, Ulrike Schuerkens (2023a) highlighted the links that can exist between the worlds of academia and business. Her analysis shows that in a context marked by the deterioration in conditions of access to employment for young graduates, the implementation of university programmes, modules, and incubators is now an integral part of the strategy of business schools to encourage and support students in setting up their own businesses. Betty K. is one of those students who have been introduced to entrepreneurship as part of their university studies. During her studies at the prestigious *Ecole Supérieure Polytechnique de Dakar*, she was a member of a student club like the American NGO Enactus,[16] whose aim was to design and implement social projects in rural areas. Betty K. sees this experience as a decisive factor in her career, because "knowing how to make an impact on people's lives"[17] gave her the desire to become an entrepreneur, especially in a context where "we can no longer wait for the state to give students jobs [...], there aren't enough places for all those who graduate each year". That's how she came up with the idea, long before she graduated as a public health engineer, of launching a project to produce "100% Made in Senegal" cheeses. This project, which she led with two friends from the entrepreneurs' club, benefited from the technical support of the school's teaching staff. After winning several prizes for their project, these student-entrepreneurs have now graduated and moved on to marketing their products.

There is also another form of student entrepreneurship outside the university context, as illustrated by the story of Cathy D. A half-scholarship holder of the Senegalese government when she left secondary school, Cathy D. launched an informal micro-business hiring out cutlery and kitchen utensils for weddings, christenings, and other events. Her aim was to pay her school fees following the death of her father: "I had enormous difficulties. That was my first idea, to make money".[18] Thanks to her better grades, she was finally able to get a full scholarship to study for a degree in management. At the time of the survey, Cathy D. was studying for an MBA at a private British institute in Dakar, which she financed through her job as a sales manager. With her "busy" schedule requiring "organisation and sacrifice", Cathy D., who describes herself as someone who "enjoys researching and sharing information", devotes her weekends to her YouTube channel, which she set up in 2020. Her videos, which offer "business ideas for Senegal and Africa", are viewed by an average of 500 internet users, but have not yet reached the minimum monetisation threshold of 1,000 subscribers.

The sociologist Akindès recently proposed the term "*youth paradox*" to characterise a situation that is evident in Africa, where young people and youth are the subject of political rhetoric promising them a better future, while, faced with both the increasing precariousness of jobs and the tougher conditions for accessing them, "their present eludes them and leaves them few prospects for transforming their living conditions" (2022: 95). While the trajectories of these two student-entrepreneurs may serve to illustrate this youthful paradox, it seems to me that they also reflect an awareness of an epochal change. As Ulrike Schuerkens has pointed out, many Senegalese graduates now see a career as an entrepreneur as a "realistic alternative to employment" (2023b: 289). This observation is confirmed by Cathy D., who sees herself as an entrepreneur while remaining employed:

> I expected to have my qualifications and a very good salary, a very good job, a car, that's what I honestly expected. But things have changed. In the beginning, our parents told us that we had to work, that we had to learn, that we had to go to school and get good grades to get a job. But nowadays that doesn't guarantee you a job, or a good salary [...], things aren't like they used to be.

Women Entrepreneurs in Times of Pandemic

In Senegal, as elsewhere in sub-Saharan Africa, the COVID-19 crisis has had a considerable negative impact on economic growth and household well-being (World Bank, 2020; Razafindrakoto and Wachsberger, 2021; Schuerkens, 2023a). Businesses have borne the brunt of the measures taken by governments to prevent the spread of the disease. My sample, essentially made up of young businesses, provides a better understanding of the effects of COVID-19 on entrepreneurial activity. The case of Mariama T. speaks for itself. With her dance business, she was led to offer online courses, without success because "few people in Africa consume paid content online".[19] This entrepreneur considers the period of confinement to be one of the greatest challenges she has had to face in her ten years in business: "We were closed for a few months, I don't know how long, but I tend to tell people that it disturbed me so much that I started drinking coffee".

But the disruptive effects of the pandemic were not all negative. Latifa D., who runs a family business that provides training for women in rural areas on behalf of international NGOs, saw the crisis as a moment of reflection and a "wake-up call"[20] that led to the company's activities being redirected towards the agri-food sector: "COVID triggered something in me. I said to myself, well, it's time we created a brand of products following on from the training courses we were offering to rural women". So, the company set up a production unit and a label for vegetable meat, drawing on its internal resources and skills, as well as groups of women cashew nut producers. Returning to Dakar from the United States after a bachelor's degree in information technology, several professional experiences and a marriage that "didn't work out",[21] Awa D. also saw the crisis as an opportunity to set up her own business. When the multinational company specialising in STEM support for children,[22] which employed her, closed its branch for good, Awa D. decided to take over the concept. Her tutoring services in science, technology, engineering, art, and maths are now available in five public schools in Dakar.

The sample also includes two other women who this time chose to leave their jobs at the time of the crisis to become entrepreneurs. Here's what they have to say:

> During COVID, I worked for a small organisation. The person who employed me forced me to go out into the field with all the risks. I had to take precautions when I got home to my family [...], and the pay wasn't at all commensurate with the workload. I knew I was being exploited. So, I said to myself, what I'm doing now, I can do for myself. (Jeanne S., master's degree in project management, interview conducted on 18 August 2023)
>
> I was a teacher in a private American school in Dakar. [...] With COVID, we had to give online courses. They gave us a huge workload, but the pay wasn't worthwhile or enough to cover my expenses. When I came back from France, I had projects, and I took this job to be able to finance them. But I was earning so little that I didn't even have enough to save. There was no interest, so I said to myself, now's the time. (Sina G., master's graduate in literature, interview conducted on 21 August 2023)

The portraits I have just sketched are important for several reasons. Firstly, they give an insight into the profiles of women entrepreneurs who have hitherto featured very little in Africanist academic literature. In addition, by drawing on both the testimonies and the reflexive view that these women have of their respective careers, I have attempted to grasp and convey the complexity and multidimensional nature of entrepreneurship in general (Fayolle, 2004) and more specifically that of women (Constantinidis, 2014). From the descriptions provided, these women's commitment to entrepreneurship stems from a variety of factors linked to personal dispositions, individual or family aspirations, the discovery of business opportunities, economic constraints, and even exceptional circumstances such as the recent COVID-19 pandemic. Finally, and from a macro-social perspective, I have attempted to describe these new forms of female entrepreneurship in the light of the global and local dynamics that are traversing and transforming contemporary societies in sub-Saharan Africa, such as the migration phenomena of expatriation and return, the increased responsibility of women in the household economy, and the tightening of conditions of access to employment for young people. It now remains to be seen how these women go about developing their businesses.

Resources and Subjectivity in the Entrepreneurial Act

Several sociological studies (Granovetter, 2000; Grossetti and Reix, 2014) have emphasised that, over and above the reasons that may lead an individual to become an entrepreneur, business creation is first and foremost a question of economic, social, and even institutional resources. After highlighting the different resources on which the women entrepreneurs rely to develop their businesses, this section supports the hypothesis that the nature of the resources available to these women entrepreneurs and the ways in which they access them lead to forms of "self-assertion" as distinct from the mainstream.

Economic Resources at the Outset

Money is the driving force behind turning an entrepreneurial idea or desire into reality. Most of the women I met felt that they could not have obtained start-up finance from banking institutions. Instead, they mobilised three types of resources. As is generally the case at the start of an entrepreneurial activity, the first economic resources consisted of personal savings. This was the case for Awa D.: "I worked for a while, so I had some savings. I didn't have a lot, but I started little by little"; or Aicha D., who left Canada with her husband: "Part of it is a personal investment of savings and I reinvest what the business brings in". Sina G., for her part, explains that she left her flat to move back in with her family to free up the money to launch her business.

This first type of resource can be coupled with a second type, generally referred to as "love money", i.e., family support, as was the case for Mariama T.: "A large part of the funding was my own capital [...], and another part was paid for by my father so that we could run advertising campaigns"; or financial support from friends and family, as Aissatou L. explains: "At the beginning, I had a lot of money worries, so it were friends who helped me by lending me money to pay salaries".

In addition to these first two resources, there is a third: salaries. Some women entrepreneurs, particularly those whose businesses have not yet reached a satisfactory level, have salaried jobs. They are both entrepreneurs and consultants (N'Deye N., Awa D.), programme managers (Yandé T.), or communications managers (Cathy D.). For N'Deye N., this double-hatted strategy of using her salary as a source of finance can have a negative impact on the development of the business:

> I dream of the time when I'm going to put an end to this consultancy because my entrepreneurial activity takes up 120% of my time. [...]. I can't be as productive as I want to be. In Senegal, if you're not behind every member of your staff as an entrepreneur, you break your back. As soon as you let go of your business for a while, you can quickly run into surprises. It's enough to make you tear your hair out.

Cognitive Resources

In developing their businesses, the women I met also rely on cognitive resources. Most of them have higher education qualifications and express what I might consider to be a "capacity to learn how to learn". Indeed, the terms "reading up", "doing research", or "learning as you go along" were regularly used. Several testimonials illustrate this willingness to learn:

> Sometimes I read up on the Internet about management, or how to develop my business, or how to get good visibility on social networks and so on. (Aissatou L.)
>
> We research and learn. [...]. I read up on lots of things, I'm really interested in the subject. I'm interested in new technologies, in ways of modernising agriculture [...]. There are short courses that don't make you an engineer,

> but at least you learn something. As soon as I see agriculture somewhere, I stop and try to see what I can learn. (N'Deye N.)
>
> I've read many, many books on management, project management and so on. And a lot of Learning by Doing. But a lot of entrepreneur podcasts, a lot of books and that's it, I think that's essential. (Mariama T.)
>
> You can't evolve by sticking to what you've got, because everything is renewed. I didn't understand English, but I signed up on a website to attend the Master Classes in Shanghai, for which I paid 200 dollars. And when I work on international productions with people who have worked on major projects, I also learn techniques and ways of doing things [...]. The best training is when you learn from people who are good. (Kalista S.)

The Social and Institutional Environment

The literature on what is known as "entrepreneurial ecosystems" (Isenberg, 2010; Laperche et al., 2019; Cao and Shi, 2021; Stam and Van de Ven, 2021) emphasises the importance of the social, cultural, and institutional environment, in other words the "social worlds" in the development of entrepreneurial activity. At the start and throughout their entrepreneurial careers, the women I met also benefited from resources drawn from their respective social worlds.

Social and Professional Environment

These resources can be interpersonal in nature. Mariama T. explains that she lived in an environment made up of young people who, like her, had returned from migration and were carrying out their business project:

> At the time, there were about ten of us young people returning from Morocco, France, or the United States, and we were together almost all the time, having drinks together to talk about the challenges of our different projects, because we all started out more or less at the same time. There were also those who had preceded us by a few years. [...] I was reluctant to start my own business and they were the ones who helped me get over the hurdle.

Fatou D. also confides that her career was marked by her involvement in the charity of the Senegalese rapper *Fou Malade,* known in the literature as one of the leaders of *Y'en a Marre*, a political protest movement from the suburbs of Dakar that promotes an ethos of success through effort and work (Dimé, 2017; Mbaye, 2021). She believes that it was this rapper who "helped her see [her] potential" and "invest herself in her community". Fatou D. has set up an association which, every year since 2022, has organised an economic forum specifically dedicated to the suburbs because, in her view, "there are a lot of entrepreneurs in the suburbs, but the problem is that we don't get any support from the start".

For those who are both entrepreneurs and employees, the professional world is not just a means of acquiring economic resources. In some cases, such as that of

Cathy D. (employee and Youtube artist), the professional activity can be a place to draw on other types of resources:

I'm in marketing and communications. So, I asked for training on Adobe Première Pro paid for by the company. I was trained for a week, and it helped me to edit my videos on YouTube.

Incubators and Support Programmes for Entrepreneurs

The careers of these women are also marked by their participation in networking events, competitions, training, or incubation programmes organised by local private or voluntary organisations involved in entrepreneurial support. In fact, 11 of the 15 women entrepreneurs I met had taken part in this type of event at least once in their careers, and five of them had been through Orange Corners and MVP Lab 221, two incubation programmes (see Figures 8.1 and 8.2). These selective programmes, which last several months and offer monthly stipends, are recognised by those who have taken part as being decisive for their development:

> The fact that I trained as an accountant and had no idea of anything to do with business management, anything to do with management, anything to do with entrepreneurship, so I had to learn, and it was through Orange Corners that I learnt a lot of things. (Latifa D.)

Figure 8.1 MVP Lab 221 incubation programme poster showing the number of applications received.

Figure 8.2 Orange Corners incubation programme poster showing the number of applications received.

With Orange Corners and the training courses on artificial intelligence and business, this is what opened my eyes and enabled me to set up parallel activities such as e-service. (Jeanne S.)

We'd actually done a market study to find out about our competitors, but we didn't know how to understand the market, how to enter it and what strategy to adopt. These six months of incubation at Orange Corners enabled us to do just that. (Betty K.)

With the MVP Lab, it's education. You learn different things that you didn't think about when you were starting out. It gives you useful skills. (Awa D.)

As an entrepreneur, you're really on your own, you're in your own bubble, you think you know. But that's not always the case. The MVP Lab is all about practical experience. It's very intense, but that's really what an entrepreneur need. (Aicha D.)

The Institutional Environment

Finally, the resources of the institutional environment can be highlighted to some extent. In Senegal, various mechanisms have been put in place by the public authorities to support business start-ups. These include the General Delegation for Rapid Entrepreneurship for Women and Young People (DER/FJ). Kalista S. received funding from this agency when she launched her business, while N'Deye N. was awaiting a response to a funding application submitted in 2021. As for Sabrina C., the creation of this public agency played an indirect but decisive role in the development of her consultancy structure for small and medium-sized enterprises: "With the advent of the DER, businesses received mass information telling them: if you want to have access to funding, well, you have to structure and formalise yourself. That helps us get customers".

"Not Everyone Can Be an Entrepreneur"

All the women I met were positive about their commitment to entrepreneurship. They see it not only as a form of personal fulfilment and financial independence but also as a way of having a say in the world around them. The terms "value creation", "social impact", and "contribution to development" are regularly used in their discourses, and some of them, like Kalista S., see themselves as pioneers of a new generation: "When you are a pioneer in a field, you have to do things well, you have to be rigorous, hard-working, respectful and have everything you need to reassure the older generation, but also to guide the younger generation to follow in our footsteps".

These women also used terms such as "resilience", "perseverance", "courage", "abnegation", "sacrifice", "ability to manage difficulties", "risk-taking", "financial education", and "patience" to describe their commitment to entrepreneurship. These terms are accompanied by a phrase that comes up regularly in the interviews: "Not everyone can be an entrepreneur". This is easy to understand because the justification that completes it generally says in substance: "That employees are also needed to work for those who create businesses". While this can be understood as a criticism of the new rationale of global, neo-liberal capitalism, which pushes individuals to think of themselves as, or become, entrepreneurs (Foucault, 2004; Dardot and Laval, 2009; Boltanski and Chiapello, 2011), it can also be interpreted as an expression of the trials and tribulations experienced by these women during their entrepreneurial careers.

These challenges can be seen at different levels. First and foremost, in terms of social relationships. Many of the women I met felt that their social life was restricted because of their entrepreneurial commitment. This is the case, for example, with Kalista S., who says that she "works late into the night" some weeks, to the point of becoming a "zombie with no social interaction". Cathy D. also confides that she has very little time for going out at weekends, while Siny S. stresses the need for her to put her business ahead of her social obligations: "If I have a site visit and a wedding at the same time, I go to my site visit first because that's what life as an entrepreneur is all about".

Furthermore, most of these women entrepreneurs explain that they made the choice to become entrepreneurs despite their parents' initial reservations and doubts. The case of Sina G. is illustrative. Although she also has a brother who is an entrepreneur, she explains that "the patience they [her parents] had with him as a man was not the same with me as a woman, because I am a mother, wife and daughter". N'Deye N. also recounts a scene from her father's point of view at the start of her business:

> A former colleague of mine and I had come up with the idea of opening a consultancy. I asked her to come to my house so we could have a chat. I was living with my parents at the time. We were in the middle of talking about how we were going to set up the business and all the other things we needed to do. My father stopped by when he saw us in the living room thinking about it. His comment was: "Are you dreaming?" We never continued the discussion [...], that was our first and last meeting.

Although it should be emphasised that the people close to these women eventually supported them in their endeavours, the fact that they went against family authority appears here to be another form of hardship experienced by these women entrepreneurs. A final type of hardship, no less significant, can be seen at the level of intimacy and marital relationships. The cases of Fatou D. and Yandé T. have already shown how women's constrained entrepreneurship can help redefine gender roles within Senegalese and African households. Mariama T.'s account is along the same lines. In her second marriage, she sees her commitment to her business as one of the reasons for her divorce. For Kalista S., entrepreneurship as a conscious choice is a matter of negotiating gender relations. Married to an engineer "who tends to come and join [her] in the recording studio" when she's working late, she believes that "when you choose your life partner, he has to understand the world you live in and what you're in for".

Standing Out from the Crowd

It seems to me that the meaning of the phrase "not everyone can be an entrepreneur" is best understood by going through these different social trials. A phrase which thus becomes the expression of a form of "self-affirmation" in distinction to the many. This expression, which ran through all the interviews, was used above all by those whose businesses had reached a relatively high level of development:

> I don't see myself as a woman and an entrepreneur, I see myself as an entrepreneur, meaning that I can do everything a man can do and do it ten times better. I run my business on my own [...]. Women are born leaders and managers at the same time. (Awa D.)
>
> I did it all on my own, with no help from anyone. Not everyone can do what I did. (Aissatou L.)
>
> I did it [starting a business] because I was motivated, and I had an opportunity. I had the resources, and the resources were financial, but they were also mental and psychological. (Mariama T.)
>
> When I started out, I had nothing, I didn't know anyone. There was no one to show me the ropes. I was just lucky to come across a production company.

> They let me get on with it and the result is there. But I worked hard; it's hard work. (Kalista S.)

It is undoubtedly paradoxical that these women entrepreneurs have not only relied on their own personal resources to create and develop their businesses, but also on the resources of the social worlds in which they live. But the contradiction is only apparent. On the one hand, we need to bear in mind the social hardships experienced by these women entrepreneurs. On the other hand, it should be emphasised that entrepreneurship is one of the economic activities that relies most heavily – especially at start-up – on individual resources and dispositions. Furthermore, it was pointed out that the resources of their ecosystem, including access to finance and incubation programmes, are only obtained through an institutional selection process. Finally, entrepreneurship is about doing business, and this necessarily involves the market, which excludes those least able to compete. It is clear, therefore, that if the entrepreneurial careers of these women are expressed as generally positive experiences, they are so through social structures and institutions that lead to forms of "self-affirmation" as distinct from the mainstream.

Conclusion

As part of a comprehensive sociology of entrepreneurial activity, the aim of this chapter was to provide an account of the subjective meaning that women entrepreneurs in Dakar give to their activities and the ways in which they are carried out. By drawing on the life stories and reflective views of 15 contemporary women entrepreneurs, this chapter highlighted the complexity and multidimensional nature of entrepreneurial commitment. In the cases studied, this commitment reflects the affirmation of personal dispositions, individual or family aspirations, the discovery of business opportunities, and even economic constraints. But entrepreneurial activity takes place in a wider socio-economic context. We have shown how it can be understood in the light of factors such as migration, the increased responsibility of women in the household economy, the tightening of conditions of access to employment for young people, and the recent pandemic of COVID-19; all phenomena that are affecting contemporary Senegalese and African societies. There was also discussion of the economic, cognitive, social, and institutional resources on which these women rely to develop their businesses. Insofar as a large proportion of these resources are acquired or have been acquired despite social hardship and institutional selection processes, it was argued that these women's entrepreneurship is experienced and expressed as a form of "self-affirmation" in contrast to the mainstream.

In the field of academic research, this study is a contribution that enriches the rare works testifying of the emergence of new figures in women's entrepreneurship in sub-Saharan Africa (Sylvanus, 2006, 2008; Toulabor, 2012; Vampo, 2021; Schuerkens, 2023c). Between the images of the businesswoman as part of transnational trade networks and those of the trader in the informal economy, which are the dominant images in the literature, it now seems clear that sub-Saharan Africa has contemporary female entrepreneurs who are characterised by a high level of education and by the fact that their businesses operate in the formal sector. While it is understood that these women represent a minority in economies dominated by informality, the fact remains that with the demographic growth underway and the continuing progress made in the schooling of young girls in Africa (Antoine et al., 2001; Lange, 2021), we can expect an increase in their numbers in the years to come. In my view, the advent of these new women entrepreneurs opens new avenues for academic research.

Finally, this research is part of a political reflection on entrepreneurship in Africa. As we know, this is an increasingly well-publicised phenomenon (Larcher, 2021): Entrepreneurship has recently become a political issue, as many decision-makers and funding agencies see it as a key factor for development (Chapus et al., 2021). As we have seen, Senegal has set up an agency such as the *Délégation à l'Entrepreneuriat Rapide des Jeunes et des Femmes* (DER/FJ), which assists project creators and supports local private-sector players and associations involved in entrepreneurial support. While these initiatives, which exist in Senegal as in other African countries, are to be encouraged in contexts where there is an acute shortage of successful entrepreneurs, it seems to me that the categories of female entrepreneurs identified in this study suggest that new elements should be introduced into entrepreneurship policies in Africa. The links between higher education and business creation have been highlighted by the category of "student-entrepreneur". The importance of work experience in business creation is seen in the description of "ordinary female entrepreneurs" and "pandemic female entrepreneurs". The cases of "expatriate entrepreneurs" lead me to reflect on the entrepreneurial return of the African diasporas. Finally, with the "returning female entrepreneurs", we saw how the return from student migration could lead to the creation of a business. If these categories can provide a better understanding of business creation, the way forward is not for entrepreneurship policies in Africa, but for a political economy favourable to entrepreneurship. This would include not only initiatives to promote and support entrepreneurship, as is currently the case, but also policies on school enrolment and access to higher education, policies on access to employment for women and young people, and policies to encourage the return of student and diasporic migrants.

Notes

1 The fieldwork for this study was financed by the European project ManaGlobal and was realised in July and August 2023 in Dakar, Senegal.

2 The two-month field survey (July and August 2023) was carried out as part of the ManaGlobal programme supported by the European Union's Horizon 2020 Framework Programme through Marie-Sklodowska Curie Grant Agreement 82374.

3 I got in touch with the *Délégation Générale à l'Entrepreneuriat Rapide des Femmes et des Jeunes* (DER/FJ), a public body whose mission is to support entrepreneurial initiatives. In addition to this public body, contacts have been established with private support structures such as ImpactHub, PitchPalabre, and JokkoLabs. Managers of investment funds specifically dedicated to women entrepreneurs, such as Women Investment Capital (WIC), were also contacted as part of the survey. Finally, inter-

views were conducted with the managers of the SenStartup association, one of whose missions is to represent entrepreneurs to political decision-makers. I would like to thank the managers of this association for their warm welcome and for the opportunity they gave me to use their offices and facilities during my stay. Finally, I would like to express my gratitude to the friendly, enterprising women who accepted my interview requests.

4 Source: *Agence Nationale de la Statistique et de la Démographie du Sénégal.* https://www.ansd.sn/Indicateur/donnees-de-population, accessed on 4 April 2023.
5 Interview conducted on 7 August 2023.
6 Interview conducted on 18 August 2023.
7 Interview conducted on 14 August 2023.
8 Interview conducted on 27 July 2023.
9 Interview conducted on 19 July 2023.
10 Interview conducted on 21 July 2023.
11 See: https://forbesafrique.com/fatou-kine-diop-creatrice-de-tontines-digitales/, accessed on 15 March 2024.
12 Interview conducted on 17 July 2023.
13 See: https://www.bbc.com/afrique/region-50059133,accessed on 27 March 2024.
14 Interview conducted on 3 August 2023.
15 Interview conducted on 25 July 2023.
16 See: https://enactus.fr/
17 Interview conducted on 24 July 2023.
18 Interview conducted on 5 August 2023.
19 Interview conducted on 16 August 2023.
20 Interview conducted on 27 July 2023.
21 Interview conducted on 21 July 2023.
22 STEM stands for Science, Technology, Engineering and Mathematics.

References

Adjamagbo, A. and A.-E. Calvès (2012) "L'émancipation féminine sous contrainte", *Autrepart*, 61 (2): 3–21. https://doi.org/10.3917/autr.061.0003

Akindès, F. (2022) "Le paradoxe jeune: Un défi pour les politiques publiques en Afrique", in Agence française de développement (ed.) *L'économie africaine 2022*, pp. 95–108. Paris: La Découverte. https://www.cairn.info/l-economie-africaine-2022--9782348073601-p-95.htm

Alexandre, L. (2016) "A typology of entrepreneurs, a gendered approach", *Revue de l'Entrepreneuriat / Review of Entrepreneurship*, 15 (3): 109–127. https://www.cairn.int.info/article.php?ID_ARTICLE=E_ENTRE_153_0109

Antoine, P., M. Razafindrakoto, and F. Roubaud (2001) "Contraints de rester jeunes? Évolution de l'insertion dans trois capitales africaines: Dakar, Yaoundé, Antananarivo", *Autrepart*, 18 (2): 17–36. https://doi.org/10.3917/autr.018.0017

Balachandra, L., T. Briggs, K. Eddleston, and C. Brush (2019) "Don't pitch like a girl!: How gender stereotypes influence investor decisions", *Entrepreneurship Theory and Practice*, 43 (1): 116–137. https://doi.org/10.1177/1042258717728028

Banégas, R. and J.-P. Warnier (2001) "Nouvelles figures de la réussite et du pouvoir", *Politique africaine*, 82 (2): 5–23. Cairn.info. https://doi.org/10.3917/polaf.082.0005

World Bank (2020) *Economic Impact Assessment of COVID-19 and Policy Responses in Sub-Saharan Africa* (21; Africa's Pulse, p. 12), World Bank Group. https://documents1.worldbank.org/curated/es/950981586462612240/pdf/Executive-Summary.pdf, accessed 13 March 2024.

Becker, H. S. (2013) *Les ficelles du métier: Comment conduire sa recherche en sciences sociales* (Continued from 1st printing). Paris: La Découverte.

Bellier, A. and A. Idi Cheffou (2019) "Investissements et projets entrepreneuriaux face aux stéréotypes de genre", *Management & Avenir*, 108 (2): 43–62. https://doi.org/10.3917/mav.108.0043

Blanchet, A. and A. Gotman (2017) *L'entretien*. Paris: A. Colin.

Boateng, A. (2018) "Contextualising women's entrepreneurship in Africa", in A. Boateng (ed.) *African Female Entrepreneurship*, pp. 3–33. Cham: Springer International Publishing. https://doi.org/10.1007/978-3-319-65846-9_1

Boltanski, L. and E. Chiapello (2011) *The New Spirit of Capitalism* (1st ed. 1999). Paris: Gallimard.

Boni, S. T. (2008) *Que vivent les femmes d'Afrique?* Paris: Panama.

Boutillier, S. and A. Tiran (2016) "The theory of the entrepreneur, its evolution and its contextualization", *Innovations*, 50 (2): 211–234. https://doi.org/10.3917/inno.050.0211

Bréant, H. (2019) "Retours sur capital(e): Socialiser les émigré-e-s au retour", *Actes de la recherche en sciences sociales*, 225 (5): 54–66. https://doi.org/10.3917/arss.225.0054

Bréant, H. (2020) "Réinstallations d'émigrés africains: Les usages sociaux des diplômes étrangers", *Migrations Société*, 180 (2): 83–96. https://doi.org/10.3917/migra.180.0083

Cao, Z. and X. Shi (2021) "A systematic literature review of entrepreneurial ecosystems in advanced and emerging economies", *Small Business Economics*, 57 (1): 75–110. https://doi.org/10.1007/s11187-020-00326-y

Cassarino, J.-P. (2004) "Theorising return migration: The conceptual approach to return migrants revisited", *International Journal on Multicultural Societies (IJMS)*, 6 (2): 253–279.

Cerase, F. P. (1974) "Expectations and reality: A case study of return migration from the United States to Southern Italy", *The International Migration Review*, 8 (2): 245–262. https://doi.org/10.2307/3002783

Chapus, Q., J.-P. Berrou, and Y. Onibon Doubogan (2021) "Le retour du héros? L'entrepreneur, itinéraire d'un concept chez les "développeurs" en Afrique", *Revue internationale des études du développement*, 245 (1): 11–39. Cairn.info. https://doi.org/10.3917/ried.245.0011

Charmes, J. (2005) "Femmes africaines, activités économiques et travail: De l'invisibilité à la reconnaissance", *Revue Tiers Monde*, 182 (2): 255–279. https://doi.org/10.3917/rtm.182.0255

Chasserio, S., P. Pailot, and C. Poroli (2016) "L'entrepreneuriat est-il genré", *Regards croisés sur l'économie*, 19 (2): 62–75. Cairn.info. https://doi.org/10.3917/rce.019.0062

Constantinidis, C. (2014) "Women entrepreneurs", in P.-M. Chauvin, M. Grossetti, and P.-P. Zalio, *Dictionnaire sociologique de l'entrepreneuriat*, pp. 287–300. Paris: Presses de Sciences Po. https://www.cairn.info/dictionnaire-sociologique-de-l-entrepreneuriat--9782724616408-page-287.htm

Coquery-Vidrovitch, C. (2012) *Les Africaines: Histoire des femmes d'Afrique subsaharienne du XIXe au XXe siècle*. Paris: La Découverte. (Original edition 1994)

Cordonnier, R. (1987). *Femmes africaines et commerce: Les revendeuses de tissu de la ville de Lomé, Togo*. Paris: L'Harmattan.

D'Andria, A. and I. Gabarret (2016) "Women and entrepreneurs: Thirty years of research in female entrepreneurial motivation", *Revue de l'Entrepreneuriat / Review of Entrepreneurship*, 15 (3–4): 87–107. Cairn.info. https://doi.org/10.3917/entre.153.0087

Dardot, P. and C. Laval (2009) *La nouvelle raison du monde: Essai sur la société néolibérale*. Paris: La Découverte.

Dieng, S. A. and D. Diaw (2023) "Un état des lieux de l'économie sénégalaise", in U. Schuerkens (ed.) *Entreprises, entrepreneurs et travail au Sénégal*, pp. 43–74. Paris: L'Harmattan.

Dimé, M. (2017) "De bul faale à Y'en a marre: Continuités et dissonances dans les dynamiques de contestation sociopolitique et d'affirmation citoyenne chez les jeunes au

Sénégal", *Africa Development / Afrique et Développement*, 42 (2): 83–105. https://www.jstor.org/stable/90018192

Drori, I., B. Honig, and M. Wright (2009) "Transnational entrepreneurship: An emergent field of study", *Entrepreneurship Theory and Practice*, 33 (5): 1001–1022. https://doi.org/10.1111/j.1540-6520.2009.00332.x

Fayolle, A. (2004) "À la recherche du cœur de l'entrepreneuriat: Vers une nouvelle vision du domaine", *Revue internationale P.M.E. Économie et gestion de la petite et moyenne entreprise*, 17 (1): 101–121. https://doi.org/10.7202/1008453ar

Flahaux, M.-L. (2015) "Intention et réalisation de migration de retour au Sénégal et en République démocratique du Congo", *Population*, 70 (1): 103–133. https://doi.org/10.3917/popu.1501.0103

Foucault, M. (2004) *Naissance de la biopolitique: Cours au Collège de France, 1978–1979*. Paris: Gallimard.

Gabarret, I. and B. Vedel (2015) "Pour une nouvelle approche de la motivation entrepreneuriale", *La Revue des Sciences de Gestion*, 271 (1): 13–20. https://doi.org/10.3917/rsg.271.0013

Gartner, W. B. (1988) "Who is an entrepreneur? Is the wrong question", *American Journal of Small Business*, 12 (4): 11–32. https://doi.org/10.1177/104225878801200401

Gartner, W. B. (1989) "Some Suggestions for Research on Entrepreneurial Traits and Characteristics", *Entrepreneurship Theory and Practice*, 14 (1): 27–38. https://doi.org/10.1177/104225878901400103

Goyal, P. and V. Yadav (2014) "To be or not to be a woman entrepreneur in a developing country?", *Psychosociological Issues in Human Resource Management*, 2 (2): 68–79. https://go.gale.com/ps/i.do?p=AONE&sw=w&issn=2332399X&v=2.1&it=r&id=GALE%7CA392573250&sid=googleScholar&linkaccess=abs, accessed 5 January 2024.

Granovetter, M. (2000) "The economic sociology of firms and entrepreneurs", in R. Swedberg (ed.) *Entrepreneurship: A Social Science View*, pp. 244–275. Oxford: Oxford University Press. https://doi.org/10.1093/oso/9780198294627.003.0013

Grossetti, M. and F. Reix (2014) "Parcours biographiques et carrières entrepreneuriales", in P.-M. Chauvin, M. Grossetti and P.-P. Zalio (eds) *Dictionnaire sociologique de l'entrepreneuriat*, pp. 412–431. Paris: Presses de Sciences Po. https://doi.org/10.3917/scpo.chauv.2015.01.0412

Gruenhagen, J. H., P. Davidsson, and S. Sawang (2020) "Returnee entrepreneurs: A systematic literature review, thematic analysis, and research agenda", *Foundations and Trends® in Entrepreneurship*, 16 (4): 310–392. https://doi.org/10.1561/0300000096

Gupta, V. K. and D. B. Turban (2012) "Evaluation of new business ideas: Do gender stereotypes play a role?", *Journal of Managerial Issues*, 24 (2): 140–156. http://www.jstor.org.distant.bu.univ-rennes2.fr/stable/43488130

Isenberg, D. (2010) "How to start an entrepreneurial revolution", *Harvard Business Review*, 88 (6): 40–50.

Jamid, H., L. Kabbanji, A. Levatino, and K. Mary (2020) "Les migrations pour études au prisme des mobilités sociales", *Migrations Société*, 180 (2): 19–35. https://doi.org/10.3917/migra.180.0019

Kane, N. and R. Chroqui (eds) (2021) *L'entrepreneuriat féminin en Afrique, entre bricolage et survie*. Paris: L'Harmattan.

Kenney, M., D. Breznitz, and M. Murphree (2013) "Coming back home after the sun rises: Returnee entrepreneurs and growth of high-tech industries", *Research Policy*, 42 (2): 391–407. https://doi.org/10.1016/j.respol.2012.08.001

Kirzner, I. M. (2009) "The alert and creative entrepreneur: A clarification", *Small Business Economics*, 32 (2): 145–152. https://www.jstor.org/stable/40344540

Lange, M.-F. (2021) "Une discrète révolution mondiale: La progression de la scolarisation des filles et des jeunes filles dans les pays du Sud", *Autrepart*, 87 (3): 3–33. https://doi.org/10.3917/autr.087.0003

Laperche, B., M. Lima, E. Seulliet, and B. Trousse (eds) (2019) *Les écosystèmes d'innovation: Regards croisés des acteurs clés*. Paris: L'Harmattan.

Larcher, L. (2021). "La médiatisation de l'entreprise et de l'entrepreneuriat en Afrique", *Revue internationale des études du développement*, 245 (1): 227–237. https://doi.org/10.3917/ried.245.0227

Lin, D., J. Lu, X. Liu, and X. Zhang (2016) "International knowledge brokerage and returnees' entrepreneurial decisions", *Journal of International Business Studies*, 47 (3): 295–318. https://www.jstor.org/stable/43907573

Locoh, T. (1996) "Changements de rôles masculins et féminins dans la crise: La révolution silencieuse", in J. Coussy and J. Vallin (eds) *Crise et population en Afrique. Crises économiques, programmes d'ajustement et dynamiques démographiques*, pp. 445–470. Paris: Les Études du CEPED.

Locoh, T. (2013) "Genre et le marché du travail en Afrique subsaharienne", in M. Maruani (ed.) *Travail et genre dans le monde*, pp. 171–181. Paris: La Découverte. https://doi.org/10.3917/dec.marua.2013.01.0171

Mary, K. (2014) "Le retour difficile des jeunes Maliens formés en l'Amérique du Nord", *Hommes & Migrations*, 1307 (3): 39–46. https://doi.org/10.4000/hommesmigrations.2876

Mbaye, J. F. (2021) "Culture politique et politique culturelle du Hip Hop Galsen", *Présence Africaine*, 199–200 (1): 147–174. https://doi.org/10.3917/presa.199.0147

Mbembe, J.-A. (2013) *Sortir de la grande nuit: Essai sur l'Afrique décolonisée*. Paris: La Découverte.

Noy, C. (2008) "Sampling Knowledge: The Hermeneutics of Snowball Sampling in Qualitative Research", *International Journal of Social Research Methodology*, 11 (4): 327–344. https://doi.org/10.1080/13645570701401305

International Labour Organization (2016) *Women at work. Trends 2016* [Executive summary]. International Labour Organization. https://www.ilo.org/wcmsp5/groups/public/---dgreports/---inst/documents/publication/wcms_457537.pdf, accessed 5 February 2024.

International Labour Organization (2021) *Building a more equitable future: Women's rights at work and in the workplace at the heart of post-COVID recovery* [Briefing note]. International Labour Organization. https://www.ilo.org/wcmsp5/groups/public/---dgreports/---gender/documents/publication/wcms_814505.pdf, accessed 5 February 2024.

Paillé, P. (2011) "L'analyse par théorisation ancrée", *Cahiers de recherche sociologique*, 23: 147–181. https://doi.org/10.7202/1002253ar

Pesqueux, Y. (2012) "Entrepreneur, leader... Des figures bien étranges", *L'Expansion Management Review*, 147 (4): 30–41. https://doi.org/10.3917/emr.147.0030

Pinard, É. (2016) "Les femmes propriétaires à Pikine, au Sénégal: Entre nouvelles responsabilités familiales et désir d'autonomie", *Recherches féministes*, 29 (2): 43–62. https://doi.org/10.7202/1038720ar

Pruthi, S. (2014) "Social ties and venture creation by returnee entrepreneurs", *International Business Review*, 23 (6): 1139–1152. https://doi.org/10.1016/j.ibusrev.2014.03.012

Qin, F., M. Wright, and J. Gao (2017) 'Are 'sea turtles' slower? Returnee entrepreneurs, venture resources and speed of entrepreneurial entry", *Journal of Business Venturing*, 32 (6): 694–706. https://doi.org/10.1016/j.jbusvent.2017.08.003

Razafindrakoto, M. and J.-M. Wachsberger (2021) "Édito. L'entrepreneur et le COVID-19 en Afrique", *Revue internationale des études du développement*, 245 (1): 5–7. https://doi.org/10.3917/ried.245.0005

Sagna, O. (2022) *Rapport sur la situation de l'enseignement supérieur: Sénégal*. UNESCO National Commission in collaboration with the Ministry of Higher Education, Research, and Innovation (MESRI). https://whec2022.net/resources/Country%20report%20-%20Senegal.pdf, accessed 3 March 2024.

Saxenian, A. (2002) "Transnational communities and the evolution of global production networks: The cases of Taiwan, China and India", *Industry and Innovation*, 9 (3): 183–202. https://doi.org/10.1080/1366271022000034453
Schuerkens, U. (ed.) (2008) *Globalization and Transformations of Local Socioeconomic Practices*. New York: Routledge.
Schuerkens, U. (ed.) (2023a) *Entreprises, entrepreneurs et travail au Sénégal*. Paris: L'Harmattan.
Schuerkens, U. (2023b) "Les étudiant.e.s-entrepreneur.e.s: Apprentissage professionnel, entre études et entreprises", in U. Schuerkens (ed.) *Entreprises, entrepreneurs et travail au Sénégal*, pp. 289–311. Paris: L'Harmattan.
Schuerkens, U. (2023c) "Les femmes entrepreneures au Sénégal et le contexte géographique plus large de l'Afrique et de l'Europe", in U. Schuerkens (ed.) *Entreprises, entrepreneurs et travail au Sénégal*, pp. 312–335. Paris: L'Harmattan.
Schuerkens, U., M. Seye, and P. Manga (2023) "Manager dans l'ère de la glocalisation actuelle: La nouvelle génération des entrepreneurs dakarois appartenant aux nouvelles classes moyennes du Sénégal", in U. Schuerkens (ed.) *Entreprises, entrepreneurs et travail au Sénégal*, pp. 213–256. Paris: L'Harmattan.
Schumpeter, J. A. (2021) *The Theory of Creative Destruction* (G. Fain, ed.). Paris: Payot. (Original edition 1951)
Shapero, A. and L. Sokol (1982) "The social dimensions of entrepreneurship", in C. Kent, D. Sexton, and K. Vesper (eds) *Encyclopaedia of Entrepreneurship*, pp. 72–90. Engelwood Cliffs: Prentice Hall.
Stam, E. and A. Van de Ven (2021) "Entrepreneurial ecosystem elements", *Small Business Economics*, 56 (2): 809–832. https://doi.org/10.1007/s11187-019-00270-6
Sylvanus, N. (2006) "L'habileté entrepreneuriale des Nana Benz du Togo", *Africultures*, 69 (4): 179–184. https://doi.org/10.3917/afcul.069.0179
Sylvanus, N. (2008) "Rethinking 'Free-trade' practices in contemporary Togo: Women entrepreneurs in the global textile trade", in U. Schuerkens (ed.) *Globalization and Transformations of Local Socioeconomic Practices*, pp. 174–191. New York: Routledge.
Sylvanus, N. (2009) "Commerçantes togolaises et diables chinois. Une approche par la rumeur" (V. Foucher, Trad.), *Politique africaine*, 113 (1): 55–70. Cairn.info. https://doi.org/10.3917/polaf.113.0055
Toulabor, C. (2012) "Les Nana Benz de Lomé. Mutations d'une bourgeoisie compradore, entre heurt et décadence", *Afrique contemporaine*, 244 (4): 69–80. Cairn.info. https://doi.org/10.3917/afco.244.0069
Vampo, C. (2021) "Des Nana Benz aux cheffes d'entreprise contemporaines à Lomé, au Togo: L'entrepreneuriat dit 'moderne' en question", *Revue internationale des études du développement*, 245 (1): 145–169. https://doi.org/10.3917/ried.245.0145
Weber, M. (2008) *Économie et société. Les catégories de la sociologie*. Paris: Plon.

9 Relational Biographies of Women Social Entrepreneurs in Senegal[1]

Sadio Ba Gning

Introduction

For a long time, the Social and Solidarity Economy (SSE) has rarely been approached from the angle of its entrepreneurs, the focus being more often on its alternative aims to the market economy and its relationship with the informal economy. Yet the notion of the entrepreneur has already been studied in its capitalist dimension by Max Weber (2003 (1904–1905: 50)), then by Joseph Schumpeter (1912), who theorised it as an innovative function of "creative destruction". Ronald Burt introduced the figure of the employee entrepreneur, who exploits "structural holes" in the company's relational network to position himself (Burt, 1992). Following on this relational network approach, this research is based on the theory of embedding (Granovetter, 1985) and decoupling (White, 2002), taken up in France by Michel Grossetti and Jean François Barthe (2008). Its aim is to study gender dynamics in the SSE based on entrepreneurial figures, in this case, women. The portraits of the women studied in this chapter immediately raise two questions: How is the figure of the social entrepreneur constructed? What role do relational networks play? This research is based on the life stories and egocentric networks of a hundred heads of social enterprises, reconstructed as part of the FRES programme,[2] using qualitative survey methods that combine participant and direct observation, life histories, and repeated interviews, including with members of their entourage, particularly men. The women, aged between 30 and 70, come from a variety of social backgrounds, and are of Muslim or Christian faiths.

After presenting in the first part profiles of the women entrepreneurs studied and my methodological choices, I describe the space of women entrepreneurs' networks, before finally analysing in the third part the embedding of professional paths in multiple relational links (family and associative) in networks (personal, institutional, and professional) that reveal the diversity of women social entrepreneurs' profiles.

Profiles of Female Social Entrepreneurs: Field Data

Methods

The qualitative data from the FRES survey was collected between September 2016 and October 2017. It traces the career paths of women entrepreneurs and their

DOI: 10.4324/9781003492931-12

family and associative (including religious and political) histories, in relation to their professional activities. The development of a common interview guide, tested and stabilised during an exploratory phase, facilitated the collection of data. It combines direct observation and iterative in-depth individual interviews. Around a hundred women entrepreneurs were interviewed in three regions of Senegal (Dakar, Saint-Louis, and Ziguinchor).

The women entrepreneurs were chosen because of their activities and their position as managers of social enterprises. Targeting was carried out in two stages: (1) firstly by the technique of purposive sampling with key informants; (2) then by snowball effect. In the absence of databases, I first had to rely on contacts provided by key informants based on predefined criteria (activity and elective position in a family business or associative organisation). Secondly, contacts were provided by women entrepreneurs who had already been surveyed and who agreed to put me in touch with other women with similar characteristics. In this way, the data collected reflects the general characteristics of women entrepreneurs in Senegal and the diversity of their profiles.

Socio-demographic Characteristics

Despite their wide diversity, the women entrepreneurs surveyed share some common characteristics, particularly in terms of networking and reconciling work and family life. Most were married, polygamous or monogamous, with an average of three to five children. They tend to work in sectors that are traditionally dominated by women (catering, market gardening, dyeing, agri-food, processing, marketing, etc.), where they have built up significant social capital. Associations and professional circles are seen as levers for the creation and growth of their businesses.

Overall, the women studied manage at least one social enterprise with a legal status. They may come from the informal, formal, or rural entrepreneurial sectors. The average number of employees in their businesses was between 10 and 20. The rest are members of associations. They can be found in networks of women entrepreneurs that they manage in the form of Economic Intervention Groups (EIGs), cooperatives, mutual cooperatives, or local development, religious or political associations (parties, social movements).

In terms of values, women entrepreneurs consider ethics and social responsibility to be paramount. While religion is a springboard in their professional careers (Gning, 2019), the level of education does not seem to be a determining factor in network dynamics; the most educated women, who are often salaried or retired, are no more networked than their less educated counterparts. Most female employees, who make up almost a third of our sample (21), are Catholics. Table 9.1 completes this description.

Table 9.1 Sociodemographic characteristics

<table>
<tr><td>Number</td><td colspan="8">70</td></tr>
<tr><td>Age</td><td colspan="8">35–75 years</td></tr>
<tr><td rowspan="2">Marital status</td><td colspan="4">Brides: 45</td><td rowspan="2">Widows: 16</td><td rowspan="2">Singles: 2</td><td rowspan="2">Divorced: 7</td></tr>
<tr><td colspan="2">Monogamous: 21</td><td colspan="2">Polygamous: 24</td></tr>
<tr><td>Number of children</td><td colspan="8">2–8</td></tr>
<tr><td rowspan="3">Religion/Type and level of education</td><td colspan="4">Muslim women: 59
Average length:</td><td colspan="3">Catholics: 11
Average length:</td></tr>
<tr><td rowspan="2">Coranic school/literacy: 4</td><td colspan="3">French school</td><td colspan="3">French school</td></tr>
<tr><td>Primary: 18</td><td>Secondary: 30</td><td>University: 6</td><td>Primary: 1</td><td>Secondary: 7</td><td>University: 3</td></tr>
<tr><td>Position within the association</td><td colspan="3">President: 68</td><td colspan="3">General secretaries: 2</td><td></td></tr>
<tr><td>Business sectors GEI/ Associations</td><td>Catering</td><td>Processing of local products/ local cereals/ fishery products</td><td>Rice</td><td>Market garden blocks</td><td>Soap making/ Detergent and bleach manufacturing</td><td>Dyeing/Sewing/ Screen printing</td></tr>
<tr><td>Nature of the social enterprise</td><td>GEI: Group of economic intervention</td><td>Sports and cultural association</td><td>Credit union (AVEC)</td><td>Cooperative</td><td>A family business</td><td></td></tr>
<tr><td>Spouse's occupation</td><td>Livestock Development Officer/ Security Officer</td><td>Fisherman</td><td>Retailer</td><td>Bank staff member High school teacher</td><td>Horticultural technician</td><td>Mason/ Joiner</td><td>SENELEC agent/ Mayoral staff member/ Bank staff member</td><td>Retired</td></tr>
<tr><td>Parents' occupations</td><td>Marabout</td><td>Farmer</td><td>Teacher</td><td>Employees</td><td>Technicians</td><td>Retailer</td><td>Marabout</td><td></td></tr>
</table>

Typology of Female Entrepreneurs

Based on these elements, the women entrepreneurs are classified into four groups (Table 9.2). To highlight the wide diversity of profiles and backgrounds, and to identify the relational characteristics of women social entrepreneurs, we felt that the criteria relating to religion, age, marital status, and education were important.

At the end of this classification (9.2), it is important to stress that the categories are not exclusive. An entrepreneur may combine or have some of the same characteristics from one category to another. For example, a senior woman may be a local development activist, just as a conciliatory woman may have started her career as a senior or junior woman. This illustrates the bifurcated nature of the career paths of the women entrepreneurs studied.

The Space of Women Entrepreneurs' Social Networks: Multiple Anchors

Talking about professional, family, religious, political, associative, and institutional links at the same time is tedious at first sight, but above all, it reflects the interweaving of these groups in the trajectories of women entrepreneurs. If embeddedness corresponds to situations where the roles of individuals overlap in several social spaces (Granovetter, 1974), this notion makes it possible to grasp the entanglement of economic relations and social relations (kinship ties, friendships, neighbourhood ties, religious ties, political ties) in the trajectories of women entrepreneurs. As an evolving construct, embeddedness makes possible the dynamics of social networks (Mitchell, 1969), insofar as social ties are built, strengthened, or broken according to the issues at stake and the preferences of individuals.

Analysing social embeddedness means considering the multiplexity of the spaces of interaction and the links that result from them, depending on the roles and interests of each agent (Mitchell, 1969; Vergrugge, 1979). Multiplexity makes it possible to understand the degree to which the trajectories of women entrepreneurs are embedded in inherited (family) and socially constructed relationships (neighbourhood, institutional, professional, associative, friendly one). The distinction between, on the one hand, family social ties and, on the other, professional social ties, overlaps with the distinction between social capital "inherited" by the agent and social capital "built up" through a strategy of accumulation (Ferrary, 2010). This distinction between the two forms of social capital makes it possible to reconcile a structuralist approach of social networks that considers the effects of "inherited" social capital and a more "actionist" approach that analyses social capital accumulation strategies through embedding choices. For Mark S. Granovetter (1974), this takes the form of "strong" social ties (family-social contact) and "weak" social ties (work contact) accumulated through professional activities. For Granovetter (1973), "weak" ties are therefore more effective than "strong" ties in the search for a job since they enable agents to obtain better information about the labour market. Embeddedness can therefore be understood as both a "status" and a "process" (Grossetti and Bes, 2003). As a process of increasing the dependence of one social entity on another, it is weakened by decoupling, which corresponds to the process of autonomation of these links (Grossetti and Barthe, 2008). To study

Table 9.2 Typology of female entrepreneurs

	Muslim women entrepreneurs	*Catholic women entrepreneurs*
1st category **Seniors**	Head of a social enterprise Aged (60–70+) Member of several associations Elective and social responsibilities Members of an association Multiple roots (family, professional, and local associations, etc.) Low level of education/no formal education Informal/Retired/No formal education Widowed or in a polygamous marital union and living separately Family, professional, political, and institutional ties	Head of a social enterprise Aged (60–70+) Member of several associations Elective and social responsibilities Multiple roots (family, professional, and local associations, etc.) Retired women Widows Family, religious, political, professional, and institutional ties
2nd category **The militants**	Head of social enterprises Aged between 50 and 59 Elective responsibilities in local associations (religious and/or political) Members of an association Monogamous/polygamous Graduated/ employed/no formal education Professional experience/local development/educated Family, professional, political/ religious ties	Head of social enterprises Aged between 50 and 59 Elective responsibilities in local associations (religious and/or political) Monogamous Graduates/Employees Family, professional, and religious ties
3rd category **The conciliators**	Aged between 40 and 49 Head of an association Elective functions in associations Members of an association Sole trader/family/informal business owner Graduates/educated/no formal education Monogamous/polygamous Family, political and religious ties	40–49 years old Head of an association Association responsibilities Sole proprietor/family business Monogamous Graduates/educated/no formal education Family, religious and professional ties
4th Category **The cadets**	40–30 years old Individual activity Associative responsibilities (CSA) Instructed/no formal instruction Members of an association Polygamous/monogamous Family and religious ties	40–30 years old Individual activity Associative responsibilities (CSA) Graduates/instructed Members of an association Educated Family and religious ties Monogamous

the place of these ties in the trajectories of women entrepreneurs, and their role in access to material resources (financing, access to land) and immaterial resources (legitimacy, recognition, social position), it is necessary to describe them first. We are focusing here on family, neighbourhood, associative (including religious and political), institutional, and professional ties.

Family, Neighbourhood, and Community Links

Family ties are any form of relationship based on biological or social kinship. This definition highlights the strong ties forged with close family, as opposed to weak (professional) ties (Granovetter, 1973, 1985). In the economic literature, some studies show the negative effects that family ties can have on the transition of microenterprises to a more modern system, particularly because of "forced solidarity" and redistribution norms that weigh on certain members (Grimm et al., 2013) Other studies show that in times of crisis, the family circle facilitates access to useful resources for entrepreneurs (information, financial support, etc.) (Berrou and Combarnous, 2011). In a more limited context, the use of family labour plays an important role in microenterprises (Nordman and Vaillant, 2014). Maintaining these family ties gives rise to economic exchanges during family ceremonies (weddings, christenings, deaths, etc.). Put another way, investing in these relationships that can be mobilised for instrumental purposes takes on the meaning of an important commitment for each woman. They devote time to them through their participation in family ceremonies and essentially redistribute parts of the wealth they have accumulated to build up their social capital. This is the idea suggested by the title: "The franc is intimately associated with grace and recognition" (Fall and Guèye, 2003; my translation).

By neighbourhood ties, we mean all the informal ties that play such a central role in the trajectories of women entrepreneurs. They refer to any form of geographical or relational proximity (neighbours, acquaintances) maintained on an interpersonal basis or through collectives by women in their social environment. As an informal method of financing and a classic form of community organisation, the tontine polarises these neighbourhood relationships. It is largely based on inter-acquaintance, which enables individuals linked by professional, relational, and/or geographical proximity to pool resources. In a narrower sense, it refers to any financial transaction whose purpose is to pool funds to be shared among members at a given time. More precisely, according to a periodicity established by consensus (daily, weekly, or monthly), the members contribute the same amount which is paid to each of them in turn. Based on the principle of mutuality, tontines enable women to demonstrate their ability to maintain relationships based on trust, the foundation of their future entrepreneurial collaboration. Diversified according to the needs identified, the tontines have proved to be a significant source of funding for economic activities, helping to get income-generating activities off the ground.

Following on from the logic of tontines, women entrepreneurs are also led to maintain associative links, which may emerge from different circles formed at several levels (local, national, and regional). These associative links can be structured around collectives depending on the activity, geographical origin, religion, etc. Under the impetus of development organisations and micro-finance institutions, and to access greater resources offered by these organisations, women entrepreneurs are encouraged to organise themselves into networks in the form of savings and credit cooperatives (SCC), village associations of savings and credit (VASC), and women's promotion groups (WPG) made up of groups of economic intervention (GEI), which are collective enterprises. Through these organisations, women entrepreneurs are involved in associative relationships that imply participation in economic and social activities based on shared values and common objectives.

Associative links can include a significant religious dimension. We refer to this as any form of religious closeness maintained individually or collectively by women entrepreneurs. They are often based on long-standing family ties (depending on the denomination of the parents or the husband), neighbourhood ties such as the Basic Ecclesiastical Communities, known as BEC,[3] or new ties (women's groups set up to promote religious education). These religious communities take the form of urban religious associations called *dahira* or a group of "street children's godmothers", called *ndéyou daara*. They are likely to encourage the creation of bonds of trust between women entrepreneurs at community level and to win the sympathy of influential local religious figures who act as informal guardians – who are consulted and informed to collect prayers and blessings. For these entrepreneurs, religious activities provide an opportunity to renew their religious ties, which they can use in the future to resolve specific problems (e.g., administrative or tax red tape, loans, and the obtaining of contracts).

When women entrepreneurs focus on political relations, they do so within the framework of associative organisations (parties, groups, etc.) to support influential political figures. To become militants, they renew pre-existing family or friendship ties in other social settings (religious associations, women's promotion groups, tontines, etc.) or create new ones through political activism, seen as a means of accessing and securing various resources (bank financing, technical support, etc.). Women entrepreneurs can then set up movements to support candidates in the continuity of their militant trajectory by mobilising a diversity of new and old relationships. The reverse is true, with women favouring new relationships forged in the political sphere, particularly when they are involved in political mobility. At the level of these political networks, women entrepreneurs must prove their electoral mobilisation capacity to be able to negotiate *quiproquos* in terms of institutional and/or banking facilities. But these relationships, which may appear to be clientelist, turn out to be much more complex than they appear. They involve women entrepreneurs taking part in meetings and mobilising women's groups, they manage to satisfy the electoral goals of candidates who are keen to broaden their base and who are willing to reward their support. In addition to the links forged in the community, women entrepreneurs are involved in other personal, institutional, and professional relationships.

Institutional, Professional, and Personal Links

Analysing the social networks of women entrepreneurs also means considering the technical, material, and organisational environments in which they are formed and structured. It is not just a matter of looking at the influence of networks in terms of access to institutional support systems for women's entrepreneurship (funding, training), but also of understanding the role of these systems in the construction of social links and the structuring of networks and, conversely, how they interact. The contractual (legal provisions) and organisational (companies, development agencies, NGOs, government departments, associations, etc.) environments constitute resources and contingencies for developing individual strategies and building institutional links. We use this concept here to refer to the relationships that women entrepreneurs have with actors in microfinance organisations, civil society organisations, ministries, tax authorities, chambers of commerce, municipalities, NGOs, banks, and development organisations, which can give them access to several forms of resources (information, credit, training, technical support). We distinguish institutional links from professional links, which we use here to refer specifically to the working relationships that women entrepreneurs have with each other in the context of their economic and social activities – relationships between associative enterprises within the same group or between groups.

A final type of relationship is worth describing. These are interpersonal links that may emerge from different circles (family, association, institutions, etc.). These are elective links with childhood friends, neighbours, associative partners, former colleagues, religious or political figures, etc. All these relationships, which are relatively sustainable, are "mediation resources" (Grossetti, 2008) that enable women to build their entrepreneurial careers around networks. Considered in the embedding process, these multiple relationships can be activated throughout the life trajectory.

The figure[4] below sets out the circles from which the networks of women entrepreneurs emerge, which in the final analysis are sets of multi-sited links in different domains and at different levels that coexist, overlap, and interact daily. Among the possible social configurations, the simplest one may consist of at least one link, with several circles within it. But the relational configuration of the network can be more complex when it involves more than two types of links. For example, between associative ties (neighbourhood, religious and political), family ties (siblings, co-wives, husband, and children), and professional ties, a social network is formed that crystallises part of each of these relationships.

Associative Dynamics and the Embedding of Pathways and Networks

It is not always easy to identify the historical points of reference that enable us to grasp the dynamics of the networks because of this embeddedness, which reveals that the construction and expansion of women entrepreneurs' networks from these spaces of relationships is far from being part of a linear and unilateral process. It involves considering the dynamics of associations (local, political, religious,

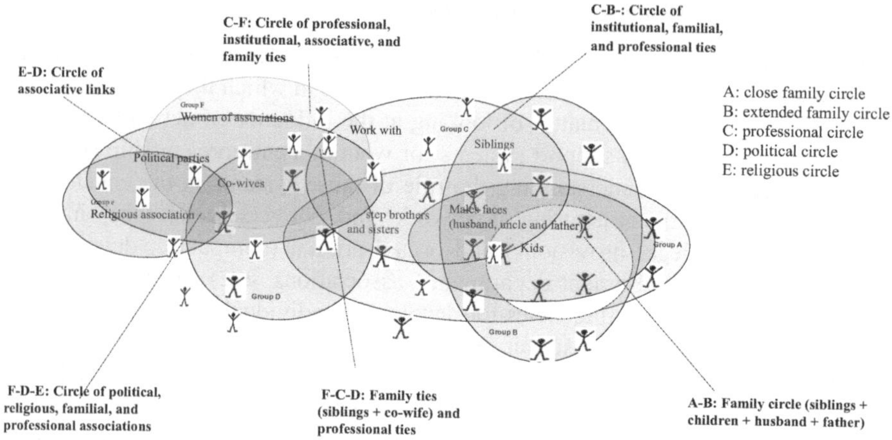

Figure 9.1 Space of social entrepreneurs' relational networks

social), which significantly interfere in the networks specific to each entrepreneur and at different stages of her career. To support our argument, four typical portraits drawn from our typology (Korka B., Habsa D., Marième L., and Justine F.) are presented.

Pioneering Women: Family and Associative Ties (Professional and Political) Embedded in Personal Networks

Aged 60–70 and over, elderly women make up a third of our sample. They steer several national and regional social initiatives through the networks of women entrepreneurs they manage. As well as being socially recognised, they also benefit from a few mechanisms for the advancement of women (funding from the State, development organisations, etc.). Most of them are Muslims, with strong family and associative roots (religious, political, and professional). By contrast, their Catholic counterparts in the same group are retired or former activists in religious associations. They run social initiatives at local, national, and regional levels. The career paths of these pioneer women surveyed are influenced in different ways by their multiple memberships in different social circles (family, political, religious, institutional, and personal). By virtue of their central position, they accumulate diverse links in the form of social capital, which is just as important as economic capital. But by acting as a bridge between members, and sometimes between networks, these social leaders make themselves inescapable, arbitrating not only interactions but also the allocation of resources. They consolidate their elective position by controlling the most informal networks that are useful to the other women entrepreneurs in their groups. In this way, within these network spaces, they ensure the coexistence of interdependent social links (family and associative) and economic links (professional).

Case 1: Korka B.

Korka B. is 61 years old at the time of our study. After an early and difficult start in the informal sector, Korka B. gradually moved towards the SSE. Before that, however, she had been occupied for 19 years by a family life that included a succession of maternities (1971–1981). She then looked after her children's education until at least the 1990s. To develop her business, she diversified both her products and her relationships, to build a bridge with the SSE by creating a social enterprise in the form of a GEI (Group of economic interest) in 1996. To stabilise this new social enterprise, Korka B. took advantage of the local and political roots of her grandmother, who raised her. She then relied on organisations of women entrepreneurs in various fields (professional and associative), within which she held several responsibilities (President of the northern women farmers' network, Treasurer of the northern rice mill, opposition politician, local councillor) for around ten years (2001–2012).

Korka B. became involved in politics in the early 2000s, having previously had this dual support (family and community). She entered politics to attract funding and diversify her partnerships. At the request of a political friend, who is the granddaughter of a friend of her grandfather, Korka B. joined the presidential coalition. Between 2004 and 2008, she was elected as a local councillor. From 2001 onwards, Korka B. experienced a turning point in her career as an entrepreneur, having used her professional links at the institutional level with women farmers in the north and rural areas to consolidate her base until 2017. Since then, her political alliances have been renewed at each election, enabling her to negotiate *quidproquos* (provision of premises, access to machinery and funding, participation in international trade fairs, etc.). Between alliances and break-ups (2012), her relationships have changed and have been rebuilt, drawing on new links (friends, local leaders, ministers) and attracting resources (creation of the first rice mill in the north and plans for a second). Korka B. has been able to build up her professional address book at the institutional level and maintain a recognised leadership position (twice Grand Prix Head of State 2008 and 2015).

Women Militants' Backgrounds: The Interweaving of Family and Association Ties (Religious, Professional, and Political) within Institutional Networks

These women are aged between 50 and 59 and make up two-thirds of our sample. This very heterogeneous intermediary group has common characteristics in terms of their associative responsibilities. There are more Muslim women than Catholics. The deep-rootedness of family and community ties is also obvious in the institutional networks. On the one hand, many women, whether employed or retired, draw on their professional experience either in development or in a trade (teacher, secretary, trainer, rural leader, etc.). Comparing the practices of women entrepreneurs, militants draw on their cultural resources as educated women, while mobilising their social membership of religious and political families to woo institutional networks (banks, government departments). On the other hand, those who come from the informal sector may have little or no education, or be failing at school. They are aware of the rhetoric around access to more rights for women, to citizenship in terms of access to land or reproductive health, which they do not hesitate to take on board.

Case 2: Habsa D.

Habsa D. is 53 years old at the moment of our study. Her father is a marabout, and her mother is a shopkeeper. After taking her A-levels in 1987, her mother advised her to set up her family business. She gave her the necessary capital. Within a few months, her business had 15 members, including neighbours and other entrepreneurs (processors, agricultural producers, etc.). With the help of her parents, 30 hectares were sold to Habsa D. on her uncle's land.

To increase her agricultural production, Habsa D. applied for a loan from the agricultural bank. She had previously joined a farmers' association. Moussa C. is its president. He is a friend of Habsa D.'s older sister, a political leader in the same party. It was with this group that she was able to obtain 50 hectares in the extensive project initiated by a cooperation partner in 1995. The funding benefited eight groups in their association. As the association's supply and stock manager in 1995, Habsa D. attended many of the training courses offered by her partners, rubbed shoulders with many people from development and cooperation organisations, and got to know other women entrepreneurs in the process.

In 2000, the association went into a crisis after Moussa C. left the organisation after being elected as a member of parliament. Habsa D. then turned to a friend, a rural entrepreneur she had met in training courses. The two of them set up the Northern Women Entrepreneurs Network. Habsa D. became the general secretary and her friend the president. In 2006, a conflict arose between the two friends. In 2008, Habsa D. and a number of trusted members set up the *Réseaux des Femmes Entrepreneures Rurales* (REFER), which has grown from 13 to 15 groups, with over 800 members. Habsa D. is also the General Secretary of a religious foundation. Thanks to her sister, a member of the Economic and Social Council who supports Matar R., the son of Habsa D.'s marabout, a friend of her older brother and brother-in-law (his wife is Habsa's D. cousin), she was able to get a ticket to Mecca as a reward for her political support as the daughter of a religious leader.

Conciliating Women: The Interweaving of Community Ties within Professional Networks

Aged between 40 and 49, the conciliating women have similar characteristics as the first two groups in terms of associative and relational dynamics. The search for compromise with grassroots community organisations is very important. They rely on the social roots of religious groups (brotherhoods or ecclesiastics) to legitimise their activities and on local women's solidarity to set up social and solidarity-based economic initiatives. What is special about these women entrepreneurs is that they are very active in neighbourhood and village political and religious associations, from which they recruit other women entrepreneurs by setting up credit unions and forming groups or tontines, which tend to merge with the aims of these associations.

Case 3: Marième L.

Marième L. is a 46-year-old entrepreneur at the time of our study. Married with one son, she lives in the north of France. After failing out of school, she became involved in the youth movement in her municipality, managing a community telecentre for five years. She inherited the position of village chief when her father retired and handed it over to her. As such, she looks for income-generating activities for women. It was also a way for her to give them the benefit of her experience gained during her various training courses.

Marième L. became involved in politics in 1999, at the request of her grandfather, who put her in touch with a politician. Her plan was to develop her own multiservice business and grow onions on a family plot, financed by the politician, who happened to be a friend of her father.

Running the telecentre has enabled Marième L. to make a name for herself, especially through her participation in debates on Saint-Louis radio. That's why, when it came time to choose a coordinator for the women's promotion groups in the municipality, she was nominated by the other women entrepreneurs in 2005. Marième L. set up her group in 2012, which now has 70 members involved in farming, rice growing, livestock rearing, and market gardening, facilitated by the financing of three hectares of land from a cooperation partner.

The daughter of a marabout, Marième L. is the president of a religious association she set up with the women of her village, some of whom are entrepreneurs. The association is run by her marabout, whom she met at a talk organised by the *Badiénou Gox* neighbourhood women's association, which Marième L. heads. Since 2012, Marième L. has been President of the DRIFEL women's livestock-breeders' association in her municipality, which has over 2,000 members. She is the departmental treasurer of the Network of Women's Organisations for Pastoral Development (ROSOPP).

Career Paths of Younger Women: Embedding Family Ties within Professional Networks

Finally, the so-called "cadettes" are aged between 30 and 40. Being very few in our sample, they have individual or family business or agricultural activities, which they tend to combine with associative activities (tontine, cultural and sports association, savings and loan association). As far as their level of education is concerned, Catholic women are better educated than Muslim women. In addition, these women entrepreneurs have greater family responsibilities than those mentioned above, due to their greater domestic and educational responsibilities. Family and neighbourhood ties are at the heart of social initiatives. Husbands and in-laws play an important role. By extension, they also draw on religious ties or use politics to drive social initiatives. On the other hand, while it is important for them to have a good reputation and the recognition of their (in)families, the constraints linked to their family responsibilities do not always allow them to emerge or occupy leading positions in social entrepreneurship. The few who manage to do so remain exceptions, like Justine F.

Case 4: Justine F.

Justine F. (34 at the time of our study, married, two children, baccalaureate – Deputy Mayor of her commune – President of the *Réseau des fédérations femmes rurales du Sud* – President of the women's association in her municipality – Project manager in a women's promotion association.)

Born into a royal, animist family, Justine F. became a Christian after her marriage and has a wealth of experience in community work, acquired since secondary school. Displaced by the conflict in Ziguinchor, she returned to her husband's village to start a new life. Thanks to her husband, who was a rural animator for the NGO Caritas, Justine F. was encouraged to start her own business. At first, she used her husband's political connections to do her training, before getting involved in her municipality, relying on the women's organisations set up around the Catholic associative movement. Justine F. uses the federations of social enterprises she runs as her political base. Some of these women are also parents of students at the seminary, volunteers, or customers at the "open doors" activities organised each year to raise funds through the sale of meals (if they don't cook, they buy) by the Saint Joseph seminary. Her brother-in-law is the village priest. The seminary serves as a showcase for Justine F. to promote the women's federation. In return, Justine F. uses her position at the town hall to obtain financial and material support for the seminary.

Justine F.'s strategy for gaining access to all the visible spheres of public life is also a political one. At the last municipal elections, she was nominated as deputy mayor. Thanks to this position, Justine F. is promoting the federation of women that is multiplying their opportunities to change things. It was in this spirit that the Rural Women's Network was set up, to work towards a sub-regional goal of promoting market garden blocks as a strategy in the fight for peace. The network reflects women's commitment to earning an income that will enable them to meet their children's health and education costs.

Following an in-depth analysis of the detailed qualitative portraits, the career paths of these social entrepreneurs are embedded in relational networks, following a long process of building, deconstructing, and breaking multiple links. While family and religious relationships serve as anchoring strategies that run through all the paths of the women entrepreneurs surveyed, we observe a decentring and a logic of conquest of different associative spaces (local, professional, denominational, or political) in the dynamics of the expansion of their activities and in their stabilisation. In many respects, the way in which family ties and associative ties are embedded in career paths reflects the multiplexity of ties in various domains, old, and new, strong, and weak (family, businesses, associations).

This multiplexity, which operates through the mediation of interpersonal links and the prism of interference, highlights the juxtaposition, superimposition, and entanglement of the links mobilised. In fact, these women can be managers of a social enterprise and negotiate access to more arable land for the women in their groups, as town councillors, neighbourhood delegates, or political leaders, just as they can access bank loans as chairwomen of a collective of women entrepreneurs thanks to the interpersonal links they maintain with influential players (political or religious ones).

These women take part in the agenda of institutional players by participating in their activities on an ad hoc basis, particularly through training courses. They may choose to take advantage of a visit to an influential political figure to demonstrate their ability to mobilise people for electoral purposes (for one day), or of a visit to their marabout (once or three times a year) to meet local political authorities who can provide them with business opportunities. Although each type of link has its own specific temporality, the tendency to develop personal networks at the institutional level and professional networks at the local and community levels testifies to the ability of women social entrepreneurs to use their multiple anchors (family, religious, political, economic ones, etc.) and to bring these links into a coherent dialogue to make their way in the social economy.

Similarly, the life cycle of female entrepreneurs is also an important factor in shaping the career paths of social entrepreneurs. They become important figures from the age of 50 once they can withdraw from domestic and educational responsibilities. The conditions for such empowerment may lie in delegating tasks to other, younger women, depending on their position within their household and their economic power to pay for the services of a domestic helper. While up to the age of 45, the strategies of anchoring (family, religious ones) are stronger, the logic of conquering political and institutional spaces dominates. The dynamic interplay of these two approaches – anchoring and conquering – means that a bond built up in one area of sociability may endure or disappear in other cases. The sum of all these links gives women entrepreneurs the power to negotiate material and immaterial resources.

Conclusion

The aim of this research was to study the dynamics of networks in the trajectories of female social entrepreneurs and to show the extent to which they are embedded in multiplex links to access the resources available in their networks. In the first part, we presented the data from our survey, showing the general and specific characteristics of these women entrepreneurs. The second part of our presentation described the space of these networks by showing a series of sometimes overlapping links that cross the trajectories. In the third part, the overlap of these old, recent, and new social relationships enabled us to show, in a dynamic way, how family and associative ties are embedded in pathways and networks, through the regularities, continuities, changes, ruptures, and (re)configurations during entrepreneurial trajectories.

The diversification of networks at the heart of these trajectories reveals a long and complex process of embedding and decoupling. The multiplex nature of these networks reflects the ability of women entrepreneurs to embed their professional trajectories in relationships that *ultimately* prove instrumental, enabling them to achieve their goals through the synchronisation of different time horizons. The dual strategy of anchoring (family and religion) and conquering (political and institutional) both serve to legitimise and moralise women's entrepreneurship, which in turn fosters recognition and enhancement of the career paths of social entrepreneurs. Through the plurality of anchors and logics of totalising conquests, the construction of women entrepreneurs' paths reveals both the complexity of the embedding process and the decoupling, which through these interdependent, interwoven, and multiplex relational links, allows us to grasp the multidimensional character of the woman entrepreneur and her plural figures.

Notes

1 This chapter was published in French: Gning, Sadio Ba (2021) "Biographies relationnelles d'entrepreneures sociales au Sénégal", *RECMA*, 362 (4): 66–80 and is here published with the kind authorisation of the review.

2 The results that are presented here are part of the research programme "Women, social/religious networks and entrepreneurship in Senegal" funded by the *Institut de Recherche pour le Développement* (IRD) between 2016 and 2019 and coordinated by Sadio Ba Gning. The survey involved 100 female social entrepreneurs and 20 key informants. It took place from September 2016 to October 2017 in Dakar, Saint-Louis, located in the north of Senegal, and Ziguinchor, in the south.

3 A good example of this is the Caritas network, which is structured around the Basic Ecclesiastical Communities (BECs), which are family organisations overseen by the parish priest and the bishop at diocesan level.
4 This diagram summarises the network of women entrepreneurs, which is made up of links in different areas and at different levels. It was drawn up after analysing the qualitative portraits of the women surveyed. In the configuration of these networks, links from family, professional, and community circles play a pivotal, cross-cutting role.

References

Berrou, J.-P. and F. Combarnous (2011) "Testing Lin's social capital theory in an informal African urban economy", *The Journal of Development Studies*, 47 (8): 1216–1240. https://doi.org/10.1080/00220388.2010.547937

Burt, R. S. (1992) *Structural Holes: The Social Structure of Competition*. Cambridge: Harvard University Press. https://www.jstor.org/stable/j.ctv1kz4h78

Fall, A. S. and C. Guèye (2003) "Derem ak Ngerem: Le franc, la grâce et la reconnaissance Les ressorts de l'économie sociale et solidaire en Afrique de l'Ouest", *Revue de MAUSS*, 21 (1): 97–112.

Ferrary, M. (2010) "Dynamique des réseaux sociaux et stratégies d'encastrement social", *Revue d'économie industrielle*, 129–130 (1–2): 171–202. https://doi.org/10.4000/rei.4153

Gning, S. B. (2019) "La religion, une ressource pour l'entrepreneuriat féminin au Sénégal", *Sociologies pratiques*, 39 (2): 133–144.

Gning, S. B. (2021) "Biographies relationnelles d'entrepreneures sociales au Sénégal", *RECMA | Revue internationale de l'économie sociale*, 362 (4): 68–80.

Granovetter, M. S. (1973) "The strength of weak ties", *American Journal of Sociology*, 78 (6): 1360–1380.

Granovetter, M. S. (1974) *Getting a Job: A Study of Contacts and Careers*. Chicago: University of Chicago Press.

Granovetter, M. (1985) "Economic action and social structure: The problem of embeddedness", *American Journal of Sociology*, 91 (3): 481–510.

Grimm, M. et al. (2013) "Kinship ties entrepreneurship in Western Africa", *Journal of Small Business and Entrepreneurship*, 26 (2): 125–150. https://doi.org/10.1080/08276331.2013.771854

Grossetti, M. (2008) "Réseaux sociaux et médiations dans les activités d'innovation", *Hermès, La Revue*, 50 (1): 19–27. https://doi.org/10.4267/2042/24148

Grossetti, M. and J. F. Barthe (2008) "Dynamique des réseaux interpersonnels et des organisations dans les créations d'entreprises", *Revue française de sociologie*, 49 (3): 585–612. https://doi.org/10.3917/rfs.493.0585

Grossetti, M. and M.-P. R. Bes (2003) "Dynamiques des réseaux et des cercles. Encastrements et découplages", *Revue d'économie industrielle*, 103 (1): 43–58.

Mitchell, J. C. (1969) *Social Networks in Urban Situations: Analyses of Personal Relationships in Central African Towns*. Manchester: Manchester University Press.

Nordman, C.J. and J. Vaillant (2014) "Entreprenariat informel et genre à Madagascar: Le rôle des normes de solidarité et des responsabilités domestiques dans les écarts de performances", *Mondes en développement*, 166 (2): 59–72. https://doi.org/10.3917/med.166.0059.

Schumpeter, J. (1912) *Theorie der wirtschaftlichen Entwicklung*. Leipzig: Duncker and Humblot.

Vergrugge, L.M. (1979) "Multiplexity in adult friendships", *Social Forces*, 57 (4): 1286–1309.

Weber, M. (2003) *L'éthique protestante et l'esprit du capitalisme: Suivi d'autres essais.* Paris: Gallimard.

White, H. C. (2002) *Markets From Networks: Socioeconomic Models of Production.* Princeton, NJ: Princeton University Press.

10 Social Entrepreneurship in Dakar

Reasons for the Disaffiliation of Members of the Association of Women Seamstresses of the Marché Colobane (A.F.C.)

Aboubacar Diallo and Paul Mamba Diédhiou

Introduction

Research into the problems of the artisanal textile sub-sector has identified 23,106 businesses in Senegal, half of which are estimated to be occupied by textile artisans (Sadji 2004: 11; Azevedo, 2016). However, because of global competition and the restructuring of the national economy (Schuerkens et al. (eds) 2019; Schuerkens (ed.) 2023), women dressmakers are struggling to develop their business. Senegal's women dressmakers must contend with a lack of improvement in the state's import control system (dumping and second-hand goods).

In the Integrated Framework (IF) report on the diagnosis of trade integration (Rapport d'étude, 2013), it is mentioned that the State does not very often explore all the possibilities offered by the rules of the World Trade Organisation (WTO) and the specific agreements between it and the European Union to improve the conditions for exporting and importing textile products (Rapport d'étude, 2013). Similarly, the West African Economic and Monetary Union (Ndoye, 2003) considers that the lack of financial resources is the main cause of the difficulties faced by women dressmakers in Senegal because there are not enough credit lines targeting the informal sector in which they find themselves. The International Trade Centre (Rapport d'étude, 2013) states that the informal situation in which Senegalese women dressmakers find themselves explains the problems they face. Most women dressmakers in Senegal do not have their own shop. Many of their activities take place in the local markets and neighbourhoods (houses).

However, these places are often unsuitable for the practice of their activities because of the lack of hygiene and insecurity (Sadji, 2004). Similarly, the sector's problems are linked both to the low level of educational qualifications and professional skills, as most tailors working in sewing and dressmaking have received on-the-job training. These forms of apprenticeship do not guarantee real professional skills. The level of initial training is very low due to the lack of training for trainers. Further training and capacity-building are also inadequate. The training frameworks available, workshops, and vocational training centres are inadequate for the numbers to be trained. Training programmes are not redefined, and there is also the problem of space, as often only 10 to 20 square metres are available for production, the showroom, the office, and the storage of goods and manufacturing inputs (Sadji, 2004: 22). Against this backdrop, the Senegalese Tailors' Movement

DOI: 10.4324/9781003492931-13

(*Mouvement des Tailleurs du Sénégal* – M.T.S), made up of around a hundred associations in 42 departments, has identified this problem as "a top priority" in its demands. This would provide women tailors with a suitable space in which to carry out their activities, with a view to improving their living and working conditions.

In response to these problems, the Senegalese government has put in place several strategies which, in essence, aim to find viable solutions to the problems faced by those working in the informal sector, particularly women dressmakers. These include organising the following into formal associations of craftswomen and women seamstresses by the contribution of dressmaking to job creation, the promotion of local production units, the quality and labelling of services, trade promotion to ensure better positioning of products on the national and international market, capacity-building for the actors, the updating of static data, the improvement of the legislative and regulatory framework, and protection measures for craftswomen dressmakers and their families (Délégation à l'Entreprenariat Rapide – DER, 2024).[1]

The State has set up the *Agence pour la Promotion et le Développement de l'Artisanat* (APDA): the aim of which is to boost and relaunch the Senegalese craft industry with a budget of 28 billion F-CFA financed by the African Development Bank and the Islamic Bank of Senegal among other financial partners.[2] Then there is the *Délégation Générale de l'Entreprenariat Rapide (DER),* which has a budget of 30 billion F-CFA to finance people (aged between 18 and 40) wishing to set up business in the following sectors: agriculture, animal husbandry, and in the sewing sector, with a repayment rate of 5%, at 500,000 F-CFA of the total amount.[3] Finally, there is also the National Craft Development Strategy, which promotes craft businesses in every region of the country, as well as provides funding for the expansion and modernisation of craft businesses.[4]

In response to directives from the Senegalese government, the women dressmakers at Marché Colobane have decided to create the *Association des femmes couturières du Marché Colobane* (A.F.C.). Such an organisation would enable women dressmakers to move from the informal sector to the formal sector, thanks to public initiatives. The association was set up in 2015 with the aim of bringing together the women dressmakers of Marché Colobane into a structure capable of bringing their demands to the attention of the authorities, but also a structure responsible for pooling the women's efforts to resolve the various problems facing its members. These include problems relating to the financing of their activities, the reduction in the payment of the licence fee to the town hall (considered very costly), the problem of insalubrity, the problem relating to insecurity, and the problem relating to the acquisition of spaces or workshops. A.F.C.'s recognition, thanks to the receipt it has obtained from the State for its partners, has enabled the seamstresses to gain visibility on a national level. This recognition can be attributed to the creation of a special fund in 2015, with a view to becoming financially independent. This is funded by a contribution of 500 F-CFA per member per month. The fund enables to help women seamstresses experiencing social difficulties, such as weddings, christenings, illnesses, or death.[5]

As a result, the association became a member of the Senegalese Tailors' Movement (STM). In 2017, a body to which all the associations of tailors in Senegal (some 100 associations in 42 departments) belong. In other words, it is the umbrella organisation for the micro-associations of tailors working in Senegal's markets and neighbourhoods. It defends the tailors' cause with the supervisory authorities, in this case the ministry responsible for the craft industry, as well as government structures dedicated to entrepreneurship in the craft industry. Moreover, in 2019, the STM got into a tussle with the State because the latter wanted to grant the Diamniadio site to a Chinese entrepreneur to set up his textile industry. So far,[6] the matter continues to arouse the anger of the movement, which wants the site to be allocated to Senegal's tailors, who are looking for a specific space in which to practise their trade. Similarly, the A.F.C., between 2017 and 2018, began participation in certain meetings: training workshops with craft chambers, craft fairs, and exhibitions at the Dakar International Fair (FIDAK), and meetings of craft chambers).

As part of this process, the A.J.T.C. has also managed to obtain from the Town Hall an agreement on the annual payment of licence fees with a grouping of receipts for a sum of 1,000,000 F-CFA (whereas previously it was around 25,000 to 30,000 F-CFA per year for each pruner). With the support of other trades, the association has managed to obtain a subsidy of 700 million F-CFA from the State, with the support of the World Bank, to repair not only the damage caused by the fire at Marché Colobane in 2018, due to recurrent power cuts, but also to finance their activities. Part of this envelope was used to set up a security cordon to watch over Marché Colobane, in general, and the sewing workshops in particular. It also made it possible to help dressmakers who found themselves "unable" to pay their rent, to the tune of 50,000 to 60,000 F-CFA per month, depending on the size of the shop, ranging from 20 to 25 m^2. Moreover, in collaboration with delegates from Marché Colobane and other trades, the A.F.C. has succeeded in lowering the rent from 35,000 to 30,000 F-CFA per month, depending on the size of the shop.

In addition, this funding has enabled to improve the wastewater treatment system[7] at Marché Colobane. Similarly, in 2019, the A.F.C. set up a haggling post to facilitate the sale of products. This strategy has attracted both domestic and foreign customers (Republic of Guinea, Guinea-Bissau, Mali, etc.). In addition, in 2020, the Gueule Tapé-Fasse-Colobane town hall granted a sum of 32,000,000 F-CFA to be distributed to the various corporations operating at the Marché Colobane to help them cushion the impact of the crises caused by COVID-19. The A.F.C. was able to enter a partnership with PAMECAS[8] for financial assistance for seamstresses in distress to help them start or restart their businesses. This partnership resulted in a donation of 500,000 F-CFA, with a requirement from PAMECAS of a repayment rate of 25% with an interest rate of 1%.

Despite these achievements, women dressmakers are disaffiliating themselves from the A.F.C. In other words, of the 100 members of the A.F.C. in 2018, 85 disaffiliated between 2018 and 2024, i.e., a rate of 85%.[9] In the light of these findings, this study focuses on the following questions: What are the reasons why women seamstresses disaffiliate from the A.F.C. even though it is the key to their success? To what extent does the functioning of the A.F.C. explain the disaffiliation? How did the practices of the A.F.C. leaders have influences on disaffiliation?

Research Methodology

Understanding the factors that explain the disaffiliation of women seamstresses at A.F.C. is the major concern of this chapter. Considering that disaffiliation can only be understood through the speeches, opinions, and perceptions of the actors involved, the qualitative research methodology seemed appropriate for this study.

To scientifically validate the relevance of the choice of this approach, we referred to James Rule's rational analysis (2002), on the understanding that each theory has its own methodological implications. Semi-structured interviews were used to gather information. Around 30 in-depth individual interviews were carried out, enabling data to be collected on the reasons why the women seamstresses left the A.F.C. These interviews were conducted in May 2024 with the women dressmakers who are no longer members of the A.F.C. and based at Marché Colobane, as well as with the actors in charge of the A.F.C. The collection of this data was based on the following selection criteria: whether they were women seamstresses who were disaffiliated from the A.F.C., and whether they were A.F.C. leaders. This means that we used the "reasoned or theoretical choice sampling technique" (N'Da, 2015: 106). In addition, this information was exfoliated using the categorical thematic content analysis technique (N'Da, 2015), which consists of identifying the themes most discussed and most cited in the individual interviews conducted with the disaffiliated women dressmakers of the A.F.C. and with their leaders. These topics of discussion were related to the operation of the A.F.C., the attitudes and practices of the leaders, and the search for funding, which seems to be better mastered by middle-aged women because of their experience (strong and weak links) and their political affiliations (social safety nets). Illustrative quotes on these themes have been selected to support our analysis.

The study took place at Marché Colobane, located in the commune of Gueule Tapée-Fass-Colobane, the largest commercial area in the country's capital and one of Dakar's 19 arrondissements. The market is part of the Dakar Plateau arrondissement, bounded to the north by the HLM district, the Cité Port, and the Cité des Douanes, to the south by the Gibraltar district, to the east by the Hann-Bélair district separated by the autoroute (Seydina Limamou Laye), to the west by the Fass district and to the south-west by the Medina district.

This market stretches along the Colobane roundabout, which runs alongside Autoroute A, the Seydina Limamou Laye motorway, from Cité Port (near the family roundabout), Cité Douane (near the HLM district) to the Samba Diéry Diallo barracks. Within this market, there is a shopping centre "Cheikh Ahmadou Bamba" located between the Colobane urban bus station, Cité Barack, Robinet Sérère, and Baye aye.

Overview of the Association of Women Dressmakers in Colobane (A.F.C.)

Description of the A.F.C.

Historically, Marché Colobane is one of the oldest and largest markets in Dakar. It was created in 1964 after the displacement of Marché FASS. Since its creation, it has always been home to women dressmakers. At the time, the market was plagued by safety and sanitation problems, which gave it a bad image nationally, sub-regionally, and internationally, which meant that women tailors found it difficult to carry out their activities. The insiders call it "Black Market" because it's a favourite hawker's market. It's here where many burglars and muggers from all walks of life sell their loot after committing their crimes. His real name is "Cheikh Ahmadou Bamba", a name that has been given to it for almost 20 years, but which is unknown to the people who frequent the market today.

It should also be pointed out that, despite these problems, there has never been an umbrella organisation of tailors to deal with them. Today, these problems are a regular occurrence at Marché Colobane. It was against this backdrop that the women dressmakers at Marché Colobane[10] decided to set up a respected and respectable association to identify and propose appropriate solutions to their problems. After all, it is a market that supplies not only the country, but also the West African sub-region, Central Africa, Europe, and North America, to name but a few. These figures demonstrate the importance of creating an association like the A.F.C. From 2015 to 2017, this association had 100 members in 470 shops or sewing workshops.

However, it is important to point out that we have no knowledge of the existence of official documents attesting to the legality of the A.J.T.C., including the statutes or internal regulations that govern it. Ignorance of the statutes and internal rules can affect the association's visibility and reliability and contribute to its destabilisation. It can also undermine the association's survival and provoke a kind of "retention", i.e., a lack of confidence and doubt in the members of the A.F.C. (Ly et al., 2002). In the same vein, Emmanuel Dione (2000) shows in his study, that this lack of knowledge of the statutes and internal regulations is linked to the fact that they have not been widely disseminated. According to him, failure to disseminate an association's statutes and internal rules deprives it of credibility among its members.

The women interviewed describe this as a constraint which destroys the ambition and desire of the dressmakers to remain members of the A.F.C. This lack of knowledge of the statutes governing the functioning of the association is a sign of discouragement for the women dressmakers who believe that it is necessary for them to belong to the association:

> I don't even believe that the A.F.C. has any internal rules governing its operations. Or even if it does, it's only in words. What's more, the association is badly designed, and its internal rules are not known to all its members. For example, every member should have a badge and a number. That's how

> it works elsewhere. I'm willing to stay, but the way the Association works doesn't give me the courage to stay. The fact that the Association's internal rules have not been translated into the local language has contributed to the friction and the rift. Finally, the fact that the internal regulations have not been made public makes me doubt its existence and discourages me from continuing to belong to this Association. Penda N., aged 36, disaffiliated from the A.F.C., May 2024.[11]

These comments reveal a lack of knowledge of the statutes and internal rules, and a failure to publicise them, all of which contribute to the fragility of the A.F.C. What's more, the seamstresses point out that the association does not require a legal and legitimate character, which translates into a lack of credibility and guarantee to international standards. In other words, the gap in the usual procedure (written and accompanied by certain sanctions and legal fines) explains this wave of exits by members of the association. This lack of familiarity with the statutes and regulations is due to the fragility of the membership procedure, which is oral.

Objectives, Mission, and Purpose of the A.F.C.

The overall objective of the A.F.C. takes the form of support and mutual collaboration between members, which is in line with the development of national skills with a view to accelerating their participation in wealth creation, in accordance with the objectives of the Senegal Emerging Plan (PSE). A.F.C. has stimulated the government, thanks to its financing structures dedicated to entrepreneurship in the craft sector, to investigate the difficulties its members are facing. With this request, the government is seeking to encourage financial backers to increase their investment. It is also seeking to identify and draw on available resources to meet the specific needs of women dressmakers. The aim is to help women seamstresses pool their efforts and profits, by solving problems related to the financing of their activities and the reduction in the payment of the licence fee to the town hall, by solving the problem of insalubrity and insecurity, and by solving the problem related to the acquisition of spaces or workshops. The government's mission is to ensure equal opportunities for women dressmakers. Such a mission would enable women dressmakers to gain recognition from the State to benefit from subsidies through funding structures dedicated to entrepreneurship such as the DER and their partners. Acquiring these subsidies should enable the association to solve the various problems that these women face daily and guarantee the continuity of their activities or jobs. The establishment of the A.F.C. should enable its members to better defend their professional interests. In other words, it should generate benefits enabling women to exercise their profession under favourable conditions. However, evidence from the field shows that the initial objectives and missions of the A.F.C. are not being met.

We agree with Emmanuel Dione (2000) that the misappropriation of the purpose and mission of associations is one of the main causes of their dysfunction. Moreover, this misuse justifies and legitimises the disaffiliation of its members.

These women have given up because they can no longer see the advantages and benefits that compel them to stay. From this point of view, James Rule (2002) states that individuals are instrumentally motivated by a utilitarian logic of "cost-benefit" and "benefit-benefit" and can modify their behaviour if these are not achieved. In fact, the replies received from the respondents show that, often, women dressmakers leave the A.F.C. because of the lack of advantages and benefits due to non-compliance with the objectives and missions assigned.

Ethnography of the A.F.C.: The Organigramme

The A.F.C. is registered as a socio-economic and profit-making organisation. It is made up of a president, a general secretary, a treasurer, a person in charge of information and a person in charge of merchandising. The president is the legal entity of the association. Her role is to organise and direct the meetings of the executive committee, ensure strict compliance with the statutes and internal regulations, and order and control the various activities. She also authorises expenditure and has all the powers necessary for the management of the association. As president, she contributes to the promotion, development, and search for financial and material resources.

The General Secretary is the central executive body. She is responsible for the practical implementation of the programme and directives issued by the General Meeting. She reports to the Executive Committee, under the supervision of the Chairman, and keeps the association's head office permanently open. She draws up the minutes of meetings, incoming and outgoing correspondence, and keeps a register. She coordinates membership applications from new members as well as from the association's branches, assists them with their integration, and updates the membership file and the duty roster. The Treasurer is the custodian of the association's funds; she is responsible for all financial and accounting operations. She operates the account(s) opened in the name of the association with a banking institution (e.g., PAMECAS). It settles the expenditure orders issued by the President.

The Information and Communications Officer is responsible for the association's internal and external policy. She oversees relations with the press and internal information management. She is also responsible for informing the Board of press articles, publications, and other information of interest to the association. She is the spokesperson and responsible for motivating and managing human relations between members of the A.F.C. The role of the bargaining agent is to find markets/offers to enable members to sell their goods. However, a closer look reveals that the haggling post is considered by the members to be a clandestine post, set up to meet the specific needs of the association's leaders. In other words, it seems to have been created by certain members of the group leaders to promote the sale of their products. Even if the women leaders try to justify the legality and legitimacy of this position and others in general:

> Contrary to what detractors say, this post does exist and is recognised by everyone. This post is designed to help women dressmakers, without distinction,

> to find markets where they can sell their goods. Seamstresses often find it difficult to sell their products after having spent so much energy making them. That's why we decided to set up this post to alleviate these difficulties. So, it's a job that will benefit all the members of our association, not just the leaders, as the saboteurs think. Fatou T., aged 50, canvasser[12] for the A.F.C., May 2024.

This extract shows the existence of a disagreement between the directors and the members over the allocation of posts that determine the running of the association. This casts suspicion on the character and legal basis of the association because many of its members do not believe in its legal existence. As far as they are concerned, the association only exists in name. What's more, there are no official legal documents presented by the members to attest to its legality. For this reason, some of the interviewees clearly stated that the posts and the people occupying them had been chosen haphazardly. This situation not only justifies the illegality but also underlies the failure to consider the criteria required for the operation of traditional organisations in Senegal, in this case, associations. The law states that all Senegalese traditional organisations must meet the criteria for Economic Interest Groups (EIGs), namely: object; name; registered office; duration; allocation of responsibilities; term of office; decision-making body for the group's operation (Azevedo, 2016).

A closer look reveals that the A.F.C. does not comply with these criteria, because it does not have a registered office; its duration is not determined at all; the duration of mandates is not complied with either and in addition, the allocation of responsibilities is not respected. This shows the extent to which the women dressmakers feel almost total disinterest in this association because of the lack of an adequate structure of the organisation. All these shortcomings are forcing many women dressmakers to discredit the association. This discrediting led them to delegitimise the A.F.C., given that the legal fundamentals of an association are not respected. This is what gives rise to the notion of "cost" (Rule, 2002). Indeed, all our respondents think that remaining in the A.F.C. with this poor structure is a "real waste". Their membership of this association, because of its legal shortcomings and poor structure, would be surfing on a huge "cost". This corroborates James Rule (2002) when he says that individuals cannot continue to belong to a group for so long when the cost is higher than the benefits, they can derive from it.

Communication Measures of A.F.C. Leaders: The End of Disaffiliation

Increasing Dissatisfaction among Communications Professionals

Communication is a precious and essential tool, without which the smooth running and achievement of an organisation's objectives become almost impossible. However, within the A.F.C., there is an acute communication deficit. It manifests itself in the privatisation of information. The communication deficit in an organisation makes it impossible to establish and maintain a balance of information among all the organisation's stakeholders (Cornelissen, 2017):

> Within the A.F.C., the directors don't communicate very well. There is a privatisation of information, i.e. information concerning the survival of the association is limited to the level of the directors. What's more, decisions within the association are taken unilaterally, without informing most of its members. We are told nothing about what goes on within the association. That's why I've decided to leave the association. Amina S., aged 37, disaffiliated from the A.F.C., May 2024.

These comments show that the lack of communication is perceived by disaffiliates as a privatisation of information on the part of the governing body. This situation leads to discouragement and encourages them to give up because they feel excluded. As a result, this lack of communication can lead to confusion, if not total or partial withholding, resulting in a mode of exclusion between those who have the information and those who do not (Ly et al., 2002). Putting these remarks into context, it must be said that within the A.F.C., women dressmakers have a poor perception of communication players. These perceptions are due to the bad impression given by the communication players who embody a certain political attitude that makes it difficult for most (apolitical) women dressmakers to give credence to the sincerity of their communication. This way of operating has created a dispute with women dressmakers who do not like politics or who do not share the same political opinions. In addition, this situation has led to dysfunction as women dressmakers who suffer the effects of this practice without benefiting in any way decide to leave the organisation.

The work of Fatou Sarr (1998) shows that associations that try to comply with political directives are not as successful in Senegal as associations that evolve without them. There is greater personal development and financial growth in associations that self-regulate than in those that do not. In addition, this politicisation of communication has led to unequal sharing of information, but also of resources. This unequal sharing of information is a factor that most often leads to the dissolution of associations (Ly et al., 2002). Similarly, some of the women interviewed said that the association had enabled some seamstresses who previously had only one workshop to enrich themselves illegally through the plundering of their members. It is believed that people join a group less out of a desire to succeed than in the hope of deriving some benefit from their membership (Festinger, 1953). Strategic analysis theorists agree that the behaviour of actors is not predictable because it is changeable (Crozier and Friedberg, 1977). These authors state that the actor constantly adjusts his behaviour to the data he encounters in the pursuit of his objective. This means that the disaffiliated members of the A.F.C. have adopted this behaviour in response to new circumstances (Rule, 2002). Their reasons for choosing disaffiliation are due both to the lack of communication and to the political attitudes of the women involved:

> My decision to leave the A.F.C. is due to the fact that we are often deprived of information about possible funding. Just recently, I heard that the World Bank has offered us funding, the exact amount of which I don't know. But our

> chiefs, in collusion with the delegates from Marché, ate the money without informing us beforehand. And the seamstresses who tried to challenge this practice were stifled and reprimanded (either by imprisonment or by bribing the challengers) by the guards at the Marché police station. That's why I say that this association only benefits an illegitimate minority. Marieme B., aged 25, disaffiliated from the A.F.C., May 2024.

The obstacles encountered by members of A.F.C. in accessing finance support Rule's (2002) view that individuals change their minds when they find that the situation has turned against them. In the same vein, our interviewees pointed to the lack of personality of the seamstresses responsible for passing on information, which explained the willingness of members to break the "*social pact*". This lack of personality on the part of these actresses underpins their failure to embody leadership and creates a conflict of competence within the A.F.C. Indeed, we have noticed that communication is under the control of a single person, who is none other than the president who carries out a dual function within the association. This interference is seen by some of the members surveyed as a factor blocking the flow of communication. This situation supports the idea that the lack of leadership among women managers in an organisation would generate quarrels within it (Asnal, 2011). This is to say that this lack of leadership is applicable to A.F.C., which in turn would have encouraged the disaffiliation of these members.

Influence of Information Received: Perceptions, Assessments, and Rationales

Within the A.F.C., there is no transparency in the communication procedures. This lack of transparency is attributable to the rumours that has been receiving recently about this association:

> I withdrew from this association as soon as I felt that I couldn't prosper by staying. What's more, the people we put at the head of this organisation don't play fair with us. Often, when the funding comes, they don't tell us, and it's only then that we hear the echoes in the workshop corridors. Recently, I heard that the Gueule Tapé-Fasse-Colobane town hall had given 32 million F-CFA to be distributed to the various guilds operating in this market to help them cushion the impact of the crises caused by COVID-19. But to date, we still don't know where this money, the seamstresses' share, has gone. My comrades and I protested to claim our share. This protest ended in a general quarrel and was echoed by the media, who travelled to find out more. Aïda S., aged 32, disaffiliated from the A.F.C., May 2024.

These comments highlight the imperfections of communication within the A.F.C. Instead of reassuring means of communication, women dressmakers are forced to give credence to information generated by rumours. This emphasis on rumours has led to misunderstanding within the group. This is in line with James Rule's (2002) view that individuals pursue stable ends by adapting their actions to new circumstances and changing information (Rule, 2002). In the same sense, we can say that the information that the women seamstresses received from rumours led them to disaffiliate themselves from the organisation. Even though within the A.F.C., several communication channels exist in the digital age – WhatsApp, Facebook, Messenger, telephone SMS, etc., but they are not sufficiently exploited:

> We haven't set up information groups using social networks because people aren't engaged. When we have information to pass on, we take advantage of our downtime to pass it on quickly by word of mouth. Binta K., aged 56, president of the A.F.C., May 2024.

The failure to use communication channels clearly shows that those in charge lack good strategies enabling them to minimise the imperfections linked to rumours and to have control over this communication and the people targeted by its information. And yet, the use of channels (e.g., WhatsApp, Facebook, etc.) could be an asset for smooth operations (insurance, release of money, funding opportunities, etc.). In the same vein, it is essential for all stakeholders in a group to communicate with each other so as not to attract hatred within the group (Kumcu, 2001). This confirms the position of rational choice theorists who assert that individuals calculate their actions in the light of perceived rewards and act according to these calculations (Rule, 2002; Niosi, 2002).

Attitudes and Practices of A.F.C. Women Managers: Factors Influencing Disaffiliation

Within the A.F.C., the attitudes and practices of its leaders are viewed negatively, as many women dressmakers explain their reasons for leaving the organisation. This negative assessment of these attitudes and practices explains the deterioration in relations between leaders and members of this organisation. Moreover, this deterioration in relations is due to the lack of consideration that the association's leaders feel towards its uneducated members:

> The reason why I decided to leave this association is the low status that its leaders reserve for us members who have hardly been to school. In fact, we illiterate women dressmakers are often dissociated from the organisation's decision-making bodies. However, most of the seamstresses who make up this organisation are barely literate. Mariama D., aged 35, illiterate and disaffiliated with the A.F.C., May 2024.

This interview extract shows that the low educational status of some members seems to be a sign of contempt on the part of the leaders of the A.F.C. This contemptuous attitude towards these members often unleashes their anger, which underpins their disaffiliation. As for the governors, they think that these illiterates know nothing about the running of an association. This misunderstanding between the managers and the illiterate members makes working together complex, incomprehensible, and even impossible. However, at A.F.C., there are also illiterate members in the management team. As a result, there is a degree of affinity in this treatment, especially as some traditional women in this category (illiterate) are not subjected to this ordeal:

> I'm illiterate, but I wasn't subjected to the ill-treatment described by my comrades who decided to leave our association. I've also never seen or witnessed this kind of scene. As far as I'm concerned, what these people are saying is nothing more than a diversion to legitimise their decision to leave. Maïmouna D., aged 36, illiterate and affiliated to the A.F.C., May 2024.

This extract shows that the deterioration in relations was not just between the leaders and the members, but also between the members of the A.F.C. For some seamstresses, however, the fact that the leaders took matters concerning the organisation into their own hands without involving them was just a pretext used to protect their own interests and those of their own political persuasion:

> The leaders of the A.F.C. associate certain illiterate women with their political affiliation to the APR (Alliance pour la République). In fact, during the 2019 presidential elections, they organised a meeting in honour of this ruling party. If you want to make money, you must be in their party. Similarly, if you want to benefit from the privileges and the opportunities that arise in the association, you must belong to their political party. That's why they call us auxiliaries, because they don't need our input in meetings and decision-making. Quite simply because, politically speaking, we're not on the same wavelength. Nafi S., aged 31, illiterate and disaffiliated from the A.F.C., May 2024.

These comments show that the attitudes and practices of the A.F.C. leaders, linked to their political affiliation (APR, the party in power from 2 April 2012 to 2 April 2024), constitute a factor that legitimises the desire of women dressmakers to disaffiliate, which would cause the dysfunction. This situation is contrary to the thesis made by Samba Diouf (2011) on "Le groupement féminin '*Sante Yalla*' à Ziguinchor". According to the author, the group is a good alternative, because it helps to improve the living conditions of the women who join or are integrated into it. In other words, women acquire much greater financial autonomy than they would have on their own. Similarly, it should be remembered that women's living conditions improve much more within the group than if they were on their own. However, this analysis by Samba Diouf (2011) contrasts with the realities of our study, as the A.F.C. does not contribute to improving the living conditions of the women seamstresses who belong to it. What's more, these women seamstresses are not financially independent. The complexity of relations between the association's leaders and members, due to the unequal sharing of resources, runs counter to this analysis.

Multiple Identities within the A.F.C.: Indicators of Disaffiliation

Within the A.F.C., there is inconsistency in the multiplicity of players (plural identities) who make it up. Within this association, we note the membership of individuals who do not practise the sewing trade, in particular the fabric and shoe sellers and the delegates from Marché Colobane. The presence of these persons belonging to other professional groups raises misunderstandings, especially as their membership is contrary to the criteria of belonging to the association because each of the categories will be able to develop their own strategies and maximise their interests. This game of profit by these heterogeneous players weakens the social cohesion of the members of the A.F.C. Those who are most vulnerable or victims of this game of interests may look for ways out of this compartmentalisation, which is neither beneficial nor advantageous to them. Such is the logic of those who think that their presence in this association is fortuitous because they have realised that it is not designed to defend and safeguard the sole general interest of women dressmakers. This finding corroborates the logic of James Rule (2002) because he does not focus on the reason for the appearance of a change in the ends pursued but on the existence of calls to do so. The disaffiliation of women dressmakers is thus motivated by the intrusion of outside tradespeople (e.g., fabric and shoe sellers), whom they see as a serious threat to their interests.

From another point of view, within the A.F.C., an identity problem arose between members of foreign origin and those of Senegalese origin. This problem led most foreign dressmakers to distance themselves from the organisation:

> I've been at since 2005. The tailors were not united. It was every tailor for himself, God for all. I'm a part of the tailors who encouraged the setting up of this association in 2015. But as soon as I started, I began to be targeted by people who didn't like the positions I took. For example, when you have 1,000,000 F-CFA, some women can ask for 60,000 F-CFA to present to their religious leader. My comrades and I (referring to foreigners, non-Senegalese women) were opposed to this idea because it was contrary to our basic culture. Since then, we've been the main target of their attacks. They didn't tell us anything about what was going on inside the association. We were no longer considered. We were even excluded from decision-making bodies. So, my comrades and I decided to distance ourselves once and for all from them and from the association. Esther C., aged 26, disaffiliated from the A.F.C., May 2024.

The words of this Congolese woman, disaffiliated from the A.F.C., show that the cultural difference has contributed to the weakening of relations which have led to a definitive break between these two parties. The cultural diversity (e.g., between Senegalese and Congolese women) is thus a threat to the cohesion of the A.F.C. culture. This reflects the fact that African organisations often suffer from this aversion to outsiders which, far from uniting the group around the essentials, tends instead to encourage grouping into ethnic sub-groups (Faye, 2008). This notion of sub-group was felt within the A.F.C., especially with this label of Senegalese origin and foreign origin. In addition, Mariam Faye (2011) argues that the management model proposed in an association is at the origin of cultural and denominational cleavages. In her view, associations need to develop an organisational management model that breaks with the traditional management methods of socio-cultural or religious associations, which are highly hierarchical. They must be based on the principles and rules of good governance, which is also a prerequisite for economic competitiveness. This observation applies to A.F.C., which has not managed to overcome its weaknesses.

The Experience of A.F.C. Members: An Asset in the Search for Funding

Experienced People for the Smooth Running of A.F.C.

Several studies have shown the importance of the presence of experienced people in voluntary organisations. In fact, the study carried out by Oscar Bravo (2015) in Peru on associative participation through volunteering showed that experienced persons are an asset to the smooth running of an association. These people are seen by both society and the State as viable partners in their organisations (Bravo, 2015). This shows how involving people in volunteering would highlight the great value of education and the civic participation that comes with it, as a means of tackling poverty and social exclusion. Moreover, the surveys conducted for this research showed that the task of raising the funding that is essential to the smooth running of A.F.C. falls to members aged over 40. They are the ones who know how to find, mobilise, and capture financial resources, and aid through their relationships (social safety nets). This is the case with the partnership between PAMECAS and A.F.C., made possible thanks to the efforts and relations of the management team, in this case the president, who has enabled certain members to take out loans to finance their activities:

> We have helped some of our members to obtain funding from PAMECAS. This has prevented many dressmakers from going bankrupt. We've achieved this thanks to the trust we've built up with PAMECAS agents. Trust based on respect and consideration. Bintou K., aged 56, President of the association, May 2024.

This extract shows the predominant role played by middle-aged people within the A.F.C. This shows that age is not an obstacle to the smooth running of the A.F.C., but rather a financial safety valve. Moreover, the work of Isabelle Marchand and Olivier Laau-Laurin (2024) has shown that middle-aged people are pillars in the development of local communities. The authors go on to point out that, contrary to popular belief that middle-aged people are passive recipients of care, they can act as the driving force behind collective action. They are part of the local system of action and develop initiatives that encourage socio-territorial innovation in response to a social problem. Their participatory contributions foster the development of rich, resilient communities. This situation was confirmed by our interviewees, who showed that A.F.C. members with associative experience have played important roles in its operation. They know how to access the opportunities presented to the association:

> Thanks to our experience, we were able to obtain the partnership agreement with PAMECAS, the reduction in the cost of rent for shops at Marché

> Colobane, etc. Our experience enables us to know the right moments, i.e. when to talk to the landlord, but also how to get together with the players from other trades to ensure that Marché Colobane runs smoothly, and in particular to protect the interests of the A.F.C. Mame C. aged 50, member of the association, May 2024.

These interview extracts show the know-how of experienced people who have been involved in the voluntary sector for a long time. This length of time in the business world implicitly gives them the power to manage in the interests of the A.F.C.

Political Relations with Experienced Persons, as an Important Aspect of Attracting A.F.C. Funding

Over and above the experience of middle-aged people in the voluntary sector, our interviewees highlighted the importance of networking. This data corroborates Marc Granovetter's network actor theory (1973), which shows that distant and close social acquaintances ("strong ties and weak ties") are assets for accessing opportunities. The political "links" between the female leaders of A.F.C. and the party in power at the time (APR) should be seen in this light. In fact, their attachment to this political party (APR) made it easier for them to obtain allegiances linked to lower shop or sewing room rents:

> Our comrades often say that we are politicians. No! We've understood that in this country, if you don't get involved in politics, you can't win your case. The people who are appointed to head the funding structures dedicated to entrepreneurship are politicians. So, to attract their attention, you must be on their political side. That's why we're often seen near the delegates at Marché Colobane for the dressmakers' cause. Khady D., aged 54, communications officer at A.F.C., May 2024.

This passage shows that the politicisation referred to by the members is not necessarily an obstacle to the smooth running. On the contrary, it contributes to its smooth running. In other words, these people, often experienced and with a political background, act as social safety nets for the A.F.C., in the sense that they help to attract the funding that is essential to its smooth running.

Current Situation of Women Seamstresses Disaffiliated from the A.F.C.

Because of the dysfunction of the A.F.C. due to its politicisation, women dressmakers disaffiliated themselves from it. In fact, the A.F.C., even if it has financial consequences, has enabled them to return to the informal sector. The reason for this is that they prefer to work on their own in complete autonomy:

> I'd rather go back to my job where I was on my own before joining the A.F.C. I feel better in that than staying in an organisation with no better and uncertain future. I plan to start my own business, which will enable me to

> remain financially independent. Mariama C., aged 26, disaffiliated from the A.F.C., May 2024.

Although the A.F.C. remains a formal framework, these women have returned to an informal framework, but this time with the experience acquired within the A.F.C. and much more enterprising initiatives such as participation in tontines (EIG), online sales, and annual religious events.

Participation in Tontines: An Empowerment Strategy

The term "tontine" comes from the Italian name "Tonti Lorenzo", a Neapolitan banker who is said to have invented this system of financial exchange within a group of people (Bidzogo, 2012). A tontine would be defined as an association of people contributing to a common fund, the amount of which is paid in turn to each of them. The term fits in well with the stated aim of "reconciling the economy and society". As such, the tontine contributes to social cohesion and promotes relationships based on trust and friendship, hence the name "society of friends". The principle is simple: a group of friends or relatives meet regularly to pool their savings, with each contributing a fixed sum on a regular basis (Bidzogo, 2012). Participation in tontines is one of the strategies used by disaffiliated women dressmakers at A.F.C. to ensure their financial viability and self-financing:

> Since I left the A.F.C., I joined a tontine where we each contribute 5,000 F-CFA for ten days, and each time one person receives the money. This system of mutual aid has enabled me to be financially self-sufficient, allowing me to finance my services. Bineta S., aged 25, disaffiliated with the A.F.C., May 2024.

As soon as they left the A.F.C., these women dressmakers decided to set up a tontine called "Naate" in Wolof, with 20 members. This tontine operates based on a contribution of 5,000 F-CFA per day per person and after 10 days, one person receives,[13] through a draw, a total amount of 1,000,000 F-CFA. The tontine, which has a social and mutual aid character, will enable these women to buy or renew their work equipment such as sewing machines at an estimated cost of 175,000 F-CFA, clothing fabrics at 3,500 F-CFA per kilogram, and workshop hire costs. The amount acquired from this tontine would also be used to finance non-work items, such as family care: accommodation bills, meals, school fees, etc. Thanks to this ongoing tontine system, the women are also able to buy plots of land and gradually build their homes. In addition to this system of mutual aid, these women dressmakers take advantage of annual religious events such as the Magal Touba, Gamou Tivaouane, etc., to sell their ready-made goods.

Online Sales: A Product Distribution System

Since the COVID-19 pandemic, local Senegalese businesses have accelerated the digitisation process (Diédhiou, 2023: 276). This involves selling items or products online from a company's website. The disaffiliated members of A.F.C. sell online via WhatsApp Business, Facebook, TicToc, etc. These disaffiliated members put their products on the Internet via their own websites. These disaffiliates use their WhatsApp statuses to put online articles/products (e.g., clothes) made to attract a mass of customers who want their models. They work with "Thak-thiak" motorbike taxi drivers, which means "go quickly or quickly done", to facilitate deliveries after orders and purchases (Diédhiou, 2023: 276):

> I'm banking heavily on online sales, because the experience of COVID-19 has shown how often online sales are a profitable business. I post my products as statuses on WhatsApp and thanks to my contacts who reproduce the same statuses, I manage to capture the attention of many customers from the country, the sub-region and the diaspora. Ndeye Fatou S., aged 37, disaffiliated with the A.F.C., May 2024.

They mainly target Dakar's inhabitants, Senegalese from the interior, women traders from Guinea, Mali, Guinea-Bissau, Sierra Leone, Liberia, Côte d'Ivoire, Burkina Faso, Benin, Togo, and certain Central African countries such as Gabon, Cameroon, Congo, and Europe, and North America. They encounter these outside customers through a network of people known as "brokers" based in Dakar or at the Marché Colobane. These people also make a profit from each customer they send. This is a source of financial profitability for these women dressmakers.[14] Deliveries are made to customers in Dakar by "Thak-thiak" motorbike taxis. If the customers are outside Dakar, but inside the country, the "brokers" work with them to collect their parcels from pick-up points such as Médina,[15] Colobane, Pikine, Grand-Yoff, Thiaroye, Stade Amitié, etc. These localities are often the stopping-off points for the "Thak-thiak" motorbike taxis but also for regional bus schedules (e.g., Ziguinchor, Tambacounda, Fouta, Kolda). As for buyers outside Senegal, i.e., in Europe and the sub-region, it is the "*brokers*" or "*démarcheurs*" who take direct charge of loading the parcels via the GPS. Deciding to leave the A.F.C., which was dysfunctional because of its politicisation by the leaders, the women dressmakers prefer to return to the informal sector by self-financing. They have found success in participating in tontines and selling their products online.

Conclusion

The creation of the A.F.C. with recognition (a receipt) allowed women dressmakers who were formerly in the informal sector to move into the formal sector, thanks to public initiatives (e.g., the DER). However, the recent divisions within the A.F.C. are no longer in line with this logic and, as a result, members, no longer seeing their interests in these groupings, are starting to disaffiliate.

The qualitative approach used in this research enabled in-depth semi-structured interviews to be carried out with young women dressmakers and the managers of the A.F.C. Thus, the analysis of categorical thematic content shows that the A.F.C. is dysfunctional, key to the disaffiliation of women tailors. This disaffiliation is the result of the A.F.C.'s having been diverted from its original mission and objectives, since instead of being an association providing social assistance (financial support), it has become a political instrument. Added to this is the poor communication of those responsible for disseminating information, which is a major factor in disaffiliation. In fact, these communication officers do not take enough time to inform members about any decisions taken to ensure the smooth running of the A.F.C. This attitude is described by the interviewees as a sign of incompetence and a lack of leadership on the part of the staff responsible for communication. However, the privatisation of information would not allow the A.F.C. members to take advantage of existing opportunities (financial accessibility). Moreover, the attitudes and practices of the A.F.C.'s managers, based on a selective strategy linked to the granting of opportunities according to the political position of the members and bad rumours, have led women dressmakers disadvantaged by these practices to leave the A.F.C.

This situation is closely related to the logic of James Rule (2002), who states that instrumentally motivated individuals act according to a utilitarian *benefit and advantage* logic. The non-use of experienced people in the operation of the A.F.C. is an indicator of disaffiliation. And yet, experienced people would be an indispensable asset in the search for funding, because of their experience, social networks, and political affiliations. This has created generational and identity-based differences within the association, resulting in selective governance and, in turn, influencing disaffiliation. In addition, disaffiliated members of the A.F.C. have found other alternatives, such as participating in tontines and selling their products online, to boost their activities, and become independent. The bottom line is this: the decision to disaffiliate from the A.F.C. is due to the disadvantages associated with the lack of benefits faced by its members. The A.F.C. does not live up to the expectations of these Colobane women dressmakers.

Notes

1 www.fpaa.gouv.sn, accessed 26 January 2024.
2 Statement by Ibra Ndiaye, Director General of the *Agence pour la Promotion et le Développement de l'Artisanat (APDA)*, (6 December 2013), written by www.leral.net, accessed 9 August 2024.
3 https://financements.der.sn, accessed 28 February 2024.
4 Report by the Ministry of Crafts and Informal Sector Transformation on the draft budget 2024. www.bigwww.big.gouv.sn, accessed 27 September 2024.
5 This was the case of a woman who was seriously ill and unable to pay the hospital fees. The association came to her bedside with the sum of 350,000 F-CFA.
6 https://www.seneweb.com, accessed 29 January 2024.
7 Talking of the reinforcement of the sanitation system, we allude to the fact that SONAGED vehicles, which used to pass by once a day, now pass by twice a day.
8 PAMECAS is the union of mutual societies of the *Partenariat pour la Mobilisation de l'Épargne et du Crédit au Sénégal* (Partnership for the Mobilisation of Savings and Credit in Senegal), which grew out of a project that gave rise to the first savings banks in 1956.
9 These data were collected from the A.J.T.C. (*Association des jeunes tailleurs de Colobane*) Registers, 2024. To find this value, we need to multiply the partial headcount (85) by 100 divided by the total headcount (100) under normal conditions.

10 All kinds of clothing models are made here. Ready-to-wear for modern consumers, traditional clothing for events, military outfits, and so on. According to the President of the A.F.C., these clothes can only be found at Marché Colobane, thanks to the professionalism of the women dressmakers.
11 These verbatims (quotations) quoted throughout the text are taken from the interviews. These quotations are taken from a textual transcription from Wolof to French.
12 It is the link between the A.J.T.C. and its customers. Its aim is to find customers to sell products quickly.
13 The person who wins the draw says in Wolof "Damay teggui sama naate", a literal translation of "I am the person who collects the jackpot".
14 These women make all kinds of clothes, for both men and women.
15 Médina, rue 25, 45 near Sham and the Beaux Maraichers, and AIBD urban bus stations remain the biggest boarding points.

References

Asnal, S.-H. (2011) *Le monde rural à l'épreuve de la micro finance: cas du projet de micro-crédit de la mission inter Sénégal avec le groupement des femmes de Mbadatte (région de Fatick)*. Master thesis, M. Tamba (dir.) Université Cheikh Anta Diop de Dakar, Faculté des Lettres et Sciences Humaines, Département de Sociologie.

Azevedo, J. (2016) *L'économie solidaire et sociale au Sénégal*. Master thesis, B. Thiboud (dir.) Université Montaigne, Bordeaux, Faculté des sciences de territoires et de la communication, Département interdisciplinaire des dynamiques africaines.

Bidzogo, E. (2012) "Vers un véritable autofinancement de l'investissement en Afrique? Témoignage en forme de projet, de souhait, de suggestion sur les tontines au Cameroun", *Revue des Sciences de gestion*, 255–256 (3–4): 167–170.

Bravo, O. (2015) "La participation des personnes âgées grâce au volontariat", *Revue Éducation des Adultes et Développement*, 82: 1–7.

Cornelissen, J. (2017) *Corporate Communication, A Guide of Theory and Practice*. London: Sage.

Crozier, M. and F. Friedberg (1977) *L'acteur et le système. Les contraintes de l'action collective*. Paris: Seuil.

Démart, S. (2018) "L'épuisement des dynamiques de la fédération des associations afro-descendantes", *BAMKO-CRAN*, 31: 72–96.

DER (2024) *Rapport de la Délégation à l'Entreprenariat Rapide. Offre de services.* https://elevage.sec.gouv.sn/sites/default/files/Offre%20de%20services%20DER%20%281%29.pdf, accessed 8 August 2024.

Diédhiou, P.-M. (2023) "Ethnographie d'une boutique locale: Cas d'*Auchan Keur Massar* à Dakar", in Ulrike Schuerkens (ed.) *Entreprises, entrepreneurs et travail au Sénégal*, pp. 255–280. Paris: L'Harmattan.

Dione, E. (2000) *Le don et le recours de l'économie urbaine*. Dakar: Enda Tiers-Monde.

Diouf, S. (2011) *Les femmes dans les groupements de promotion féminine dans la ville de Ziguinchor: L'exemple du groupement Sante Yalla*. PhD thesis, Boubacar Ly (dir.) Université Cheikh Anta Diop de Dakar, Faculté des Lettres et Sciences Humaines, Département de Sociologie.

Faye, M. (2011) *La gouvernance associative des organisations paysannes*. Master Thesis, P. Diédhiou (dir.) Université Cheikh Anta Diop de Dakar, Faculté des Lettres et Sciences Humaines, Département de Sociologie.

Faye, O.-N. (2008) *Analyse sociologique d'une organisation non gouvernementale féministe*. Master thesis, M. Tamba (dir.) Université Cheikh Anta Diop de Dakar, Faculté des Lettres et Sciences Humaines, Département de Sociologie.

Festinger, L. (1953) *Group Attraction and Membership*. New York: Darwin Cartwright.

Geertz, C. (1998) "La description dense: Vers une théorie interpretative de la culture", *Enquête*, 6 (October): 73–105.
Granovetter, M. S. (1973) "The strength of weak ties", *American Journal of Sociology*, 78 (6): 1360–1380.
Kumcu, A. (2001) *De fil en aiguille: genèse et déclin des ateliers de confection turcs d'Amsterdam.* Amsterdam: Thesis UVA-FAC.
Lam, I.-T. (2018) *Entreprendre en Afrique, la clé d'une réussite.* Paris: L'Harmattan.
Ly, H., M. Soumare and S. Wade (2002) *Organisations et associations des quartiers en milieu urbain ouest-africain.* Dakar: Enda Tiers-Monde.
Marchand, I. and O. Laau-Laurin (2024) "La participation sociale des personnes ainées: un pilier au développement des communautés locales", *Revue Interventions Économiques*, 71: 1–39.
N'Da, P. (2015) *Recherche et méthodologie en sciences sociales et humaines: Réussir sa thèse, son mémoire de master ou professionnel et son article.* Paris: L'Harmattan.
Ndoye, M. (2003) *Expansion du commerce interrégional entre les pays de la CEMAC et de l'UEMOA.* Rapport d'étude, UEMOA: Dakar.
Niosi, J. (2002) "La théorie du choix rationnel: un commentaire", *Sociologies et Sociétés*, 34 (1): 79–88.
Rapport d'étude du Centre de Commerce International (2013) *Étude diagnostique sur l'intégration du commerce: Sénégal.* https://unctad.org/system/files/official-document/aldcinfd2_fr.pdf, accessed 21 August 2024.
Rule, J. (2002) "Les leçons du choix rationnel", *Sociologies et Sociétés*, 34 (1): 51–66.
Sadji, A. (2004) *Le sous-secteur du textile artisanal.* Rapport d'étude, Dakar: Ministère de l'Économie et des Finances du Sénégal.
Sarr, F. (1998) *L'entreprenariat féminin au Sénégal.* Paris: L'Harmattan.
Schuerkens, U. (ed.) (2023) *Entreprises, entrepreneurs et travail au Sénégal.* Paris: L'Harmattan.
Schuerkens, U., M. Branine and A. Mamman (eds) (2019) *Pour une sociologie du management en Afrique et dans le monde arabe.* Collection Vivre l'entreprise. Série Management et ressources humaines. Paris: L'Harmattan.

Part 4

Women Entrepreneurs and New Challenges

11 Participatory Financing in Senegal and Its Role in Financing Female Entrepreneurship

An Empirical Case Study

Mamadou Ndione, Marie-José Scotto, and Hicham Sbai

Introduction

Entrepreneurship is one of the solutions to poverty, the inability of governments to respond favourably to the many demands for jobs, and the low hiring rates of large companies in developing countries (e.g., Naudé, 2010; Quinn and Woodruff, 2019). The projects, which are mostly small scale with little prospect of growth, rely mainly on network phenomena (Chabaud and Ngijol, 2010) to develop income-generating entrepreneurial activities and thus improve people's well-being.

However, in developing countries such as Senegal, most entrepreneurs suffer from a lack of finance (Ndione and Dang, 2022). The informal nature of many entrepreneurial activities and the lack of guarantees or legitimacy of governments in drawing up policies to increase the supply of loanable funds are one explanation for this situation. In fact, finding sources of finance is a recurring problem for entrepreneurs, particularly women, and in this context, crowdfunding is becoming an alternative for them. Crowdfunding consists of a project owner using a funding platform to present a project and obtain funds from a group of contributors, known as a crowd, in exchange for pre-defined or undefined benefits. It is an exchange of funds, outside the traditional financial circuit, using a technological interface (Mollick, 2014).

While several studies have looked at participatory financing around the world, few to our knowledge have looked at its practical implementation in developing countries such as Senegal, and its role in financing women's entrepreneurship. This raises a few research questions: How does participatory financing work in Senegal and what role does it play in financing women entrepreneurs?

Africa has the highest rate of female entrepreneurship in the world and the economic role of African women is one of the most important in the world (Stivell and Zhan, 2014). Furthermore, Senegal has the highest percentage of women entrepreneurs on the African continent, at 36.8% of the country's active entrepreneurs, by way of comparison, this rate is 5.9% in South Africa (Alexandre and Ndour, 2021). In the light of this information, the choice of Senegal is justified. Furthermore, Senegal, a member of the West African Economic and Monetary Union (UEMOA[1]), is one of the most stable countries in Africa. It has long enjoyed social and political stability and is one of the most attractive and competitive countries in sub-Saharan

DOI: 10.4324/9781003492931-15

Africa. By way of illustration, the wealth created in 2020 was estimated at 23 million euros. This places Senegal in the group of middle-income countries.[2]

We will begin by presenting our theoretical framework. Next, we will provide a definition and typology of participatory financing while examining the specific case of Senegal and its women entrepreneurs. The research methodology and results will then be presented. Finally, we will conclude this chapter with a discussion and a conclusion.

Theoretical Framework: Social Bricolage in the Entrepreneurial Context

In developing countries, a large proportion of the population develops entrepreneurial activities to meet their primary needs in a "fragile" financing environment, according to Owusu and Janssen (2013). It is therefore necessary to talk about social bricolage. This concept was developed by the French anthropologist, Lévi-Strauss (1962), who defined bricolage as a person's ability to make do with the scarce resources of the environment. It was in this context of scarcity that Baker and Nelson (2005) adapted the concept to the field of entrepreneurship. According to them, to cope with the scarcity of funding sources, women entrepreneurs have to "tinker" to create and sustain their entrepreneurial activities. These authors have defined bricolage as the ability to combine pre-existing resources to solve various problems or to reuse them differently to pursue other opportunities. Baker and Nelson (2005) consider that *bricolage* involves the combination of two "constructs": resourcefulness and a willingness not to be limited by environmental or institutional constraints (Razgallah et al., 2016). In Senegal, particularly with the development of the *Système D*, do-it-yourself (DIY) is highly developed among entrepreneurs. Entrepreneurs will mobilise their skills and efforts to obtain available financial resources quickly and "within reach" (Ntep, 2021). In fact, some entrepreneurs call on their entourage to access sources of finance, or they call on socio-cultural actors to resolve conflicts of interest within their entrepreneurial activities (Ndione and Dang, 2022). Di Domenico et al. (2010) add a dimension of improvisation which, combined with the bricolage approach, creates the conditions for organisational resilience (Weick, 1998).

We note that women entrepreneurs, especially in the context of a low-resource environment, will mobilise different strategies (Razgallah et al., 2016), including those involving the processes of bricolage and effectuation. Entrepreneurship is defined as the exploitation of economic potential and, to do this, it is essential to develop a business plan and identify the resources needed to exploit this economic opportunity (Shane, 2000). However, it must be recognised that developing a business plan does not guarantee success in the activities undertaken (Lange et al., 2007). In some developing countries, the informal nature of the business and the low level of education of some entrepreneurs mean that they have no business plan, and yet these entrepreneurs manage to build genuinely sustainable and lucrative businesses. It is in this uncertain context that the theory of effectuation is extremely useful. This theory highlights the ability of entrepreneurs to make their business activities sustainable and viable by combining the resources at their disposal with the demands of their environment (Sarasvathy, 2001). This author was at the origin of the theory of effectuation. She draws a distinction between the classic entrepreneurial model, described as causal, and the effectual logic, based on entrepreneurial contingency. In causal logic, the entrepreneur bases his activity on a well-defined business plan that will enable him to achieve his objectives. In effectual logic, the resources available to the entrepreneur determine his choices and objectives. In other words, causal logic is based on prediction, whereas effectual logic is based primarily on available resources. It is in this context that Wiltbank et al. (2006) consider the entrepreneur's identity, experience, and social capital to be important resources in the context of effectuation.

As we indicated earlier (Alexandre and Ndour, 2021), most women entrepreneurs in Senegal (62.9%) set up their business to seize an opportunity rather than out of necessity. In this context, what can participatory financing offer as an alternative method of financing?

Crowdfunding in Senegal: An Overview

Definition and Typology of Participative Financing

Using a platform such as the Internet, participatory funding enables an entrepreneur to present a project to a qualified audience of "backers"[3] and, in return, hope to receive funding free of charge or on pre-defined terms (Belleflamme et al., 2013; Onnée and Renault, 2013). Participatory funding involves a specific project owner (humanitarian, artistic, or entrepreneurial), an intermediary or a technological interface such as an online platform, and individuals likely to finance the project, either through donations, loans with or without interest, or capital investment.[4] Contributions are generally small amounts, but the large number of subscribers has an impact on the funds raised. Participatory financing is therefore an alternative for a business, from the start-up phase through to maturity (Rossi, 2014). That said, the participatory financing model predates the development of the Internet. These new technologies have enabled its development and wider access, but "tontine" systems, popular in financing African entrepreneurship, have existed for a long time.[5] Participatory financing gives greater visibility to a business since the platforms are consulted by several specialised individuals and fundraising is generally accompanied by information on the feasibility of the project. It also helps to attract potential customers and strengthens a company's image. Equity crowdfunding platforms offer two ways of raising funds: AON (all *or* nothing) or KIA (keep *it all*). Depending on how the funds are raised, they may or may not be made available to the project owner. In the case of the AON, the rule of the game is to reach the sum to be raised within a set period. If the project owner fails to do so, the contributors will be reimbursed. In the KIA mode, the project owner can recover the sums raised.

There are several models of participatory financing:

- The counterparty model, the participatory financing model, then crowdlending, and the donation model.
- The *quid pro quo* model means that people's support is conditional on a previously defined *quid pro quo*. This may be in the form of tangible assets (products) or intangible assets (thanks).
- The equity crowdfunding model represents a traditional equity investment in a company.

In this case, the platforms offer interested individuals the chance to finance the project by holding shares. There are two possible models: the "club" model, which is a closed group comprising only wealthy individuals, and the "holding" model, which pools funds raised from different individuals for reinvestment in promising projects. The latter model has the advantage of facilitating the post-investment phase since the project owner will certainly need advice and support if the platform does not offer this service. On the other hand, protecting the interests of small shareholders may seem complex because of the diffuse nature of the ownership structure and the difficulty of gathering the opinions of all stakeholders.

There is also "crowdlending", or financing in the form of a loan. In return for their contributions, crowdfunders are reimbursed at pre-defined dates and under pre-defined conditions.

Finally, the last model is based on donations. This is the most widely publicised form of funding (Vulkan, 2016). It is used to fund charities and humanitarian initiatives. Belleflamme et al. (2013) discussed *royalty-based crowdfunding* or profit sharing. Authors such as Calmé et al. (2016) summarise the different categories of participatory financing in two models: (1) the "community" model, or without financial consideration, and (2) the model with financial consideration.

Participatory Senegal

Historically, it is very difficult to place the advent of participatory finance in Senegal, and for good reasons: the tontine system, organised by women, has existed for a long time. While women entrepreneurs in Senegal suffer from a notorious problem of financial sources, there is reason to hope that participatory finance will provide an alternative way of boosting entrepreneurial activities, since, according to Hemer (2011), crowdfunding makes it possible to finance activities that seem too risky for conventional financial structures (Onnée, 2016). This model has the advantage of limiting time constraints, geographical distances, and transaction costs, unlike traditional financing. Participatory finance can play an important role in the development of women's entrepreneurship at the same time as that of mobile telephony. The mobile telephony ecosystem has given a significant boost to the West African economy, creating economic added value of 37 billion dollars in 2017[6] (or 6.5% of GDP). In West Africa, where around half the population lives in rural areas, mobile telephony is playing an increasingly important role in reducing inequalities in access to and use of key services. In Senegal, for example, less than 25% of adults have access to a bank account. In rural areas, this percentage is barely 10%. As most Senegalese have no access to any type of credit, they are often seen in traditional informal rotating savings associations called tontines. Tontines are managed informally, and the risks of fraud and litigation are very high, which limits their potential[7].

Research Methodology

Context of the Study: Women Entrepreneurship in Senegal, between Necessity and Opportunity

Research conducted on the subject in Senegal confirms the role of female entrepreneurship in terms of jobs, innovation, and growth (Kane and Chroqui, 2023). The *Global Entrepreneurship Monitor* (GEM) report considers Senegal to be the leading country in sub-Saharan Africa for the creation of businesses by women (Simen, 2023). Research conducted in other African countries converges in considering female entrepreneurship as a key element of development and employment (Stivell and Zhan, 2014). The rate of entrepreneurial activity among women in Senegal has risen by 10%, with the gap between men and women narrowing to just 5% (Simen, 2023). According to World Bank figures,[8] women still represented only 34% of the working population in 2021. However, the number of women running businesses rose from less than 10% in 2006 to 32% in 2016, according to the latest general business census conducted by the ANSD (National Agency for Statistics and Demography).[9] This trend is particularly noticeable among women aged between 35 and 54, in a desire not to be dependent on men (Simen, 2023). However, these businesses are still too small to be truly productive.

Senegal is one of the African countries most committed to gender equality and women's autonomy. The development of women's entrepreneurship is one of the Senegalese government's major development priorities, and the country has ratified numerous international conventions since the Beijing Conference in 1995. The creation of a Ministry for Women's, Family and Children's Rights, as well as the creation in 2017 of various "gender" units in other sectoral ministries, demonstrate a desire for a cross-cutting approach. Several observatories have been set up, such as the ONDF (National Observatory for Women's Rights) in 2008 and the ONP (National Parity Observatory) in 2011. The PSE (Emerging Senegal Plan) aims to develop women's entrepreneurial activity through self-employment or the creation of income-generating activities and to promote gender equality in Senegal (Simen et al., 2018). Other structures have also been set up to facilitate access to credit and strengthen women's entrepreneurship, namely the FNPEF (National Fund for the Promotion of Women's Entrepreneurship), the FNCF (National Credit Fund for Women), and various other projects. Senegal has also put in place a national strategy for the empowerment of women (SNAEF) to enable them to develop their potential and to contribute to the development of the economy. National and international NGOs play a major role in Senegal, sometimes taking the place of the state. Created in 1982, CONGAD is a harmonising body for all NGOs operating in the country. Local development most often relies on external projects run by international bodies or NGOs (Piveteau, 2005). There is a three-way relationship between the local government, the informal sector, and NGOs, which underpins Senegal's economic development (Diop and Dartiguenave, 2021). Despite criticisms of formatting and standardised training modules, NGOs are a key player in the development of associative life in Senegal (Fall, 2011), particularly women's entrepreneurship.

Simen (2023) has defined the socio-economic characteristics of women entrepreneurs based on several criteria, including motivation, management style, financing, use of networks, not forgetting family status, educational, economic, and social level, and self-limitation (Simen, 2023). Other obstacles include funding constraints (Winn, 2005), less access to vocational training, and the stereotypical perception of women in their traditional roles. However, the study by Gning (2019) confirms the ability of women entrepreneurs to integrate into networks of influence in the market economy, particularly religious networks.

Difficulties in accessing finance are a recurring problem for women entrepreneurs (Leitch et al., 2018). The traditional method remains the tontine, a model in which collective savings finance capital requirements. Women's tontines are widely used in West Africa and their development is a marker of the spheres of activity of women and men (Orhan, 2001; Elotmani, 2022). The principle is simple: "The sum of accumulated contributions is given, in turn, to each participant. A saving or loan is thus released at each tontine round for the benefit of a different beneficiary" (Semin, 2007: 4). Microfinance programmes, also promising at the outset, do not seem to have lived up to their promises. According to Ndione et al. (2021), this lack of effectiveness is due to the excessively high interest rates applied to micro-credits.

A Mixed Approach

Our qualitative exploratory approach was deployed in two stages: Firstly, by identifying the players in participatory finance in Senegal, and then through a survey of 43 women entrepreneurs in Senegal (southern region), in the Ziguinchor region[10] – whereas most studies focus on Dakar. This region was chosen partly for methodological reasons, as one of the authors had several contacts in the region who could interview women entrepreneurs, but also to study more precisely the impact of motivations and access to finance, which may be stronger in this area than in the region of Dakar, the administrative and economic capital. It is also an area where NGOs are more present and active, due to the geopolitical situation, and can provide more sustained support for entrepreneurial projects.

Documentary Study: Identifying the Players in Participatory Finance

We consulted the *Google* search engine for information on participatory financing platforms in Senegal and the results revealed two platforms (see Table 10.1): One dedicated to financial inclusion (MaTontine) and another specialising in participatory financing through *royalties* (Waalam Invest). To our knowledge, these platforms are the most active in Senegal. We identified and collected the information available on the two websites of these platforms. The information was collected by *web scraping*,[11] using the *Python* program in October 2021. This recent technique has been used by Yu et al. (2017) and Jang and Chu (2022), among others.

The data was processed in two stages. Firstly, we re-read the information for each platform to order and check the consistency of the information gathered. Secondly, we manually analysed the data using a thematic grid derived from the literature review and international documentation.

Qualitative Approach: Questionnaire Administered

In the second part, we wanted to find out what the women had to say by means of a questionnaire. We administered a questionnaire to an atypical population. This population is in the poorest area of Senegal and is affected by armed conflict, which has an economic impact on the local population. However, a recent study (Simen, 2023) shows that women in this region are highly organised within formal and informal networks. Ziguinchor is also considered to be one of the three cities representative of female entrepreneurship in Senegal (Simen, 2023). The questionnaire was administered over two months, in February and March 2022, to 43 women entrepreneurs. This was a convenience sample. The women entrepreneurs were part of the incubator at the University of Ziguinchor, which brings together most of the women entrepreneurs in the region. The measurement scales used to administer our questionnaire are all nominal and the questions were pre-tested within a sample of 10 women entrepreneurs, to ensure that our questions (Yin, 2018) were in line with the expectations of local women entrepreneurs. We administered the questionnaire face-to-face to ensure a high response rate and to control our sample (Linsky, 1975). The responses obtained were not subject to any control or adjustment procedure. To ensure that the questions asked were clearly understood and the answers complete, we translated the questionnaire into *Wolof*. Wolof is the most widely spoken language in Senegal and is spoken by nearly everyone.

- The first questions (questions 1 to 5) included information on the respondent's age, marital status (single, married, divorced, widowed, separated), and social status. For income, we used a scale from 1 to 4 (modest, average, well-off, rich) and coded the variable from 1 (modest) to 4 (rich). Similarly, for the level of education, four choices were offered: elementary, baccalaureate, higher or no formal education.
- A second block of questions (questions 6 to 9) dealt with the characteristics of the company: legal status, number of employees, main business activity, geographical scope.
- Questions 10 and 11 dealt with the reasons for setting up the company. The choices were: to survive, to innovate, to keep the tradition, with the possibility of "another" choice.

- Question 12 offered several answers to the question about sources of funding: state, bank, family, participatory funding, and always the possibility of choosing "other".
- Question 13 was an open-ended question about how the business is run: "How do you manage your business"?
- The last three questions (14 to 16) focused on the difficulties encountered and the outlook: "What is the nature of the problems you have encountered or are encountering?", "How have you overcome them?", and "What is your goal for the future?

For all the questions (and for the closed questions), the questionnaire administrator left room for comments.

Results

The Players in Participative Financing

The results presented in Table 11.1 show that participatory financing is not very widespread in Senegal. There are only a limited number of equity crowdfunding platforms, and the only ones that exist are not well known. The information published on their websites is not exhaustive, resulting in information asymmetry. The most active platforms are:

- MaTontine, specialising in financial inclusion and created in 2015 to facilitate access to credit for the most vulnerable stratum. Its customers are mainly women and associations that are involved in a collective dynamism. Before accessing credit, members take part in tontines, where funds are collected *via* a technological interface and each participant in turn recovers the amount of their deposited funds. All participants are graded based on their punctuality in making contributions and compliance with pre-established rules. Because of a score awarded to each member, the platform's partner microcredit organisations can grant a loan to a member. The platform earns its fees from the commissions it collects from the microcredit organisations, as well as from commissions on tontine advances. It can, for example, provide its members with training in accounting or distribute inputs to members working in agriculture.
- The Waalam Invest platform focuses specifically on entrepreneurs and project leaders in Africa. It encourages the African diaspora to participate in job creation and the promotion of income-generating activities in Africa. The platform was launched in Senegal in 2016. It has raised more than €262,000 to finance projects and has created around 87 direct and indirect jobs. This platform analyses the company's situation before integrating and supporting it on a crowdfunding campaign. It monitors, audits, and manages *royalties*.

Table 11.1 Participatory financing players in Senegal: main characteristics

Themes	*MaTontine*	*Waalam Invest*
Geographic scope	Senegal	Africa
Sector	Financial inclusion	Entrepreneurship
Year of creation	2015	2016
Type of crowdfunding	Crowdfunding with a financial contribution	*Royalty-based* equity financing
Legal form	Information unavailable	Information unavailable
Target population	Women and farming associations	Entrepreneurs/project leaders
Method of financing	Financial structures (partners)	Coupon investment
Partners	*Cofina* and *Sunu Assurances*, *Orange Money*, *Yup* or *via* money transfer (*Wari*)	Information not available
Objectives	Digital platform for financial services: it facilitates access to financial and non-financial services for those excluded from the traditional financial system, through collaboration with organisations working in the field of financial inclusion.	Giving African entrepreneurs the opportunity to raise funds without capital dilution
Number of projects funded	Information unavailable	Information unavailable
Amounts financed	Information unavailable	+ more than €262,000
Popularity of the platform	Around 27,200 results (47 seconds)	Around 14,000 results (44 seconds)
Duration	The tontine is fixed for a specific period. The duration of the loan granted by micro-finance institutions depends on the amount of the loan.	Depending on the stakeholders
Support for project leaders	Access to energy, access to finance, financial products, and agricultural inputs	Company analysis; company introduction; campaign support; monitoring, audit and *royalty* management
Operating mode	Tontines are used as a first step on the road to financial inclusion. A loan file, generated using an algorithm, facilitates decision-making; rapid loan.	A minimum investment of 15 euros
Benefits for the platform	Gain advance (6% commission). Other financial products such as insurance	Commissions
Benefits for customers	Easier access to finance	Easier access to finance Benefit from support throughout the term of the contract to help them run their business successfully
Rights or Exit, Governance	Information unavailable	Information unavailable
Ethics charter; Legal protection	Information unavailable	Information unavailable

These platforms lack visibility and the lack of information on their sites may be a barrier to some investors. In fact, none of the platforms provided information on their websites about their system of governance, respect for human rights, ethical charters, legal protection – both for investors and project sponsors –, management of intellectual property, and socially responsible investment.

Survey of Women Entrepreneurs: Analysis of Questionnaire Results

We analysed the profile of women entrepreneurs according to three criteria: age, family, and social situation. On the age of the women entrepreneurs we interviewed, we found that they were not young, which is consistent with the data collected in our literature review. Sixty per cent of our sample are concentrated in the 31–40 and 41–50 age brackets. Twenty-eight per cent of women are over 50 (Figure 11.1).

In terms of marital status, the majority are married, which is consistent with the age distribution, but nearly 20% are single (Figure 11.2).

In terms of household income, over 70% of our sample considered themselves to have modest to very modest incomes based on their response to the question on estimated income levels (Figure 11.3), and this in a country where, according to

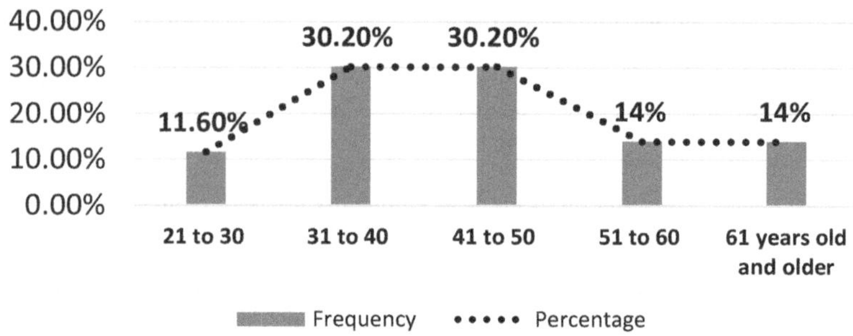

Figure 11.1 Socio-demographic characteristics of the sample: age

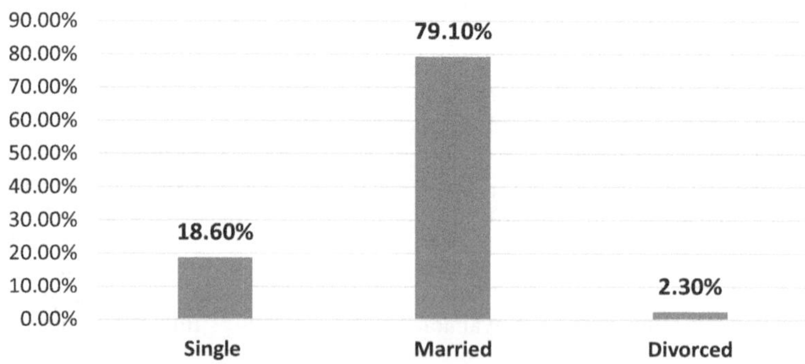

Figure 11.2 Socio-demographic characteristics of the sample: family situation

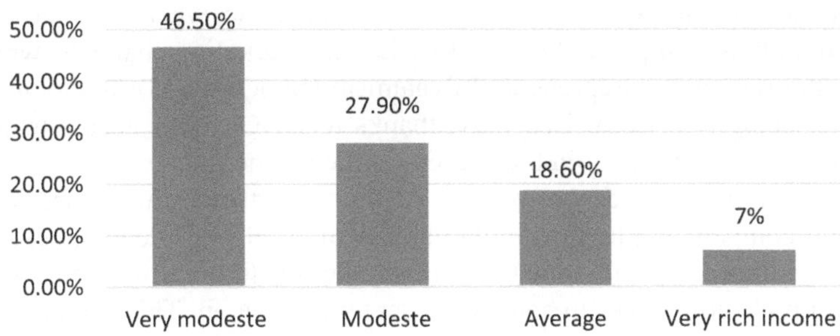

Figure 11.3 Socio-demographic characteristics of the sample: Very rich income

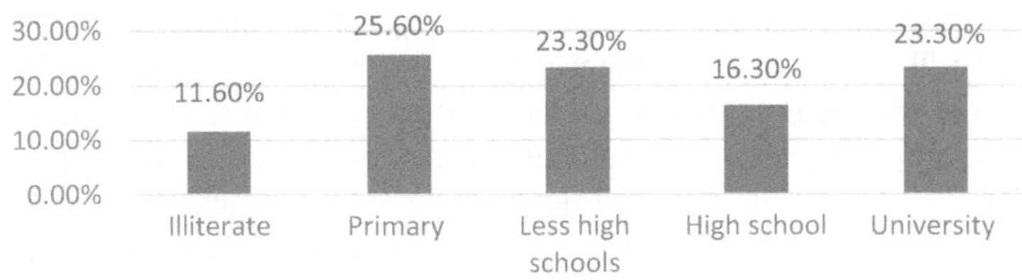

Figure 11.4 Socio-demographic characteristics of the sample: level of education

World Bank data, the gross monthly salary per capita in 2019 is $119. These very low-income levels may confirm that entrepreneurship, in a region where work is scarce and unemployment high, is a way of creating one's own employment.

Regarding their level of education, we noted a relatively low percentage of illiterate women: less than 12% (Figure 11.4). Eighty-eight per cent of the women in our sample had a level of education from elementary to higher education, and 46.6% answered that they had a certificate or a higher level. If we combine the results on baccalaureate level and the above figures, we obtain a score of almost 40%. According to Wiltbank et al. (2006), most of our respondents had received an education that helped them in their entrepreneurial project.

We also looked at the characteristics of the company. Most businesses created (76.7%) are in the form of an economic interest group (EIG), a structure that facilitates sources of funding. The Ziguinchor region is home to many NGO projects. They target women on a territorial basis – grouping women together according to affinities. The funding targets groups of women in a collective dynamic. These initiatives to promote women's entrepreneurship can be found in most emerging countries, particularly in India. The Indian model, known as the "Self-Holding Group", requires women to organise themselves beforehand or form an association.

The NGO can then offer them financing (credit) and support. An economic interest group (EIG) is a structure that attracts funding from NGOs and local authorities. Just over 16% of businesses are in fact individual sales activities ("informal" response in our questionnaire). This part of Senegal, despite an unstable political situation (war), is a rich region with a flourishing agriculture. This frontier zone, with its abundant natural resources, is also a trading zone, where local people have access not only to equipment but also to sales and marketing channels, which also explains the region's entrepreneurial dynamism (Simen, 2023). It should also be noted that being part of an EIG may, thanks to NGOs, give access to training, which is an important factor in the success of the business.

In terms of size, the responses were vague. Nevertheless, these are small and very small companies. The maximum number of employees does not exceed ten. Despite the imprecise and sometimes contradictory figures, we noted the large number of male employees in companies set up by women. This can be explained by the need for labour for heavy work tasks (transport) and security: roughly speaking, one woman employs two men.

The businesses are diversified. The responses show the heterogeneity of the activities – essentially small food shops, small equipment shops, or livestock product shops (milk, meat) with frequent networking and "subcontracting" to supply the product to the customer when needed. In their comments, 36.5% of our sample stressed the importance of professionalism in their activities, as well as quality (of product or work). The fields of activity show a significant export activity to the neighbouring country (Guinea-Bissau). Local activities, meanwhile, take place via a network of regional and cross-border markets, the *loumos* (the term used to describe a weekly market in the local Fulani language). These *loumos* are veritable commercial hubs that have taken advantage of the shortcomings of national product marketing circuits (Diallo, 2016). We have already highlighted the intensity of trade in this border area. Local products (food and livestock products, palm oil, honey, local handicrafts) are sought after and exported to the capital, where they are appreciated for their quality. One of the questions asked concerned the motivation for setting up a business. The need to survive and create a job accounted for 16,3% of the motivations, which is consistent with the low incomes indicated earlier in our analysis (Figure 11.5). This is not always the main reason given. For 39.5% of respondents, the majority, tradition was a strong motivation. Here we find

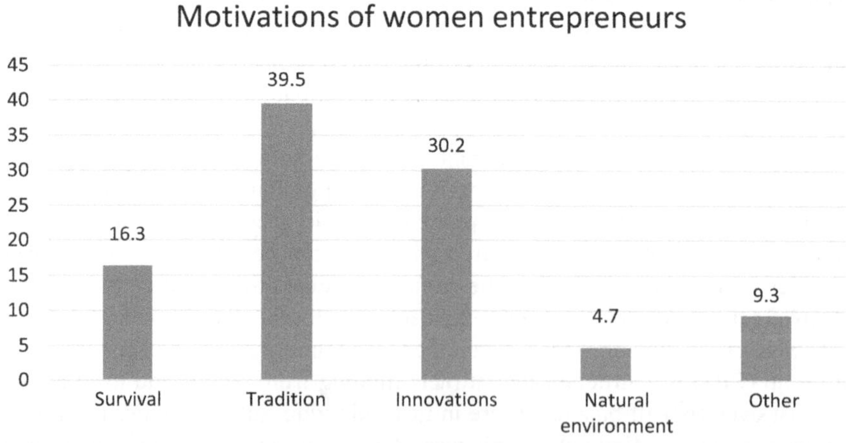

Figure 11.5 Motivations given as a percentage

the tradition, for the woman, of supporting the family and to ensure the children's future and therefore the need to help (the children, the family, the husband), the traditional role of a mother in Senegal. For a second group (30.2%), innovation was indicated as the main motivation. Finally, 4.7% are motivated to exploit environmental opportunities, while 9.3% give other reasons.

This is also consistent with the literature on the motivations of women entrepreneurs in Senegal (Alexandre and Ndour, 2021).

When it comes to funding their activities, our group of respondents cited the State and its new initiatives. The Senegalese government provides substantial funding for EIG through local authorities and town halls, for both economic development and electoral purposes. The limited use of banks is consistent with the literature. However, we were surprised to see no mention of NGOs in the responses, even though they are a major player in the Ziguinchor area. The low use of participatory financing should also be noted. Only 7% of our respondents had used it, and even then, we must understand that this is classic tontine financing. The platforms were not mentioned. We believe that the question was understood because our questionnaire was translated into Wolof. What's more, 40% of our sample was made up of women with a bachelor's degree or higher. However, women have no desire to change the way they do things because the tontine and mutual aid systems are a legacy of the "old times". Participatory financing is a new form of financing. Here again we see the influence of tradition. Changing their model is also a way of abandoning their culture and the security of the historical financing model, which is rooted in mutual aid and "social bricolage" (Figure 11.6).

One of the questions asked was: "How do you manage your business"? The main concern here is to maintain margins. For the women interviewed, this was the answer that represented good management.

The last three questions (14 to 16) focused on the difficulties encountered and the outlook. The main problems identified by our respondents were restrictions on the sale of certain products following new government regulations on seafood and livestock products, and the lack of commercial opportunities due to problems in transporting products to purchasing areas. In fact, it is not the lack of finance that appears to be the main problem for these women entrepreneurs, but the lack of

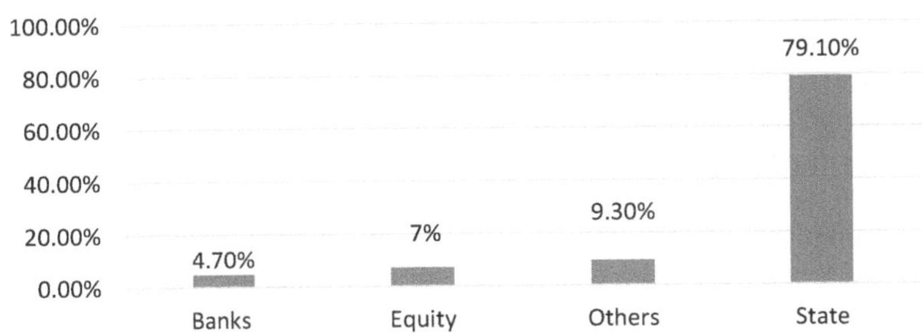

Figure 11.6 Methods of financing

Table 11.2 Main difficulties encountered by women entrepreneurs

Reasons identified	*Percentage*
Decline in customer numbers	23.3%
Lack of customers	14.0%
Lack of controls	11.6%
Lack of funding	2.3%
Lack of goods	2.3%
Lack of products	11.6%
Mortality	4.7%
Customer problems	2.3%
Delay in government payments	2.3%
Late delivery	2.3%
Out of stock	9.3%

customers, due to the poverty of the population and the low level of local purchasing power.

Nearly half (48.9%) of the respondents said that the main problems they encountered were related to the decline or lack of customers, and therefore orders. This was followed by a shortage of products and goods and stock-outs (23.2%). Financing only came 6th at 2.3%, on a part with late deliveries or late payments from the government. Another source of problems identified is the "mortality" (in the sense of fragility) of businesses, which are very small, a reminder that this region is a conflict zone and that businesses suffer the repercussions of this instability, just like people.

Our question 15 sought to identify how these women entrepreneurs resolved their difficulties. Help from family or friends remains a possibility (14%). Participatory financing was cited by 9.3% of our sample as a possible solution. But overall, the main strategy in the event of a problem remains patience and waiting for better days, which is in line with our theoretical framework of "social bricolage", in which we clearly see strategies for adapting to the situation and improvisation mechanisms. As far as their vision of the future is concerned, 81.5% of them said, they wanted their business to grow.

Discussion

Our results show that participatory financing can help to strengthen financial inclusion. It enables poor people to carry out income-generating activities and meet their commitments. As Hulme and Mosley (1996) point out, the MaTontine platform reduces the problems of detection and non-compliance with contracts. The platform checks the creditworthiness of project sponsors by organising an electronic tontine. Compliance with deadlines and commitments is assessed, which helps the partner microfinance institutions in their decision-making. The MaTontine platform also gives entrepreneurs the opportunity to benefit from several services, such as training in financial management. This training facilitates the sustainability of activities once financing has been obtained. Our results concur with those of Rossi

(2014) regarding the influence of participatory finance on the maturity of projects undertaken. We also note that the MaTontine platform gives individuals the means for their own development (Maystadt, 2004), particularly in the financing of agriculture (Rutherford, 2000).

The MaTontine and Waalam Invest platforms offer entrepreneurs the advantage of reducing the transaction costs involved in obtaining credit. Indeed, MaTontine, thanks to its financial partners and accurate information on project owners, facilitates access to sources of finance for people who are at risk from the traditional financial sector. So, as Hemer (2011) develops, crowdfunding makes it possible to finance risky activities. The Waalam Invest platform pre-studies a company before it enters a campaign.

Our results show that the use of financing platforms in Senegal represents a means of testing community interest in projects. It also enables project leaders to benefit from support at several levels (Onnée and Renault, 2013). Through the training sessions, project sponsors can contact the trainers directly to be guided in their choices. In fact, there is interaction between project sponsors and the teams of trainers or platform advisers. Social capital plays an important role in participatory financing in Senegal, particularly with the MaTontine platform. MaTontine trains and assists women's EIGs, who generally know each other, as well as farms made up mainly of family members. It is easier to finance networked groups that are used to working as a team. Participatory finance platforms are committed to project leaders and this commitment, in the sense of Walthoff-Borm et al. (2018), facilitates innovation in entrepreneurial activities. These results support those of Bouglet and Garmilis (2018), who highlighted that the commitment of platforms strengthens the quality of the governance of funded companies. Using these platforms is an opportunity for project sponsors. Indeed, the platform gives more visibility to the project owner and strengthens its image.

Our results still show that participatory financing is not very popular among our sample, which is generally the case in Senegal. It is still an emerging phenomenon, as discussed by Bessière et al. (2020), and the lack of communication and reliable information on participatory finance platforms hampers its development. However, according to the World Bank, crowdfunding is set to grow significantly, given the estimated financing needs of the sub-Saharan region, estimated at between $140 billion and $170 billion. In Senegal, crowdfunding projects raised a total of €23 million in 2018 (Ndione et al., 2021). We also note that there is no mention of NGOs. This seems surprising to us because the Ziguinchor region is a region of Senegal in which NGOs are present in supporting entrepreneurship projects. This may be due to the limited nature of the sample.

However, women entrepreneurs are wary of participatory financing, and the reason is that they are not familiar with the different ways in which it works. We also noted in the first part of our study that the information provided by the platforms does not give investors complete information. We might add that the literacy rate for women is low in Senegal and that most female entrepreneurs cannot read or write in French, hence the need to have our questionnaire translated into Wolof. As a result, language and education are barriers to development and the use of funding platforms for a large proportion of women entrepreneurs. Even though the women in our sample were well educated (only 11% considered themselves illiterate), we found the same lack of information and knowledge about the possibilities of participatory financing. The informal nature of many entrepreneurial activities is also a factor to be considered, in line with our theoretical framework of the *bricolage* of women creating small structures. In Senegal, according to figures from the *National Agency for Statistics and Demography*, in 2017 the informal sector accounted for 96.4%[12] of jobs created, compared with 3.6% for the formal sector. What's more, 80% of jobs created nationwide are in the informal sector. The country's authorities therefore need to introduce appropriate measures to organise entrepreneurial activities. In addition, the risks of plagiarism need to be taken into account, as there is also a risk that a woman entrepreneur (or a man entrepreneur) could see her project plagiarised, particularly with the Waalam Invest platform. The platform has not communicated the intellectual property protection mechanisms on its website. Another risk to consider is the systemic risk, which is all the greater when the environment is unfavourable due to political crises or demonstrations that can undermine the growth prospects of SMEs benefiting from participatory financing. All these factors are holding back the development of participatory financing in Senegal.

Conclusion

This research was a first step in our analysis of the use of participatory financing by women entrepreneurs in Senegal. Our sample, however limited, shows the low use of traditional loans and the lack of information on the possibilities of participatory financing, perhaps due to the area in which we made our observations. A larger study of women entrepreneurs in Dakar or in another large city (Touba, the country's second largest city, for example) could yield different results. A more qualitative approach could also provide us with precise information about the methods of financing women's business projects, the degree of knowledge of these methods, and knowledge of participatory financing and its possible use. The profile and experiences of these women entrepreneurs could also provide additional elements of analysis to explain their entrepreneurial motivations. Among the obstacles or accelerators, the development of telephone and Internet networks is also a significant indicator of a favourable technological environment. Participatory financing is still in its infancy in Africa, particularly in Senegal, but it offers major prospects because, according to World Bank figures, sub-Saharan Africa will have to cover financing needs estimated at between €140 million and €170 million.[13] A recent study (Bollaert et al., 2021) on African countries confirms the importance of digital financial technology solutions, such as participatory financing, and their potentially greater effectiveness than the traditional solutions offered by banks and venture capital.

Our research has confirmed the theoretical knowledge on women's entrepreneurship in Senegal, and in particular the work of Ntep (2021) on women's microentrepreneurship. It also shows the obstacles to the development of participatory finance in the UEMOA, but also the emergence of local initiatives aimed at putting project leaders in touch with potential funders. At the same time, our chapter highlights the resilience and resourcefulness of women entrepreneurs in a region ravaged by more than 30 years of armed conflict. Despite the war and the displacement of the population, women have been able to adapt and promote income-generating activities by exploiting the advantages of their environment, forming groups to expand their activities, relying on the tontine system, and using their friends and family to overcome the difficulties of accessing sources of finance. Under these conditions, both international and state organisations will need to strengthen information systems to better structure the entrepreneurial activities of women creators and formalise their activities, with the aim of enabling them to access more sources of finance, by developing access to participatory finance, and to be part of a desire for growth, and to contribute to national development. Our research may be limited by the fact that we do not consider platforms in Europe that finance activities in Senegal. Future research of a more qualitative nature is planned, to make a comparison with other neighbouring countries. Another fruitful line of research could be to investigate the role of the Senegalese diaspora in the development of participatory financing.

The aim of this future research is to continue the study of the place of participatory financing in female entrepreneurship and to establish whether Senegal represents a special case, given the strength of its female entrepreneurship: 36.8% of the country's entrepreneurs, as we indicated earlier by referring to the work of Alexandre and Ndour (2021), or whether this development is similar in neighbouring countries, such as those of the UEMOA.

Notes

1 This is an organisation made up of eight West African countries. The treaty establishing this organisation was signed in Dakar in 1993 by Benin, Burkina Faso, Côte d'Ivoire, Mali, Niger, Senegal, and Togo. The treaty officially came into force in 1994. The only non-French-speaking country in this union is Guinea-Bissau, which joined the intergovernmental organisation in 1997.
2 https://www .banquemondiale .org /fr /country /senegal /overview #1.
3 Anyone who knows about the platform: potential funders.
4 https://www.economie.gouv.fr/cedef/financement-participatif
5 And not just in Africa: the Statue of Liberty, donated by France to the United States of America in 1886, was already a model of participatory funding: 100,000 French citizens took part in its financing .
6 https://www.gsma.com/subsaharanafrica/wp-content/uploads/2018/11/2018-04-11-dd7760bf439236e808ea61ee986845eb.pdf
7 For more information, please visit the GSMA website: www.gsma.com.
8 https://donnees.banquemondiale.org/indicator/SL.TLF.CACT.FE.ZS?locations=SN
9 Agence Nationale de la Statistique et de la Démographie (ANSD) (2017), *Rapport Global du Recensement Général des Entreprises 2016.*
10 The Ziguinchor region is one of Senegal's 14 administrative regions. Bordering Gambia in the north and Guinea-Bissau in the south, it forms the western part of Casamance, known as Basse Casamance. Communication with Dakar is almost exclusively by sea or through Gambia.

11 In essence, this is a technique that extracts data (content or information) from websites.
12 https://lequotidien.sn/poids-du-secteur-informel-dans-leconomie-lansd-affiche-ses-chiffres/
13 Crowdfunding's Potential for the Developing World. 2013. infoDev, Finance and Private Sector Development Department. Washington, DC: World Bank.

References

Alexandre, L. and M. Ndour (2021) "Community groups as triggers of female entrepreneurship, the case of Senegal's food sector", *Recherches en Sciences de Gestion*, 145 (4): 45–71.

Baker, T. and R. E. Nelson (2005) "Creating something from nothing: Resource construction through entrepreneurial bricolage", *Administrative Science Quarterly*, 50 (3): 329–366.

Belleflamme, P., T. Lambert, and A. Schwienbacher (2013) "Individual crowdfunding practices", *Venture Capital*, 15 (4): 313–333.

Bessière, V., E. Stéphany, and P. Wirtz (2020) "Crowdfunding, business angels, and venture capital: An exploratory study of the concept of the funding trajectory", *Venture Capital*, 22 (2): 135–160.

Bollaert, H., F. L. De Silanes, and A. Schwienbacher (2021) "Fintech and access to finance", *Journal of Corporate Finance*, 68 (C): 1–14.

Bouglet, J. and G. Garmilis (2018) "L'equity crowdfunding, une régulation traditionnelle pour un modèle innovant?" *Revue Française de Gestion*, 44 (273): 107–133.

Calmé, I., S. Onnée, and É. A. Zoukoua (2016) "Plateformes de crowdfunding et acteurs de l'écosystème entrepreneurial: Quelle(s) coopération(s), quels business modèles?", *Revue Française de Gestion*, 42 (259): 139–154.

Chabaud, D. and J. Ngijol (2010) "Quels réseaux sociaux dans la formation de l'opportunité d'affaires?" *Revue française de gestion*, 206 (7): 129–147.

Diallo, M. M. (2016) "Frontières et activités marchandes en Afrique de l'Ouest: Logiques d'acteurs et fonctionnement scalaire", *Territoire en mouvement: Revue de géographie et aménagement*, 29: 1–21.

Di Domenico, M., H. Haugh, and P. Tracey (2010) "Social bricolage: Theorizing social value creation in social enterprises", *Entrepreneurship Theory and Practice*, 34 (4): 681–703.

Diop, J. and J. Y. Dartiguenave (2021) *Dynamiques locales et construction du développement au Sénégal: L'intelligence territoriale stratégique au service des territoires*. Paris: L'Harmattan.

Elotmani, S. (2022) "Determinants of women's entrepreneurial success: The case of Senegal", *Revue Management & Innovation*, 5 (1): 117–134.

Fall, M. A. (2011) "Les experts globaux du développement local au Sénégal", *Multitudes*, 47 (4): 71–77.

Gning, S. (2019) "La religion, une ressource pour l'entrepreneuriat féminin au Sénégal", *Sociologies pratiques*, 39 (2): 133–144.

Hemer, J. (2011) "A snapshot on crowdfunding", *Working Paper R2/2011*, Fraunhofer Institut.

Hulme, D. and P. Mosley (1996) *Finance Against Poverty*. London and New York: Routledge.

Jang, H. and W. Chu (2022) "The effect of message features on donations in donation-based crowdfunding", *Journal of Consumer Behavior*, 21 (6): 1464–1477.

Kane, N. and R. Chroqui (2023) *L'entrepreneuriat féminin en Afrique, entre bricolage et survie*. Paris: L'Harmattan.

Lévi-Strauss, C. (1962) *La Pensée Sauvage*. Paris: Plon.

Lange, J. E., A. Mollov, M. Pearlmutter, S. Singh, and W. D. Bygrave (2007) "Pre-start-up formal business plans and post-start-up performance: A study of 116 new ventures", *Venture Capital*, 9 (4): 237–256.
Leitch, C., F. Welter, and C. Henry (2018) "Women entrepreneurs' financing revisited: Taking stock and looking forward", *Venture Capital*, 20 (2): 103–114.
Linsky, A. S. (1975) "Stimulating responses to mailed questionnaires: A review", *Public Opinion Quarterly*, 39 (1): 82–101.
Maystadt , J.-F. (2004) "Microfinance au Nord: Un effet de mode importé du Sud?", *Mondes en développement*, 126 (2): 69–82.
Mollick, E. (2014) "The dynamics of crowdfunding: An exploratory study", *Journal of Business Venturing*, 29 (1): 1–16.
Naudé, W. (2010) "Entrepreneurship, developing countries, and development economics: new approaches and insights", *Small Business Economics*, 34 (1): 1–12.
Ndione, M., M.-J. Scotto, and E. Vernier (2021) *Financement participatif au sein de l'UEMOA: opportunités et limites pour l'entrepreneuriat*. Paper presented at the 14th Annual Conference of CERI, Istec Business School, Paris.
Ndione, M. and R. Dang (2022) "Les mécanismes de gouvernance classique et transversale au sein des PME sénégalaises", *Question(s) de management*, 40 (3): 37–48.
Ntep, F. (2021) "Un cas de bricolage: le financement de la création de toutes petites entreprises par les femmes à Thiès (Sénégal)", *Journal of Small Business and Entrepreneurship*, 35 (1): 130–152.
Onnée, S. (2016) "Vers une compréhension du rôle joué par la foule", *Annales des Mines-Réalités industrielles*, 1 (17): 12–16.
Onnée, S. and S. Renault (2013) "Le financement participatif: atouts, risques et conditions de succès", *Gestion*, 38 (3): 54–65.
Orhan, M. (2001) "Women business owners in France: The issue of financing discrimination", *Journal of Small Business Management*, 39 (1): 95–102.
Owusu, A. and F. Janssen (2013) *Social entrepreneurship: Effectuation and bricolage approaches to venture establishment in West Africa*. Paper presented at the 4th International Research Conference on Social Enterprise, Belgium, Liège.
Piveteau, A. (2005) "Décentralisation et développement local au Sénégal. Chronique d'un couple hypothétique", *Revue Tiers Monde*, 181 (1): 71–93.
Quinn, S. and C. Woodruff (2019) "Experiments and entrepreneurship in developing countries", *Annual Review of Economics*, 11 (1): 225–248.
Rossi, M. (2014) "The new ways to raise capital: An exploratory study of crowdfunding", *International Journal of Financial Research*, 5 (2): 8–18.
Razgallah, M., O. Zeribi, and A. Maalaoui (2016) *Social entrepreneurship and DIY: perceptions of social entrepreneurs*. Paper presented at the XXVth Conference of the International Association of Strategic Management, Hammamet, Tunisia.
Rutherford, S. (2000) *The Poor and their Money*. New Delhi: Oxford University Press.
Sarasvathy, S. D. (2001) "Causation and effectuation: Toward a theoretical shift from economic inevitability to entrepreneurial contingency", *Academy of Management Review*, 26 (2): 243–263.
Semin, J. (2007) "L'argent, la famille, les amies: Ethnographie contemporaine des tontines africaines en contexte migratoire", *Civilisations*, 56: 183–199.
Shane, S. (2000) "Prior knowledge and the discovery of entrepreneurial opportunities", *Organization Science*, 11 (4): 448–469.
Simen, S. F. (2023) "Perception des femmes entrepreneures face aux exigences de garanties des organismes de crédit au Sénégal: quelle influence des réseaux d'affaires", *Journal of Small Business & Entrepreneurship*, 35 (1): 1–22.
Simen, S. F., S. B. Coulibaly, and A. Diabate (2018) "Quels facteurs motivant le micro-entrepreneuriat informel féminin au *Sénégal*? L'expérience des commerçantes ambulantes de la ville de Dakar", *Revue Africaine de Management*, 4 (2): 1–14.

Stivell, M. M. P. J. and J. Zhan (2014) "The impact of microfinance on female entrepreneurial intention: Congo Brazzaville's case", *International Journal of Science and Research*, 3 (10): 1167–1175.

Vulkan, N., T. Åstebro, and M. F. Sierra (2016) "Equity crowdfunding: A new phenomena", *Journal of Business Venturing Insights*, 5: 37–49.

Walthoff-Borm, X., T. Vanacker, and V. Collewaert (2018) "Equity crowdfunding, shareholder structures, and firm performance", *Corporate Governance: An International Review*, 26 (5): 314–330.

Weick, K. E. (1998) "Introductory essay: Improvisation as a mindset for organizational analysis", *Organization Science*, 9 (5): 543–555.

Winn, J. (2005) "Women entrepreneurs: Can we remove the barriers?" *The International Entrepreneurship and Management Journal*, 1 (3): 381–397.

Wiltbank, R., N. Dew, S. Read, and S. D. Sarasvathy (2006) "What to do next? The case for non-predictive strategy", *Strategic Management Journal*, 27 (10): 981–998.

Yin, R. (2018) *Case Study Research and Applications: Design and Methods* (6th ed.). Thousand Oak, CA: Sage.

Yu, S., S. Johnson, C. Lai, A. Cricelli, and L. Fleming (2017) "Crowdfunding and regional entrepreneurial investment: An application of the Crowd Berkeley database", *Research Policy*, 46 (10): 1723–1737.

12 Factors in the Success and Failure of Public Policies to Promote Female Entrepreneurship in Cameroon

Brigitte Audrey Ekodo Bekono

Introduction

In Cameroon, it has now been established that development cannot be achieved without the active involvement of women (The Advocates for Human Rights, 2014), just as in the rest of the world, and the gender approach is now included in the public policies of all states. This can be seen from the publication of U. Schuerkens (2023), who shows that development in Africa requires not only the support for business start-ups, but above all the involvement of both women and men in this process through public policies. Public policy is a key concept in the study of the promotion of women's entrepreneurship in Cameroon. According to Vaison (1973), a public policy can be defined as a decision taken by public authorities with a view to solving a collective problem or responding to a social demand.

Howlett and Cachore (2014) stress that public policy can be understood as a set of instruments and strategies used by governments to achieve specific objectives. Stockey (1991) stresses the importance of the credibility of public policies to guarantee their effectiveness. Desrosières (2006) goes further in asserting that the essence of public policy lies in its ability to allocate resources and regulate the behaviour of social actors.

In the context of promoting female entrepreneurship in Cameroon, public policies can take different forms, such as training programmes, subsidies, tax incentives, or childcare measures, as illustrated by Muller (1990). In the same vein, Kobeissi (2010) stresses the importance of taking gender factors into account in the development of public policies to promote female entrepreneurship. Zeineb et al. (2015) stress the need for public policies to support social, female, and high-growth entrepreneurs.

As the phenomenon of women's entrepreneurship is constantly evolving (Secretary General, 2016), it raises many questions for research into its specific features. Major studies on women's entrepreneurship in Cameroon have focused on women's personal characteristics, their motivations, and the specific features of their businesses (Tchouassi, 2000; Rwenge et al., 2013; Nkolo, 2015; Tsambou and Kamga, 2016; Toche, 2020; Yen, 2022; Simo, 2023). However, recent research has highlighted the importance of socio-political factors in supporting women to set up and run their own businesses.

DOI: 10.4324/9781003492931-16

A growing number of researchers are highlighting the importance of examining the impact of public policies for entrepreneurship on the entrepreneurial decision (Ahl, 2010). According to Boussetta (2011), the support of public policies, support structures, and financial institutions are decisive factors in the success of women entrepreneurs. Consequently, state institutions play a decisive role in the emergence of female entrepreneurship in Cameroon. According to O'Rourke (2020), women in Cameroon face significant challenges in accessing employment and entrepreneurship, particularly due to social norms and gender stereotypes. However, public policies can help to reduce these barriers and promote female entrepreneurship. Mahadea and Kabange (2019) examined the influence of government regulations and institutions on entrepreneurial performance in Cameroon and found that public policies can have a positive impact on the performance of women-led businesses.

This chapter sets out to identify and understand the success and failure factors of Cameroonian public policies for the promotion of women's entrepreneurship, by conducting a qualitative study with 20 women entrepreneurs in the city of Yaoundé. I carried out this analysis according to three categories of impact of public policies on Cameroonian women entrepreneurs: firstly, the regulation and administration of Cameroonian public policies for women entrepreneurship; secondly, public policies concerning support and capacity-building structures for women entrepreneurs; and thirdly, public policies concerning financing structures.

Review of Literature

The Regulation and Administration of Public Policies to Promote Women's Entrepreneurship

Law 2010/001 of 13 April 2010 on the promotion of small and medium-sized enterprises applies uniformly to men and women. This uniformity is supposed to guarantee equal opportunities, but it does not consider the specific challenges faced by women entrepreneurs. Bagher Gorji and Paria (2011) have shown that simple administrative procedures encourage business start-ups. However, this simplification is often insufficient for women, who must overcome additional obstacles such as gender discrimination and lack of access to professional networks. In general, Singh and Belwal (2008) highlight the lack of institutional support as a major obstacle to female entrepreneurship. De Bruin and Welter (2007) have highlighted the need for more targeted government plans and strategies to promote women entrepreneurs. Their research shows that current policies fail to provide the necessary institutional support, leaving women without the right support to overcome entrepreneurial challenges.

In the case of Cameroon, the creation of the Ministry for the Promotion of Women and the Family (Décret présidentiel n° 320, 2004) marked a significant step forward in the fight against gender disparities, particularly in entrepreneurship. This ministry was created with the aim of eradicating disparities between men and women, as Ella (2019) points out. The ministry runs awareness campaigns on pay inequalities and gender discrimination, as explained by Brun (2019) and Etoundi (2013). In 2009, a national action plan (Ministère de la promotion de la femme et de la famille, 2009) was put in place by MINPROFF, for the development of female entrepreneurship in Cameroon, with four main objectives: the creation of a legislative and regulatory framework conducive to the development of businesses (Bandibenoand Nkonga, 2019), the strengthening of women's managerial and entrepreneurial skills to make them more productive and competitive as explained by Kamdem (2011) and Tchouassi (2018) who believe that a good knowledge of the entrepreneurial ecosystem and adequate skills enable better economic development. Finally, the implementation of financial mechanisms has to be mentioned that are better adapted to the needs of businesses promoted by women, as discussed by Nkakleu (2007) and Nkakleu et al. (2013), and the strengthening of entrepreneurial networking to facilitate access by women entrepreneurs to regional, national, and even international opportunities.

However, these efforts, while laudable, remain largely theoretical and are struggling to bring about concrete changes on the ground. The persistence of economic disparities shows that public policies need to be better adapted and more rigorously implemented. The Gender, Climate Change and Agriculture Support Programme (Recha et al., 2014) has set ambitious targets for promoting women's entrepreneurship, such as creating a favourable legislative framework and strengthening women's managerial skills. However, the lack of effective monitoring and rigorous evaluation limits the impact of these initiatives. Research shows that without in-depth knowledge of the specific needs of women entrepreneurs and appropriate implementation, public policies often fail to achieve their objectives. This is demonstrated by the work of Abousaid (2023) on the issue of factors impacting women's entrepreneurship.

Existing studies highlight significant shortcomings in the regulation and administration of public policies for the promotion of women's entrepreneurship in Cameroon. Other research emphasises the lack of institutional support and persistent structural obstacles despite the policies in place (Assoumou Menye and Guetsop Sateu, 2017). In addition, Tchouassi (2002) stresses the need to consider intrinsic determinants such as motivation, self-confidence, and entrepreneurial skills, which are often neglected in current approaches.

The limitations raised by the regulations governing women's entrepreneurship justify the development of an empirical test that will make it possible to gather essential quantitative and qualitative data, to understand the current dynamics and identify the factors of success and failure of existing initiatives in this area for the promotion of women's entrepreneurship in Cameroon.

Awareness-Raising and Capacity-Building Structures

The Cameroonian government has also introduced a policy of institutionalising, structuring, and organising microfinance with the aim of facilitating access to finance for entrepreneurs, particularly women entrepreneurs (Baturin, 2014). Women entrepreneurs can now benefit from the system of savings and credit cooperatives, which is more affordable or accessible for them and they are no longer limited to financing by tontines and women's groups. The *Fond National de l'Emploi*

(FNE)[1] and several professional associations, such as the *Association des Femmes pour la Promotion de l'Entrepreneuriat Vert* (AFEPEV)[2] and the UKUZOLA association,[3] also provide women micro-entrepreneurs with capacity-building and training opportunities for more effective and sustainable management (cf. Hisrich and Brush, 1984; Meli and Nodem, 2021).

The National Action Plan for the Development of Women's Entrepreneurship (PAN-DEF, 2009) is one of the major initiatives that Cameroon has put in place to encourage women to set up their own businesses. The Cameroonian government's strategy is based primarily on creating an environment conducive to female entrepreneurship, building institutional capacity to promote female entrepreneurship, and developing support tools and services for Cameroonian women entrepreneurs. However, Cameroon's 6th periodic report under the Convention on the Elimination of All Forms of Discrimination against Women (2014–2019) showed uneven implementation and inadequate monitoring, preventing greater awareness of gender equity issues in entrepreneurship in Cameroon. Training and capacity-building initiatives are often fragmented and lack continuity, which limits their long-term impact.

Various training and capacity-building programmes have been set up to help women develop entrepreneurial skills. Galloway and Brown (2002) stress that these initiatives are essential for improving the productivity and competitiveness of women entrepreneurs. However, these programmes are not always accessible to all women, particularly those in rural areas. According to Stephan (2007), developing an entrepreneurial culture is essential for success in entrepreneurship, and the best way to implement it is through university teaching to enable students to learn the fundamentals of entrepreneurial activities. However, the lack of resources, appropriate content, post-training follow-up, and ongoing support makes it difficult to apply the skills in practice, once they have been acquired, as Fayolle (2017) argues. With the aim of further strengthening capacities, networking is considered by Cameroonian public policy to be a key factor in the success of businesses (Wassila, 2010).

Although efforts have been made to encourage networking among women entrepreneurs, these networks often remain limited in scope and impact. This is what Simone Desjardins and Annette St-Onge (2009) explain in their article. Access to international networks on a wider scale is particularly limited, reducing the opportunities for growth and overall development of businesses run by Cameroonian women. This is a challenge that has not yet been met by Cameroon, as described in the National Development Strategy 2020–2030 (Simo, 2023).

It is therefore worth setting up an empirical test to determine the real impact of awareness-raising and capacity-building structures on women's entrepreneurship in Cameroon. This will make it possible to gather the quantitative and qualitative data needed to understand the current dynamics, and identify the factors behind the success and failure of existing initiatives for Cameroonian women, justifying this continuing unfavourable situation.

Financing Structures for Women Entrepreneurs

Through its strategy for the development of small and medium-sized enterprises, the social economy, and handicrafts, promoted by the Ministry of Small and Medium-sized Enterprises, the Social Economy and Handicrafts in 2009, the Cameroonian government is encouraging the creation of microfinance, and savings and credit cooperatives to facilitate access to finance for women entrepreneurs. These structures are intended to offer more accessible solutions than traditional financing systems, which are often inaccessible to women. Faced with certain economic obstacles, a few microfinances designed to promote women's entrepreneurship in Cameroon are floundering, as Ateba (2022) explains. However, despite these initiatives, studies show that many Cameroonian women entrepreneurs continue to encounter difficulties in accessing these resources. High interest rates, collateral requirements, multiple discrimination, and lack of awareness of available services remain major obstacles for Cameroonian women entrepreneurs, as demonstrated by Sariette Batibonak (2022).

The *Programme d'Appui à la Création et au Développement des PME* (PACD/PME) designed by the Ministry of Small and Medium-sized Enterprises MINPMEESA (Tsambou, 2016), aims to facilitate women entrepreneurs' access to technologies, financing, feasibility studies, and specific training. However, despite the existence of this programme, access to finance remains a challenge. Studies show that complex procedures, lack of information, and low penetration of financial services in rural areas hamper the effectiveness of the PACD/PME.

In 2011, the Cameroonian government created the *Cameroon Rural Financial Corporation* (Ministère de l'Économie, 2014) and the *Banque Camerounaise des PME* to facilitate access to finance for SMEs, including those run by women. Although these institutions are a step in the right direction, their real impact on women's entrepreneurship remains limited by operational and structural challenges. Women, particularly in rural areas, continue to face obstacles in accessing such finance due to bureaucracy, required collateral, and lack of information on available services.

Existing studies show a significant gap in the understanding and effective implementation of financing structures for women entrepreneurs in Cameroon. Research by Dabiç et al. (2022) highlights that, despite efforts to create accessible financing structures, women continue to face considerable barriers. Empirical data on the impact of these initiatives is limited, fragmented, and often not representative of rural and urban socio-economic realities.

To overcome the obstacles and obtain data that are more representative of the current situation, an empirical test will enable us to collect quantitative and qualitative data to assess the real impact of the financing structures approved by Cameroonian public policies for the promotion of women's entrepreneurship. By closely examining the specific barriers faced by women, this study will be able to provide evidence-based recommendations for improving public policy and funding initiatives.

Women's Entrepreneurial Education

At educational level, the Cameroonian government is gradually introducing modules on entrepreneurship at higher education level, specifically at ESSEC (*École*

Supérieure des Sciences Économiques et Commerciales) and ENSET (*École Normale Supérieure d'Enseignement Technique*) since 2002 and 2009, respectively. Tchouassi (2002) also stresses the importance of entrepreneurial education for women in Cameroon. In addition, some universities are entering into partnerships with private agencies such as AGRO-PME Fondation[4] to set up clubs within their establishments that enable male and female students to familiarise themselves with the concepts of entrepreneurship to encourage vocations. Tafelefack (2019) even believes that to make the education system more effective and women more independent, entrepreneurial education is needed in schools and universities.

Higher education institutions in Cameroon have integrated entrepreneurship training programmes into their academic curricula to meet the growing institutional demand for entrepreneurship education, as explained by Villette (2011). Universities such as the University of Yaoundé and the University of Douala offer specialised courses and degrees in entrepreneurship. These programmes aim to provide students with the skills they need to set up and run businesses. However, the impact of these initiatives on business creation by young graduates remains largely understudied. Research often shows a mismatch between the skills taught and the real needs of the market, as suggested by the study of Gay et al. (2014) that states that there is a need to rethink the teaching of entrepreneurship in African universities, to better prepare future entrepreneurs for the realities on the ground.

In addition, the Cameroonian government, in collaboration with non-governmental organisations, has set up several entrepreneurship training programmes. The *Programme National de Développement Participatif* (PNDP) is an example of initiatives to promote female entrepreneurship (Meli and Nodem, 2021). These programmes aim to strengthen the entrepreneurial capacities of young people and women. However, the effectiveness of these programmes is often limited by logistical challenges, a lack of sustainable funding, and limited geographical reach.

Educational institutions in Cameroon are often faced with a lack of resources and adequate infrastructure to provide quality entrepreneurial education, particularly for women entrepreneurs. Teachers sometimes lack specific training in entrepreneurship, and teaching resources are often insufficient or obsolete (Kede, 2023). In addition, training programmes are theoretical and lack the practical components essential for developing genuine entrepreneurial skills.

There is also a significant gap between the skills taught in entrepreneurial education programmes and the skills required by the labour market. This is a phenomenon already described by Pépin (1997). Young graduates often find themselves ill-prepared to face the challenges of the real entrepreneurial world. This mismatch limits the impact of educational programmes on business creation and economic growth.

It should also be noted that entrepreneurial education programmes are not always accessible to all, particularly rural populations and women. Socio-cultural barriers, lack of information and the costs associated with training are major obstacles to inclusiveness, as can be seen in the Annual Report of the 61st Commission on the Status of Women from 2017. In addition, training initiatives are often concentrated in urban areas, leaving rural populations with little or no access to these opportunities.

Research carried out to date on entrepreneurship education in Cameroon highlights considerable efforts but also significant gaps. Studies by Tchouassi (2000) highlight structural and operational challenges that limit the effectiveness of programmes for Cameroonian women entrepreneurs. However, there is a lack of robust empirical data on the actual impact of these initiatives on entrepreneurship and economic growth.

With a view to providing additional data to understand and improve the situation of Cameroonian women entrepreneurs, an empirical test will allow us to assess the real impact of entrepreneurial education programmes through quantitative and qualitative data. By closely examining the specific barriers faced by women entrepreneurs, this research will be able to provide evidence-based recommendations for improving public policy and government initiatives for women's entrepreneurship in Cameroon.

Methodology

In this study, I chose a qualitative methodology based on an exploratory-hybrid approach. I opted for abductive reasoning because this research was constructed through back and forth between the literature and the data collected in the field. I adopted an interpretivist paradigm, which assumes that the nature of the object of study is not clearly defined and that it is up to the researcher to clarify its understanding.

In the empirical approach, I used semi-structured interviews based on a pre-established interview guide. This guide was used as a reference to bring out the themes that the interviewee would not address spontaneously. To draw up this interview guide, I relied on both the lines of enquiry arising from the main research question and the fieldwork.

Before conducting the final interviews, an exploratory pre-test phase was carried out. This phase included five pre-interviews to test and improve the interview guide. The final interviews were conducted with 20 women entrepreneurs aged between 30 and 70, with children, who had set up very small and small businesses in the city of Yaoundé.

The information collected was sorted and classified using Nvivo 12 software and analysed using content analysis. I decided to use manual analysis for its advantages, such as accurate understanding of language and consideration of context, the respondent's personal experience, figures of speech, and use of symbols and gestures. The software provides a summary analysis that may not be able to capture the complexity of manual analysis.

Presentation and Analysis of Results

Women entrepreneurs are critical of the administrative services and regulations in force. They are particularly affected by the effects of regulations during the start-up phase of their business. They report that the problems they encounter are mainly linked to the process of formalising their business. The women interviewed mentioned the excessive length of the procedures and the huge quantity of documents to be provided as major difficulties. I can quote some of the women entrepreneurs who said:

> The real difficulty in this matter of legalising a company is that the information is not available to everyone. I tried to look even on the internet to put together my file, but I had to do it twice because the information I received here and there was never the same. (Marie-Laure N., 35, two children, makes food products (yogurts, mayonnaise, salad dressing, and jam))

All the women interviewed for this study said that they had not received any help from the State to facilitate the process of formalising their structure. "I've never received any help from the State to get started; on the contrary, I'll spare you the money I've spent to help my business move forward" (Clarisse D., 38, six children, supplies chicken for cutting).

Another said: "I know that the State gives a lot of help to women in agriculture, but I don't know if there is any help for me in my field" (Akwah B., 33, two children, produces tea, infusions, and body balms).

The women in my sample said they wanted to receive effective help from the state, support that would make it easier for them to enter the entrepreneurial field, and above all that would enable them to be supported. It was in this context that one of them said:

> We can't really evolve because it's out of our profits that we pay the rent, eat, and so on. We're constantly going round in circles, and that's a shame. The State should be able to support us with subsidies, help with illnesses or even help with sending children to school (Liliane H., 52, five children, care provider for the elderly).

All 20 women interviewed agreed that Cameroon's administrative services and regulations are "inefficient". My results show that Cameroonian women entrepreneurs find public policy procedures discouraging and not conducive to entrepreneurship. Cumbersome regulations, complex administrative circuits and procedures, and administrative complications are the main obstacles to female entrepreneurship in Cameroon. Although the State of Cameroon provides numerous support programmes for women entrepreneurs, it was found that the women interviewed had not benefited from any of these programmes. In addition, they complained that the administrative process was cumbersome, complex, and costly, even if it was just to apply, to participate in a project or programme organised by the state. They also complain that they only receive information when it is too late for them to take part, because the information circulates in a network, whereas it should be accessible to everyone.

This highlights the nature of the underlying problem, which could be linked to the quality and relevance of communication and information dissemination to Cameroonian women entrepreneurs.

Support and Capacity-Building Structures

The women entrepreneurs in my sample also expressed dissatisfaction with the lack of support from organisations that help women entrepreneurs. In this context, the lack of support from the Cameroonian government and the resulting obstacles are a real brake on their activities.

Their feelings are illustrated by the words of one of the business owners interviewed when she deplores the lack of effective support initiatives: "Sometimes you see advertising posters or adverts about a programme or project organised for women entrepreneurs, sometimes I even take time out to take part in these seminars and training courses, but I can assure you that it doesn't achieve much because there is no follow-up afterwards" (Farida D., 42, three children, estate agent).

Another company director confirmed this, saying: "I've stopped taking the training courses and seminars that the government and my associations organise because they waste more of my time than anything else. These are things you can get on the internet and sometimes some training courses aren't even adapted to our reality" (Thérèse F., 29, one child, makes baby porridge).

The statements made by the women interviewed reveal that they share the view that they have not benefited from an effective support service or structure, particularly in terms of support, guidance, and training. Although some respondents mentioned that they had attended training courses provided by a support structure, this structure did not provide the necessary support they needed to set up and sustain their businesses.

Financing Structures

When it comes to financing their activities, the results of this study show that the women entrepreneurs in the sample are reluctant to take out a bank loan to start their business. They say they prefer personal financing (personal savings) and help from their family or tontines. This is what Amélie N. (63, three children, dressmaker) told me when she said: "I started sewing at home at the age of 22 and I've never taken out a bank loan. What's more, I had no guarantees to give them".

Another entrepreneur in the same vein told me: "I don't think you should take out any credit. It's better to start out with what little you have, rather than getting into debt and entering a spiral of debt that won't stop. I had a small amount of savings from my previous job and that's what got me started" (Monique R., 38, four children, interior designer).

"When I saw the bank take away my friend's land for a loan that had not been repaid on time, I said I would never take out a bank loan. It's all one thing after another and it gives you an illusory sense of security. Not to mention the interest rates, which are often high. No, really, no bank loan for me" (Falonne R., 63, two children, bookshop).

And one last woman said: "Even if I wanted a bank loan, I couldn't take it out because I don't have the guarantees" (Suzanne D., 52, four children, restaurant).

Women who have tried to take out a bank loan to supplement their savings have reported significant difficulties. One young businesswoman recalls how, despite having submitted several loan applications, none of them were successful. No bank would grant her a loan. That's when she said: "When I wanted to start my business, I tried everything to get a bank loan, but no one would give it to me without guarantees. I come from a very poor family, and it was finally thanks to a tontine that I was able to start my business" (Claire B., aged 47, six children, hairdresser).

The sample also showed that there are women who don't really need to raise funds to launch their businesses, including Agathe N., 34, two children, who is a masseuse and beautician and says: "I started massages and beauty treatments at home with the equipment I had and above all my skills, which enabled me to use the natural products I had. Then I started offering low-cost training courses and was able to put money aside to open my own business".

My interviews reveal that most small Cameroonian women entrepreneurs are self-financing in one way or another. This is partly because they set up businesses based on activities that do not require significant financing. It can also be explained by the existence of substantial savings on the part of these women before they launch their activities, or by their use of tontines.

On the other hand, the mistrust of banking institutions towards the businesses of the women interviewed explains their tendency to self-finance. These women believe that the guarantees required by banks are sometimes unattainable for some of them, even when they are prepared to accept high interest rates.

Discussing the Results

Recent studies show that the Cameroonian state is increasingly implementing public initiatives to enable the growth of female entrepreneurship, but these remain largely unknown to women entrepreneurs.

Firstly, the National Employment Fund (FNE) offers grants and soft loans to support women's entrepreneurship projects according to Okah-Efogo and Timba (2015). This initiative is important because it allows women entrepreneurs to access funds with affordable interest rates, which is essential for the viability of their business. According to Kenmegni (2023), the characteristics of entrepreneurs, such as gender, can therefore influence access to credit for small and medium-sized enterprises (SMEs) in Cameroon. In this way, the FNE can help to reduce gender inequalities in access to finance.

In addition, the government has launched the *Programme de Promotion de l'Entrepreneuriat Féminin* (PPEF) which aims to increase women's access to credit and encourage investment in women-led businesses (Njinyah and Pendati, 2021). This initiative is important because it recognises that women entrepreneurs have specific financing needs and face barriers in accessing credit. Mayoux (2001) argues that microcredit can be an effective tool for women's empowerment in Cameroon, but that it needs to be accompanied by capacity building and social support measures to be sustainable.

The creation of the *Banque Camerounaise des PME* (BC-PME) is another important initiative to facilitate access to finance for women entrepreneurs in Cameroon. The BC-PME offers financial products and services tailored to the needs of women entrepreneurs, including short-, medium- and long-term credit, guarantees, and advisory services (Tadie et al., 2021). This initiative is important because it recognises that women entrepreneurs have specific financing needs and require financial services tailored to their needs.

The *Fonds Spécial d'Équipement et d'Intervention Intercommunale* (FEICOM) offers grants and soft loans to finance women's entrepreneurship projects in local authorities decentralised by the Ministry of Decentralisation and Local Development. This initiative is important because it recognises that women entrepreneurs have specific financing needs and require funds to start up and develop their businesses.

Finally, the *Fonds de Garantie des Crédits aux PME* (FOGAPE) is a guarantee fund designed to facilitate access to bank credit for SMEs. It offers guarantees to women entrepreneurs who do not have sufficient collateral to obtain a bank loan from the Ministry of Finance. This initiative is important because it recognises that women entrepreneurs often find it difficult to provide sufficient guarantees.

However, my conclusions reveal that despite the political implementation of aid programmes, projects, and regulations in favour of Cameroonian women entrepreneurs, the services provided by the Cameroonian administration to women project owners are still limited, insufficient, and of low quality.

Regulation and Administration of Policies to Promote Women's Entrepreneurship

Regarding the regulation of public policies to promote women's entrepreneurship, there are still factors of failure that hamper the effectiveness of public policies. There is a lack of interministerial coordination, as public policies to promote women's entrepreneurship are often implemented by different ministries and government agencies without effective coordination, as Dié and Asseko (2021) show. As a result, there is overlap, duplication, and inconsistency in programmes and activities, which can reduce their effectiveness and impact.

There is a lack of consultation with women entrepreneurs, as public policies to promote women's entrepreneurship are often designed without adequate consultation with Cameroonian women entrepreneurs themselves (Desjardins et al., 2009). This can lead to a poor understanding of their needs and challenges, and to programmes and activities that do not meet their expectations (Asse, 2015).

There is a lack of monitoring and evaluation, as public policies to promote women's entrepreneurship are often implemented without adequate monitoring and evaluation. This can lead to misallocation of resources, poor management of programmes and activities, and an inability to measure their impact, and make improvements (Ahouissou, 2011). According to Desjardins and St-Onge (2009), the factors affecting women's businesses in Cameroon are many and varied, ranging from the difficulty of accessing credit to the poor education and training of women entrepreneurs. According to Jean-Pierre Warnier (1993), 30 years ago, entrepreneurship in Cameroon was often hampered by corruption and clientelism, which could affect the management of programmes and activities aimed at women entrepreneurs.

Without adequate transparency and accountability, it is difficult to report results and impacts to stakeholders, which can lead to a loss of confidence in public policies.

The administrative red tape, complicated regulations, and difficult access to the network were major factors in discouraging the women entrepreneurs in my sample about the success of Cameroon's public policies to promote women's entrepreneurship.

Support and Capacity-Building Structures

Regarding support and capacity-building structures, public policies to promote women's entrepreneurship are often poorly understood or poorly communicated to women entrepreneurs (Badiang and Biboum, 2014). This can lead to low participation in programmes and activities, as well as a lack of awareness of the opportunities and resources available. The lack of sustainability, and longevity of programmes and activities is a major factor in failure. According to Abonge (2012), women's enterprises in Cameroon have a positive impact on household livelihoods and survival, but they face major challenges in terms of sustainability and growth. Without proper planning and the implementation of the sustainability and longevity of programmes and activities, there can be an over-reliance on external funding and an inability to maintain long-term outcomes and impacts.

The lack of understanding of the specific needs and challenges of women entrepreneurs is one of the factors leading to the failure of public policies to promote women's entrepreneurship. The programmes and activities proposed do not always correspond to the real needs of women entrepreneurs and are sometimes not adapted to the Cameroonian context, which can lead to a poor allocation of resources and low effectiveness with women entrepreneurs. In the same vein, Mouchingam Mefire (2018) believes that public policies must consider the specificities of women based on their family, financial, social, and environmental situation in order to be effective in their support proposals and capacity building.

A few authors are now focusing on support and capacity building for women entrepreneurs. Lebègue (2011) stresses the importance of support tailored to the specific needs of women entrepreneurs (cf. Villette, 2011).

He demonstrates in his research that many women do not find the training and programmes offered by the state to be to their liking, and that they have very mixed opinions about these support structures. This confirms the results of this study, as several women entrepreneurs stated that they had not gained anything from the training they had taken part in. Furthermore, Lebègue (2015) reiterates his assertions by demonstrating that state support and capacity building for women entrepreneurs is an inescapable condition for their success.

Financing Structures

Funding structures for public policies to promote women's entrepreneurship are often underfunded and under-resourced. This can lead to a limited capacity to implement effective programmes and activities, as well as an inability to respond to the needs and challenges of women entrepreneurs (Assoumou, 2017). In the case of this study, the women entrepreneurs were mostly self-financed. The involvement of these financing structures in their entrepreneurial activities is therefore fairly low (Brush, 2014). Women's reluctance to approach banking institutions is sometimes due to bad experience, the complex documentation required to put together an application, a lack of guarantees, or simply the banks' reputation.

In the case of this study, most women entrepreneurs already had savings to launch their activities, others had financial support from their families, and others had recourse to tontines. They had already realised that Cameroon's banking system was reluctant to assess the risks involved in granting credit to very small and small businesses.

Ascher (2012) stresses that the source of start-up capital is one of the determining factors in entrepreneurial success. It's important not to get into debt from the outset, as one of the business owners I interviewed said. However, the larger the business grows, the more funds it will need, and so it will be necessary to seek larger sources of finance, particularly from banking institutions (Bhattachary and Londhe, 2014).

Conclusion and Recommendations

The Cameroonian women entrepreneurs in my sample encounter many difficulties in carrying out their entrepreneurial activities. Cameroon's public policies for promoting women's entrepreneurship, although favourable in theory, do not yet enable the women entrepreneurs interviewed to develop their businesses to the full, whether in terms of the regulations in force and administrative procedures, the support and capacity-building structures that are supposed to help them to develop better, or the financing structures that are supposed to facilitate their access to bank loans and guarantees. For the most part, they are unaware of the opportunities available to them and are often unconvinced of the contribution these proposals can make to their business activities.

I can therefore conclude that the public policies put in place to promote female entrepreneurship in Cameroon are an important step in the right direction to reduce gender inequalities and promote gender equality (cf. Zeineb, 2015). However, it is important to consider all the success and failure factors of Cameroonian women entrepreneurs, including intrinsic factors, if these public policies are to be effective and make a real contribution to stimulating the country's economic growth. Business support programmes must be designed to consider local specificities and the needs of Cameroonian women entrepreneurs, encouraging entrepreneurial innovation, collaboration, and cooperation between businesses, digitalisation, business performance, and taking into account the intrinsic factors of success for women entrepreneurs (Vergnaud, 1995).

This study carried out on the success and failure factors of Cameroonian public policies to promote women's entrepreneurship has certain limitations. Firstly, the study was carried out on a limited sample of Cameroonian women entrepreneurs, which may affect the generalisability of the results. In addition, the study focused mainly on national public policies, without considering local or regional initiatives that may also have an impact on the promotion of female entrepreneurship.

Another limitation of the study is that it did not consider external factors that can influence the success or failure of public policies, such as economic, political, or social changes. In addition, the study did not examine the long-term effects of public policies on the promotion of women's entrepreneurship, which may be important for assessing their real impact.

In terms of future research perspectives, it would be interesting to conduct more in-depth studies on the intrinsic factors of successful female entrepreneurship, such as motivation, self-confidence, and entrepreneurial skills. Comparative studies could also be conducted to examine regional differences in the promotion of female entrepreneurship in Cameroon, as well as effective practices in other African countries.

It would also be important to conduct research into the specific obstacles faced by women entrepreneurs in certain sectors of activity, such as agriculture, technology, or services, and to examine how public policies can be adapted to meet these challenges. Finally, longitudinal studies could be carried out to assess the long-term impact of public policies on the promotion of female entrepreneurship and identify the key factors in their success or failure.

Based on the results of this study and the analysis of public policies to promote women's entrepreneurship in Cameroon, several recommendations can be made to improve their effectiveness and impact.

Firstly, it is recommended that inter-ministerial coordination be strengthened to ensure coherent and effective implementation of public policies. The various ministries involved in promoting women's entrepreneurship should work closely together to avoid duplication, overlap, and gaps in policy implementation. Effective coordination would also maximise the use of resources and improve the impact of public policies.

Secondly, it is important to consider the specificities of women entrepreneurs in the design and implementation of public policies. Public policies should be tailored to the specific needs of women entrepreneurs, particularly in terms of access to finance, training, mentoring, and networking. Public policies should also consider the socio-cultural and economic constraints faced by women entrepreneurs, such as restrictive social norms, family responsibilities, and lack of family support.

Thirdly, it is essential to set up a system for monitoring and evaluating public policies to measure their impact and effectiveness. The data collected through monitoring and evaluation should be used to adjust and improve public policies in line with needs and realities on the ground. The results of evaluation should be made public to ensure the transparency and accountability of policymakers.

Fourthly, it is recommended that the capacities of actors involved in the implementation of public policies be strengthened, civil servants, service providers, and civil society organisations. Actors should be trained on gender issues, the specificities of women entrepreneurs, and best practices in promoting women's entrepreneurship.

Finally, it is important to promote awareness and communication around public policies to promote female entrepreneurship. Women entrepreneurs should be informed of the public policies available, and the opportunities offered. The media, social networks, and civil society organisations can play an important role in raising awareness and communicating about public policies.

Based on the 3C model by Solava Ibrahim (2017), here is a model of effective support for women entrepreneurs from Cameroonian public policies (Table 12.1).

This model aims to effectively support Cameroonian women entrepreneurs in their entrepreneurial journey by considering the intrinsic and extrinsic factors of their success. The aim is to make them aware that they are discriminated against and disadvantaged, to support them in their social transformation towards autonomous entrepreneurship, and to work with the State to provide a legal framework for their entrepreneurial activity. The concrete actions proposed in this model are

Table 12.1 3C model of support for women entrepreneurs

Steps	*Description*	*Concrete actions*
Awareness	Raising awareness among Cameroonian women of their discriminated and disadvantaged status	- Raising awareness of women's rights and gender equality - Training on entrepreneurial skills and female leadership - Setting up networks of women entrepreneurs to encourage the exchange of experience and good practice
Conciliation	Social transformation where women decide to move from being discriminated against to becoming autonomous entrepreneurs.	- Personalised support for women entrepreneurs in setting up and developing their businesses - Setting up support and capacity-building structures tailored to the needs of women entrepreneurs - Facilitating access to finance and bank guarantees for women entrepreneurs
Collaboration	Working with the State to provide a legal framework for women's entrepreneurial activity	- Strengthening interministerial coordination to ensure coherent and effective implementation of public policies - Adapting public policies to the specific needs of women entrepreneurs, particularly in terms of access to finance, training, mentoring and networking. - Setting up a system for monitoring and evaluating public policies to measure their impact and effectiveness

based on the conclusion and recommendations set out above. However, as this is a study during a doctoral thesis, other results will be obtained soon.

Notes

1 The National Employment Fund (FNE) is a Cameroonian public body responsible for promoting employment throughout Cameroon.
2 AFEPEV is a Cameroonian non-profit association that helps empower women and vulnerable communities to build a healthy and sustainable environment.
3 Ukuzola is an association offering innovative solidarity coliving to young entrepreneurs in developing countries (60 per cent women). By supporting them and enabling them to devote themselves 100% to their projects, Ukuzola stimulates social innovation and aims to build a more sustainable and equitable future for all.
4 AGRO-PME Foundation is a non-profit organisation created in 2014 in Cameroon to promote agricultural and agri-food entrepreneurship. Its mission is to support small and medium-sized enterprises (SMEs) in the agri-food sector by offering them training, consulting, coaching, and financing.

References

Abonge, C. V. (2012) "Assessing the impact of women's enterprises on household livelihoods and survival: Evidence from the North West Region of Cameroon", *Greener Journal of Social Sciences*, 2 (5): 147–159.

Abousaid, F.-Z. and M. Hilali (2023) "Les défis de financement pour les femmes entrepreneures: Une question de genre", *Revue du contrôle, de la comptabilité et de l'audit*, 7 (1). https://www.revuecca.com/index.php/home/article/view/891, accessed 24 July 2024.

Ahl, H. and T. Nelsson (2010) "Moving forward: Institutional perspectives on gender and entrepreneurship", *International Journal of Gender and Entrepreneurship*, 2 (1): 5–9.

Ahouissou, B. A. (2011) *Financement de l'entrepreneuriat rural dans la région du centre au Cameroun.* PhD thesis in management, Université de Liège. ORBI-University of Liège. https://orbi.uliege.be/handle/2268/99282

Ascher, J. (2012) "Female entrepreneurship: An appropriate response to gender discrimination", *Journal of Entrepreneurship Management and Innovation (JEM),* 8 (4): 97–114.

Asse, G. P. N. A. N. (2015) *Les femmes entrepreneures dans la société politique camerounaise.* PhD in political science, Université de Bordeaux. https://core.ac.uk/download/pdf/46811082.pdf.

Assoumou, M. O. and F. A. S. Guetsop (2017) "L'entrepreneuriat féminin au Cameroun: Enjeux et perspectives", *Revue congolaise de gestion*, 24 (2): 11–42.

Ateba, J. C. (2022) *Le développement de l'entrepreneuriat féminin au Cameroun: Cas de la CEC-PROM MATURE.* Saarbrücken: Editions Universitaires Européennes.

Badiang, M. A. and A. D. Biboum (2014) "Succès et échec des micro-entreprises: Une analyse par la pratique contexte du marketing entrepreneurial en Afrique", https://www.academia.edu/39984331/Entrepreneurial_Marketing, accessed 4 August 2024.

Bagher, G. and R. Paria (2011) "The study of barriers to entrepreneurship in men and women", *Australian Journal of Business and Management Research*, 1 (9): 31–36.

Bandibeno, I. K. and L. Nkonga (2019) Gouvernance et développement local au Cameroun. *Revue d'Etudes en management et finance d'organisation*, 3 (8). https://revues.imist.ma/index.php/REMFO/article/download/13351/8711, accessed 24 July 2024.

Batibonak, S. (2022) *Discrimination et entrepreunarialité des femmes au Cameroun, Cahier de recherche* n°5, Observatoire francophone pour le développement inclusif par le genre. https://ofdig.org/wp-content/uploads/2022/12/Cahier-de-recherche-05–2022.pdf, accessed 4 August 2024.

Baturin, C. (2014) *Land as a determinant of power in Cameroon and the role of the Mutuelle d'Epargne et du crédit pour la promotion de l'entrepreneuriat féminin (MUDEF) in women obtaining it.* Wellesley College. https://repository.wellesley.edu/object/ir1006, accessed 24 July 2024.

Bhattacharya, S. and B. R. Londhe (2014) "Micro Entrepreneurship: Sources of Finance and Related Constraints", *Procedia Economics and Finance*, 11, 775-783. https://doi.org/10.1016/s2212-5671(14)00241-x, accessed 24 July 2024.

Boussetta, M. (2011) "Entreprenariat féminin au Maroc: environnement et contribution au développement économique et social", Research Report No. 10–11, Investment Climate and Business Environment Research Fund, Dakar.

Brun, D. (GENCAP) (2019) *Data on gender equality in Cameroon.* Gender Standby Capacity Project (GenCap). file:///C:/Users/audre/Downloads/data_on_gender_equality_in_cameroon-hno_2020-17_oct_19.pdf, accessed 4 August 2024.

Brush, C. G. (2014) "Exploring the Concept of an Entrepreneurship Education Ecosystem", in S. Hoskinson and D. F. Kuratko (eds) *Innovative Pathways for University Entrepreneurship in the 21st Century* (*Advances in the Study of Entrepreneurship, Innovation and Economic Growth, Vol. 24*), pp. 25–39. Leeds: Emerald Group Publishing Limited.

Comité de pilotage cellule opérationnelle Minpmeesa (2009) *Stratégie de développement des petites et moyennes entreprises, de l'économie sociale et de l'artisanat.* Document 2 et 3: Stratégie du secteur et Plan d'Actions Prioritaires, https://www.minpmeesa.cm/site/?media_dl=846, accessed 24 July 2024.

Dabić, M., L. P. Dana, D. M. Nziku, and V. Ramadani (eds) (2022) *Women Entrepreneurs in Sub-Saharan Africa: Historical Framework, Ecosystem, and Future Perspectives for the Region.* Cham: Springer Nature.

de Bruin, A., C. G. Brush, and F. Welter (2007) "Advancing a framework for coherent research on women's entrepreneurship", *Theory and Practice*, 31 (3): 323–339.

Décret présidentiel n° 320 (2004) https://www.minfopra.gov.cm/recueil/REPARATIONS/DECRET%20N°%202004-320%20DU%208%20DECEMBRE%202004%20portant%20organisation%20du%20gouvernement.pdf

https://www.minfopra.gov.cm/recueil/REPARATIONS/DECRET%20N°%202004-320%20DU%208%20DECEMBRE%202004%20portant%20organisation%20du%20gouvernement.pdf

Desjardins, S. and A. St-Onge (2009) *Les facteurs qui affectent les entreprises féminines: Perspectives de croissance: Le cas du Cameroun.* Working Paper. Geneva: International Labour Office Publications.

Desrosières, A. (2006) "De Cournot à l'évaluation des politiques publiques", *Prisme, Cournot Centre for Research in Economics*, 7: 7–51.

Dié, M. D. and M. F. E. Asseko (2021) "Contexte socio-institutionnel et économique et développement de l'entrepreneuriat scientifique au Cameroun", *Science Technologie Développement*, 1 (1). https://doi.org/10.21494/iste.op.2021.0669, accessed 4 August 2024.

Ella, E. (2019) "Sociologie de la politique nationale genre du Cameroun: Acquis et défis majeurs du début du XXIe siècle", *Cahiers de l'IREA*, 36: 23–110.

Etoundi, A., N. Chameni, and A. Meva (2013) "Écarts de salaire entre hommes et femmes au Cameroun: Discrimination ou Capital humain? Une approche par sous-groupes". [Gender wage gap: Discrimination or Human Capita? A subgroup approach]. *MPRA Paper*. https://ideas.repec.org/p/pra/mprapa/64761.html, accessed 24 July 2024.

Fayolle, A. (2017) *Entrepreneuriat: Théories et pratiques, Applications pour apprendre à entreprendre*. Paris: Dunod. https://doi.org/10.3917/dunod.fayol.2017.01, accessed on 24 July 2024.

Galloway, L. and W. Brown (2002) "Entrepreneurship Education at University: A Driver in the Creation of High Growth Firms?" *Education & Training,* 44 (8/9): 398–405.

Gay, M., C. Ibrahim, and O. Curbatov (2014) *Repositioning universities in the development of Africa*. IAUPL (International Association of University Professors and Lecturers). Impressum: CH: Oleg Curbatov, 978-9975-4089-5–0. ⟨hal-01423211⟩, accessed 24 July 2024.

Hisrich, R. D. and C. Brush (1984) "The Woman Entrepreneur: Management Skills and Business Problems", *Journal of Small Business Management*, 22 (1): 30–37.

Kamdem, E. et al. (2011) *Pratiques d'accompagnement et de performance. Très petites et petites entreprises camerounaises en phase de démarrage*. Dakar: Ed. CODESRIA.

Kede, N. and N. R. Tsafack (2023) "Effet de l'inclusion financière sur la formalisation des petites et moyennes entreprises au Cameroun", *Journal of Small Business & Entrepreneurship*, 35 (1): 56–85.

Kenmegni, N. G. R. (2023) "Some Entrepreneurs' Characteristics and Cameroonian Small and Medium Size Enterprises' (SMEs) Access to Credit", *Global Academic Journal of Economics and Business*, 5 (1): 1–12. https://doi.org/10.36348/gajeb.2023.v05i01.001, accessed 24 July 2024.

Kobeissi, N. (2010) "Gender factors and women's entrepreneurship: international evidence and policy implication", *Journal of International Entrepreneurship*, 8 (1): 1–35.

Lebègue, T. (2011) *Le processus entrepreneurial des femmes en France*. PhD thesis in Management Sciences, Université de Bretagne Occidentale.

Lebègue, T. (2015) "La réussite de carrière entrepreneuriale des femmes", *Revue de l'entrepreneuriat*, 1 (14): 93–127.

Mahadea, D. and M. Kabange (2019) "Influence of government regulations and institutions on entrepreneurial performance in Cameroon," *Journal of Developmental Entrepreneurship (JDE)*, World Scientific Publishing Co. Pte. Ltd. 24 (4): 1–17.

Mayoux, L. (2001) *Emplois, genre et petites entreprises: comment adapter l'environnement politique?* Document de travail SEED n° 15, Série sur le développement de l'entrepreneuriat féminin et le genre dans les entreprises (WEDGE).

Meli, D. S. and C. Nodem (2021) *Le Genre et la Performance des Entreprises au Cameroun*. Policy paper n° 776. Other Policy Briefs. African Economic Research Consortium. https://publication.aercafricalibrary.org/handle/123456789/3177, accessed 4 August 2024.

Ministère de l'Économie, de la Planification et de l'Aménagement du Territoire (2014) *Guide de l'investisseur*. https://f2icameroon.com/documents/Guide_de_Investisseur.pdf, accessed 24 July 2024.

Ministere de la Promotion de la Femme et de la Famille (2009) *Plan d'action pour le développement de l'entrepreneuriat féminin au Cameroun (PAN-DEF) 2010–2014*. FAO, *FAOLEX*. https://faolex.fao.org/docs/pdf/cmr147303.pdf, accessed 24 July 2024.

Mouchingam, M. L. (2018) *Politiques publiques, programmes et projets sensibles au genre: cas de la communauté Mandjara au Cameroun*. Collections thèses et mémoires électroniques de l'université de Montréal.

Muller, P. (1990) *Les politiques publiques*. Paris: Presses Universitaires de France.

Njinyah, S. Z. and M. Pendati (2021) "Awareness and Usage of Government Policies by Women Tourism Entrepreneurs in Cameroon", in M. Z. Ngoasong, O. Adeola, A. N. Kimbu, and R. E. Hinson (eds), *New Frontiers in Hospitality and Tourism Management in Africa*, pp. 173–192. Cham, Switzerland: Springer Nature.

Nkakleu, R. (2007) *Capital social et identification et exploitation d'opportunités entrepreneuriales en contexte camerounais: une étude pilote*. Paper presented at the 5th International Congress of the Academy of Entrepreneurship, Innovation and Evolution of Entrepreneurial Practices, Canada, Sherbrooke.

Nkakleu, R., A. Biboum, and A. Badiang (2013) *Accompagnement des Entrepreneurs et Performance Post Création des Petites Entreprises Camerounaises et Sénégalaises / Support for Entrepreneurs and Post Creation Performance of Cameroon and Senegalese Small Businesses*. Senegal: Trust Africa.

Nkolo, A. S. (2015) *Les femmes entrepreneures dans la société politique camerounaise.* PhD Political science. University of Bordeaux.

Okah-Efogo, F. and G. T. Timba (2015) "Female entrepreneurship and growth in Cameroon", *African Journal of Economic and Management Studies*, 6 (1): 107–119.

Pépin, Y. (1997) "Savoirs pratiques et savoirs scolaires: une représentation constructiviste de l'éducation", *Revue des sciences de l'éducation*, 20 (1): 63–85.

Recha, J. W., M. Kapukha, A. Wekesa, S. Shames, and K. Heiner (2014) *Sustainable Agriculture Land Management Practices for Climate Change Mitigation: A Training Huide for Smallholder Farmers. The CGIAR Research Program On Climate Change, Agriculture And Food Security (CCAFS).*

Rwenge, M. J., K. Njeri, and L. Maina (2013) *Facteurs Explicatifs de l'Entrepreneuriat Feminin en Afrique Subsaharienne: Cameroun et Kenya / Explanatory Factors of the Female Entrepreneurship in Sub-Saharan Africa: Cameroon and Kenya*, TrustAfrica. Senegal. https://policycommons.net/artifacts/1445261/facteurs-explicatifs-de-lentrepreneuriat-feminin-en-afrique-subsaharienne/2077023/, accessed 12 July 2024.

Schuerkens, U. (2023) *Entreprises, entrepreneurs et travail au Sénégal.* Paris: L'Harmattan.

Secretary General (2016) Women's Economic Empowerment in the Changing World of Work*: Nations Unies Conseil Économique et Social*, E/CN.6/2017/3. https://digitallibrary.un.org/record/856760/files/E_CN-6_2017_3-FR.pdf, accessed 12 July 2024.

Simo, A. P. (2023) "Le déploiement controversé de l'ODD 16 au Cameroun. Peace and governance in a contested political context", *Revue internationale des études du développement*, 253: 95–117.

Singh, G. and R. Belwal (2008) "Entrepreneurship and SMEs in Ethiopia: Evaluating the role, prospects and problems faced by women in this emergent sector", *Gender in Management: An International Journal*, 23 (2): 120–136.

Stephan, U. (2007) *Culture of Entrepreneurship* (C-Ent), Dresden University of Technology. PhD in Natural Sciences. https://archiv.ub.uni-marburg.de/diss/z2008/0146/pdf/dus.pdf?, accessed 12 July 2024.

Stockey, L.-N. (1991) "Une politique publique crédible", *Journal de dynamique et de contrôle économiques*, 15 (4): 627–656.

Tadie, T. K., C. E. Ambassa, L. A. Fono, and J. Sadefo-Kamdem (2021) "Critères de choix du mode de financement par crédit-bail dans les Petites et Moyennes Entreprises (PME) au Cameroun", *Revue du Contrôle de la Comptabilité et de l'Audit*, 5 (1): 181–202.

Tafelefack, J. and M. A. Atemkeng (2019) Contribution de la « *géogouvernance locale* » et de « *l'éducation entrepreneuriale* » à la limitation de la contreperformance du système éducatif camerounais d'enseignement secondaire general, *Djiboul*, *Spécial* 8. https://djiboul.org/wp-content/uploads/2023/03/Tire-a-part_37.pdf, accessed 12 July 2024.

Tchouassi, G. (2000) "Femmes entrepreneurs au Cameroun: une approche par les récits de vie", *Revue Congolaise de Gestion*, 2–3: 63–77.

Tchouassi, G. (2002) "Entreprendre au féminin au Cameroun: possibilités et limites", in *Actes du 2e Congrès de l'Académie de l'Entrepreneuriat sur le thème: champs de l'entrepreneuriat et dynamique des sociétés*, pp. 433–445. Bordeaux: Académie de l'entreprenariat.

Tchouassi, G., N. Ngwen, O. H. Tékam, and S. Temfack (2018) "Youth and women's entrepreneurial knowledge and economic development", *International Journal of Organisational Science*, 19 (1): 57–79.

The Advocates for Human Rights (2014) *Cameroon Committee on the Elimination of Discrimination Against Women 57th Session.* https://www.theadvocatesforhumanrights.org/Res/cameroon_cedaw_vaw_february_2014%202.pdf, accessed 12 July 2024.

Toche, C. L. M. (2020) *Analyse des dynamiques entrepreneuriales des femmes dans la création d'une entreprise collective: le cas de la création d'une coopérative féminine dans la région de l'Ouest du Cameroun*. PhD thesis in society and economy, Université Rennes 2. https://theses.hal.science/tel-03405447/, accessed 12 July 2024.

Tsambou, A. D. and B. A. F. Kamga (2016) "Analyse micro structurelle des caractéristiques managériales et performance des entreprises au Cameroun", *Revue africaine de management*, 1 (1): 112–132.

Vaison, R. (1973) "A note on 'public policy'", *Canadian Journal of Political Science/Revue canadienne de science politique*, 6 (4): 661–666.

Vergnaud, G. (1995) "Quelle théorie pour comprendre les relations entre savoir-faire et savoir", in A. Bentolila (ed.) *Savoirs théoriques et savoirs d'action*, pp. 5–20. Paris: Nathan.

Villette, M. (2011) "How to respond to the institutional demand for teaching entrepreneurship. An ethnographic account of a teaching experiment", *Revue française de socio-économie*, 1 (7): 83–101.

Warnier, J.-P. (1993) *L'esprit d'entreprise au Cameroun*. Paris: Karthala.

Wassila, L. (2010) *Le réseautage: Un outil d'apprentissage entrepreneurial chez les femmes entrepreneures algériennes*. Université Mohamed Khider, Biskra. https://me.univ-biskra.dz/images/me_seminaire/2014/pdf_fr/smf1214.pdf, accessed 12 July 2024.

Yen, D. G. B. (2022) "Entrepreneuriat féminin et croissance économique: Cas du Cameroun", *Revue Internationale du Chercheur*, 3 (2): 131–154. https://doi.org/10.5281/zenodo.6614741, accessed 4 August 2024.

Zeineb, D. D. (2015) "Le rôle de la politique publique dans l'encouragement de l'entrepreneuriat féminin en Algérie: Réalité et perspectives", *Recherches Économiques Manageriales*, 9 (2): 15–34.

13 Women Entrepreneurs in Côte d'Ivoire's Philanthropic Landscape

Jean-Claude Kouadio

Women's Philanthropy: The Emergence of a Long-Invisible Phenomenon

Women's philanthropy is a little discussed and little studied phenomenon, leading people to believe that philanthropy only has a male face. Yet history shows that women have been involved in philanthropy since the Middle Ages. We refer here to the research of Fagnart and L'Estrange (2011), which bears witness to this tangible reality. In the same vein, Cohen (2010) traces the involvement of women philanthropists in Quebec society from the end of the 19th century to the middle of the 20th century. In addition to these studies, the journal *Voluntas* published a special issue in 1996, entitled "Women and philanthropy", which takes stock of women's philanthropic activities in various parts of the world, in both northern and southern societies (McCarthy, 1996).

The fact that women's philanthropy has long gone unnoticed is explained by historical and legal facts. Firstly, modern philanthropy was strongly influenced by the donation of money by wealthy businessmen in the 19th century (Zunz, 2012). This activity has largely contributed to thinking about philanthropy through the prism of giving money, often ignoring its other forms, such as volunteering and giving oneself. Women have been the victims of this collective representation of philanthropy, especially as their philanthropic actions have mostly been associated with volunteering and the feminist movement for greater rights (Belliard, 2009). Belliard explains that women's specialisation in volunteering took place in a historical context where women were financially subordinate to their husbands. According to the laws of the time in France, and in countries such as Western Germany, women had no right to earn or spend their own money without a man's permission. Under these conditions, it was difficult for women to devote themselves to financial philanthropy. According to Alalouf-Hall (2020), the law of the time therefore helped to keep women out of financial philanthropy and made men the main donors.

Over time, this reality has changed. The various feminist movements in favour of economic and social equality, which have fostered major changes in the roles of women and men in the West, have enabled women to become involved in financial philanthropy, where they now devote money to social causes. Various studies by the *Women's Philanthropy Institute*[1] including those from 2015 and others, clearly

DOI: 10.4324/9781003492931-17

show the commitment of a growing number of women on the financial philanthropy scene (cf. Mesch et al., 2015a and 2015b). For example, in her book, De Nowell (1996) profiles fourteen Canadian women philanthropists who have each donated between $1.25 million and $500 million to support the arts, health, and the construction of university buildings. More recent data shows that Canadian women philanthropists gave a total of $3.3 billion in 2012 (Alalouf-Hall, 2020). Vasavada (2012) shows the rise of women's philanthropy in India through women's ability to fund and manage philanthropic institutions.

The emergence of women's financial philanthropy is also correlated with the increase in the number of women's great fortunes. The list of billionaires for the year 2023 published by Forbes Magazine includes 340 women[2] from 39 different geographical areas (Lafranco and Paterson-Withorn, 2023). An analysis of this list shows that their sources of income are diversified. Some have inherited the family business, such as Françoise Bettencourt-Meyers ($69 billion in assets), who inherited L'Oréal from her mother; or inherited it from their husband, as in the case of Julia Koch ($59 billion in assets), who inherited Koch Industrie on the death of her husband. Another category of women built their fortunes with their husbands. Rafaela Aponte-Diamant ($31.2 billion) falls into this category. She and her husband each own 50% of MSC, the world's largest shipping company. In this list, a final category of women has built their fortunes on their own, as in the case of Gina Rinehart ($27 billion), who made her fortune by investing in iron ore.

These great female fortunes are a force for philanthropy and a hope for the future of humanity. Melinda Gates (2019) and recent research findings show that women give more than men (Loehr, 2018). A concrete example is the donation of $6 billion in 2020 by Mackenzie Scott (on the list of billionaires in 2023) to charitable organisations. This example can be backed up by that of another great fortune by the name of Zhonghui You (on the 2019 list of billionaires), founder of the educational software company Shenzhen Seaskyland Technologies, who has joined the *Giving Pledge*[3] *initiative,* spearheaded by Bill and Melinda Gates and Warren Buffet (Alalouf-Hall, 2020). While generosity and altruism may at first sight appear to be the main motivations for women's philanthropy, according to studies by the *Women*'s *Philanthropy Institute* (2015), it should nevertheless be noted that surveys carried out by Astruc (2019) on the activities of the Bill and Melinda Gates Foundation show the extent to which taxation and the conquest of new business opportunities can prove to be essential motivations for women philanthropists. The author points out that the former couple's various donations to international organisations and charities serve to protect their wealth from tax, enhance their image, and create influence to gain access to business opportunities. Hence the title of his book, "*The Art of False Generosity*" indicates that the couple's generosity is associated with self-interest. It also implies that women's philanthropy is not devoid of self-interest.

In addition, the current dynamics of women's philanthropy can also be seen in Africa through women who are organising themselves into networks to make themselves visible in the African philanthropic landscape.[4] Among these, we will look at the case of businesswomen philanthropists in Côte d'Ivoire. We will draw up a profile of these women and analyse their relationship with philanthropy. Finally, we present their areas of intervention and some of the results of their work.

Businesswomen Philanthropists in Côte d'Ivoire

The rise of women entrepreneurs is a reality in the Ivorian business world. Côte d'Ivoire's government statistics show that more than 20% of formal businesses are run by women.[5] They can be found in the agri-processing sector, such as Kanté Coulibaly, manager of DISTRIPREST; in services, such as Huguette Kohoue Lawson, founder and managing director of SAGES CI; and in finance, such as Laureen Kouassi-Olsson, founder of Birimian ventures. The other striking fact is that the philanthropic landscape is increasingly registering the presence and activity of these businesswomen. Philanthropy in Côte d'Ivoire is no longer the preserve of businessmen and politicians, nor of first ladies and wives of politicians. It is also made up of women entrepreneurs who, after rising through the business world, decide to invest in philanthropy. These women, with their diverse profiles, get involved in one or more areas linked to events they have experienced during their social career, or linked to the passion they have developed for a cause. The data collected shows that they are interested in the fields of entrepreneurship, art and culture, health, and education.

Businesswomen Philanthropists Involved in Entrepreneurship

Businesswomen philanthropists involved in entrepreneurship fall into two categories. The first category concerns those whose actions are aimed at all young entrepreneurs, regardless of gender. The second category relates to those whose actions are dedicated solely to women, with a view to encouraging and boosting female entrepreneurship. Whatever the category, for each philanthropist it is a question of helping her target group based on the experience she has acquired in the course of her career. In the first category, we look at Bénédicte Janine Kacou Diagou, founder of the BJKD foundation, and in the second, Séphora Kodjo, founder of the SEPHIS foundation.

Box 13.1

Biography of Bénédicte Janine Kacou Diagou, Founder of the BJKD Foundation

- **Birth and Family**

  Bénédicte Janine Kacou Diagou is an Ivorian businesswoman, born in 1973 in Abidjan. She is the daughter of Ivorian businessman Jean Kacou

Diagou, one of Côte d'Ivoire's richest people according to the 2023 ranking published by *Sika Finance* business magazine.

- **Studies**

Bénédicte Janine Kacou Diagou graduated from *Cours Sainte-Marie de Hann* in Dakar, Senegal, with a *baccalauréat* in science. After completing her baccalauréat, she went on to study at the *Institut franco-américain du management* in Paris, where she obtained a *Bachelor of Business Administration*. She then obtained a Master's degree in Financial Engineering from Middlesex University in London.

- **Career Path**

Bénédicte Janine Kacou Diagou is currently Chief Executive Officer of the NSIA Group, a pan-African group specialising in bancassurance, represented in twelve African countries. Before taking up this position, she climbed several rungs up the corporate ladder. After graduating in 1995, she joined the finance department of CITIBANK NA in Abidjan, before moving on to the Mobil ACOE group, where she worked as an internal auditor.

In 1999, she joined the NSIA Group, where she initially held the position of Director of Audit and Management Control. In 2004, she was appointed Chief Financial Officer of NSIA Côte d'Ivoire. Here, she played a major role in the takeover of BIAO, one of the oldest banks in Côte d'Ivoire. From 2008, she spent three years as Central Director in charge of strategy and finance. In this new role, she was involved in the acquisition of a stake in NSIA by the American investment fund ECP. In 2015, she successfully managed the exit of ECP and the entry of the National Bank of Canada and Améthis Finance into NSIA's capital. In 2017, she played a major role in the takeover of Diamond Bank. Following the takeover, she was appointed Chairman of the Board of Diamond Bank S.A. Bénédicte Janine Kacou Diagou is also a director of BGFI Bank Côte d'Ivoire.

All of her background and accumulated professional experience formed the basis of her current position. In 2014, she was appointed by the Head of State as a member of the Economic and Social Council of Côte d'Ivoire.

Bénédicte Janine Kacou Diagou was recognised in 2017 by *Jeune Afrique* magazine as one of the 50 most influential businesswomen on the African continent.

Source: https://www.yeclo.com/bio-cv-qui-est-benedicte-janine-kacou-diagou and *Sika Finance* Magazine (2023), Official portal of the government of Côte d'd'Ivoire (2023).

Bénédicte Janine Kacou Diagou, a Philanthropist Dedicated to Youth Entrepreneurship

Bénédicte Janine Kacou Diagou is the founder of the BJKD foundation. She is a finance expert and director of several companies. In 2018, she created her foundation in response to several years of soliciting, mentoring, and helping young people to carry out their projects.[6] In setting up the foundation, she wanted to give legal form to several years of informal philanthropy. Her decision is in keeping with the spirit of "give back".[7] She said: "I owe it to myself to give back to the world what life has given me".[8] This was the basis of her motivation. In this way, the foundation is based on the values of sharing, service, and self-giving (Fraternité Matin, 2020). This philanthropist is passionate about art and culture. As a result, she is also involved in these areas. But entrepreneurship remains the area that receives the most attention from her, with its desire to help reduce unemployment and contribute to the economic and social development of people. Each year, the foundation organises a competition called the "BJKD prize", during which the most deserving candidates are selected and rewarded with financial support for a business project. The competition is aimed at young entrepreneurs to help them develop their entrepreneurial skills and business.[9] To date, the foundation is in the sixth year of this award and has supported a total of 29 young people for a total amount of 214 million F-CFA distributed to the winners.[10] Thanks to the support of its network, i.e., a group of donors made up of companies, international institutions, diplomats, and public institutions, the foundation was able to extend all its activities very quickly to 14 African countries south of the Sahara.

Box 13.2

Biography of Séphora Kodjo, Founder of the SEPHIS Foundation

- **Birth and Family**

  Séphora Kodjo was born in 1992. She is married and has three children.

- **Studies**

  Séphora Kodjo holds a Bachelor's degree in Business Administration and a Master's degree in Development Studies. Her ambitions led her to complete her training in peace and security issues in The Hague (Netherlands). She also trained in preventive diplomacy in Johannesburg (South Africa). After graduating from the Obama Foundation's YALI programme, she trained in strategic project management at Harvard University.

- **Career Paths**

  Séphora Kodjo is the Founding President of the SEPHIS Foundation and Managing Director of the SEPHIS Group. She began her career in public administration as a researcher at the Ministry of Youth. She then became

Director of the Government Spokesperson's Office at the Ministry of Communication and Media, where she was responsible for organising all press briefings and releases at national and international levels. Subsequently appointed to the post of technical adviser, she resigned in 2019 to devote herself full-time to her foundation, and her business. She is also a peace mediator accredited by the African Union.

Sources: Fanucchi (2021) "Sefora Kodjo, PCA of the Sephis Foundation Côte d'Ivoire: L'empowerment of women is our priority, and they must make their own way", *AfricaPresse.Paris:* https://www.africapresse.paris/Big2021-Sefora-KODJO-PCA-de-la-Fondation-Sephis-Cote-d-Ivoire-L-autonomisation, accessed 6 July 2024.
Official portal of the government of Côte d'Ivoire (2023) "Citizen in the spotlight: Sefora Kodjo, symbol of winning sisterhood", https://www.gouv.ci/_actualite-article.php?recordID=14847&d=1, accessed 6 July 2024.

Séphora Kodjo, a Promoter of Female Entrepreneurship and Leadership

Unlike the previous philanthropist, Séphora Kodjo, founder of the Sephis Foundation, is a feminist who is active in the economic empowerment of women through entrepreneurship. She has an atypical philanthropic background. The idea of setting up the foundation came to her while she was still a student in 2009, without any major financial resources. What we know from her story is that she wanted to run for the post of president of the students' union at the University of Abidjan, for which no woman had ever applied (Fanucchi, 2021). Séphora Kodjo was confronted with many sexist prejudices. Notwithstanding these prejudices, she was able to compete for the job she wanted. This prejudice was the trigger for her philanthropic commitment to women's leadership and entrepreneurship. After working in administration for more than three years after her studies, she resigned in 2019 following the creation of her company, Groupe SEPHIS, which specialises in services. Since then, she has devoted herself to her foundation and her company.

This foundation is present in thirteen African countries and supports the continent's women entrepreneurs through its various programmes[11] such as *African Women of the Future* (AWF) and *Forum International du Leadership Féminin* (FILF). The foundation helps women to formalise and structure their businesses, conquer markets, and access credit. As part of its AWF programme, the foundation receives financial and technical support from the German Development Cooperation (*Deutsche Gesellschaft für internationale Zusammenarbeit*/invest for jobs). This support has enabled the philanthropic institution to assist more than 200 SMEs run by women in various sectors. The foundation has also succeeded in negotiating two lines of credit with a financial institution in Côte d'Ivoire and Senegal, for a total of two billion F-CFA to enable the women it supports to have access to the bank credit they need to develop their businesses. The foundation has more than 10,000 beneficiaries under its various programmes.[12] On the strength of these results, the foundation has positioned itself as a strategic player in the growth of SMEs run by women in Africa. These results have earned it several international awards, including the 2018 African Union prize for the best training initiatives for women in Africa and a tweet from former President Barack Obama.[13]

Businesswomen Philanthropists Involved in Art and Culture

Art and culture are other favourite areas for some philanthropists. Setting up a foundation is a way of promoting Africa's cultural heritage and encouraging the work of local artists. Their activities include collecting works of art, organising cultural and artistic events, and providing financial support to artists. Philanthropists involved in art and culture include Bénédicte Jeanine Diagou Kacou (Fondation BJKD), Zanouba Omaïs (Fondation Omaïs), and Illa Ginette Donwahi (Fondation Donwahi). We will be looking here at Illa Ginette Donwahi, a philanthropist who has made this her field of choice compared with others who are also involved in other areas.

Box 13.3

Biography of Illa Ginette Donwahi, President of the Charles Donwahi Foundation

- **Birth and Family**

  Illa Ginette Donwahi is an Ivorian economist and businesswoman born in 1959. She is the daughter of Charles Bauza Donwahi, a former political figure in Côte d'Ivoire. Her brother Alain Richard Donwahi is a politician and current member of the Ivorian government (2024).

- **Studies**

  Illa Ginette Donwahi has a degree in economics. She studied at Clermont College in California, USA.

- **Career Path**

  Illa Ginette Donwahi returned to Côte d'Ivoire after studying in the United States and initially worked for private companies operating in the agri-food sector. In 2000, she became President of the *Groupement des exportateurs de café et de cacao de Côte d'Ivoire*. From 2008 to 2011, she was vice-president of the *Comité de gestion de la filière café-cacao* on behalf of the Ivorian government. She remains active in the agri-industry as a rubber and bergamot essential oil producer. She set up the Charles Donwahi Foundation for Contemporary Art in 2008.

Source: Sylvestre-Treiner (2018)

Illa Ginette Donwahi, Passionate about Contemporary Art

Illa Donwahi is a company director operating in the agri-industry in Côte d'Ivoire. Her passion for contemporary art led to the creation of the Donwahi Foundation in 2008 with the help of some of the continent's leading figures in the field, including Simon Njami[14] and Marème Samb.[15] Her passion for art runs in the family. She inherited it from her father, who was an art collector. The creation of the foundation is a form of tribute to her father.[16] For the founder, the Donwahi Foundation is a space for promoting African culture. Its purpose is to support and promote the work of Ivorian and African artists. But from a broader perspective, this philanthropist sees the Donwahi Foundation as a space where the arts and cultures of the world can engage in dialogue (Sylvestre-Treiner, 2018). The foundation promotes local and international creation. The foundation hosted an exhibition of works by the famous Spanish artist Antoni Clavé in 2022. With an operating budget of 200 million F-CFA a year, the foundation has organised several artistic events since its creation, the most important of which are Sindika Dokolo's photographic collection and the works of Samuel Fosso and Ananias Leki Dago (Simonet, 2015 and Sylvestre-Treiner, 2018).

Businesswomen Philanthropists Working in Education and Health

Most foundations in Côte d'Ivoire focus on health and education. These include foundations such as *Atef Omaïs* and *Children of Africa,* founded and run by philanthropic businesswomen. In the area of health, these foundations focus on building and renovating health centres, caring for the sick, and running public health campaigns (awareness-raising, vaccinations, screening for diseases such as breast and cervical cancer, HIV AIDS, etc.). These philanthropists also donate medicines and equipment to health facilities. In the field of education, they build and renovate school infrastructure (classrooms and canteens), distribute school kits at the start of each new school year, reward the best pupils, etc. Below, we look at the example of Dominique Ouattara, the First Lady in 2024, a philanthropist active in the fields of health and education.

Box 13.4

Biography of the Founding President of the *Children of Africa* Foundation

- **Family**

Dominique Ouattara, born Dominique Claudine Nouvian, is the First Lady of Côte d'Ivoire. She was born on 16 December 1953 in Constantine,

Côte d'Ivoire, and is the wife of Dr Alassane Ouattara, President of the Republic of Côte d'Ivoire. Dominique Ouattara has two children.

- **Studies**

1989: Real estate expert diploma in Paris (France)
1987: FNAIM property administrator diploma (France)
1975: DEUG in languages with economics option, University of Paris X (France)
1972: *Baccalauréat* in economics, Strasbourg (France)

- **Career Path**

Dominique Ouattara, First Lady of Côte d'Ivoire, enjoyed a brilliant career as a company director, particularly in the property sector, before her husband became President of the Republic of Côte d'Ivoire. In 1979, she became CEO of the AICI international group, which operates in Africa and Europe. After strengthening her presence in Côte d'Ivoire, notably in Yamoussoukro, Bouaké, San-Pédro, and Jacqueville, Dominique Ouattara set up AICI in Europe in 1989, choosing France as her international showcase. After opening a first office in Paris, AICI continued its development in the South of France in 1991 with the launch of an agency in Cannes.

In 1993, a co-ownership management company, "Malesherbes Gestion", which manages more than 200 buildings in Paris, completed the expansion of the AICI International group. AICI International continued to expand in 2001, setting up operations in Gabon, followed by Burkina Faso in 2006.

In 1996, Dominique Ouattara was also appointed CEO of EJD Inc., which manages the Jacques Dessange Institute in Washington. In 1998, she acquired the Jacques Dessange franchises in the United States and became CEO of *French Beauty Services*, which manages all the brand's American franchises.

Currently First Lady of Côte d'Ivoire, she devotes her time to her role as First Lady and to her foundation.

Source: *Children of Africa Foundation* Annual Report 2017 and 2022.

Madame Dominique Ouattara, a Philanthropist Devoted to the Causes of Children and Mothers

Dominique Ouattara has a double hat. She has been First Lady of Côte d'Ivoire since 2011. But she is also recognised as an entrepreneur with a proven track record in the business world.[17] It was in 1998, when she was a company director, that she decided to carry out a project that had been close to her heart since she was very young. This project was to help the weakest and the most deprived (*Children of*

Africa Foundation Report, 2022). The creation of the foundation then became the channel for fulfilling this desire. The choice to focus on children was the one that met her expectations. The foundation's vision explains this choice. It believes that "the future of the country lies with children".[18]

Supported by this vision, she has seen the need to invest in the future of the children who will meet the challenges of development in Africa. Hence the primary mission of the *Children of Africa* foundation, which is "to provide assistance to the children of Africa"[19] as well as to their mothers. Since its creation, the foundation has carried out numerous activities in the fields of health and education. According to the statistics in the foundation's 2022 annual report, to date more than 84,027 children have been vaccinated against meningitis and typhoid fever; 103,000 children have been monitored by the ophthalmology caravan and 169,000 children have been de-wormed. In addition, the mother and child hospital was built in 2018 at a total cost of 25 billion F-CFA. In the field of education, the Foundation has given more than 385,000 children free access to reading materials through its mobile libraries and the distribution of 158,000 school kits. The foundation has also built school infrastructure, notably the Dominique Ouattara high school in the town of Kong, and recently built the *Children of Africa* school of excellence in the town of Abobo, at a cost of 1.65 billion F-CFA. To this list can be added 11 multimedia rooms, the aim of which is to introduce children to computer tools. The foundation has reception centres for children who are victims of trafficking and labour exploitation, street children, and orphans. These destitute children are cared for (housing and schooling). The foundation carries out indirect actions in favour of children. These indirect actions are aimed at mothers. The foundation believes that by helping mothers, they will be able to ensure the well-being of their children, within the family unit. This is the aim of the *Fonds d'Appui aux Femmes de Côte d'Ivoire* (FAFCI) set up by the foundation in 2012. This fund has benefited more than 360,000 women since its creation. These results demonstrate Dominique Ouattara's commitment to the cause of children in Africa. Her commitment has not gone unnoticed by public decision-makers and international institutions. In 2008, for example, she won the international prize for the best president of a charity in West Africa. And in 2009, she was made an Officer of the Côte d'Ivoire Order of Merit for Solidarity (*Children of Africa* Foundation Report, 2022).

Motivations of Ivorian Businesswomen Philanthropists

The different profiles of businesswomen philanthropists that we have drawn up highlight various motivations for their philanthropic commitment. We distinguish between overt and secondary motivations.

Declared Motivations

The reasons given are those put forward by philanthropists. In this respect, the primary motivation identified by women philanthropists is to give back to society. For some businesswomen philanthropists, giving to others means giving back to society some of the assets they have amassed over the course of their lives. This motivation is associated with the theory of gift-giving, which evokes the idea of returning the initial gift (Mauss, 2012). This can be seen very clearly in the example of Bénédicte Janine Kacou Diagou, who set up her foundation with a view to redistributing some of the assets that society had enabled her to acquire. The second motivation is the desire to pay tribute to a third party. In this case, the foundation is set up to continue the work of a person who has marked the philanthropist's life. The case of Illa Ginette Donwahi is a good illustration of this motivation. She created the Donwahi Foundation as a tribute to her late father, who was also involved in art and culture. A third motivation identified is the passion developed for a cause that the philanthropist has always kept in mind. The example of Dominique Ouattara shows that she had a passion for the cause of the weak and disadvantaged from an early age. The last motivation identified is awareness because of an event experienced, as was the case with Séphora Kodjo who, after having been the victim of sexist prejudice, committed herself to take action in favour of women's leadership and entrepreneurship.

Secondary Motivations

In addition to the above-mentioned motivations, data from the field reveals other self-interested motivations. Philanthropy is also a way for these businesswomen to raise their profile in the public sphere. This gives them prestige, privilege, recognition, and influence. This is most evident in the case of Séphora Kodjo and Dominique Ouattara, who have won several accolades for their philanthropic activities. The former has received a tribute from the Ivorian government and recognition from the African Union and from former US President Barack Obama.[20] The latter has also received several awards, including the international prize for the best president of a charitable organisation in West Africa, the African Women's Award for Excellence from the African Union and UN Women, and a distinction from the United Nations Population Fund for her work on behalf of children and the empowerment of women. In addition, she was made an Officer of the Côte d'Ivoire Order of Merit for Solidarity (*Children of Africa* Foundation Report, 2022). The major consequences of these awards are increased credibility and a denser network of contacts for the recipients, which can benefit both their foundation and their business (Kouadio, 2022). This phenomenon is best understood through the analyses of Depecker et al. (2018), who see philanthropy as an *investment*. For these authors, the initial economic capital invested in philanthropic actions is transformed into other capital in the form of symbolic and social capital, making it possible not only to recover the initial capital but also to generate profits. Some data from the field is in line with these authors' position. Indeed, most businesswomen's foundations are financially supported by the companies they run. For example, the BJKD foundation is supported by the NSIA group, which is headed by the foundation's founder. Similarly, the Atef Omaïs foundation is supported by the SOTICI company and the Tiama hotel, which is also run by the foundation's president. This support is not freely given when you consider that the Ivorian tax system provides a tax reduction for companies that make donations to charitable organisations (Direction Générale des Impôts, 2018). This means that taxation is also one of the motivations for the philanthropic commitment of businesswomen. In a way, what is spent on social actions is taxed back. Finally, philanthropy is a business strategy (Godbout, 2008) used by women in business.

Whatever the motivation behind their commitment, the visibility of the work these women do and the positive impact of their actions[21] demonstrate their effectiveness in the Ivorian philanthropic landscape. Through transparency and performance indicators, they receive both technical and financial support from major donors such as international organisations, governments, companies, and celebrities. For example, the Sephis Foundation's list of donors includes the US and Canadian governments, the German development agency GIZ, the European Union, PROPARCO, UNICEF, UN Women, and major companies such as SIFCA, Bank of Africa, Ecobank,[22] etc. The same applies to the BJKD Foundation and the *Children of Africa* Foundation, which benefit from the support of donors of the same order.[23] This is proof that financial transparency is a source of opportunity for Ivorian foundations (Kouadio and Saouré, 2022). It is therefore easy to see from the above that these philanthropic businesswomen represent a new market for donors and potential donors looking for serious and effective charities to support philanthropic causes in Côte d'Ivoire and other countries on the African continent.

Conclusion

This chapter highlights the emergence of women's philanthropy, particularly that of women entrepreneurs in Côte d'Ivoire. The cases presented show the dynamism of these women and the motivations associated with their commitment. It emerges that their commitment is motivated by personal values based on altruism, empathy, and generosity. However, these motivations are often associated with interest (social, tax, and economic benefits). In any case, Douglas (2004) has already warned that "there is no such thing as a free gift". She goes so far as to say that "there would never have been a single gift in the world" if giving were to be devoid of any interest (Douglas, 2004: 204). These words from this anthropologist allow us to focus on the dynamism of these businesswomen, who offer a glimmer of hope for Ivorian philanthropy, which is struggling to prove its worth in terms of contribution and social impact (Kouadio, 2022). The visibility and impact of the foundations' actions is attracting growing interest from donors. As a result, these women are becoming the preferred partners of donors for projects on the African continent.

Notes

1 Created in 1991 within the Lilly Family School of Philanthropy at Indiana University in the United States, the Women's Philanthropy Institute is the first research institute on women's philanthropy. Its aim is to promote women's philanthropy by highlighting their potential in this area.

2 This number is considerable compared to the 2019 list, where women billionaires numbered 244 (Alalouf-Hall, 2020).

3 This is a movement of philanthropists who pledge to donate the majority of their wealth to charitable causes, either during their lifetime or in their wills on their death.
4 *Centre on African philanthropy* (2023) "Women in African initiative: reflection of launch", accessed 4 January 2024 at https://capsi.co.za/launch-women-in-african-philanthropy-initiative/.
5 Official portal of the government of Côte d'Ivoire (2023): "Entrepreneuriat féminin: plus de 20% des entreprises formelles dirigées par des femmes", accessed 4 January 2024 at https://www.gouv.ci/_actualite-article.php?recordID=14923
6 Excerpt from remarks by the President of the BJKD Foundation in the newspaper *Fraternité Matin*, published by the State of Côte d'Ivoire on 24/02/2020 in the focus section, and available on:
https://www.fratmat.info/article/202138/focus/olga-djadji-presidente-de-la-fondation-benedicte-janine-kacou-diagou-nous-voulons-aider-a-reduire-le-chomage-
7 *Give back* is the motivation found in the literature about some American philanthropists. It means giving back to society or one's community.
8 Comments taken from the foundation's website: https://fondationbjkd.com/organisation, accessed 5 January 2024.
9 https://fondationbjkd.com/entrepreneuriat/detail/le-prix-bjkd-pour-lentrepreneuriat-jeunes-i764, accessed 5 January 2024.
10 https://fondationbjkd.com/entrepreneuriat/detail/le-prix-bjkd-pour-lentrepreneuriat-jeunes-i764, accessed 5 January 2024.
11 Information collected on the foundation's website: https://fondationsephis.org/mission/:, accessed 5 January 2024.
12 See the foundation's website: https://fondationsephis.org/mission/
13 Official portal of the government of Côte d'Ivoire (2023) "Citizen in the spotlight: Sefora Kodjo, symbol of winning sisterhood", https://www.gouv.ci/_actualite-article.php?recordID=14847&d = 1, accessed 5 January 2024.
14 Writer and curator.
15 Senegalese businesswoman and founder of the MAM gallery for contemporary art in Cameroon.
16 For example, in 2019, the Charles Bauza Donwahi arts centre was built in Soubré (Nawa region) as a tribute to her father.
17 She was voted best businesswoman of the year 2000 at Vénice at the Annual Gala of the American consulting firm Star Group (*Children of Africa Foundation* Report, 2022).
18 Interview of 27-06-2019 with Ms Cissé of the Children of Africa foundation that I had with the foundation during my PhD research (Kouadio, 2022).
19 https://childrenofafrica.org/aider-les-enfants-dafrique, accessed 5 January 2024.
20 Cf. Official portal of the government of Côte d'Ivoire (2023) "Citoyen à l'honneur: Sefora Kodjo, symbole de la sororité gagnante", https://www.gouv.ci/_actualite-article.php?recordID=14847&d=1and https://fondationsephis.org/mission/, accessed 5 January 2024.
21 This visibility and the impact of their actions have enabled some of them to win awards and recognition at international and local level.
22 See the foundation's website: https://childrenofafrica.org/aider-les-enfants-dafrique, accessed 5 January 2024.
23 See the BJKD Foundation website (https://fondationbjkd.com/) and the Children of Africa website (https://childrenofafrica.org/partenaires/).

References

Alalouf-Hall, D. (2020) "Have we really grasped the potential of women in philanthropy?", *PhiLab.* https://philab.uqam.ca/blogue-accueil/avons-nous-reellement-saisi-le-potentiel-des-femmes-dans-le-secteur-de-la-philanthropie/

Astruc, L. (2019) *L'art de la fausse générosité: La fondation Bill and Melinda Gates*. Arles: Actes du Sud.

Belliard, C. (2009) *L'émancipation des femmes à l'épreuve de la philanthropie*. Paris: L'Harmattan.

Centre on African Philanthropy (2023) Women in African initiative: Reflection of launch. https://capsi.co.za/launch-women-in-african-philanthropy-initiative/

Children of Africa Foundation Annual report (2017). https://childrenofafrica.org/wp-content/uploads/2021/04/Rapport-COA-2017.pdf

Children of Africa Foundation Annual report (2022). https://childrenofafrica.org/wp-content/uploads/2023/09/Rapport-Children-Of-Africa-2022.pdf

Cohen, Y. (2010) *Femmes philanthropes. Catholiques, protestantes et juives dans les organisations caritatives au Québec (1880–1945)*. Montréal: Presses de l'Université de Montréal.

De Nowel, I. (1996) *Women Who Give Away Millions: Portraits of Canadian Philanthropists*. Ontario: Dundurn Group.

Depecker, T. et al. (2018) "Philanthropy as investment. Contribution à l'étude des stratégies de reproduction et de légitimation des élites économiques", *Politix*, 121: 9–27.

Direction Générale des Impôts (2018) ''Note de service N° 2432/SEPMBPE/DGI-DLCD du 20 juin 2018. Objet: régime fiscal des associations et autres organismes sans but lucratif'', Direction Générale des Impôts de la République de Côte d'Ivoire.

Douglas, M. (2004) *Comment pensent les institutions* followed by *La connaissance de soi* and *Il n'y a pas de don gratuit*. Paris: La Découverte.

Fagnart, L. and E. L'Estrange (eds) (2011) "Le mécénat féminin en France et en Bourgogne (XVe-XVIe siècles). Nouvelles perspectives." Proceedings of the international study day held at the University of Liège, 10 May 2010. *Moyen Age: Revue d'Histoire et de Philologie,* 117 (3–4): 467–602.

Fanucchi, B. (2021) "Sefora Kodjo, PCA of the Fondation Sephis Côte d'Ivoire: L'autonomisation des femmes est notre priorité, et elles doivent s'imposer par elles-mêmes", *Africa Presse Paris.* https://www.africapresse.paris/Big2021-Sefora-KODJO-PCA-de-la-Fondation-Sephis-Cote-d-Ivoire-L-autonomisation.

Fraternité matin (2020) ''Olga Djadji, présidente de la Fondation Bénédicte Janine Kacou Diagou: nous voulons aider à réduire le chômage'', *focus.* https://www.fratmat.info/article/202138/focus/olga-djadji-presidente-de-la-fondation-benedicte-janine-kacou-diagou-nous-voulons-aider-a-reduire-le-chomage-.

https://www.fratmat.info/article/202138/focus/olga-djadji-presidente-de-la-fondation-benedicte-janine-kacou-diagou-nous-voulons-aider-a-reduire-le-chomage-https://www.fratmat.info/article/202138/focus/olga-djadji-presidente-de-la-fondation-benedicte-janine-kacou-diagou-nous-voulons-aider-a-reduire-le-chomage-https://www.fratmat.info/article/202138/focus/olga-djadji-presidente-de-la-fondation-benedicte-janine-kacou-diagou-nous-voulons-aider-a-reduire-le-chomage-

Gates, M. (2019) *The Moment of Lift: How Empowering Women Changes the World*. New York: Flatiron Books.

Godbout, J. (2008) "Quand les gens d'affaires se font les cadeaux", in P. Chanial et al. (eds) *La société vue du don. Manuel de Sociologie anti-utilitariste appliquée*, pp. 85–100. Paris: La Découverte.

Kouadio, J.-C. (2022) *Philanthropie et développement en Afrique. Étude de cas en Côte d'Ivoire.* PhD thesis in sociology, under the supervision of Ulrike Schuerkens, Université de Rennes 2.

Kouadio, J.-C. and K. Saouré (2022) "La transparence des fondations africaines: Entre opportunité, tension et contrainte", *L'Année Philanthropique*, 4: 43–46.

Lafranco, R. and C. Paterson-Withorn (2023) "World's billionaires list. The richest in 2023", *Forbes.* https://www.forbes.com/billionaires/#5e5dd6f5251c

Loehr, K. E. (2018) *Gender Matters: A Guide to Growing Women's Philanthropy.* Washington, DC: CASE.
Mauss, M. (2012) *Essai sur le don. Forme et raison de l'échange dans les sociétés archaïques.* Paris: Presses Universitaires de France.
McCarthy, K. D. (1996) "Women and philanthropy", *Voluntas*: *International Journal of Voluntary and Nonprofit Organizations*, 7 (4): 331–335.
Mesch, D. et al. (2015a) *Do Women Give More? Findings from three unique data sets on charitable giving.* IUPUI Women's Philanthropy Institute.
Mesch, D. et al. (2015b) *How and Why Women Give. Current and Future Directions for Research on Women's Philanthropy.* IUPUI Women's Philanthropy Institute.
Official portal of the government of Côte d'Ivoire (2023) "Citizen in the spotlight: Sefora Kodjo, symbol of winning sisterhood". https://www.gouv.ci/_actualite-article.php?recordID=14847&d=1
Official portal of the government of Côte d'd'Ivoire (2023) "Entrepreneuriat féminin: plus de 20% des entreprises formelles dirigées par des femmes". https://www.gouv.ci/_actualite-article.php?recordID=14923
Sika Finance (2023) "The 10 Biggest Fortunes in Côte d'Ivoire". https://www.sikafinance.com/marches/les-plus-grandes-fortunes-de-cote-d-ivoire-numero-3-jean-kacou-diagou_41809
Simonet, D. (2015) "Ici Abidjan - À la rencontre des faiseurs d'art". *Le Point.* https://www.lepoint.fr/culture/ici-abidjan-a-la-rencontre-des-faiseurs-d-art-28-05-2015-1931870_3.php
Sylvestre-Treiner, A. (2018) "Côte d'Ivoire: la Fondation Donwahi, un havre d'art et de paix à Abidjan", *Jeune Afrique.* https://www.jeuneafrique.com/mag/529540/culture/cote-divoire-la-fondation-donwahi-un-havre-dart-et-de-paix-a-abidjan/#:~:text=Ouvert%20%C3%A0%20tous%20les%20genres,attract%20les%20lyc%C3%A9ens%20et%20%C3%A9tudiants
Vasavada, R. (2012) "A cultural feminist perspective on leadership in non-profit organizations: A case of women-leaders in India", *Public Administration Quarterly,* 36 (4): 462–503.
Zunz, O. (2012) *La Philanthropie en Amérique. Argent privé,* affaires *d'État.* Paris: Fayard.

Web links

https://childrenofafrica.org/aider-les-enfants-dafrique
https://fondationbjkd.com/entrepreneuriat/detail/le-prix-bjkd-pour-lentrepreneuriat-jeunes-i764
https://fondationbjkd.com/entrepreneuriat/detail/le-prix bjkd pour-lentrepreneuriat-jeunes-i764
https://fondationbjkd.com/organisation
https://fondationsephis.org/mission/
https://www.fratmat.info/article/202138/focus/olga-djadji-presidente-de-la-fondation-benedicte-janine-kacou-diagou-nous-voulons-aider-a-reduire-le-chomage-
https://www.yeclo.com/bio-cv-qui-est-benedicte-janine-kacou-diagou

14 Business Sustainability Adoption by Ghanaian Women Entrepreneurs

Kathy-Ann Fletcher, Philomena Asante, and Sharon L. Forbes

Introduction

Understanding the rate of sustainability adoption in business is a priority for various stakeholders from academics, activists, and practitioners (Boonsand Lüdeke-Freund 2013).

Sustainability remains at the core of the UN's sustainable development goals, particularly goal nine which focuses on promoting sustainable industrialisation and innovation and goal twelve which speaks to supporting sustainable consumption and production patterns. Academic interest in sustainability adoption has been established, including accounting for cultural differences (Caprar and Neville, 2012), gender and generation (Gazzola et al., 2020), and country of origin (Cowan and Guzman, 2020), among other factors. Sustainable development has itself been defined as "development that meets the needs of the present without compromising the ability of the future generations to meet their own needs" (Brundtland, 1987).

There is a knowledge gap regarding the implementation of Sustainability Design Theory in SME business practice generally and in Ghana and emerging markets more specifically. Addressing this gap will benefit a range of stakeholders from businesses, employees, and citizens as well as the wider economy of the country under investigation. The chapter will make three main contributions. Firstly, we are providing insight to businesses and entrepreneurs on how to embed sustainability thinking in their business through planning and goal setting. Secondly, we are giving policymakers and government officials a clear understanding of the drivers and barriers that exist to either support or restrict sustainability adoption by SMEs. This is an important process in providing an evidence-based rationale for supporting the removal of those barriers and creating a facilitating environment for sustainability adoption among SMEs. Thirdly, we give academic researchers an approach for applying the Sustainability Design Theory to sustainability adoption among businesses by focusing on women entrepreneurs in Ghana.

This chapter's structure will explore the importance of the study, review relevant literature on sustainability and entrepreneurship, introduce the theoretical framework in line with Sustainability Design Theory, and illustrate the methodology of the study. Additionally, we will outline the findings of the study and discuss how it advances the knowledge in the discipline and end with our conclusions and recommendations for future research.

DOI: 10.4324/9781003492931-18

Importance of the Study

Researchers have identified a critical requirement for sustainable systems in society that meets the needs of all stakeholders within society (Geissdoerfer et al., 2017; Carbo et al., 2014). Sustainability is an established source of positive reputation, sales, revenue growth, and customer retention (Ameer and Othman, 2012; Baah and Jin, 2019) for organisations. Furthermore, sustainability has been linked to the viability of the organisation (Hoverstadt and Bowling, 2005; Sonego et al., 2018; Baldassarre et al., 2020). This relationship has been proven in relation to studies globally as well as to a range of countries in Africa, e.g., South Africa (Wachira, Berndt and Romero, 2020), Nigeria (Vu and Nwachukwu, 2020) and Ghana specifically (Abubakari and Thuranira, 2021). However, it is crucial for this study to investigate the role of adoption specific to gender as women represent the fastest growing segment of entrepreneurs across the globe (Cardella, Hernández-Sánchez, and Sánchez-García, 2020) and therefore, hold a growing influence on all matters of business and the wider economy, including business sustainability. Bocken et al. (2013) note like other researchers that businesses can strategically generate social, environmental, and economic value by embedding sustainability within the core of their business. They note the growing population amplified with consumption patterns poses challenges to health and well-being and the natural environment calls for new systems as the way of addressing these challenges. The demand for more production to meet the needs of the growing population will pose an even greater threat to the ability of future generations to meet their needs. Despite the importance of addressing matters of social and environmental sustainability in business, these challenges are not clearly outlined across the globe, especially in some of the areas that are at greater threat of harm in an unsustainable system. This chapter contributes therefore by providing insights into the drivers, barriers, and impacts of sustainability adoption in SMEs in Ghana. The purpose of this insight is to guide entrepreneurs, policymakers, and academics in creating a facilitating environment for entrepreneurs to design sustainability into their business practice.

This study draws its sample from women entrepreneurs in Ghana. This is a significant contribution because it addresses several challenges identified at the intersection of women entrepreneurship and sustainability adoption. Firstly, while it is established that women-owned businesses are essential for economic growth through job creation, wealth generation, income distribution, and innovation (Neneh and Welsh, 2022), they are underrepresented in research (Kaciak and Welsh, 2020). Fang et al. (2022) note that women entrepreneurs in the US and Europe range from 20 to 40%. The World Economic Forum shows that women entrepreneurship numbers are growing all over the world, noting that there are 8–10 million small- to medium-sized enterprises in emerging markets with at least one owner who is a woman and citing the World Bank that one in three businesses are owned by women (Masterson, 2022). Ghana specifically is a global leader in the rate of women entrepreneurship with 37.2% in 2022 according to a Mastercard Index of Women Entrepreneurs (Oluwole, 2021). Secondly, while it is not solely women entrepreneurs' responsibility to address the challenges solved by sustainable approaches, Grimes et al. (2018) and Conger et al. (2018) are among those researchers who identify women's leadership in driving the environmental and social changes needed especially through business and entrepreneurship. Much of the research speaks to women being at the greatest risk of harm from environmental and social challenges (Warth and Koparanova, 2012; Eastin, 2018). However, the wider society will also benefit from the transformations driven by sustainability adoption within their organisations. Therefore, supporting innovations and improvements in business practices such as sustainability enhances the social, environmental, and economic prospects of the economy that is driven by small- to medium-sized enterprises. Addressing these various challenges will align our chapter with an international agenda to support women entrepreneurs (Dal Mas and Paoloni, 2020). This study provides rationale for more financial and infrastructural support to create a facilitating environment for sustainability adoption by identifying the barriers to adoption thus providing policymakers with insight into demand, drivers, and challenges faced by women entrepreneurs in embedding sustainability in their companies.

Literature Review

Entrepreneurship

The term "entrepreneurship" has been variously defined in academic literature. For example, Kao (1993) stated that entrepreneurship is the process of doing something new and something different for the purpose of creating wealth for the individual and adding value to society. In earlier research, Gartner (1990) surveyed the views of academics, business leaders, and politicians to identify the themes that constitute the concept of entrepreneurship. The eight constituent themes of entrepreneurship were: the entrepreneur, innovation, organisation creation, creating value, profit or non-profit, growth, uniqueness, and the owner-manager (Gartner, 1990). More recent definitions have discussed entrepreneurship in terms of its ability to generate job opportunities and lead to economic development (Barot, 2015; Hessels, 2019). Although there is no single widely accepted definition of entrepreneurship, what is consistently accepted is the important contribution of entrepreneurship to the economic growth of nations (Weeks and Seiler, 2001; Chinomona and Maziriri, 2015).

Brush and Cooper (2012) state that women are the fastest growing category of entrepreneurs globally. Given this, women entrepreneurs play an important role with regard to economic growth and employment creation (Akhalwaya, 2012; Nxopo and Iwu, 2015). Similarly, to the term "entrepreneurship", definitions for "women entrepreneurs" are also varied in the academic literature. In Manerkar's (2015) study of women entrepreneurs in India, the respondents were simply defined as females or a group of females initiating, organising, and running a company. Della-Giusta and Phillips (2006: 1059) undertook case study research in Ghana and defined women entrepreneurs as "women who had undertaken independently an economic activity which generated income". In their South African study, Chinomona and Maziriri (2015: 839) defined a women entrepreneur as "the female front-runner of a business who takes the initiative of introducing a new venture, who accepts the associated risks and who is effectively responsible for its day-to-day activities". Other definitions of women entrepreneurs have focused on aspects such as the percentage of ownership in a company, the way that ownership was obtained (e.g., founded, purchased, inherited), self-employment or employer of others, management role, and goals of the company (e.g., profit motive versus self-sufficiency) (see the summary in Avolio, 2011).

Whilst there is quite extensive research conducted on women entrepreneurs in developed nations (Avolio, 2011), there is a comparative lack of research on women entrepreneurs in developing nations (Della-Giusta and Phillips, 2006). Much of the literature in this area has focused on identifying the constraints that limit or prevent women from starting entrepreneurial endeavours; these have been found to include a lack of education and training, culture and customs, gender discrimination, lack of support mechanisms, and access to finance or other resources (Chitsike, 2000; Brush, 2006; Della-Giusta and Phillips, 2006). Some literature has focused specifically on the issues faced by women entrepreneurs in Africa, including research in Rwanda (Nsengimana, Tengeh, and Iwu, 2017), Nigeria (Sajuyigbe and Fadeyibi, 2017), South Africa (Chinomona and Maziriri, 2015; Okeke-Uzodike, 2019) and Ghana (Quagrainie, et al., 2021). Resulting from these constraints, Everts (1998) notes that women's enterprises tend to be small in scale, based on part-time work, and located in the home or close to it.

The Increasing Focus on Sustainability and Sustainable Development

There is little doubt that the concept of sustainability is an increasingly important one for business owners and managers. Sustainability is most frequently defined as "meeting the needs and aspirations of the present generation without compromising the ability of future generations to meet their needs" (Brundtland, 1987: 292). The concept of sustainability is generally understood to consist of economic, environmental, and social dimensions. In other words, sustainability is about balancing economic, human, and environmental activities, based on the notion that organisations exist in an ecosystem and not in isolation (Orobia et al., 2020). Similarly, Higgins (2014) describes sustainability as an integrated system consisting of three overlapping dimensions. Business sustainability is defined as the discovery, creation, and exploitation of entrepreneurial opportunities that contribute to sustainability by generating social and environmental gains for others in society (Hockerts and Wustenhagen, 2010; Pacheco, Dean, and Payne, 2010; Shepherd and Patzelt, 2011).

Business sustainability is important in terms of meeting the UN's Sustainable Development Goals (SDGs). All member states have committed to achieving the 17 SDGs, which were established under the United Nations 2030 Agenda. It has been noted that although the achievement of the SDGs is at a nation level, the goals cannot be achieved without the involvement of the business sector (Sachs, 2012). In his seminal paper, Elkington (1994) also noted that businesses must play a central role in achieving the goals of sustainable development. Some research on African women entrepreneurs has focused on the relationship of these business owners to the achievement of the SDGs. For example, Quagrainie et al. (2021) reported that women micro-entrepreneurs in Ghana are a critical part of the sustainable development process; women micro-entrepreneurs increase their own income and that of their local community and thus help to achieve SDG#1 ("*No poverty*"). Similarly, Sajuyigbe and Fadeyibi (2017) found that the involvement of Nigerian women in entrepreneurship is a catalyst to sustainable economic development. Khumalo and Mutobola (2014) state that support for women-owned businesses is essential in addressing the challenges of inequality, economic growth, and sustainable development for a nation.

Sustainability and Drivers/Business Benefits

Elkington (1994) first suggested that businesses could gain benefits through the adoption of environmentally sustainable strategies. For example, sustainability has been reported to result in improved financial performance and profitability (Epstein and Roy, 2003; Whelan and Fink, 2016). The drivers of business sustainability have also been identified; these have been found to include management commitment, adherence to regulatory requirements, improved efficiencies, decreased operating costs, increased revenues, reputational gain, competitive advantage in the market, enhanced employee morale, and pressure from consumers or other key stakeholders (see: Epstein and Roy, 2003; Lorenzand Lützkendorf, 2008; Caprar and Neville, 2012; Wolf, 2014; Paulraj, Chen, and Blome, 2017; Ghadge et al., 2021; Adams, Donovan, and Topple, 2022).

As most of the sustainability literature has focused on corporations and developed nations, there has been a limited focus on the benefits of sustainability in the context of African businesses. Thorpe and Prakash-Mani (2004) reported that the benefits of sustainability for businesses in emerging markets include cost reductions, increased sales, reduced risks, development of human capital, building reputation, and enhanced access to capital. This study also identified the benefits specifically relating to businesses in the sub-Saharan region of Africa; these are focused on (1) the management of human resources, leading to benefits such as increased productivity, improved motivation, and lower staff turnover, and (2) environmental practices in the agricultural and tourism sectors, which lead to revenue gains (Thorpe and Prakash-Mani, 2004). In research with small- and medium-sized enterprises in Ghana, Adomako (2020) found that sustainable innovation is positively associated with business growth.

Sustainability and Barriers

Whilst the benefits and other factors are drivers of business sustainability, there are also barriers which impede the ability of businesses to adopt sustainable strategies. Previous research has identified barriers such as resource limitations, high costs, a lack of knowledge or information, unclear returns of investment, a lack of perceived benefits, technology issues, consumer resistance, and price increases (see: Schaper, 2002; Hillary, 2004; Walker, Sisto, and McBain, 2008; Karakaya, Hidalgo, and Nuur, 2014; Cooney, Dencik, and Marshall, 2022). Again, there is limited exploration of the barriers to business sustainability in an African context. In a study of small and medium-sized firms in South Africa, Fatoki (2019) reported that the major barriers to the implementation of sustainable manufacturing practices are financial, management, and social factors.

Business, Gender, and Sustainability

Previous research on business sustainability and gender has reported that having greater gender diversity at a board level will have a positive impact on both the social and environmental performance of a company (Walls, Berrone, and Phan, 2012; Hussain, Rigoni, and Orij, 2018). In particular, the level of philanthropic giving has been found to be higher when a company has women directors or managers (see for example: Marquis and Lee, 2013; Glass, Cook, and Ingersoll, 2016; Horbach and Jacob, 2018; Zhang, Han, and Yin, 2018). Boards with greater gender diversity are also associated with an increased disclosure of information relating to sustainability, corporate social responsibility (CSR), or environmental, social and governance (ESG) performance (Liao, Luo, and Tang, 2015). It has been suggested that the results relate to specific characteristics of women, such as having a greater sustainability orientation and being more stakeholder oriented (Helfaya and Moussa, 2017; Hossain et al., 2017), or being more focused on achieving social outcomes rather than commercial activities (Dimitriadis et al., 2017). In addition, previous research has found that women entrepreneurs, compared to their male counterparts, have greater environmental attitudes, and are more involved in green issues (Braun, 2010; Hechavarria et al., 2012).

In the context of sub-Saharan Africa, Thorpe and Prakash-Mani (2004) suggest that the primary focus of businesses on social aspects of sustainability may derive from an unwillingness or inability of governments to provide community services; however, this report did not examine the gender of the entrepreneurs. In their South African study of small businesses, Van Vuuren and Groenewald (2007) noted that women entrepreneurs play an important role in terms of creating jobs, alleviating poverty, and uplifting living standards; again, this suggests the contribution and focus of African women entrepreneurs on the social dimension of sustainability. In a study of women entrepreneurs and executives in developing nations (including Nigeria), more than half of the respondents indicated they manage their businesses in ways that minimise adverse effects on the environment (Ambepitiya, 2016). In terms of social sustainability, Ambepitiya (2016: 176) states "these businesses focus on trading with the poor, helping the community to develop skills and abilities, paying fair prices and receiving fair payments, [and] encouraging fair treatment of all staff".

Given the growth of women entrepreneurs and their importance in terms of achieving the UN's SDGs, it is critical that the sustainability of these businesses is examined, particularly in the context of developing nations. This research with women entrepreneurs in Ghana:

(a) explores their views and actions with regard to environmental and social sustainability;
(b) identifies the factors that are drivers of, or barriers to, their implementation of sustainable business practices;
(c) examines the value of these sustainable practices to their business; and
(d) determines the priority (i.e., past, current, and future) for their business in terms of economic, environmental, and social sustainability.

Theoretical Framework: Sustainability Design Theory

Extant research discusses the range of motivations and barriers for adopting business sustainability practices for a range of sectors and economies (Caprar and Neville, 2012; Zhang, Oo, and Lim, 2019; Wang, Si, and Fahad, 2023). Such a diverse series of studies have applied a variety of theories and models to the decision-making process for organisations in choosing to adopt business sustainability practices. This chapter applies a theory that speaks to the creation of a process that solves sustainability-related challenges (Baldassarre et al., 2020); this is the Sustainability Design Theory (SDT). We are applying this theory, which focuses on the process of creating built environments (e.g. products, buildings, etc.) with positive environmentally responsible, socially equitable, and economically viable outcomes (Holmström, Liotta, and Chaudhuri, 2017) to the adoption of sustainable practices among women entrepreneurs in Ghana. Baldasarre et al. (2020) highlight the importance of understanding the role of Sustainability Design Theory in business transition due to the impact on the entire socio-economic system. This chapter will provide insight into the decisions to adopt sustainability practices in the business for women entrepreneurs, either new or established, in the business journey and is essential due to the influence SMEs possess in the strength of Ghana's socio-economic development.

Baldassare et al. (2020) argue that Sustainability Design Theory must be tied to the objectives of the organisations. Within our study, we link a proactive approach to embedding sustainability into business practices by exploring whether initial understanding of sustainable needs (social and environmental) is then addressed in the entrepreneurs' planning for their business in these aspects. Baldassare et al.'s (2020) application of the model in a framework comprises a set of themes, some of which are relevant to the research conducted in Ghana. We extend the process by discussing not only environmental sustainability but also social sustainability. We cover the main themes of strategic objectives, core activities, the terminology of sustainable designers, and the challenges of the design process.

Research has identified a range of benefits to sustainable design (Geissdoerfer et al., 2017), such as energy conservation, reduction of pollution, and occupational health, and productivity (da Silva et al., 2021). The overall benefit of improved sustainable practices among businesses, governments, and citizens includes a more habitable and equitable earth (Geng et al., 2019). Further benefits to businesses extend to competitive advantage, positive customer perceptions in the market, and increased sales, revenues, and profits for business (Pieroni, McAloone,

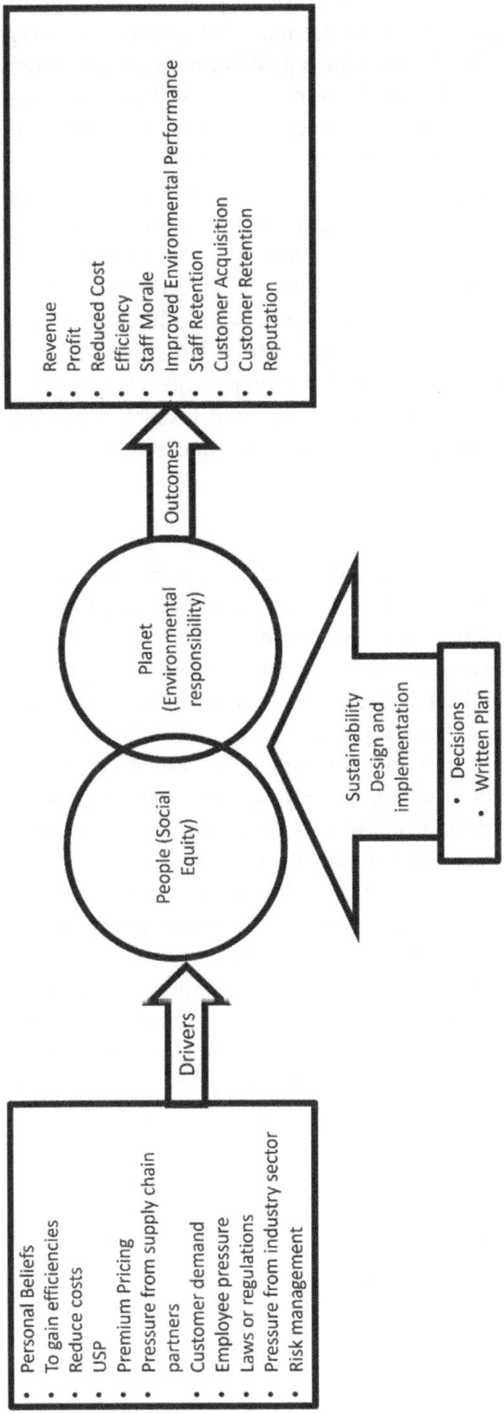

Figure 14.1 Thematic framework as applied in the study

and Pigosso, 2019). The challenges posed by climate change, resource scarcity, and growing social inequity drive the need for sustainable design more urgently (Wiegleb and Bruns, 2018), to create a positive outlook for current and future generations. Research has identified key principles in SDT to apply to the design of products, buildings, systems, and processes throughout the lifecycle (Baldassere et al., 2020). We apply this to the process of planning and implementing sustainability in the business processes of an organisation. We are applying SDT as a framework by which the entrepreneurs in the study are minimising their social and environmental impact on their society. We focus on environmental and social factors to consider when designing a business solution that is accessible, equitable, and affordable for all stakeholders. Figure 14.1 outlines the theoretical framework designed for the execution of this study. The motivations, such as personal beliefs, reduced costs, and USPs, drive the sustainable design along social and environmental elements of the triple bottom line and lead to positive outcomes for the business such as revenue, profit, reduced cost, and staff morale.

Method

Following a quantitative methodology, data was collected from participants to evaluate the sustainability adoption among female entrepreneurs in those populations. This questionnaire data collection began in March 2023 via Qualtrics software and focused on recruiting through entrepreneurial organisations with women memberships such as (1) Association of Ghana Industries-women in Business, (2) Women in Agribusiness Ghana, (3) Business Hub, and (4) CAMFED women business growth programme network through email. Potential respondents were given a period of two weeks in which to complete the questionnaire and two reminder messages were sent during this period to encourage participation. A total of 44 Ghanaian respondents completed the questionnaire.

The questionnaire was developed following a review of the sustainability literature discussed below. The questionnaire was pre-tested by three academic experts and modified prior to the data collection phase. The final questionnaire consisted of a variety of open and closed questions, including some Likert-scaled items (refer to the Appendix for a copy of the questionnaire). The collected data were analysed in SPSS, with descriptive analytics and Pearson Correlation testing to explore the relationships between the drivers, the planning and implementation, and the outcomes for the businesses, with significance being tested at the 0.5 level.

Results

We analysed the data using SPSS version 28 and exploratory factor analysis (EFA) to examine the factors within this data set. Since this phase of the study is exploratory and without hypotheses, we have used EFA to identify the relevant patterns in the data and support the development of hypotheses for future stages of data collection. We start this report of the results with the descriptive statistics associated with the study.

Business Demographics

There was a spread of businesses from those operating for less than two years to those established more than 20 years ago. Table 14.1 shows that the highest single percentage are those businesses established over 20 years ago.

The participants came from a range of sectors highlighted in Table 14.2 from agriculture to construction, to fashion, to hospitality, and manufacturing among others. This therefore means that the findings can theoretically be applied to a range of context rather than one sector.

The participants who responded largely fell within the delineation of small businesses, with 87 % having fifty or less employees in the company. Table 14.3 shows the full outline of the business size.

Table 14.4 shows the spread of the ages of the participants from under 20 years to 60-plus years.

Table 14.1 Age of Business

Age of business	*Number*	*Percent*
Under 2 years	5	11.4
2 to 5 years	7	15.9
6 to 10 years	7	15.9
11 to 15 years	3	6.8
16 to 20 years	2	4.5
Over 20 years	10	22.7
Total	34	77.3
Missing	10	

Table 14.2 Sectors represented in the study

Sector of business	*Number*	*Percent*
Accommodation and food service activities	4	9.1
Agriculture, forestry, and Fishing	5	11.4
Administrative and support service activities	1	2.3
Beauty and personal care	2	4.5
Construction	1	2.3
Fashion and clothing	6	13.6
Hospitality and tourism	1	2.3
Information and Communication	2	4.5
Manufacturing	4	9.1
Other	6	13.6
Total	32	72.7
Missing	12	

Table 14.3 Size of business

Size of business	*Number*	*Percent*
Less than 10	18	40.9
Between 11 and 50	10	22.7
Between 51 and 250	4	9.1
Total	32	72.7
Missing	12	

Table 14.4 Age of business owner

Age of participant	*Number*	*Percent*
Under 20 years	1	2.3
20–29 years	3	6.8
30–39 years	10	22.7
40–49 years	6	13.6
50–59 years	7	15.9
60 or older	5	11.4
Total	32	72.7
Missing	12	

Environmental Sustainability

Over 65% of the valid respondents often think about the environmental impact of their businesses, with none of the participants responding never to this question. Our result is a significant signal that the women entrepreneurs in our study are cognisant of the potential environmental impact of their businesses. This is also an early indicator that environmental sustainability is a factor in business decision-making. A further signal of the entrepreneur's consideration of sustainability in decision-making comes through the statistics that 92.3% of the valid responses showed that their consideration of the environmental impacts has led them to improve relevant practices in their business. While this is not often reflected in the creation of a written plan, with only 20.5% of valid responses having a written plan, the strength of the decision making is seen in the implementation of various environmental improvement actions. In this study, we found that each of the pre-set types of environmental actions listed in the questionnaire were used by members of the population as well as an additional measure, which is recycling waste into building materials and energy.

Our research shows that the entrepreneurs appreciate the value of implementing sustainable practices in their businesses with the premier value reported being reduced costs, closely followed by improved environmental performance, improved reputation, and increased profits. This shows that values as both financial, environmental, and social count for the businesses. Our investigation displayed that there were a range of motivations for implementing environmental sustainability within the company, with personal beliefs being the leading motivation, followed by achieving efficiencies and reducing costs. The first four motivations are a mix of business and personal motivations, but they have the same outcome in terms of driving the organisation to implement environmental sustainability within the company's operations. There is a range of barriers from the company specifics (e.g., financial costs 31.8% and lack of motivation 15.9%) to wider socio-economic barriers (e.g., lack of technology and innovation 22.7%) that prevent more wholesale adoption of environmentally sustainable business practices. Over 88% of the respondents noted that without those barriers, they would be in a better position to adopt environmentally sustainable practices.

Social Sustainability

The research shows that 69.6% of the respondents think about the social impact of their business, slightly more than those who consider their environmental impact. They also select a consideration for the social impact with none selecting never for this question. This also shows the first indication that social sustainability is a consideration within business decision-making. This is also supported by 81.8% of the respondents who improve social sustainability practices in their business based on their consideration of the impact. However, like the environmental sustainability, only around 26.1% have a written plan for implementing social sustainability in the business. Ultimately, they have implemented largely all the options of improving sustainability in their business with philanthropy the leading action implemented, closely followed by staff development, training and education, and staff wellbeing policy.

The companies recognise the value of social sustainability within their organisation with the leading response being improved staff morale (33.3%), improved reputation (27.8 %), improved social performance (22.2%), and reduced costs (11.1%). The motivations for implementing were like environmental sustainability with personal beliefs being the primary motivation with 47.6% of the responses, followed by reducing costs (14.3%), reducing risks (14.3%), and gaining efficiencies (9.5%). These motivations were somewhat prevented from going to fuller implementation due to several identified barriers, such as the financial costs (25%), inaccessible technology and lack of innovation (18.2%), lack of knowledge/skills/experience (18.2%), and uncertainty over return on investment (13.6%). Understanding these barriers is important as more respondents (95.5%) stated they would adopt more socially sustainable practices if barriers were removed.

Sustainable Priorities

The research shows that the priorities around implementing sustainability are not static and are prone to change over time potentially due to changing contexts in society. The respondents in the study show that their present priorities are social and environmental while their future priorities are economic and social. Overall, social is the priority, sharing the lead in both the short and long terms. Our study showed these priorities in providing definitions from the perspective of the entrepreneurs.

These definitions also show the nature of the sustainable priorities to be "comprehensive and necessary for practice", in the words of our respondents, to cover the environment, society, and the economy. Some of these definitions include the following:

> "It's about conserving the natural resources of the economy to support and protect the health and wellbeing of the people in a country".
>
> "What has to be done to keep the environment safe for posterity".
>
> "Activities and processes that prevent environmental deterioration as a result of our economic activities".
>
> "Ensuring that business operations are not harmful to the environment".
>
> "Having reduced or zero negative impact on the environment".
>
> "The ability to maintain or sustain a suitable environment or place of work for the betterment of your business".

Pearson Correlation

Our initial Pearson Correlation to examine the relationships depicted in the theoretical framework demonstrated a positive correlation between thinking about impact (social and environmental) and a written plan for implementing sustainable practices (0.84). The data also showed a positive correlation between thinking about impact (social and environmental) and actual implementation of the sustainable actions (0.81). While our sample is small, this is a positive indication that women entrepreneurs are thinking about the environmental and social impact of their business practice, are designing sustainability into their operations, and implementing these actions within their organisation.

Discussion

Our chapter builds on the work by Quagrainie et al. (2021) who noted the critical role of women entrepreneurs in the sustainable development process by demonstrating that these entrepreneurs are thinking about the impact of their business and building on these considerations in planning as well as implementation. Therefore, governmental support through legislation, funding, training, and technological backing is essential to assist the further sustainability design and implementation within these organisations due to the benefits to the organisations and national sustainable development as identified by Khumalo and Mutobola (2014). These benefits to the company specifically have been identified in terms of financial performance and profitability by Epstein and Roy (2003) and Whelan and Fink (2016) among others. This chapter shows that while reduced costs and better profitability are values observed by the company, especially around environmental sustainability, the reputation boost, and improved environmental performance are equally important to these entrepreneurs. About social sustainability, which is the enduring priority of these entrepreneurs, staff morale and reputation are the leading values observed, followed by improved social performance and reduced costs. Therefore,

Table 14.5 Sustainability design theory categories mapped onto question themes from the questionnaire

Sustainability design theory category	*Questionnaire item*
The strategic objectives	• How often do you think about the environmental/social impact of the business? • What are the motivations for sustainable implementation in your business? • Do you have a written plan for sustainable implementation in your business?
Core activities	• Implementation of sustainable practices • What is the value of the implementation of sustainable practices in your business (environmental and sustainable)?
Terminology of the sustainable designers	• Entrepreneurs providing their definitions of sustainability. • Their determination of the importance and impact of sustainable implementation.
Challenges of the design process	• What are the barriers to implementation of sustainable practices? • Would you be more likely to implement sustainable practices without the existing barriers?

while profit is a listed value, these entrepreneurs have a holistic approach to implementing and measuring the outcomes of sustainable practice in their organisations and their stakeholders.

This chapter extends the model of Sustainability Design Theory (Abed, 2021) through delineation of elements within Baldassare et al.'s (2020) discussion. These are outlined in Table 14.5 where the various elements are mapped against the data collected in our questionaire. From the perspective of the strategic objectives, thinking about business impacts and using those considerations to plan, based on certain motivations and drivers supports the demonstration of elements of the Sustainability Design Theory from the women that demonstrate from their perspective their priorities with social sustainability a short and long-term priority. This moves the terminology of the sustainable designers from simply determining jargon to establishing the basis for action. The entrepreneurs are also aware of the barriers to implementation and note as mentioned in the findings that they would be better empowered to design and action sustainability into their operations with less barriers. These barriers are challenges along economic, management, and social factors, aligned with Fatoki (2019). However, this study shows that companies are willing to take steps to overcome the barriers. This study, therefore, applies the Sustainable Design Theory in a country case whereby the activities and the structure of the theory are observed among women entrepreneurs, who like Holmström, Liotta, and Chaudhuri (2017) noted in their study, can reflect on the outcomes of the implementation for their business. These outcomes are varied and include both financial and reputational outcomes that would benefit the company, customer, and wider societal stakeholders.

This study is addressing a gap, whereby the sustainability literature has focused largely on developing countries. However, this study shows that SMEs within emerging markets are also themselves cognisant of and experiencing the benefits of implementing sustainability in their businesses, along the line of Thorpe and Prakash-Mani (2004), with the focus here being Ghana. The study's identification of lack of innovation as a barrier to sustainable adoption means that this needs to be an area of priority for policymakers and governments within Ghana and other emerging markets due to the role that sustainable innovation plays in business growth (Adomako, 2020) and subsequent development. The entrepreneurs in this study identify sustainability as positive for prosperity, growth, and health and well-being. Therefore, these entrepreneurs and the wider entrepreneurial community's empowerment for sustainability adoption would be positive for the health and growth of businesses, societies, and economies under evaluation.

Conclusion

Summary of Findings and Contributions of the Study

This chapter highlights three main findings. Women entrepreneurs within our sample are thinking about the impacts their businesses are having from an environmental and social perspective. These thoughts are correlated positively with planning and implementing sustainability into their business. Secondly, the entrepreneurs are seeing the value of implementing sustainability into their business and therefore are more willing to action this into their business should some of the identified barriers be mitigated against. Thirdly, social sustainability is the enduring priority of these entrepreneurs, tying for the lead in both present and future priorities. Environmental sustainability is a leading present priority along with social while economic sustainability is a leading future priority together with social.

In focusing on women entrepreneurs in Ghana, this chapter has made three contributions. The first sees us providing insight into how entrepreneurs can embed sustainability design in economic impact and align these with appropriate actions to get the desired outcomes. Secondly, we give policymakers and officials an understanding of the barriers to adoption and the business case for removing these barriers and creating a facilitating environment in Ghana. These are companies that are more willing to adopt because they will see the value for the company themselves and this will redound to the economic, social, and environmental development of wider society. Thirdly, we demonstrate to academic researchers, with our focus on Ghanaian women entrepreneurs, a sound approach for applying the Sustainability Design Theory.

Limitations and Recommendations for Future Research

This stage of the process has an identified small sample size which could limit the generalisability of the findings to wider Ghana and the emerging countries. However, they do give some insight from entrepreneurs who are at various stages of their development on how sustainability implementation is being approached on the ground in Ghana. This size of the sample is being addressed as we move forward with the study in finding new routes of recruitment to reach out to entrepreneurs. We are also tackling this by expanding the study to Cameroon and Scotland to be able to compare insights across developed and emerging markets. We used a quantitative approach in our research which gives a good way of exploring the relationships between the elements of our model. However, a qualitative approach may have given a more in-depth response from the participants, providing richer analysis. Future researchers can test the framework for sustainability design among entrepreneurs in other countries regardless of gender. The framework can be used to test sustainability design in particular sectors with women entrepreneurs in Ghana and other markets. Researchers can also look at exploring this study using qualitative methods.

References

Abed, S. S. (2021) "Women entrepreneurs' adoption of mobile applications for business sustainability", *Sustainability* (Basel, Switzerland), 13 (21): 11627.

Abubakari, M. and B. Thuranira (2021) "The consumer goods sector and the sustainability agenda in Ghana: A review of sustainability commitments", *Discover Sustainability,* 2 (1): 1–17. https://doi.org/10.1007/s43621-021-00037-8

Adams, D., J. Donovan, and C. Topple (2022) "Sustainability in large food and beverage companies and their supply chains: An investigation into key drivers and barriers affecting sustainability strategies", *Business Strategy and the Environment*, 32 (4): 1451–1463.

Adomako, S. (2020) "Environmental collaboration, sustainable innovation, and small and medium-sized enterprise growth in sub-Saharan Africa: Evidence from Ghana", *Sustainable Development*, 28 (6): 1609–1619.

Akhalwaya, A. and W. Havenga (2012) "The barriers that hinder the success of women entrepreneurs in Gauteng, South Africa", *International Journal of Sustainable Development*, 3 (5): 11–22.

Ambepitiya, K. R. (2016) "The role of women entrepreneurs in establishing sustainable development in developing nations", *World Review of Business Research*, 6 (1): 161–178.

Ameer, R. and R. Othman (2012) "Sustainability practices and corporate financial performance: A study based on the top global corporations", *Journal of Business Ethics,* 108 (1): 61–79. https://doi.org/10.1007/s10551-011-1063-y

Avolio, B. E. (2011) "A methodological problem associated with researching women entrepreneurs", *Journal of Women's Entrepreneurship and Education*, 1–2: 9–25.

Baah, C. and Z. Jin (2019) "Sustainable supply chain management and organizational performance: The intermediary role of competitive advantage", *Journal of Management and Sustainability,* 9 (1): 119–131. https://doi.org/10.5539/jms.v9n1p119

Baldassarre, B., D. Keskin, J. C. Diehl, N. Bocken, and G. Calabretta (2020) "Implementing Sustainable Design Theory in business practice: A call to action", *Journal of Cleaner Production,* 273: 1–17, 123113. https://doi.org/10.1016/j.jclepro.2020.123113

Barot, H. (2015) "Entrepreneurship - A key to success", *The International Journal of Business and Management,* 3 (1): 163–165.

Bocken, N., S. Short, P. Rana, and S. Evans (2013) "A value mapping tool for sustainable business modelling", *Corporate Governance,* 13 (5): 482–497. https://doi.org/10.1108/CG-06-2013-0078

Boons, F. and F. Lüdeke-Freund (2013) "Business models for sustainable innovation: State-of-the-art and steps towards a research agenda", *Journal of Cleaner Production,* 45: 9–19. https://doi.org/10.1016/j.jclepro.2012.07.007

Braun, P. (2010) "Going green: Women entrepreneurs and the environment", *International Journal of Gender and Entrepreneurship,* 2 (3): 245–259.

Brundtland, G. (1987) "Our common future – call for action", *Environmental Conservation,* 14 (4): 291–294.

Brush, C. (2006) "Women entrepreneurs: A research overview", in M. Casson, B. Yeung, A. Basu, and N. Wadeson (eds), *The Oxford Handbook of Entrepreneurship*, pp. 611–628. Oxford: Oxford University Press.

Brush, C. G. and S. Y. Cooper (2012) "Female entrepreneurship and economic development: An international perspective", *Entrepreneurship and Regional Development*, 24 (1–2): 1–6.

Caprar, D. V. and B. A. Neville (2012) "'Norming' and 'conforming': Integrating cultural and institutional explanations for sustainability adoption in business", *Journal of Business Ethics,* 110 (2): 231–245. https://doi.org/10.1007/s10551-012-1424-1

Carbo, J., I. M. Langella, V. T. Dao, and S. J. Haase (2014) "Breaking the ties that bind: From corporate sustainability to socially sustainable systems", *Business and Society Review,* 119 (2): 175–206. https://doi.org/10.1111/basr.12029

Chinomona, E. and E. T. Maziriri (2015) "Women in action: Challenges facing women entrepreneurs in the Gauteng Province of South Africa", *International Business and Economics Research Journal*, 14 (6): 835–850.

Chitsike, C. (2000) "Culture as a barrier to rural women's entrepreneurship: Experience from Zimbabwe", *Gender and Development*, 8 (1): 71–77.

Conger, M., J. S. McMullen, B. J. Bergman Jr, and J. G. York (2018) "Category membership, identity control, and the re-evaluation of prosocial opportunities", *Journal of Business Venturing*, 33 (2): 179–206.

Cooney, H., J. Dencik, and A. Marshall (2022) "Making the responsibility for practicing sustainability a company-wide strategic priority", *Strategy and Leadership*, 50 (4): 19–23.

Cowan, K. and F. Guzman (2020) "How CSR reputation, sustainability signals, and country-of-origin sustainability reputation contribute to corporate brand performance: An exploratory study", *Journal of Business Research,* 117: 683–693. https://doi.org/10.1016/j.jbusres.2018.11.017

da Silva, C., P. G. C. N. de Oliveira, J. N. Ferreira Correia, and H. N. Pujol Tucci (2021) "Evaluation of economic, environmental and operational performance of the adoption of cleaner production: Survey in large textile industries", *Journal of Cleaner Production,* 278 (3): 123855. https://doi.org/10.1016/j.jclepro.2020.123855

Dal Mas, F. and P. Paoloni (2020) "A relational capital perspective on social sustainability: The case of female entrepreneurship in Italy", *Measuring Business Excellence*, 24 (1): 114–130.

Della-Giusta, M. and C. Phillips (2006) "Women entrepreneurs in the Gambia: Challenges and opportunities", *Journal of International Development: The Journal of the Development Studies Association*, 18 (8): 1051–1064.

Dimitriadis, S., M. Lee, L. Ramarajan, and J. Battilana (2017) "Blurring the boundaries: The interplay of gender and local communities in the commercialization of social ventures", *Organization Science*, 28 (5): 819–839.

Eastin, J. (2018) "Climate change and gender equality in developing states", *World Development*, 107: 289-305.

Elkington, J. (1994) "Towards the sustainable corporation: Win-win-win business strategies for sustainable development", *California Management Review,* 36 (2): 90–100.

Epstein, M. J. and M. J. Roy (2003) "Making the business case for sustainability: Linking social and environmental actions to financial performance", *Journal of Corporate Citizenship*, 9: 79–96.

Everts, S. (1998) *Gender and Technology: Empowering Women, Engendering Technology.* London and New York: Zed Books.

Fang, S., C. Goh, M. Roberts, L.C. Xu, and A. Zeufack (2022) "Female entrepreneurs and productivity around the world: Rule of law, network, culture, and gender equality", *World Development,* 154 (2): 105846. https://doi.org/10.1016/j.worlddev.2022.105846

Fatoki, O. (2019) "Drivers and barriers to sustainability manufacturing practices by small and medium enterprises in South Africa", *Academy of Entrepreneurship Journal,* 25 (3): 1–12.

Cardella, G. M., B. R. Hernández-Sánchez, and J. C. Sánchez-García (2020) "Women entrepreneurship: A systematic review to outline the boundaries of scientific literature", *Frontiers in psychology*, 11: 1557.

Gartner, W. B. (1990) "What are we talking about when we talk about entrepreneurship?", *Journal of Business Venturing*, 5 (1): 15–28.

Gazzola, P., E. Pavione, R. Pezzetti, and D. Grechi (2020) "Trends in the fashion industry. The perception of sustainability and circular economy: A gender/generation quantitative approach", *Sustainability,* 12 (7): 2809. https://doi.org/10.3390/su12072809

Geissdoerfer, M., P. Savaget, N. M. P. Bocken, and E. J. Hultink (2017) "The circular economy – A new sustainability paradigm?", *Journal of Cleaner Production,* 143: 757–768. https://doi.org/10.1016/j.jclepro.2016.12.048

Geng, Y., T. Fujita, R. Bleischwitz, A. Chiu, and J. Sarkis (2019) "Accelerating the transition to equitable, sustainable, and liveable cities: Toward post-fossil carbon societies", *Journal of Cleaner Production,* 239: 118020. https://doi.org/10.1016/j.jclepro.2019.118020

Ghadge, A., E. Kara, D. G. Mogale, S. Choudhary, and S. Dani (2021) "Sustainability implementation challenges in food supply chains: A case of UK artisan cheese producers", *Production Planning and Control*, 32 (14): 1191–1206.

Glass, C., A. Cook, and A. R. Ingersoll (2016) "Do women leaders promote sustainability? Analyzing the effect of corporate governance composition on environmental performance", *Business Strategy and the Environment*, 25 (7): 495–511.

Grimes, M. G., J. Gehman, and K. Cao (2018) "Positively deviant: Identity work through B Corporation certification", *Journal of Business Venturing*, 33 (2): 130–148.

Hechavarria, D. M., A. Ingram, R. Justo, and S. Terjesen (2012) "Are women more likely to pursue social and environmental entrepreneurship?", in K. D. Hughes and J. H. Jennings (eds), *Global Women's Entrepreneurship Research: Diverse Settings, Questions and Approaches,* pp. 135–151. Cheltenham: Edward Elgar Publishing.

Helfaya, A. and T. Moussa (2017) "Do board's corporate social responsibility strategy and orientation influence environmental sustainability disclosure? UK evidence", *Business Strategy and the Environment*, 26 (8): 1061–1077.

Hessels, J. and W. Naudé (2019) "The intersection of the fields of entrepreneurship and development economics: A review towards a new view", *Journal of Economic Surveys,* 33 (2): 389–403.

Higgins, K. L. (2014) *Economic Growth and Sustainability: Systems Thinking for a Complex World.* San Diego: Academic Press.

Hillary, R. (2004) "Environmental management systems and the smaller enterprise", *Journal of Cleaner Production*, 12 (6): 561–569.

Hockerts, K. and R. Wüstenhagen (2010) "Greening Goliaths versus emerging Davids—Theorizing about the role of incumbents and new entrants in sustainable entrepreneurship", *Journal of Business Venturing*, 25 (5): 481–492.

Holmström, J., G. Liotta, and A. Chaudhuri (2017) "Sustainability outcomes through direct digital manufacturing-based operational practices: A design theory approach", *Journal of Cleaner Production,* 167: 951–961. https://doi.org/10.1016/j.jclepro.2017.03.092

Horbach, J. and J. Jacob (2018) "The relevance of personal characteristics and gender diversity for (eco-)innovation activities at the firm-level: Results from a linked employer–employee database in Germany", *Business Strategy and the Environment*, 27 (7): 924–934.

Hossain, M., O. A. Farooque, M. A. Momin, and O. Almotairy (2017) "Women in the boardroom and their impact on climate change related disclosure", *Social Responsibility Journal*, 13 (4): 828–855.

Hoverstadt, P. and D. Bowling (2005) "Organisational viability as a factor in sustainable development of technology", *The International Journal of Technology Management and Sustainable Development,* 4 (2): 131–146. https://doi.org/10.1386/ijtm.4.2.131/1

Hussain, N., U. Rigoni, and R. P. Orij (2018) "Corporate governance and sustainability performance: Analysis of triple bottom line performance", *Journal of Business Ethics*, 149: 411–432.

Kaciak, E. and D.H.B. Welsh (2020) "Women entrepreneurs and work–life interface: The impact of sustainable economies on success", *Journal of Business Research,* 112: 281–290. https://doi.org/10.1016/j.jbusres.2019.11.073

Kao, R. W. (1993) "Defining entrepreneurship: past, present and?", *Creativity and Innovation Management*, 2 (1): 69–70.

Karakaya, E., A. Hidalgo, and C. Nuur (2014) "Diffusion of eco-innovations: A review', *Renewable and Sustainable Energy Reviews",* 33 (May): 392–399. https://doi.org/10.1016/j.rser.2014.01.083

Khumalo, S. D. and S. Mutobola (2014) "An eminent volcanic eruption: Youth entrepreneurship", *Kuwait Chapter of Arabian Journal of Business and Management Review*, 3 (6): 1–19.

Liao, L., L. Luo, and Q. Tang (2015) "Gender diversity, board independence, environmental committee and greenhouse gas disclosure", *The British Accounting Review*, 47 (4): 409–424.

Lorenz, D. and T. Lützkendorf (2008) "Sustainability in property valuation: Theory and practice", *Journal of Property Investment and Finance,* 26 (6): 482–521. https://doi.org/10.1108/14635780810908361

Manerkar, G. A. (2015) "Women entrepreneurs in Goa: Issues and challenges", *Indian Streams Research Journal,* 4 (12): 1–8.

Marquis, C. and M. Lee (2013) "Who is governing whom? Executives, governance, and the structure of generosity in large US firms", *Strategic Management Journal*, 34 (4): 483–497.

Masterson, V. (2022) "Here's what women's entrepreneurship looks like around the world, World Economic Forum", *World Economic Forum.* https://doi.org/https://www.weforum.org/agenda/2022/07/women-entrepreneurs-gusto-gender/

Neneh, B. N. and D. H. B. Welsh (2022) "Family support and business performance of South African female technology entrepreneurs", *International Journal of Entrepreneurial Behaviour and Research,* 28 (6): 1631–1652. https://doi.org/10.1108/IJEBR-05-2021-0402

Nsengimana, S., R. K. Tengeh, and C. G. Iwu (2017) "The sustainability of businesses in Kigali, Rwanda: An analysis of the barriers faced by women entrepreneurs", *Sustainability*, 9 (8): 1372–1399.

Nxopo, Z. and C. G. Iwu (2015) "The unique obstacles of female entrepreneurship in the tourism industry in Western Cape, South Africa", *Commonwealth Youth and Development*, 13 (2): 55–71.

Okeke-Uzodike, O. U. E. (2019) "Sustainable women's entrepreneurship: A view from two BRICS nations", *Journal of International Women's Studies*, 20 (2): 340–358.

Oluwole, V. (2021) Africa claims the top three spots for highest concentration of women businesses owners in the World – Report, *Business Insider.* https://africa.businessinsider.com/local/careers/africa-claims-the-top-three-spots-for-highest-concentration-of-women-businesses/h2jcrtb, accessed 25 November 2024.

Orobia, L. A., I. Tusiime, R. Mwesigwa, and B. Ssekiziyivu (2020) "Entrepreneurial framework conditions and business sustainability among the youth and women entrepreneurs", *Asia Pacific Journal of Innovation and Entrepreneurship,* 14 (1): 60–75.

Pacheco, D. F., T. J. Dean, and D. S. Payne (2010) "Escaping the green prison: Entrepreneurship and the creation of opportunities for sustainable development", *Journal of Business Venturing*, 25 (5): 464–480.

Paulraj, A., I. J. Chen, and C. Blome (2017) "Motives and performance outcomes of sustainable supply chain management practices: A multi-theoretical perspective", *Journal of Business Ethics*, 145 (2): 239–258.

Pieroni, M. P. P., T. C. McAloone, and D. C. A. Pigosso (2019) "Business model innovation for circular economy and sustainability: A review of approaches", *Journal of Cleaner Production,* 215: 198–216. https://doi.org/10.1016/j.jclepro.2019.01.036

Quagrainie, F. A., S. Adams, A. A. M. Kabalan, and A. D. Dankwa (2021) "Micro-entrepreneurship, sustainable development goal one and cultural expectations of Ghanaian women", *Journal of Entrepreneurship in Emerging Economies*, 13 (1): 86–106.

Sachs, J. D. (2012) "From millennium development goals to sustainable development goals", *The Lancet,* 379 (9832): 2206–2211.

Sajuyigbe, A. S. and I. O. Fadeyibi (2017) "Women entrepreneurship and sustainable economic development: Evidence from Nigeria", *Journal of Entrepreneurship, Business and Economics*, 5 (2): 19–46.

Schaper, M. (2002) "Small firms and environmental management: Predictors of green purchasing in Western Australian pharmacies", *International Small Business Journal*, 20 (3): 235–251.

Shepherd, D. A. and H. Patzelt (2011) "The new field of sustainable entrepreneurship: Studying entrepreneurial action linking "what is to be sustained" with "what is to be developed", *Entrepreneurship Theory and Practice*, 35 (1): 137–163.

da Silva, C. P., G. Cardoso de Oliveira Neto, J. M. Ferreira Correia, and H. N. Pujol Tucci (2021) "Evaluation of economic, environmental and operational performance of the adoption of cleaner production: Survey in large textile industries", *Journal of Cleaner Production,* 278 (3): 123855. https://doi.org/10.1016/j.jclepro.2020.123855

Sonego, M., M. E. S. Echeveste, and H. Galvan Debarba (2018) "The role of modularity in sustainable design: A systematic review", *Journal of Cleaner Production,* 176: 196–209. https://doi.org/10.1016/j.jclepro.2017.12.106

Thorpe, J. and K. Prakash-Mani (2004) *Developing Value: The Business Case for Sustainability in Emerging Markets.* Austin, TX: Greenleaf Publishing.

Van Vuuren, J. J. and D. Groenewald (2007) "A critical analysis of the influence of start-up factors in small businesses and entrepreneurial ventures in SA", *Acta Commercii*, 7 (1): 269–280.

Vu, H. M. and C. Nwachukwu (2020) "Strategic flexibility, strategic leadership and business sustainability nexus", *International Journal of Business Environment,* 11 (2): 125–143. https://doi.org/10.1504/IJBE.2020.10029629

Wachira, M. M., T. Berndt, and C. M. Romero (2020) "The adoption of international sustainability and integrated reporting guidelines within a mandatory reporting framework: Lessons from South Africa", *Social Responsibility Journal,* 16 (5). 613–629. https://doi.org/10.1108/SRJ-12-2018-0322

Walker, H., L. Di Sisto, and D. McBain (2008) "Drivers and barriers to environmental supply chain management practices: Lessons from the public and private sectors", *Journal of Purchasing and Supply Management*, 14 (1): 69–85.

Walls, J. L., P. Berrone, and P. H. Phan (2012) "Corporate governance and environmental performance: Is there really a link?", *Strategic Management Journal*, 33 (8): 885–913.

Wang, D., R. Si, and S. Fahad (2023) "Evaluating the small and medium sized enterprises motivating factors and influencing barriers about adoption of green practices", *Environment, Development, and Sustainability,* 25 (4): 3029–3041. https://doi.org/10.1007/s10668-022-02166-0

Warth, L. and M. S. Koparanova (2012) *Empowering Women for Sustainable Development*, pp. 1–26. Geneva, Switzerland: United Nations Economic Commission for Europe.

Weeks, J. R. and D. Seiler (2001) *Women's Entrepreneurship in Latin America*. New York: Main Stop Publication.

Whelan, T. and C. Fink (2016) "The comprehensive business case for sustainability", *Harvard Business Review*, 21 October. https://doi.org/https://everestenergy.nl/new/wp-content/uploads/HBR-Article-The-comprehensive-business-case-for-sustainability.pdf

Wiegleb, V. and A. Bruns (2018) "What is driving the water-energy-food nexus? Discourses, knowledge, and politics of an emerging resource governance concept", *Frontiers in Environmental Science,* 6: 128. https://doi.org/10.3389/fenvs.2018.00128

Wolf, J., (2014) "The relationship between sustainable supply chain management, stakeholder pressure and corporate sustainability performance", *Journal of Business Ethics*, 119: 317–328.

Zhang, J., J. Han, and M. Yin (2018) "A female style in corporate social responsibility? Evidence from charitable donations", *International Journal of Disclosure and Governance*, 15 (3): 185–196.

Zhang, Q., B. L. Oo, and B. T. H. Lim (2019) "Drivers, motivations, and barriers to the implementation of corporate social responsibility practices by construction enterprises: A review", *Journal of Cleaner Production,* 210: 563–584. https://doi.org/10.1016/j.jclepro.2018.11.050

Appendix: Women Entrepreneurs and Sustainability Questionnaire

Q1 Length of time the business has been operating

Q2 Industry sector the business operates in

Q3 Number of employees in the business

Q4 Age of the business owner

Q5 Highest level of education attained by the business owner

Q6 How often do you think about the environmental impact of your business?

Q7 Have your thoughts about environmental impacts led you to take any action/s to improve the environmental performance of your business?

Q8 If there were no barriers to implementing environmentally sustainable practices, would you take action/s to improve the environmental performance of your business?

Q9 Does your business have a written plan outlining how it will adopt environmental sustainability?

Q10 How would you, in your own words, describe or define the term "environmental sustainability"?

Q11 Which of the following environmentally sustainable practices have been implemented in your business? Answers to choose: reducing energy use, producing energy from renewable sources (e.g., wind, solar, or water), reducing greenhouse gas emissions, reducing water use recycling or reusing of waste water, reducing packaging, introducing recyclable or biodegradable packaging, reducing non-organic wastes, composting of organic wastes, improving waste management.

Q12 If you have implemented any environmentally sustainable practices in your business, how would you describe the value (if any) that your business has gained as a result?

Q13 If you have implemented any environmentally sustainable practices in your business, which of the drivers (listed below) were the reason for your action/s? Answers to choose: personal beliefs, to gain efficiencies, to reduce costs, to gain a unique selling proposition, to gain a premium price in the market, pressure from supply chain partners, demand from consumers, pressure from employees, laws or regulations, pressure from industry sector to reduce risk.

Q14 If you have not implemented any environmentally sustainable practices in your business, or you have not implemented all of the environmentally sustainable practices that you would like to implement, which of these reasons are barriers that prevent you from doing so? Answers to choose: financial costs, business inertia/lack of motivation, lack of time, lack of knowledge/skills/experience, uncertainty over return on investment, inaccessible technology or lack of innovation, no interest in improving environmental performance.

Q15 Has your business gained an environmental accreditation or certification? If yes, please name the accreditation/s or certification/s.

Q16 How often do you think about the social impact of your business?
Q17 Have your thoughts about social impacts led you to take any action/s to improve the social practice of your business?
Q18 If there were no barriers to implementing socially sustainable practices, would you take action/s to improve the social performance of your business?
Q19 Does your business have a written plan outlining how it will adopt social sustainability?
Q20 How would you, in your own words, describe or define the term "social sustainability"?
Q21 Which of the following socially sustainable practices have been implemented in your business? Answers to choose: philanthropy (donation of money, products, or services), staff development, training or education, health and safety policy, equity, diversity, and inclusion plan or policy, buy local strategy, sustainable supply chain strategy, staff wellbeing policy, corporate social responsibility (CSR) plan.
Q22 If you have implemented any socially sustainable practices in your business, how would you describe the value (if any) that your business has gained as a result?
Q23 If you have implemented any socially sustainable practices in your business, which of the drivers (listed below) were the reason for your action/s? Answers to choose: personal beliefs, to gain efficiencies, to reduce costs, to gain a unique selling proposition, to gain a premium price in the market, pressure from supply chain partners, demand from consumers, pressure from employees, laws or regulations, pressure from industry sector, to reduce risk.
Q24 If you have not implemented any socially sustainable practices in your business, or you have not implemented all the socially sustainable practices that you would like to implement, which of these reasons are barriers that prevent you from doing so? Answers to choose: financial costs, business inertia/lack of motivation, lack of time, lack of knowledge/skills/experience, uncertainty over return on investment, inaccessible technology/lack of innovation, no interest in improving social performance.
Q25 Sustainability consists of three dimensions: economic, environmental, and social. Please indicate which of these three dimensions (a) has been the priority for your business in the past, (b) is your priority at present, and (c) you think will be your future priority?

Part 5

Concluding Remarks and Perspectives

15 Concluding Remarks and Perspectives

Ulrike Schuerkens

The Different Chapters' Outcomes

This edited book consists of numerous chapters that bring forward the research on female entrepreneurship in West Africa. While most of the chapters are on formal enterprises that have not been major topics in the literature on female entrepreneurship in Africa, the book starts with a chapter on the historical role of women entrepreneurs in Nigeria by analysing the life story of Simbiat Abiola. This woman was born into a Muslim elite family that made its wealth from trade as it was the tradition in pre-colonial Yoruba. She married a polygynous entrepreneur, which permitted her to contribute to the wealth of the couple as a professional life was only possible for married Muslim women. Mutiat Titilope Oladejo displays many details of her tasks in the businesses of her husband and shows the importance of her role as a supportive spouse at this time of postcolonial Nigeria. She built family wealth together with her husband as a new form of family business: a mix of traditional and modern economics. At this time, there was a rarity of having women build and manage businesses in the formal sector in Nigerian business history. In fact, family businesses "feature labour and expertise that circulate within the lineage across generations" (19). In the 20th century, "a woman was not encouraged to live outside the marital setting" (21). Nigerian business history was not interested in the few indigenous businesses that attempted to organise formally. In fact, as Simbiat's husband "was known as the founder of their businesses, Simbiat deputized and controlled the operations" (22). The postcolonial Nigerian state favoured the growth of private capital since 1972 so that a rise of indigenous entrepreneurship could soon be found.

The next chapter's aim is to show how home-based female entrepreneurship, analysed through the prism of partnership governance, contributes to learning responsible behaviour conducive to succession. This self-employment activity is a response to the need to reconcile family life with professional life. In sociocultural contexts where women are confined to family tasks, these small initiatives strengthen their social relationships and their autonomy. This is an activity whose knowledge is transmitted from one generation to the next as these home-based activities can be simultaneously undertaken with caring for children and the household. The discourses of the women who were the focus of the study of Haoua Badini Koné reveal that the family is considered an environment for entrepreneurial

DOI: 10.4324/9781003492931-20

socialisation of the younger members of the family. Distanced from public policies and support of international organisations, this type of entrepreneurship is part of a local management style, "based on the values of respect for the family, careful management of business funds, and the involvement of all members of the household, including the spouse… Women entrepreneurs at home train the younger generations in entrepreneurial activities" (42). As most African women are still in informal activities, this chapter analyses a necessity-driven decision to live as an entrepreneur in contrast to other chapters that focus more on opportunity-driven choices in the formal sector, linked to a higher educational level of these women who decide to create an enterprise.

The objective of the study of Estelle Vérine Salla Bezanga with the title "Women's "invisible" paths to empowerment in Cameroon: The case of digital companies" is to analyse the possibilities for empowering women through online sales. The aim was to assess the motivations behind women's choice of this economic activity and to take account of the environment in which they operate. The fieldwork reveals the precarious nature of the employment sector, which leads women to take up online sales as their main or secondary activity. This result can be explained, in part, by the fact that women are choosing to be autonomous and taking advantage of the opportunities offered by social networks in terms of flexibility and gain. However, as digital frontiers open, they come up against the risks of cybercrime and the uncertainties of the global economic market. Similarly, the variable informality that characterises this sector does not engage the public authorities, and the impact of this is that they are slow to make a qualitative leap forward.

The next chapter is devoted to the analysis of the motivations and constraints of pre-existing women's groups in the process of creating a collective enterprise. The case study turns around the creation of a cooperative by a women's group in Cameroon. The chapter is based on intervention research, done by Lolita Toche with a pre-existing women's group that planned an enterprise to transform avocados into oil.

Entrepreneurship has become a tool used by governments to help women, who are far from the labour market, into work. Women "are being encouraged by governments and NGOs to organise themselves collectively, in cooperatives, professional groups, and in other ways that take advantage of the collective" (60). However, as the authors could show, it is necessary in the cases of pre-existing groups, "to take into account the value of the collective dynamic, and the enhancement of the know-how and interpersonal skills of these women… Individual motivations, if they exist, are absorbed by these collective motivations" (75). Support structures have thus to consider the existing dynamics that facilitate the transition from the informal status of the group to a collective enterprise.

The next chapter, written by Paul Mamba Diédhiou, tackles local traders, particularly stallholders, who explore other sources of supply that they find in the product offers of the multinational Auchan that had in 2023 38 sub-stores in Senegal: 1 drive-through, 1 hypermarket, 20 supermarkets, and 16 convenience stores, and more than 1900 staff members in Dakar and in some other major urban spaces where a local middle class is interested to buy imported and local products that are presented in shops that introduce new sales outlets, digitisation of services (online commands), innovative managerial and marketing practices, self-service, hygiene, imported product brands, and affordability of products in particular during the festive periods. In this way, local consumers are integrated into the world food market and adopt slowly changed dietary practices. As the author argues: "Women stallholders who also own local businesses are 'relays' for Auchan among working-class consumers. They can also compete with multinational food and non-food retailers (such as Auchan) by offering a differentiated and innovative customer experience" (90). In fact, these women offer fresh products in small quantities, bought at Auchan, and sell them at interesting prices that can convince poorer customers to buy these products. Women who buy these products have thus begun to contribute to a new way of selling products that situates them between global and local products. This new practice includes goods originating from the world market with local products furnished by local agricultural practices of peasants or in the case of beverages, produced by local enterprises that transform local fruits.

The next chapter written by Ulrike Schuerkens tackles the life stories of successful women entrepreneurs in formal enterprises in Senegal that have established links with the wider African region and Europe based on what they define as their particular approach to the African continent whose development is at the heart of their enterprises: "These women put a particular emphasis on their being Africans who know the Senegalese culture and how to have success in an economic sector that they understand better than those that are not familiar with this environment" (96). These women combine their experiences made in France as a student and that of Africa in such a way as to rise to the top of economic and societal players in the African sub-region. These life stories let appear the construction of the social reality "in such a way as to reinforce the positive image they have of themselves in the eyes of the African community" (105). And Ulrike Schuerkens continues: "Acting as role models for other African women is consistent with their belief that they have a role to play to improve difficult economic situations in Africa" (105). The women presented enjoy higher income and higher educational levels than the population average. They have succeeded in transforming their social and personal situation by creating and running a successful business in Senegal and abroad, supported by their personal and professional networks. This category of entrepreneurs is a rather new phenomenon in West Africa that should be enlarged in the next years while more and more women are well-educated and look for career possibilities outside the informal sphere. Due to high aspirations, improved knowledge of management and accounting, and better access to financial support, this category of women entrepreneurs is growing and is already preparing their children to continue in their footsteps. Knowledge of these cases should be transmitted in business schools and universities that educate the next generation of women and men in West Africa. Based on traditions linked to the African continent, these women are interested to link the management education they received to their roots.

The next chapter written by Abdul-Aziz Dembélé builds on this research and tackles successful women's life stories in the digital sector. There is little existing work on these new figures of women's entrepreneurship in Africa. These women could build their success on economic, social, and institutional resources so that their entrepreneurial commitment is experienced "as a form of 'self-affirmation' in contrast to the general public" (110). They are university graduates who chose the formal sector for their business. With the emphasis put on schools and education for women in African countries, this group will be enlarged in the coming years even if they play now a mostly hidden role. Among these women entrepreneurs are returning female entrepreneurs that use their return from student migration to create a business. Political initiatives to promote and support female entrepreneurship are thus necessary to enlarge this group but also policies that encourage the return of students and diasporic migrants.

The next chapter written by Sadio Ba Gning is devoted to relational biographies of women social entrepreneurs in Senegal. This chapter "allows us to grasp the multidimensional character of the woman entrepreneur and her plural figures" (149). The chapter reveals the process of social construction of female entrepreneurs by focusing on relational networks, such as family networks, associations, such as religious or political groups, but also professional and institutional networks. Women social entrepreneurs can embed their professional trajectories in instrumental relationships. They anchor their life cycle in family and religion and conquer new paths via political and institutional strategies that serve to legitimise women's entrepreneurship. This way "fosters recognition and enhancement of the career paths of social entrepreneurs" (149). This plurality of logic reveals the complexity of the embedding process through interdependent and interwoven relational links of these female social entrepreneurs in Senegal.

This category of women entrepreneurs demonstrates that women are interested in the social aspects of enterprises and that the financial gain possible in enterprises is not the only criterion for the choice of an enterprise. As women are characterised by aspects that are linked to caring of children, of being a good partner in a couple, etc., this sort of entrepreneurship should become even more important in a time when pressure is put on life stories that include a well-functioning partnership and children. In Africa, where women who are not married and who have no children are considered as being out of a "normal" life, this sort of entrepreneurship will increase in the coming years because of its proximity to widely accepted family norms.

The chapter written by Paul Mamba Diédhiou and Aboubacar Diallo focuses on an organisation of women dressmakers that was conceived as a possibility to leave the informal status to a formal status within the A.F.C. However, this organisation has been based on weak structures not foreseen by the state. Despite the success of its leaders in obtaining funding, rumours on the utilisation of this funding by the only board and a failing communication strategy led its members to leave the A.F.C. as they could no longer see the benefit of their affiliation. Poor administrative accompanying measures and poor leadership qualities of the board led to high disaffiliation of its members entering instead tontines to assure financial assistance and to sell the clothes fabricated via the internet. Despite an adequate intention to formalise the status of these women dressmakers, rumours and a failing leadership group led to this consequence that may be overcome by the drafting of new statutes including different age groups and by accompanying the board in its tasks for the benefit of the membership.

The following chapter written by Mamadou Ndione, Hicham Sbai, and Marie-José Scotto takes stock of participatory finance in Senegal and observes its role in financing women's entrepreneurship. The study could identify the players involved in participatory financing in Senegal, as well as the lack of awareness of this method of financing among women entrepreneurs in Senegal. "Most entrepreneurs in Senegal suffer from the lack of finance" and "crowdfunding is an alternative for them" (173). Crowdfunding as an exchange of funds uses a technological interface after presenting a project and obtaining funds from a group in exchange for pre-defined or undefined benefits. While Senegal has the highest percentage of women entrepreneurs on the African continent, the role of participatory financing is still rather small. However, traditional solutions offered by banks and venture capital are rarely accepted as tontines and support by friends and families are looked for. Participatory financing needs thus strengthened information systems that permit to formalise activities of these female entrepreneurs to contribute to national development. The conclusion of the chapter is: "Participatory financing is still in its infancy in Africa, and particularly in Senegal" (188). However, it is a way to overcome the still existing financial difficulties of women to obtain funds from banks because these banks are not interested in investing in women entrepreneurs due to their role as mother and wife and prefer male entrepreneurs.

The following chapter written by Brigitte Audrey Ekodo Bekono focuses on the success and failure of public policies to promote women entrepreneurship in Cameroon. The study is structured around three categories of public policy impact: regulation and administration, support and capacity-building structures, and financing structures. In fact, the gender approach is now included in the public policies of most states. The author argues: "Public policies can take different forms, such as training programmes, subsidies, tax incentives, or childcare measures" (193). As "women in Cameroon face significant challenges in accessing employment and entrepreneurship, public policies can help to reduce these barriers and promote female entrepreneurship" (194). The study that the author has realised in Cameroon lets appear that most of these women are "unaware of the opportunities available to them and are often unconvinced of the contribution these proposals can make to their business" (205). The author concludes: "Business support programmes must be designed to consider local specificities and the needs of Cameroonian women entrepreneurs, encouraging entrepreneurial innovation, collaboration, and cooperation between businesses, digitalisation, business performance, and taking into account the intrinsic factors of success for women entrepreneurs" (206).

The following chapter is devoted to another interesting topic: Women entrepreneurs in Côte d'Ivoire's philanthropic landscape, written by Jean-Claude Kouadio. This is a new phenomenon in the philanthropic landscape of West Africa of women entrepreneurs who have succeeded in the business world. These actions mainly take the form of one-off donations to help vulnerable populations. For those who are more committed, they are creating foundations to support causes such as education, health, or the empowerment of women. The chapter presents the profiles of these Ivorian women and the commitment they show. "It emerges that their commitment is motivated by personal values based on altruism, empathy, and generosity" (224). However, these motivations are often associated with social, tax, and economic benefits. J.-C. Kouadio concludes this chapter: "The visibility and impact of the foundations' actions is attracting growing interest from donors. As a result, these women are becoming the preferred partners of donors for projects on the African continent" (224).

The next chapter tackles business sustainability adoption by Ghanaian women entrepreneurs. As Philomena Asante, Sharon L. Forbes, and Kathy-Ann Fletcher argue: While much investigation of sustainability adoption has focused on corporations and developed countries, more attention needs to be paid to emerging markets, a gap that is being addressed by this study. The authors underline that "sustainability remains at the core of the UN's sustainable development goals, particularly goal nine which focuses on promoting sustainable industrialisation and innovation and goal twelve which speaks to supporting sustainable consumption and production patterns" (228).

The chapter shows how women "entrepreneurs can embed sustainability design in economic impacts and aligning these with appropriate actions to get the desired outcomes" (242). Moreover, the authors underline that barriers must be removed to create a facilitating environment in Ghana. Focusing on sustainability will then increase the value of the companies and will redound to the economic and social development of Ghanaian society.

It is clearly shown by this research that the sustainability of enterprises is a rising topic among women entrepreneurs in Ghana, due to the social and environmental roles of African women in the past and in the present. More than men, these women are convinced on the urgent need to include sustainability measures in business plans.

Perspectives

This publication shows a field of female entrepreneurs in West Africa that is very diversified from home-based entrepreneurs, over women who lead SMEs to elite women and their enterprises that operate beyond the frontiers of the different states. Even if there should be some similarity in West African countries, recent studies have shown that Nigeria and Ghana have higher educational levels for women and a higher level of women having a bank account than a country like Cameroon. Africa as a continent has much lower educational expenses than other continents such as Europe. Religious culture and faith are also elements that influence women entrepreneurship so there are differences between Muslim and Christian women in West Africa that should be analysed in the future. Patriarchal gender relations with roles for women in couples, where the traditional male breadwinner is put in question also influence female entrepreneurship. The high number of female entrepreneurs on the continent is thus exposed to conditions these women have difficulties to overcome, such as knowing the financial rules of banks, having management knowledge for their enterprises and technical knowledge, and holding gender roles related to household and caring for children. Equalised gender relations are discussed in Senegal regarding politics, but women continue to face difficult situations regarding financial assistance to entrepreneurship, often linked to heritage rules that exclude them from land and estates. But to receive funding from banks, women need guarantees that they often cannot produce so that – due to the lack of financial support – their enterprises are smaller than those of men. Women recur to tontines or micro-credit that permit them to create small enterprises. Moreover, the low knowledge in financial affairs often leads women to renounce bank credits whose offers they don't understand. Crowd-funding, as argued in this book, may become an interesting option to be developed in the coming years that overcomes the small financial readiness of banks to give funds to women.

As Audrey Ekodo has shown in her chapter, most women in Cameroon don't receive enough assistance for leading a successful business. However, during recent years, UNDP, *GIZ-Deutsche Gesellschaft für internationale Zusammenarbeit, Agence française de développement*, Women in Africa, *Délégation Générale à l'Entrepreneuriat Rapide des femmes et de jeunes du Sénégal* (cf. Schuerkens 2023), or Bank of Africa have launched important educational programmes for women entrepreneurs in Africa. With the assistance of incubators, African women have been supported in the creation and management of their enterprises. Courses on finance, taxes, management, and technical assistance for different sectors have been offered to thousands of women in countries such as Senegal, Ghana, Nigeria, and the Ivory Coast. Long-term support has moreover been given by these organisations so that entrepreneurship could become a professional target for more and more women in Africa, faced with the employment problems of young populations on the continent where women prefer to create enterprises faced with difficulties, to be recruited by administrations and organisations that continue to prefer men with no caring and household charges. These structures of technical assistance are also in charge of facilitating bureaucratic processes such as the formalisation of enterprises that can permit to leave the informal sector if enough information has been provided to overcome the informal and not registered status. These educational and financial programmes for women entrepreneurs are the right way to overcome structural constraints linked to the entrepreneurship of African women. An ecosystem that includes women can in this way be realised on a continent where young people have difficulties finding jobs in organisations, enterprises, and administrations. The percentage of women entrepreneurs in Africa is high so their contribution to the continent's GDP is important. Neglecting these facts would mean contributing to the difficult economic situation of the continent that needs to be overcome in an intensively connected world where people have knowledge of life situations all over the world. Migrants are leaving Africa because of economic difficulties. Entrepreneurship has thus become in the last years one of the answers of development agencies and state administrations to change this situation. Networking of women is another factor that should not be underestimated as women who face similar problems can assist one another and can contribute to economic success, as Sadio Ba Gning has shown in her chapter. Women entrepreneurs' associations have been created in the last years, such as Women in Africa or *Union des femmes chefs d'entreprise au Sénégal* that promote the education of women and that give mutual support. Universities and business schools from the North cooperate with universities and business schools from the South in exchange programmes. There is thus hope that the continent's female entrepreneurs continue to improve their situation (Étude Havas Horizon, 2019).

This book has also shown that women play important roles in philanthropy and sustainability, fields that they are interested in and this more than men. Therefore, this publication can be seen as one that focuses on women entrepreneurs and their multiple and widely diversified roles that permit us to overcome the discourse on the poor African women that characterised the academic literature for the last decades (see also: Women in Africa, 2019, 2020 and 2023; Schuerkens (ed.), 2023). Africa has changed and there are now female leaders emerging that realise important tasks described in the different countries of the empirical studies of this book. Let us conclude this book with the hope that this publication can be considered useful for women entrepreneurs in West Africa and beyond, and for universities and business schools that educate the next generation of women entrepreneurs and their male counterparts who must accept the important role of women entrepreneurs on the African continent.

References

Étude Havas Horizon (2019) *Regard sur la place des femmes en Afrique: Émergence d'une nouvelle generation des leaders féminins*. Havas Paris: Women in Africa. https://wia-initiative.com/wp-content/uploads/2020/11/Etude_Havas_horizons_WIA-.pdf, accessed 22 July 2024.

Schuerkens, Ulrike (ed.) (2023) *Entreprises, entrepreneurs et travail au Sénégal.* Paris: L'Harmattan.

Women in Africa (2019) *Women in Africa: Plongée au Coeur de la ruche entrepreneuriale*. Paris: Roland Berger. https://wia-initiative.com/wp-content/uploads/2023/12/MKT_Publi_19_008_WIA_plongee-au-coeur-de-la-ruche-entrepreneuriale.pdf, accessed 22 July 2024.

Women in Africa (2020) *Accélérer la dynamique entrepreneuriale des femmes en Afrique*. Paris: Roland Berger. https://wia-initiative.com/wp-content/uploads/2023/12/Etude-RB_WIA_Accelerer_la_dynamique_entrepreneuriale_des_femmes_en_Afrique-v10112020.pdf, accessed 22 July 2024.

Women in Africa (2023) *Fiche Pays: Sénégal 2023.* Paris: Roland Berger. https://wia-initiative.com/wp-content/uploads/2024/05/WIA-FICHE_PAYS_SENEGAL-2.pdf, accessed 22 July 2024.

Websites

https://anwep-usa.org/
https://cpccaf.org/qui-sommes-nous/reseau-des-femmes-entrepreneures/
https://gender-works.giz.de/projectmap_region/senegal/
https://www.afd.fr/fr/page-region-pays/cameroun
https://www.afd.fr/fr/page-region-pays/senegal
https://www.der.sn/

https://www.facebook.com/p/Ghana-Association-of-Women-Entrepreneurs-100079646234835/?paipv=0&eav=AfZIoB4pV0ugVW-8BwfCIa8oKl5TJU1ucoMqBxRS6EqpJkv2D3DtSdncX2VMHRHnrPo&_rdr
https://www.giz.de/en/worldwide/143541.html
https://www.senegel.org/fr/mouvements/women-movements/orgdetails/124

Index

For Product Safety Concerns and Information please contact our EU representative GPSR@taylorandfrancis.com Taylor & Francis Verlag GmbH, Kaufingerstraße 24, 80331 München, Germany